P9-BAW-324

Please remember that this is a library book,
and that it belongs only temporarily to each
person who uses it. Be considerate. Do
not write in this, or any library book.

WITHDRAWN

UNDERSTANDING SOCIAL WELFARE

Harper Series in Social Work
Werner W. Boehm, Series Editor

UNDERSTANDING SOCIAL WELFARE

RALPH DOLGOFF
Adelphi University

DONALD FELDSTEIN
Federation of Jewish Philanthropies
of New York

HARPER & ROW, PUBLISHERS, New York

Cambridge, Hagerstown, Philadelphia, San Francisco,
London, Mexico City, São Paulo, Sydney

1817

Sponsoring Editor: Dale Tharp
Project Editor: Pamela Landau
Designer: T. R. Funderburk
Production Manager: Jeanie Berke
Compositor: University Graphics, Inc.
Printer and Binder: The Maple Press Company
Art Studio: Vantage Art Inc.

UNDERSTANDING SOCIAL WELFARE

Copyright © 1980 by Ralph Dolgoff and Donald Feldstein

All rights reserved. Printed in the United States of America. No part of this book may
be used or reproduced in any manner whatsoever without written permission except
in the case of brief quotations embodied in critical articles and reviews. For information address Harper & Row, Publishers, Inc., 10 East 53rd Street, New York, N.Y.
10022.

Library of Congress Cataloging in Publication Data

Dolgoff, Ralph.
  Understanding social welfare.

  (Harper series in social work)
  Includes index.
  1. Public welfare—United States. 2. Social
service—United States. 3. United States—Social
policy. I. Feldstein, Donald, joint author.
II. Title.
HV95.D64   361.6′2′0973   79-20667
ISBN 0-06-041676-9

361.6
D664u

To Eliana, Shoshana, Aaron, and Rachel,
Michael, Eric, Miriam, and Ruthie,
and to the just society
in which they deserve to grow.

35597

Contents

Preface

We have attempted to achieve two sometimes mutually exclusive objectives in this book. First, we have written a book with a point of view, one that examines social welfare issues critically, focuses on concepts, and invites challenge and alternative interpretations. We have attempted to write for an adult audience. Second, we have tried to produce a usable textbook, covering detail and fact in an organized manner, useful for all those concerned with social welfare and human services in our society. As a textbook, the volume is organized to follow many course outlines that examine social welfare programs, policies, and issues. Instructors should be aware that this text was based on a two-semester sequence, but with more or less supplementation it may be used in other formats.

The success of our work can only be judged by individual readers who we hope will be challenged to reach their own conclusions about the many issues discussed. We will have succeeded if readers attain knowledge and understanding for decisions—both as professionals and as informed and participating citizens.

We are grateful to a number of persons who read parts of or all of this book in its various stages of development and whose reactions and advice have helped us to improve it: Professors June Axinn, Barbara Bielawski, Kay Dea, Donald Fausel, Neil Gilbert, Nancy Humphreys, John Romanyshyn, Brad Sheafor, and Max Siporin, and Jacqueline Atkins, and our students Holly Delany and Phyllis Enet. We are especially appreciative for the encouragement and assistance of Professor Werner Boehm, who helped us throughout the development and preparation of this book.

Our families, from whom we have stolen time in order to prepare this book, have contributed much to its creation with their support and good humor which sustained us through several drafts. We thank them not only for making this book possible but for our lives together: Sylvia, Eliana, Shoshana, Aaron, Rachel, Shirley, Michael, Eric, Miriam, and Ruthie. A special note of appreciation is due to Sylvia Dolgoff who typed and retyped the manuscript as we drafted and revised the book.

Finally, we want to express our deep appreciation to our classroom students, whom we have taught and from whom we have learned at Adelphi, Boston, Fairleigh Dickinson, Hebrew, Bar Ilan, New York, Yeshiva, and Washington universities.

Many people have contributed to the development of this book. Nonetheless, the book is ours and we are responsible for its limitations. On each rereading we, as do all authors, become aware of things we should have written or written better. But we hope that we have come close to the expression of the ideas with which we started and that our readers find this book stimulating and helpful.

Ralph Dolgoff and Donald Feldstein

Editor's Foreword

A few years ago when Harper & Row established a textbook series in social welfare, we hoped to produce books that would serve the burgeoning undergraduate population as well as graduate social work students. In addition, we have tried to create textbooks which reflect the profession as it is now and what it will be. Obviously, as we go on with the series, we shall find that at times we have stayed too close to tradition, whereas at other times we have ventured too far into the future.

This text is destined for undergraduate and graduate students who seek an introduction into the vast and complex field of social welfare. I believe this book excels in conceptual clarity and comprehensive coverage of the intricate subject of social welfare. Major issues are clearly identified and at the same time the text contains enough detailed description of specific facets of social welfare to afford beginning students on the undergraduate or graduate level an understanding of the field, prepare them to evaluate programs, and view these in historical context. Not the least asset of the book is its pervasive value perspective which reflects both the stance of the social work profession and the commitment of the authors.

In welcoming Dr. Feldstein's and Dr. Dolgoff's work to the Harper Series in Social Work, I believe we are adding an important and enduring contribution to the professional literature.

Werner W. Boehm

UNDERSTANDING SOCIAL WELFARE

Introduction

You are a social worker on the staff of a settlement house which is setting up a summer day camp for children. What fees, if any, are necessary or desirable? Or you are a member of an advisory committee or board of a community mental health center called on to voice an opinion on how much staff time should be devoted to the treatment of troubled individuals and how much to community education and preventive work. Or you are a citizen voting on a proposal for a county nursing home for the aged. Is it needed, or are there better ways to use limited funds for the elderly?

All of the above are examples of how social workers at every level, all citizens in the welfare state, are called on time and again to make policy decisions demanding some knowledge and sophistication in social welfare. In fact, these very examples are discussed in the final chapter of this volume with the hope that the reader, by that point, will be armed with the tools for intelligent and independent judgment. Voters act on proposals for government reorganization, but it is expected that somewhere in their education they have gained some understanding of the three branches of government, of single house versus bicameral legislatures, and other elements of government. Voters act on economic issues on the assumption that they have learned about supply and demand, about inflation and depression, and other basic economic ideas. But increasingly citizens develop opinions on social welfare issues with little background in the subject.

The purpose of this volume is to introduce the student to social welfare, from a definition of common terms to a working understanding of issues. The book is organized into eleven chapters.

Chapter 1 introduces, through one major example, the idea that social values, overtly or subliminally, influence social welfare structure in society. This chapter also will introduce the reader to the biases of the authors.

Chapters 2 and 3 contain a more thorough and general examination of the relationship between the social values of any given society and social welfare. How have different societies dealt with welfare, and what is their legacy to us?

In Chapter 4 we discuss definitions and some of the basic conceptions and issues in any social welfare system in any place or time. We develop a paradigm or schema for the understanding and analysis of any welfare program.

In Chapter 5 we examine the question of who the clients of social welfare are, with special attention to some particular groups such as the poor and the handicapped.

In Chapters 6 and 7, we use the paradigm that has been developed in Chapter 4 to look at the organization of major social welfare programs in the United States in our time.

Chapter 8 discusses the emergence of social work as a profession in the social welfare arena, while Chapter 9 takes up the functions, context, and issues of social work.

Chapter 10 seeks to identify some current social trends which are likely to affect the future of social welfare in the United States.

Finally, in Chapter 11 we discuss some proposals and programs to deal with social welfare problems, alternatives to the social welfare system now in operation. We hope that our readers, at the end of this volume, will be able to choose from alternatives and to refer to a body of knowledge, and a system of analysis, which will stand them in good stead as professional social workers or as citizens of the welfare society.

Chapter 1
Blaming the Victim[1]

"Competition . . . is a law of nature . . . if we try to amend it, there is only one way in which we can do it. We can take from the better and give to the worse. We can deflect the penalties of those who have done ill and throw them on those who have done better. We can take the rewards from those who have done better and give them to those who have done worse. We shall thus lessen the inequalities. We shall favor the survival of the unfittest, and we shall accomplish this by destroying liberty. Let it be understood that we cannot go outside of this alternative: liberty, inequality, survival of the fittest, not-liberty, equality, survival of the unfittest . . . ."

William Graham Sumner[2]

Once upon a time, a husband and wife lived together in a part of the city separated by a river from the places of employment, shopping, and entertainment.[3] The husband had to work nights. Each evening he left his wife and took the ferry to work, returning in the morning.

The wife soon tired of this arrangement. Restless and lonely, she would take the next ferry into town each evening and develop relationships with a series of lovers. Anxious to preserve her marriage, she always returned home before her husband. In fact, her

[1] The term has been popularized by William Ryan, *Blaming the Victim*, New York: Pantheon, 1971.
[2] William Graham Sumner, "The Challenge of Facts," *The Challenge of Facts & Other Essays*, Albert G. Keller (ed.), New Haven: Yale University Press, 1914, p. 25.
[3] This story is similar to "Alligator River" in Sidney B. Simon et al. *Values Clarification: A Handbook of Practical Strategies for Teachers and Students*, New York: Hart Publishers, 1972, pp. 290–294. Our version comes from Herbert Bisno.

relationships were always limited. When they threatened to become too intense, she would precipitate a quarrel with her current lover and begin a new relationship.

One night she caused such a quarrel with a man we will call Lover I. He slammed the door in her face, and she started back to the ferry. Suddenly she realized that she had forgotten to bring money for her return fare. She swallowed her pride and returned to Lover I's apartment to borrow the fare. After all, she *did* have to get home. But Lover I was vindictive and angry because of the quarrel. He slammed the door on his former lover, leaving her with no money. She remembered that a previous lover, whom we shall call Lover II, lived just a few doors away. Surely he would give her the ferry fare. However, Lover II was still so hurt from their old quarrel that he, too, refused her the money.

Now the hour was late and the woman was getting desperate. She rushed down to the ferry and pleaded with the ferryboat captain. He knew her as a regular customer. She asked if he could let her ride free and if she could pay the next night. But the captain insisted that rules were rules and that he could not let her ride without paying the fare.

Dawn would soon be breaking, and her husband would be returning from work. The woman remembered that there was a free bridge about a mile further on. But the road to the bridge was a dangerous one, known to be frequented by highwaymen. Nonetheless, she had to get home, so she took the road. On the way a highwayman stepped out of the bushes and demanded her money. She told him she had none. He seized her. In the ensuing tussle, the highwayman stabbed the woman, and she died.

Thus ends our story. There have been six characters: Husband, Wife, Lover I, Lover II, Ferryboat Captain, and Highwayman. We would like you to list, in descending order of responsibility for this woman's death, all the characters. In other words, the one most responsible is listed first; the next most responsible, second; and so forth.

How did your list turn out? If you were like most people, you listed the wife first or second. Remarkably, in most American audiences, about the same number of people list the wife first as list the highwayman first! The reasons are complex. A few people list the captain first ("inhuman capitalist" or "inflexible bureaucrat") or the husband ("he should have been concerned with meeting her needs") or one of the lovers ("how mean and petty he is"). But our concern is with the largest number, who divide over whether the wife or the highwayman is most responsible. Those who select the highwayman will usually say that, after all, he did kill the woman. The equal number who find the wife most responsible will say:

—she deserved it or
—she was asking for trouble or
—she should have known better

This group will often place the highwayman *last* on the list of responsibility, because he was, after all, "doing his thing" as a highwayman. He was operating in his professional role, so to speak, whereas the wife, by committing adultery and walking lonely roads at night, had stepped out of her role as wife. In fact, when the story is retold with the word *highwayman* being replaced by *murderer,* a higher percentage holds him more responsible. *Murderer* more readily conveys guilt than the more romantic term *highwayman.*

Fundamentally, the wife is held responsible for her own murder, because of her stupidity or her moral character. The story can be retold with the wife becoming a widow who works nights to feed her hungry babies: she had to get back before the baby-sitter left. Suddenly, the results change. In that case, the highwayman is more often held responsible. But his behavior has not changed. The wife has been blamed for her murder because of her morals.

The story can be retold again—this time a black woman sits in front of a bus in a southern town in the 1950s, knowing the potential reaction in a segregated community. A white man pulls her off the bus and beats her. Who is responsible? Or an old Jewish man walks the street in Nazi Germany wearing a skullcap, although he is aware of the antisemitism that abounds. He is beaten. Who is responsible? In these cases, most people in the audience change their votes—the victim is not responsible. But a few insist that going ahead while knowing the possible consequences makes the victim responsible. Assuming poor judgment has been used, they make poor judgment equal to murder in responsibility for death.

The story is only one illustration of the tendency in American culture to blame the victim. Others abound. For generations rape victims have been held suspect—somehow they must have provoked or otherwise encouraged the rape. When mental patients fail to respond to treatment, it is rarely the therapist who is held responsible; the patient is believed to be "unmotivated" or "not ready." When one of the authors had his automobile stolen recently, he started to blame himself—he should have kept it locked and parked it in a more secure area—rather than the person who stole the car. The tendency is pervasive. Essentially it suggests that those who are disadvantaged, victimized, poor, or handicapped somehow have been responsible for their condition; if they were better or more adequate people, they would not be in a dependent position.

We begin this text with a discussion of this tendency, because it has had a profound impact on the nature of social welfare in America. There is no desire to suggest that blaming the victim is the sole, or even necessarily the major, driving force in American social welfare. American social welfare is motivated by a mixture of motives rather than one unified impelling force, such as blaming the victim. Altruism, a refusal to ignore the suffering of others, a sense of fairness, and a concern for mutual aid are also viable American values. Social welfare also functions to meet the maintenance needs of society by preventing instability and by providing for social continuity. In part one's views of the functions of social welfare depend upon one's personal perspective, but in reality our American social welfare scene is marked by ambivalent motivations rather than one pure and straightforward intention.[4]

We deal with victim blaming because it is an example of how the values of a society, even implicit values, can influence the nature of its social welfare system. Blaming the victim has several roots and several manifestations, which we shall now explore. What are the components of this American tendency to blame the victim? How does it express itself in social welfare? And what are the biases of the authors that will inform this volume?

THE AMERICAN MYTH OF THE HERO

Far across the ocean from Europe there was America. For more than four centuries people have come to America—the secular Zion, the golden nation, the land of possibilities. Leaving behind traditions, families, and the familiar, people set out for or, in the case of blacks, were taken to America. For all but those who were enslaved, America was a land of dangers but also a land full of dreams.

From the Puritan seeking religious freedom in Massachusetts, to the debtors escaping imprisonment in Georgia, the early American settlers were a mixture of craft workers, paupers, businesspeople, sailors, artisans, and adventurers. They were seeking to escape and they were searching for new horizons beyond the ocean and beyond

---

[4] The basic thrust of modern social work practice and service is oriented toward a person-situation, frequently called ecological perspective, a systems approach which attempts to avoid blaming the victim. While social work as a profession struggles with this orientation which grows in acceptance, social welfare as a social institution remains more complex in motivation. See Max Siporin, *Introduction to Social Work Practice.* New York: Macmillan, 1975, pp.17–22.

the constraints of more developed societies. As Walt Whitman later suggested, "We take up the task eternal, and the burden and the lessons . . . pioneers o pioneers, all the past we leave behind . . . conquering, holding, daring, adventuring as we go the unknown ways."

The pioneers were seen as rugged individualists, doing all for themselves. The reality was quite different from the myth. A communitarian spirit was needed in frontier territories and pioneering times. Settlements developed, and people were interdependent. Daniel Boorstin, in *The Americans*, approached the reality this way:

> But, of all American myths, none is stronger than that of the loner moving West across the land. Without having thought much about why, we have taken for granted that, on landing, the colonial traveler no longer needed his community. The pioneering spirit, we are often told, is a synonym for "individualism." The courage to move to new places and to try new things is supposed to be the same as the courage to go it alone, to focus exclusively and intensively and enterprisingly on oneself. . . . There was, of course, the occasional lone traveler and individual explorer. . . . In history, even the great explorer has been the man who drew others to a common purpose, in the face of unpredictable hardships. . . . To cross the wild continent safely, one had to travel with a group. . . . When American ways were taking shape, many, perhaps most, of the people who were the first to settle at a distance from the protected boundaries of the Atlantic seaboard, traveled in groups.[5]

Even the early American government aided the individual with mechanisms similar to those used today. Puritan communities paid a salaried town doctor—a sort of socialized medicine. During Jefferson's first administration Congress appropriated money and had highways built, including the great Cumberland Road and the Post roads.[6] These roads had many purposes, chief among them being the encouragement of travel and trade.

The complexity and specialization of modern society makes interdependence greater and more necessary than ever. Each of us can perform only a small fraction of the functions necessary to help ourselves and society to survive. The astronauts are heroic figures even while they are excellent symbols of the necessary interdependence of "heroes." They need each other's skills; they are dependent upon teams of scientists and technicians. Even so, we are left with Americans still idealizing images of self-sufficient persons, the lone eagle, and the robber baron.

The American myth includes the following components:

[5] Daniel J. Boorstin, *The Americans*, New York: Vintage Books, 1967, pp. 51–52.
[6] Charles and Mary Beard, *Basic History of the United States*, Philadelphia: Blakiston, 1944, pp. 171 and 220.

1. The best people are the rugged individualists, who are physically strong, psychologically independent, and able to flourish without help.

2. "Making it" is what counts and is to be respected. The criteria for "making it" may change but not the admiration for the achievers. An older list of great Americans would include the Carnegies, Rockefellers, DuPonts, Harrimans, Vanderbilts, and others who amassed great wealth, often without regard to means. A recent intellectual autobiography was titled *Making It*. The criteria had changed but not the respect for achievement at almost any price.[7]

3. Everything is possible. There is a constant frontier, and those who try hard enough, no matter how humble their beginnings, can "make it."

4. Humans strive for material gain. If it were not for the carrot of material gain or the stick of hunger and deprivation, motivation for work might disappear. Self-fulfillment as an end in itself or as an ethical imperative is not seen as an adequate force to keep an economy moving. Having built an economy based on material gain, we now see other motives as shadowy, unreal, or idealistic.

5. The corollary of all the above is that those who fail to make it are at least incompetent, and perhaps even lazy and immoral (synonyms). Although the entire mythology has created some of the strains in American life, it is this final corollary which is the heart of victim blaming. Somehow, if things do not go well or if one fails, then one is to blame. Other cultures—Japanese and Jewish, for example—have extolled ambition and progress. It is the combination of this striving philosophy with the corollary that the victims are themselves to blame for their victimization that makes American society particularly unusual. Not all Americans accept the mythology. At different periods it is stronger or weaker. During the Great Depression of the 1930s people felt simultaneously that they were inadequate and that the social system had failed them.[8] There are trends away from the view of the world just described, and these trends will be discussed in Chapter 10, but this view continues to have a profound effect on life in America, particularly on social welfare.

---

[7] One sports fan wrote the following in a letter to the sports editor's mailbox in the *New York Times* (August 15, 1974, Section 5, p. 2). "If he does not teach his son to be an individual and not a team player he will do him a lasting disservice. It is his obligation as a father to prepare him for a realistic world . . ."

[8] "Everybody . . . blamed himself. . . . There was an acceptance that it was your own fault, your own indolence, your lack of ability". " . . . we all had an understanding that it wasn't our fault. It was something that happened to the machinery." These contradictory excerpts are from an oral history of the Great Depression. Studs Terkel, *Hard Times,* New York: Pantheon Books, 1970, pp. 90 and 52.

This mythology needed nurture to grow and develop, and the United States supplied it. The United States has been a land of opportunity to a degree unmatched by other societies. There was and continues to be more mobility in the United States than elsewhere. One price of that mobility has been the assumption that the nonmobile were inadequate. It was only in 1912 that the continental United States was completed with states admitted to the Union. The idea of a constant frontier, according to historian Fredrick J. Turner and others, is central to the American spirit. In fact, a new, young, and vigorous national administration in 1960 named its program "The New Frontier."

Intellectual, scientific, and religious currents all fed the mythology. In Chapter 2 we discuss the relationship between the views of human nature in any society and its welfare approach and programs, but it should be noted here that the demands of industrialism, the development of the Protestant ethic (particularly the Calvinist strain), and Social Darwinism each contributed to blaming the victim.

Industrialism uprooted people from their traditional homes and pursuits, drove them to rootless cities, and encouraged mobility, material gain, and competition. Industrialism demanded the amassing of great stores of capital, something frowned on in more traditional Christian theology. It demanded a large store of low-paid working people. Religion and science were equal to the task of developing a rationale and justification for these developments. The Calvinist idea that emerged included a number of components that are discussed in the following chapter. The element of its philosophy which concerns us here is that the successful and wealthy are God's elect. God has chosen to reward them on earth for their goodness, while the poor and miserable are receiving the fruits of their evil. One need not, therefore, overly pity the poor for receiving their just desserts at the hand of God, nor should we hate the rich who are God's elect.

Scientific support came from economics and genetics. Adam Smith's ideas and the theories of laissez-faire capitalism suggested that society functions best and that the common good is furthered most when there is little or no social interference in the affairs of the market. The market is a grand anonymous stage in which each commodity finds its own value. If labor is underpaid, this is only a reflection of its market value. Any attempt to interfere by regulation lessens the ultimate good to society. All the actors in society have to play out their roles on the stage of the market.

Social scientists went further. They took the ideas of natural selection developed by Darwin and created a social equivalent. The theory of natural selection, most simply stated, is that in nature the most fit survive and the least fit die. When a herd of deer run from a pack of wolves, it is the less fleet and less able among the deer who will be caught by the wolves. This is good for the species in the long run because the weaker deer do not survive to propagate, and the stronger deer do, thus improving the strain. Thus in society, in the free market (nature), there is a natural tendency for the best to succeed and to rise in society, and any attempt to interfere with this natural selection only perpetuates and gives favor to those who cannot help society, but only harm it and bring it down.

Social welfare measures, which help the weak, only weaken society. The kindest approach, in the long run, is to let the weak fall. Laissez-faire philosophers might admit a role for charity, but more to foster uplifting the soul of the philanthropist than for aiding the victim. President Herbert Hoover claimed that enterprise builds society while charity builds character.

All of these ideas and forces had their impact in shaping the American myth. They were particularly functional to a young, vigorous, and expanding country in which there were many casualties of that expansion, from the indigenous native Americans to the black slaves, the working poor, and the waves of immigrants from different countries in each generation.

It is not our intent here to try to counter the arguments of these philosophies. They will be discussed further in Chapters 2 and 3. Most Americans reject them on face value. We live in a welfare state, and "they" are expected to be able to do something about our social problems. Most Americans believe that the destitute should be helped. But so deep and so pervasive in the American grain is the philosophy of blaming the victim that we still find ourselves, in many unconscious and subtle ways, repeating the patterns that belong to philosophies we have long since rejected. The story that opened this chapter, and the reactions of most people to it, is one example. It is a subtle mind set that demands a kind of consciousness-raising to overcome. We will discuss important ways in which this mind set is still active and particularly how it affects social welfare in America.

THE CLASSIC WELFARE CRACKDOWN SYNDROME

At the beginning of the decade of the 1960s, the city of Newburgh, New York, came into national prominence. Faced with limited funds and growing welfare rolls, a popular and demagogical city manager won fame by promising to crack down on welfare cheaters and those people who were draining the city of its wealth. The steps he took were examined by the late Samuel Mencher in an analysis of the Newburgh crisis as an example of how all communities have tended to respond to welfare problems at all periods in American history.[9]

This is how Mencher analyzed the response:

1. Make assistance as unpleasant as possible. The ways that this is done sometimes change in different places and periods. Mencher included giving relief in kind rather than money, threats of prosecution, constant reevaluation, and other difficulties. There is little attention given to the reality that a welfare cheater is not going to be dissuaded by having to stand on line for an hour, but an infirm or elderly person may be. A shy person afraid of the stigma of welfare may never make it onto the welfare rolls. Somehow the people on welfare are seen as to blame for unemployment, urban deterioration, and other social problems, and making assistance unpleasant is a social response.

2. Make recipients of relief work for the aid given. This is based partly on the fear that no one would work unless forced to and that the economy would come apart if people were assisted.

3. Keep the level of help so low that it will discourage anyone from taking relief in preference to working. This, too, is related to the work ethic, but it is also generally punitive.

4. Prevent outsiders or newcomers to the community from obtaining help: set up strict residence requirements for welfare eligibility. Because more and more welfare monies come from national sources rather than localities, this tendency has declined somewhat in local communities, but we still can see its presence in the adverse reaction to immigration during an economic recession and other fears that outsiders, newcomers, or "they" are taking jobs away from "us."

5. Encourage people to remain employed or to return to employment. Deny assistance to those voluntarily leaving jobs. Employment must be accepted regardless of its nature. Mencher discussed the dysfunctional results of such policies, which lead to the downgrading and cheapening of employment.

This is how American society has tended to respond to its poor in slightly altered forms and versions in different times and places. It illustrates one of the ways in which we continue to blame the victim for his or her afflictions. We take great pains to separate those who appear truly worthy of assistance from the unworthy, the cheaters, and the free-loaders who, in our opinion, comprise great per-

[9] Samuel Mencher, "Newburgh; The Recurrent Crisis of Public Assistance," *Social Work*, vol. VII, No. 1, January 1962, pp. 3–11.

centages of the poor despite all evidence to the contrary.[10] So that even while we no longer believe in a classical Calvinist doctrine or in Social Darwinism in its purest forms, the effects of this kind of thinking are still very much with us. As Lewis Coser has written " . . . the very granting of relief, the very assignment of the person to the category of the poor, is forthcoming only at the price of a degradation of the person who is so assigned."[11]

New Forms of Blaming the Victim

William Ryan in his book *Blaming the Victim* identifies a particularly powerful form of victim blaming current among those who have rejected the more obvious forms of this philosophy. We no longer say, points out Ryan, that the victim is evil or responsible for victimization. We may even sympathize with the victim. But we say that because the victim has been oppressed, because of all the injustices that have been done, he or she is now in such a poor state of social functioning that nothing can be done to make things better until the victim changes. In other words, the focus of our concern and our change efforts continue to be on the victim rather than on the society which has been the oppressor. In welfare planning, policy, and service delivery this point of view can take many forms. Ryan mentions one rather classic example. We "know" that the poor are incapable of deferring gratification, that they can't plan ahead or invest resources. One "proof" of this is the experiment in which the experimenter comes into a classroom of young children and offers the children a choice of one candy bar immediately or two candy bars at dismissal several hours later. In a schoolroom of middle-class children most students will opt for the two candy bars later. In a classroom in a poor neighborhood most children will opt for the one candy bar now. However, Ryan points out that this may not be due to an inability to defer gratification so much as a realistic response to prior experience. A skeptic conducted a study using the above candy bar example but added another element.

> The added factor consisted of giving the children an experience in which the promise of delayed gratification (two candy bars next week

[10] This evidence will be discussed further in Chapter 5. One example is offered here: In April 1971, the U.S. Department of Health, Education and Welfare found that less than 1 percent of welfare recipients were able-bodied men. (From *Welfare Myths vs. Facts*, Department of HEW, Social and Rehabilitation Service, Washington, D.C., SRS 72-02009.)

[11] Lewis A. Coser, "The Sociology of Poverty," *Social Problems*, vol. XIII, No. 2, Fall 1965, p. 144.

rather than one right now) was either kept or not kept. When the experiment was repeated, this was the only factor that differentiated between those who chose immediate gratification and those who chose to delay. Class and race were *not* related to delay. Those who had experienced a broken promise were the ones—not unsurprisingly—who were not willing to delay and thereby risk another disappointment.[12]

But our thinking continues to be that the problem somehow is in the psyche or the culture of the poor themselves rather than in the social conditions that continue to deny them opportunity. The children's attitudes have to change, we say, rather than the available opportunities. Thus do we blame the victim in modern terms.

Another example, perhaps apocryphal, is nonetheless worth relating. Students from a school of social work in a major university were placed in a hospital setting where a campaign against lead poisoning was being mounted. Many children grow ill and even die from chewing on the lead-based paint on windowsills and from the peeling walls of their homes. The students in the hospital began with a leaflet campaign to warn parents about the dangers of lead poisoning so that parents could supervise their children or bring them in for testing if symptoms developed. The students grew more aggressive. In this particular neighborhood they wanted leaflets and sound trucks in both Spanish and English so that people would know more about the services, and this was done. But the students grew even more thoughtful. Why should the service be focused on the victims of lead poisoning? Why not focus on the landlords who were not repairing and repainting apartments in violation of the law? So the students set out to find the landlords.

The largest single landlord in the neighborhood under consideration turned out to be the very university that was educating the students in social work to mount this campaign. This is an example of the sophisticated form of victim blaming Ryan stresses. It is putting the focus of the problem on the victim, when often this is not appropriate. In the 1960s there was the well-publicized "Moynihan Report" to President Lyndon Johnson which analyzed the problems of the Negro family.[13] Many critics felt that this, too, was a classic example of victim blaming. Although it sympathized with the problems of the Negro family and pointed out that these problems were due to generations of oppression, it suggested that little could be done to help blacks in America until the Negro family could be stabilized and strengthened. Many saw this as an invitation to focus

---

[12] Ryan, op. cit., pp. 112, 127–128.
[13] *The Negro Family: The Case for National Action*, U.S. Department of Labor, U.S. Government Printing Office, Washington, D.C., 1965.

efforts on the victims and to change them rather than to change the social conditions that created the oppression.

Thus blaming the victim is very much alive and very much with us.

> The miserable health care of the poor is explained away on the grounds that the victim has poor motivation and lacks health information. The problems of slum housing are traced to the characteristics of tenants who are labeled as "Southern rural migrants" not yet "acculturated" to life in the big city. . . . Every important social problem—crime, mental illness, civil disorder, unemployment—has been analyzed within the framework of the victim-blaming ideology.[14]

What are some of the reasons why we blame the victim? Blaming the victim serves certain purposes. It makes us feel superior; it allows us to express our hostilities toward relatively safe objects. And it also allows us subtly to defend the status quo in a society where many poor go hungry.

DO THE POOR WANT SERVICES?

An argument offered by those who blame the poor for their condition is that even if services are available, the poor do not avail themselves of these services. It has been suggested, for example, that the poor do not make use of health services because they are not really interested in health care for themselves, cannot plan for the future, expect to be disabled and ill as they get older, and so on. The major emphasis of this perspective is that poor people live in a "culture of poverty" which will not allow them to make proper use of the medical and health services.

Catherine Riessman in "The Use of Health Services by the Poor" reviewed the health care utilization patterns of lower socioeconomic groups in a number of settings. She examined the experiences of a university affiliated demonstration project, a prepaid group practice plan, and research from neighborhood health centers and decentralized family planning programs. According to her, data from these programs strongly suggest the health behavior of the poor can be altered rapidly by introducing structural changes in the ways services are offered and without seeking reasons why poor persons, because of factors intrinsic to being poor, do not use the services. Changing such factors as the cost of care, distance, and physician-patient interaction all had significant impact on the patterns of use. Similarly, in Great Britain, after the introduction of national health

---

[14] Ryan, op. cit., pp. 5–6.

insurance, it was found there was a marked increase in the use of physician and hospital services by the lower economic groups.[15]

But these findings were not really new. Four years earlier, Alan Gartner reported a whole series of examples of the use of services by the poor. He listed, among others, the following illustration. In Oklahoma, where three public health nurses had brought in 200 persons a month for immunizations, 7 paraprofessionals had brought in 2000 persons in the same service area per month.[16]

SELF-FULFILLING PROPHECIES

In recent years a discipline has arisen called *victimology*, which is the systematic study of victims.[17] Based upon an interactional approach to psychology, it suggests that the masochist needs the sadist and that the victim needs the victimizer. They are partners in the situation, and both get rewards. This may indeed be the case, where people interact in such a way that their psychological needs are met. There also may be persons who are victimization prone. The intelligent social worker and citizen will be aware of this possibility in any individual situation. On the other hand, most people who are poor do not fit into these neat categories. They obviously do not choose their victimization; it is placed upon them in large part by the way in which society is structured.

Perhaps the saddest feature of victim blaming is that people can react adversely when negative prophecies are made about them, just as they also can fulfill prophecies of a more hopeful nature. In numerous educational experiments, the intellectual achievements of children have been found to be dependent upon the expectations teachers hold for them. The labeling of poor persons, the mentally ill, and others with specific designations which serve to stereotype them has been found to strongly influence the expectations people hold for them. Tell a teacher a child is a poor learner, and he or she is likely to learn little; tell a teacher the same child has a high IQ, and he or she is likely to learn more. These expectations profoundly influence our perceptions of the poor and, simultaneously, influence the poor themselves in their expectations and self-definition.[18]

[15] Catherine Kohler Riessman, "The Use of Health Services by the Poor," *Social Policy*, Vol. 5, No. 1, May/June 1974, pp. 41–49.
[16] Alan Gartner, "Services: Do the Poor Use Them?" *Social Policy*, Vol. 1, No. 4, November/December 1970, pp. 71–72.
[17] See, for example, *Victimology*, Israel Drapkin and Emilio Viano (eds.), Lexington: Lexington Books, 1974, and *Victimology: An International Journal*, Vol. 1, No. 1 (Spring 1976) forward.
[18] Robert Rosenthal, "Self-fulfilling Prophecy," *Psychology Today*, Vol. 2, No. 4, September 1968, pp. 46–51.

THE AUTHORS' PERSPECTIVE

The reader deserves to know something about the biases of the authors. We move from a twin point of view:

1. Ultimately, individuals are responsible for their actions and behavior, if not for their fates.
2. The victims of our society are victimized primarily by the institutional structure of society and not by their own inadequacies or actions.

Both of these perspectives are important. We are as concerned about those who found the highwayman not guilty in our original story as we are about those who found the woman guilty. The highwayman may have been acting out his professional role. He also may have been a victim of oppressive forces which forced him to enter a life of crime. That may be society's fault, and it may be society's responsibility to restructure itself so that such people will be less likely to become highwaymen. Nonetheless, the highwayman is responsible for taking a life. Because of the circumstances in which people are born and raised, there are different odds confronting each individual. There are unequal capacities among people, and there are oppressive social forces. We do not deny these factors as part of the reality which confronts each individual in relation to his or her own responsibility. Also, sometimes people are so incapacitated that their impairment makes it impossible for them to control their own actions, and therefore they do not have a full measure of responsibility. These exceptions and external forces create dilemmas for human beings but, it seems to us, we have to hold people responsible for their actions *precisely* because such a claim upon them maintains their very humanity and dignity. The question is this: To what extent are people really human without assuming responsibility for their actions?

The person who kills another must ultimately be considered responsible, or we deny him his very humanity. The public official who engages in corruption because she went along with the others, the Nazi who obeyed orders, and the mugger who must support a heroin habit all are finally "to blame" or responsible for the acts they commit. There is a song in the musical *West Side Story* in which the juvenile delinquents are addressing their tormentor, Officer Krupke. After several humorous verses in which they mock society's shuttling them from judge, to psychiatrist, to social worker, the song mounts to an impassioned climax in which the delinquents insist that it is not environment or upbringing which caused their plight but, "Deep down inside us, we're no good." Although this obviously is not true, it is their way of insisting that they be recognized as individuals in their own right, that there is a certain kind of sociological jargon which is as dehumanizing as is victim blaming. If one is human, one is deserving of faith in ultimate worth, in capacity to grow. But being human implies being responsible for one's acts in spite of adversity. There is a patronizing element in portraying vandals as social revolutionaries, and ultimately there is racism in suggesting that minorities cannot be expected to live up to expectations for responsible behavior.

At the same time, we believe that poverty and other social problems derive largely from the institutional arrangements of the society in which we live. These arrangements are the result of an interplay among philosophical beliefs such as those that have been reviewed here and the demands of our society. These factors are structural in the society and not simply the byplay of individuals with equal opportunity making their demands felt in a free market economy. From the tax structure, which is not as progressive as it pretends to be, to the availability of social services and supports, to the punishments meted out by the penal system, there is vast inequality in how people are treated by society. There is a kind of "welfare" for the wealthy and for large industries (such as tax relief for mismanaged industries) not available to the poor. It is our point of view, therefore, that solutions to social problems must be sought in institutional and structural arrangements rather than in the rehabilitation of vast numbers of sick, disturbed, or uncultured people. Although as social workers we believe that individual victims may need and deserve individual services, the greatest help will come to most people through institutional change.

We live in a highly industrialized society in which we are all very interdependent. We are not the mythological autonomous and independent beings which we are led to believe is the highest order; we are, in fact, integrally dependent upon others. We cannot all assemble automobiles, grow corn, mill wheat, and teach ourselves, and we are deeply dependent upon others who are, in turn, dependent upon our own specialized skills and knowledge.

We also believe that there is an alternative reading of the information on evolution, which leads us to see cooperation and sharing rather than competition and destruction as the key elements for survival.

Ashley Montagu, the noted anthropologist, suggests:

> Clearly, the degree of sociality, of co-operativeness, prevailing in any group will constitute an important factor in influencing its fertility rate as well as its survival rate. It cannot be too often repeated that all ani-

mals are members of social groups, and that there is no such thing as a solitary animal,.even though some groups are much less integrated than others. Social life is, among other things, a means of ensuring reproduction. To the extent, therefore, that any group is less social, less fully integrated, than another, it is likely to be differentially less fertile. All other factors being equal, with the exception of the degree of social integration, it should be obvious that the group in which its members are closely integrated, are often together, is the group that is likely to leave a greater surviving progeny than the group whose members are less integratedly social.[19]

In nature there is competition, but there is also cooperation. There is selfishness, but there is also mutual aid, idealism, and self-sacrifice.

From our point of view we see the poor as victims of an imperfect system. We believe this is not the only choice in society and that other options are available. Finally, we suggest that the middle-class in our society is also a victim. Although economically less disadvantaged, the middle class, too, is caught in a snare of individualism run rampant, in which blame for one's situation and mishaps is self-directed. The middle class, often ineligible for public welfare programs and unable to pay for private ones, believes with other Americans that its problems, too, are the result of individual failure. "If we were really equal to the task, all things would be possible. Whatever our difficulties, they are the result of our failures." The over-reaction to this belief system, the other side of the coin, is the tendency among some contemporary groups to deny their own humanity, to disclaim responsibility for their behavior, to despair of achieving progress when "they" don't respond immediately to a political campaign, or to retreat to disinterested utopias. This is a kind of self-victimization.

We see victim blaming as having profoundly affected the social structure in the United States, particularly in social welfare. We see humans, however imperfectly, as being capable of adopting more humane values and of structuring a more humane society.

[19] Ashley Montagu, *Darwin, Competition, and Conflict*, New York: Henry Schuman, 1952, pp. 102–103.

Chapter 2
Social Values and Social Welfare

> "Culture is not . . . 'a response to the total needs of society,' but rather a system which stems from and expresses something had, the basic values of the society."[1]

In the first chapter we described "blaming the victim," several views of the human as victim, and some ways of understanding the poor. There will be critical differences in the social welfare institutions of the society, depending on whether, and to what degree, it blames the victim. If the victim, the poor person, is responsible for his or her plight, then at worst society will set up rather punitive, or very limited, social welfare services. At best the social welfare services will be directed to improving the victim. On the other hand, if society assumes that its own institutions and their deficiencies are responsible for poverty, then the efforts of the social welfare system may be directed toward correcting and improving those institutions. This is true in any society.

The social welfare systems a society constructs and operates are direct outcomes of the social values that are inherent in it. Often these values are implicit. They are understood as such obvious and

[1] Dorothy Lee, "Are Basic Needs Ultimate?" *Journal of Abnormal and Social Psychology*, Vol. 43, 1948, p. 395.

commonsense truth that they may not even be stated. And yet they inform the entire approach to social welfare. In this chapter, and the next, we examine how various societies, including our own, base their social welfare systems upon predominant views of human nature. While this chapter cannot be an inclusive one, covering all social welfare history, we will explore the legacy that has been bequeathed to us from the past, taking special cognizance of those social institutions and values which continue to be influential in the American social welfare structure. Primarily, we hope to make the student aware of the relationship between societal values and the organization of social welfare, so that in examining the latter the student will always look to the former for greater understanding.

MODERN VIEWS OF HUMANITY

Some people believe that humans are inherently good, and others believe humans are inherently evil. A classic statement about the evil nature of humans was made by the seventeenth-century philosopher Thomas Hobbes, who pictured human nature so "that during the time men live without a common power to keep them all in awe, they are in that condition which is called war; and such a war, as is of every man, against every man . . . continual fear, and danger of violent death, and the life of man, solitary, poor, nasty, brutish, and short."[2] No person is to be trusted, and one should anticipate the evil acts of humans rather than expect their cooperation and goodness.

More recently exponents of the fundamental, biological nature of human aggression and self-seeking behavior such as zoologist Konrad Lorenz have suggested that "the aggression drive is a true, primarily species-preserving instinct [which] enables us to recognize its full danger; it is the spontaneity of the instinct that makes it so dangerous."[3] Thus, on both philosophical and on scientific grounds, some claim that humans are untrustworthy, evil, aggressive, and dangerous.

Counter to this view of human nature is the view expounded, for example, by Jean Jacques Rousseau, an eighteenth-century philosopher. He suggested that people are naturally good and that evil does not originate in human nature but has its source in the external

[2] Thomas Hobbes, *Leviathan*, Michael Oakeshott (ed.), Oxford, England: Basil Blackwell, 1946, p. 82.
[3] Konrad Lorenz, *On Aggression*, London: Methuen, 1967, p. 40.

world. (We have contrasted "evil" and "good" for simplicity. People who believe in the capacity of the environment include those who would substitute "neutral" for "good," with the ability to be influenced either way.) Rousseau suggested we "lay down as an incontrovertible maxim that nature's first movements are always right: there is no original perversity in the human heart: there is not a single vice in it, of which I cannot say how and where it came in."[4] Arguing that humans are born good and evil derives from institutional arrangements, Rousseau, unlike Joseph Conrad, looked into the heart of humankind and saw not darkness but light.

In regard to social welfare, if we believe that humans are fundamentally evil, then we must be guarded and erect controls against evil, which can include all unacceptable behavior. Thus the causation of poverty, mental illness, out-of-wedlock pregnancies, hyperactive children, and other problems are attributed not to external forces but to the evil nature of people. Because one cannot trust statements of need or portrayals of plight, barriers are placed in front of people, and those in need are demeaned.

Rousseau's view of people as basically good fosters the idea that the societal arrangements which create evil and human problems should be altered so as to allow for the well-being of people. For instance, people should escape from the cities which are "dark, Satanic mills" and live in the countryside where they can be natural and good.

In summary, if people are considered evil, societies can explain away their needs and problems as having been created by their evil individuals. This view relieves society of the need to alter living arrangements among people and suggests that nothing can be done to change their welfare. On the other hand, if people are considered good, then one can approach social welfare as a means, in Jane Addams' memorable phrase, "to raising life to its highest value." People's lives can be improved and arrangements in society can be altered to reach higher goals for all citizens.

SELF-ACTUALIZATION VERSUS IRRITATION RESPONSE THEORIES

Just as human nature can be categorized as good or evil, theories about the *motivations* of humans can be classified into two categories: self-actualization and response to irritation. Believing that people are inherently self-actualizing or that they only respond to

[4] Ronald Grimsley, *The Philosophy of Rousseau*, (Oxford, England: Oxford University Press, 1973), p. 45.

irritation and goading has important consequences. Abraham Maslow, for example, is a major exponent of the view that humans are self-actualizing. In his view every person has a hierarchy of needs, including physiological needs, safety, belongingness, love, self-esteem, and self-actualization. Each person tries to satisfy these needs in ascending order so that more basic needs are cared for first, leaving the person free to work on the next "higher" level need. Fundamental to this point of view is the idea that there is a universal set of basic impulses found in each person to satisfy ascending sets of needs.[5]

Arguing in favor of a guaranteed annual income, Erich Fromm, a noted psychoanalyst, reflected this point of view when he suggested a human being is by nature not lazy but is basically productive and active. Problems of motivation are not, in his opinion, inherent in the nature of individuals but rest in habits of consumption, the attitudes of people, and political arrangements.[6]

Even basic needs may not be ultimate. Dorothy Lee suggested that needs are derived from values rather than basic and ultimate. She argues:

> . . . it is value, not a series of needs, which is at the basis of human behavior. The main difference between the two lies in the conception of the good which underlies them. The premise that man acts so as to satisfy needs presupposes a negative conception of the good as amelioration or the correction of an undesirable state. According to this view, man acts to relieve tension; good is the removal of evil and welfare the correction of ills; satisfaction is the meeting of a need; good functioning comes from adjustment, survival from adaptation; peace is the resolution of conflict; fear, of the supernatural or of adverse public opinion, is the incentive to good conduct; the happy individual is the well-adjusted individual.[7]

Such a view is natural in a society that believes people are born in sin and must strive willfully to overcome their inherently evil selves.

Needs also could be seen as arising from the values of a particular culture, much as in our culture we pass on through values the need for individualism and achievement. In other cultures, values determine other ways of living and viewing the world. The Arapesh, for instance, "plant their trees in some one else's hamlet, they rear

[5] Abraham H. Maslow, *Motivation and Personality*, New York: Harper & Row, 1970, pp. 35–58.
[6] Erich Fromm, "The Psychological Aspects of the Guaranteed Income," in Robert Theobald, (ed.), *The Guaranteed Income.* Garden City: Doubleday and Co., 1966, pp. 175–184.
[7] Dorothy Lee, "Are Basic Needs Ultimate?" *Personality in Nature, Society, and Culture*, New York: Alfred A. Knopf, 1956, p. 337.

pigs owned by someone else, they eat yams planted by someone else."[8] Lee is suggesting with this example, and others, that people are beyond self-actualization, that needs are not basic. Rather human behavior and needs themselves are defined by basic societal values. Given this point of view, society could just as easily be arranged in such a manner that people will work, as Fromm suggests, without being whipped or goaded. Of, if one believes in an inherent drive for self-actualization, one then can trust that those in need do not need so much to be irritated and goaded as that opportunities and social structures must be revised to enable those in poverty to achieve their aims.

Karl Polanyi also has made a similar point about the importance of basic social values as determinants of social arrangements. He has stressed the relationship of noneconomic motives to the economic system suggesting that

> The outstanding discovery of recent historical and anthropological research is that man's economy, as a rule, is submerged in his social relationships. He does not act so as to safeguard his individual interest in the possession of material goods; he acts so as to safeguard his social standing, his social claims, his social assets. He values material goods only in so far as they serve this end. Neither the process of production nor that of distribution is linked to specific economic interests attached to the possession of goods; but every single step in that process is geared to a number of social interests which eventually ensure that the required step be taken . . . but in either case the economic system will be run on noneconomic motives.[9]

The essential point of the argument by Lee and Polanyi is that the economic motivation of people and society could be subsumed in the social texture of life. Economic factors are not unreal, but instead the suggestion is made that humans and societies can be motivated by other, equally real motivations.

Given a choice, we could view people as self-actualizing as did, for example, the series of services which enable persons on public assistance to complete their high school studies and then in stages complete associate and higher degrees with the support of public funds. Such programs are based upon a belief in the self-actualizing powers of people who are poor and that there is a "payoff" for society in lower welfare costs for and taxes to be paid by the achiever and his or her family.

The irritation philosophy, on the other hand, demands that poor people live uncomfortable lives based on the theory that this will

---

[8] Ibid., p. 340.
[9] Karl Polanyi, *The Great Transformation*, Boston: Beacon Press, 1957, p. 46.

motivate them to stronger efforts to succeed. John Romanyshyn, in a discussion of the effect of viewing man as evil in nature, suggested the double-edged quality of the argument. To regard people as "naturally lazy, driven to useful work only through hunger and fear of starvation" is to suggest that "societies characterized by scarcity require an image of man that will justify social discipline required to get necessary but distasteful toil accomplished. Affluent societies can afford wider freedom of choice and can facilitate the development of new views of man more consistent, perhaps, with his true nature."[10]

So it may not be inherent in people that they need goading and irritation in order to be active; it may be that such a "reading" of people derives from scarcity in societies or from societies that do not choose to share sufficiently with those in poverty. Or it may be that such views derive from the need in a particular society to accomplish something in the future. Punitive, irritant behavior has been typical in our society for dealing with those in poverty. Low payments beneath the recognized level of subsistence, rude and punitive behavior toward the poor, and various forms of harassment are all ostensibly aimed at restoring the poor to productive lives.

The irritation response theme implicitly runs from Adam Smith to Milton Friedman and from Karl Marx to Mao Tse-tung: a human is an economic being who works for economic gain and whose behavior is economically determined. In this respect, capitalism, communism, and socialism are triplets, in that they all view people in economic terms.[11] To accept as fact the view that a human being works only for economic gain supports a punitive approach to poverty. This view makes "less eligibility" inevitable (no one on welfare can be paid as much as the lowest paid employed person in the community). Although we know in practice there are specific exceptional cases, our societal theory views less eligibility as a necessity. Persons in poverty, it is thought, can only be encouraged to rise from their impoverished state through the discomforts of low payments and a life without enough to live on. Thus, if one believes in the economic human being, then less eligibility seems to be almost inevitable, because otherwise people would not work.

Closely related to the view of the human as an economic being is the belief that a market mentality is the central and inevitable reality. Such a view is very close to the fundamentals of capitalism, communism, and socialism. This value theme also suggests that reality is

[10] John M. Romanyshyn, *Social Welfare: Charity to Justice.* New York: Random House, 1971, p. 309.
[11] Karl Marx, *Capital, The Communist Manifesto and Other Writings*, Max Eastman (ed.), New York: Modern Library, 1932; Milton Friedman, *Capitalism and Freedom*, Chicago: University of Chicago Press, 1962.

based upon the economic human being. The organization of society and the motivations of people are dictated by the market mentality, and other motives are relatively insignificant.

Polanyi has challenged this point of view and suggested that on the basis of historical evidence, as we have indicated above, economic relationships are subsumed in social relations. For example, Polanyi reports on arrangements in a number of societies where the productive and economic system was arranged so as not to threaten any person with starvation. Two such citations will suffice to make the point: "no Kwakiutl ever ran the least risk of going hungry," and "there is no starvation in societies living on the subsistence margin."[12]

A modern student of business management and the motivations of workers has hypothesized two theories, neatly entitled Theory X and Theory Y, upon which managers base their attempts to motivate workers. The assumptions of Theory X are as follows:

> ... the average human being has an inherent dislike of work and will avoid it if he can. Because of this human characteristic of dislike of work, most people must be coerced, controlled, directed, threatened with punishment to get them to put forth adequate effort toward the achievement of organizational objectives. The average human being prefers to be directed, wishes to avoid responsibility, has relatively little ambition, wants security above all.

Unlike Theory X, Theory Y holds with Maslow and Fromm that people expend physical and mental effort in work as naturally as they do in play or rest. A person will achieve organizational and personal goals through self-direction and self-control in seeking objectives to which he or she is committed. Achievement, acceptance of responsibility, creativity, and other aptitudes are widely distributed in the population.[13]

The market, the need for irritants, and the theory of the economic human being are combined in Theory X. Theory X reflects in its unity the fact that similar conclusions can be reached with either the market, the need for irritation, or the theory of the economic human being as fundamental assumptions about people.

As Polanyi has suggested, and as the world makes abundantly clear, societies have the ability to set any kind of mechanism to motivate human activity. Economic activity is certainly necessary for

[12] Karl Polanyi, "Our Obsolete Market Mentality," *Commentary*, Vol. 3, February, 1947, pp. 109–117. For other examples, see Polanyi, *The Great Transformation*, pp. 163–164.
[13] Douglas McGregor, *The Human Side of Enterprise*, New York: McGraw-Hill, 1960, pp. 33–34, 47.

the survival of society, but it can be pursued from a multitude of motives, including social ones. Harvesting, for instance, can be a religious ritual. Polanyi is critical of the split reflected in the market mentality that humans have two selves: the economic or market self and the other self, which is ideal and spiritual. With such a human-created dichotomy, economic determinism holds sway and inhibits other ways of viewing humans and society. Both capitalist and socialist societies are trapped in economic human being theories of motivation which make less probable fundamental alterations in how we view those in poverty.

From Polanyi's multimotivational point of view, social motives also serve as the engine for society and individuals, not just economic motives. Thus, from the standpoint of social welfare, assistance to poor people could just as well be based upon our social responsiblity to them. In addition, their motivation can be stronger as a result of the realization that society holds them as valued citizens and will not let them starve or be punished. Subliminal messages in this case would resound through society; poor people are to be trusted, cared for, and given to because of our higher social goals.

In our highly industrialized society strong relationships have been established between machine technology and an emphasis upon monetary motivation. According to Melville J. Herskovits this relationship has created institutions in our society which are found in no others. It is this special situation about which questions can be raised.

Herskovits has suggested that in our society

> . . . a unique focussing of economic effort on production for profit rather than for use has had repercussions on all other aspects of life. Technological unemployment is one such result, the business cycle is another; both are intimately related to a system that requires scarcity, artificially produced, if necessary, for functioning. This, in turn, makes it difficult for many persons, without regard to their ability or willingness to perform a required task, to obtain the fundamental necessities of life. In almost all non-machine societies, and in all non-literate ones, this is unknown. Resources may be meager, and subsistence difficult to obtain, but where there is not enough to go around all go hungry, as all participate when seasons of plenty provide abundance. "No one ever went hungry," among the Baganda of East Africa, "because everyone was welcome to go and sit down and share a meal with his equals," is a good expression of the tradition, universal among nonliterate folk, that none must be allowed to want in the face of plenty.[14]

[14] Melville J. Herskovits, *Man and His Works*, New York: Alfred A. Knopf, 1960, p. 267.

Peter Kropotkin has illustrated mutual aid mechanisms in all types of societies throughout history, including medieval city life and today's unions, business, political, and remarkably diverse voluntary associations. Kropotkin argues, for example, "the practice of mutual aid and its successive developments have created the very conditions of society life in which man was enabled to develop his arts, knowledge, and intelligence; and that the periods when institutions based on the mutual-aid tendency took their greatest development were also the periods of the greatest progress in arts, industry, and science."[15]

Despite the fact that it is clear industrial societies require mutual aid and cooperation, the myths remain strong that the motivations of people are dictated by the market (supply and demand) and the necessity of competition. In the following section we skim the surface of nonliterate societies, historic cultures, and nations, focusing on elements of particular interest to our understanding of human nature and alternative arrangements and on precedents which influence current social welfare. As we shall see, modern themes have very ancient counterpoints.

NONLITERATE AND ANCIENT SOCIETIES

A recent survey of hunting-gathering societies leads to the conclusion

> ... that most primitive human societies are at the same time the most egalitarian. This must be related to the fact that because of rudimentary technology this kind of society depends on cooperation more fully more of the time than any other. ... the evolution of culture has involved an evolution of technology, and thus an increasing mastery over hostile nature. Just as necessary, just as difficult, but not always so obvious, has been the mastery of man's own nature. The social inventions that have enabled societies to become larger, more complex, and stronger all have something to do with remaking or channeling man's biological needs and propensities, most of all with redirecting his selfishness.

> Food in primitive society also functions to enhance sociability rather than to be the cause of friction and competition. ... the act of sharing is so frequently a matter of polity as well as etiquette that even when food is scarce and hunger is acute generosity is more likely to prevail over hoarding simply because the maintenance or strengthening of social bonds is so important in rudimentary societies.[16]

[15] Peter Kropotkin, *Mutual Aid*, Boston, Extending Horizons Books, 1914, p. 296.
[16] Elman R. Service, *The Hunters*, Englewood Cliffs, New Jersey: Prentice-Hall, 1966, p. 30.

It may be that our complex and specialized society requires even more complicated mutual aid and cooperation. Nevertheless, we foster the myth of individual responsibility, and the "survival of the fittest" is more or less an accepted societal value.

Altruism grows out of a sociocultural reality, as does "blaming the victim." Every culture has to develop altruistic components which are required for the survival of the group. The essential factor is to recognize that the degree of cooperation and altruism, the intensity of the "blaming-the-victim" syndrome, and the role of social welfare are determined by predominant views of humans in any society, a feature which is open to choice and control.

As another aid to our sense of perspective, "blaming the victim" was unknown in pre-Colonial America. Here is a quotation from a letter written by Amerigo Vespucci describing his experience with native Americans: "They are so liberal in giving that it is the exception when they deny you anything; and, on the other hand, they are free in begging, when they show themselves to be your friends."[17]

During 1493 Christopher Columbus in a letter to King Ferdinand and Queen Isabella described the native Americans he encountered this way: "After they have shaken off their fear of us, they display a frankness and liberality in their behavior which no one would believe without witnessing it. No request of anything from them was ever refused, but they rather invite acceptance of whatever they possess, and manifest such generosity that they would give away their own hearts."[18] Their society functioned effectively and with a complex social system, using mutual aid and without an all-encompassing market mentality.

In the following brief review of ancient cultures, we will focus on elements of particular interest to our understanding of certain influences on social welfare today.

Ancient Egypt

Peasants in Egypt during the fourth through sixth dynasties (2700–2200 B.C.) have been described as planting and reaping their masters' crops. Before the first autumn crops were garnered, it was likely that peasants were close to starvation. Their lives were described as similar to the lives of animals. They were the property of the lords,

---

[17] Wilcomb E. Washburn, *The Indian and the White Man*, Garden City, New York: Anchor Books, 1964, p. 8.
[18] Jennings C. Wise, *The Red Man in the New World Drama*, Vine Deloria, Jr. (ed.), New York: Macmillan, 1971, p. 27.

beasts of burden themselves, and dependent completely upon the yield of the land and the whims of the landowners.[19]

Because of the importance of the grain harvest, the state through the king's commissioners paid special attention to planning, production, and distribution. Grain was stored for two seasons and had to be sufficient for those who were building public works, including canal and dike workers, stonemasons, and the builders of pyramids, tombs, and temples. Thus centralized planning and coordination are not inventions of the modern age and, specifically, careful provision of food supplies was a fundamental social welfare effort directly tied to national intentions and needs.

However, problems arose when there was a breakdown of the economy. For example, there is recorded an uprising in the twelfth century B.C. in which a group in the state labor corps complained: "We have been hungry for 18 days in this month. We have come here by reason of hunger and thirst, we have no clothes, we have no ointment, we have no fish, we have no vegetables. Send word to Pharoah, our good lord, and write to the vizir, our superior, in order that the means of living be provided for us."[20]

Thus we can see workers were accustomed to receiving various supplies, centrally controlled. But in times of trouble, apparently, local self-interest quickly came into play when supplies became limited, and this self-interest became the sole means of defense in the struggle for existence. One lord was quoted as saying, "When Upper Egypt was in a bad state . . . I closed the frontiers."[21] The frontiers were closed so that the available harvest and supplies would suffice for the local population. Here we see an early version of residency laws, an extreme case that drove hungry persons away and the forerunner of clashes between national and local political necessities.

There also are recorded indications as to what happened to people when the central government weakened and disintegrated. In a state of anarchy, people fed on herbs, drank water, and stole offal from the mouths of swine. "Great and Small say: 'I wish I were dead.'"[22]

But most importantly the Egyptian, like the later Judaic cultures based on religious injunctions, had obligations even toward strangers who were in need. The Egyptians believed God was a pro-

[19] John A. Wilson, *The Culture of Ancient Egypt,* Chicago: University of Chicago Press, 1951, p. 74.
[20] Herman Kees, *Ancient Egypt,* Chicago: University of Chicago Press, 1961, p. 277.
[21] Ibid., p. 58.
[22] H. Frankfort, *Ancient Egyptian Religion,* New York: Columbia University Press, 1949, pp. 85–86.

tector of the poor against the rich.[23] Thus we can see in the ancient Egyptian relationships between social welfare and societal goals, conflicts between local and other levels of government and residency laws. We can observe that centralized planning and services are not new creations but techniques used early in recorded history by a national government for its own purposes: projects, maintenance of a work force, and social control.

Ancient China

By the eighth century B.C., China had developed a political system of monarch and various subordinate groupings organized into fiefdoms. Peasants worked the land in order to support their superiors, were attached to the land, and were bestowed as vassals with the land. It is probable that peasants were assigned a piece of land to cultivate for their particular superiors and another for the use of their own families. One contemporary saying was that "dukes live on tribute, ministers on their estates, shih [a group between the power group and the ruled] on the land, and peasants on their own toil." Peasants working for their lords were the source of labor and food for the self-sufficient manorial communities, but had few rights, opportunities, or pleasures. A passage in Mencius suggests the state of affairs: "If a common man is called on to perform any service, he goes and performs it."[24]

Later during the sixth century B.C. taxes were instituted based upon the amount of land one possessed. Slowly the former responsibility of the lords to feed, house, and clothe the subordinates fell upon the peasants themselves. Emancipation from the status of manorial dependent upgraded the peasants' status and afforded them greater freedom; it also relieved the lord from many of his former responsibilities. The peasants then had only themselves to look after for livelihood. Poverty or prosperity became their own responsibility.[25]

By the fourth century B.C., Mencius expressed the Confucian ideal of the humane and righteous king and suggested that the ruler must pay attention to the people's welfare. People need the necessities of life before they can be expected to concentrate on being good. Like Maslow, Mencius hypothesized a hierarchy of needs which must be met in ascending order to meet higher level needs.

---

[23] Noel Timms, *Social Work*, London: Routledge and Kegan Paul, 1973, pp. 17–18. Timms summarizes the work of H. Bolkestein in *Charity and Poor-Relief in Pre-Christian Times* (in German).

[24] Cho-yun, Hsu, *Ancient China in Transition,* Palo Alto: Stanford University Press, 1965.

[25] Ibid., pp. 109–110.

He advised the king to avoid extravagance at court and to open parks and other state lands so people could gather wood and herbs. He also urged that public funds be used for the care of the aged, the poor, and orphans and for public assistance when natural disasters struck.

By the first century B.C., in times of natural disasters such as floods or famines, the government under a traditional relief policy took three steps. Government granaries were opened. Grain was distributed free to those who were unable to pay for it and sold to those who could afford to. The rich were called upon to give or lend grain from their personal supplies. Gifts from the imperial treasury were sent to establish relief work for the poor. Simultaneously, court commissioners were sent out to encourage the planting of grain for a new harvest. Finally, if necessary, the poor were taken from the ravaged areas and resettled on new lands.[26]

Several themes should be noted with these examples from ancient China. With the breakup of a feudal pattern, the peasant was freed from semibondage on the manor but was thrown upon his or her own resources. One can see a trade-off taking place between security, mobility, and political freedom. Further, government could and should intervene when people could not expect to care for themselves, particularly if due to a natural disaster, but in other cases as well. During a disaster, when people could not care for themselves, government help was provided. Moving from place to place to find sustenance must have been done at the expense of the government—an early governmental resettlement program. Perhaps there were additional motives, but specifically the move was made possible through governmental resources when those of the people failed. Governmental intervention in time of disaster was a clear responsibility and is an old tradition which has continued into our time. But Mencius' views are a subtle theme which also existed, that is, the government had a responsibility for the people's welfare in order to promote the "good" at all times and not just in times of disaster.[27]

Babylonia

In the early development of Babylonia, individual peasants held land either as private property or as rentals. Earlier they had been fiefs, as in China but, in this case, they worked the land for the temples. When they assumed the relatively freer state, they then had to take the onslaught of catastrophes: floods, droughts, blights, and sick-

[26] Nancy Lee Swan (trans.), *Food and Money in Ancient China*, Princeton, New Jersey: Princeton University Press, 1950, pp. 60–61.[27]
[27] See discussion, Chapter 4, of residual-institutional concepts.

ness. Before this the temple had been the owner of everything, including both land and people. When difficulties had arisen formerly, rations were distributed from the temple granaries to sustain the community through times of trouble.

When peasants were freer they were forced to borrow from the temple at interest, a fact which led to many peasants becoming seriously indebted. This resulted in friction, and there are indications some kings enacted moratoriums on debts, remission of debts, and fixed wages and prices.

During the first millenium (1000 B.C.), several types of persons were dedicated to the temples, in fact entrusted to the care of the temples. Among those were prisoners of war, slaves donated or bequeathed, and persons of free birth including children of poor families handed over in times of famine to save their lives.[28]

There are three noteworthy points to observe in the above: temples were important economic forces; governmental action was taken to relieve economic burdens and pressures, probably to avoid serious conflicts; and temples served as "social welfare" agencies, anticipating major religious institutional functions to follow in later centuries.

Hebrew and Judaic Societies

Judaic culture developed out of a desert existence in which each person had a responsibility not only to himself or herself but also to the group and the community. This tension between self-interest and group interest was neatly summed up by Rabbi Hillel: "If I am not for myself, who will be? If I am only for myself, what am I? If not now, when?"[29] With a myriad of commanded actions, Judaism established within its own sociocultural reality an altruism by commandment of God. When Abraham greets and serves three strangers who approach his tent in the desert, he establishes the principle of "caring for the stranger."

Through a series of commandments Judaism established a system of public assistance. Several illustrations demonstrate what is in essence a much more developed system of social welfare, both as an ideal and in fact. For example, Leviticus 19:9–10 states: "And when ye reap the harvest of your land, thou shalt not wholly reap the corner of thy field, neither shalt thou gather the gleaning of thy harvest.

---

[28] H. W. F. Saggs, *The Greatness that Was Babylon,* London: Sidgewick and Jackson, 1966, pp. 171–172, 198.
[29] *Ethics of the Fathers.* Philip Blackman (ed.), New York: Judaica Press, 1964, p. 44.

And thou shalt not glean thy vineyard, neither shalt thou gather the fallen fruit of thy vineyard; thou shalt leave them for the poor and for the stranger: I am the Lord your God." This commandment is essentially a tax on producers for the benefit of the poor. Many centuries later the English poor laws utilized a poor rate as a similar tax for the care of the poor.

At a later point in the book of Deuteronomy 24:19–22 the commandment is explicitly stated to forego the gleanings of the harvest in the field, olive trees, and vineyards because the remains are intended for the stranger, the fatherless, and the widow.

The emphasis upon charity of many kinds in the Old Testament did not in itself produce a redistribution of wealth or correct economic inequalities. Starvation, however, was prevented by one particular commandment:

> When thou comest into thy neighbour's vineyard, then thou mayest eat grapes until thou have enough at thine own pleasure; but thou shalt not put any in thy vessel. When thou comest into thy neighbor's standing corn, then thou mayest pluck ears with thy hand; but thou shalt not move a sickle unto thy neighbor's standing corn.
>
> [*Deut. 23:25–26*]

Public opinion, apparently, enforced this commandment, and there is no record of actual starvation in peaceful times.[30]

Among the Judaic commandments, one series of laws introduced a radical and revolutionary concept: the Jubilee year. Every fiftieth year slaves were emancipated, and property—with the exception of house property in a walled city—was to be restored to its original owners. This series of laws created a counterbalance to the possible gradual accumulation by a few of most of the property and goods. According to the Talmud and other sources, the observance of the Jubilee was a reality for many centuries.

Finally, Deuteronomy introduced the legal requirement for neighborly love. For instance, in Deuteronomy 25:35 the law states: "And if thy brother be waxen poor, and his means fail with thee; then thou shalt uphold him: as a stranger and a settler shall he live with thee."

Not only does the original five books of Moses demand taxes for the benefit of the poor such as the leket (gleanings), shikhah (forgotten produce), and pe'ah (corners of the field), but poor people were free to take food for their own use. Strangers, aliens in the land, also were free to take the produce, and apparently there was no such

---

[30] Salo W. Baron, *A Social and Religious History of the Jews*, Vol. I, *To the Beginning of the Christian Era*, New York: Columbia University Press, 1962, p. 86.

thing as a special amount of time one had to live in the land in order to receive charity or be taken care of by the community.

The prophets later stressed the importance of charity and taking care of those in need. Isaiah (58:5–7) in a statement read every year on Yom Kippur excoriates Jews because fasting and the wearing of a sackcloth and ashes are in themselves not an acceptable offering to the Lord. According to the prophet, an acceptable offering would be giving bread to the hungry, housing the poor, and clothing the naked.

Throughout later rabbinic and other Jewish literature, the performance of charitable deeds is stressed both in spirit and in the giving of things for those who need them. All human possessions belong to God (Pirke Avot 3:8) and charity is one of the three pillars of the world, along with Torah (learning) and prayer (Pirke Avot 1:2). In Talmudic times there was a fund into which people could put their hands so that others would not know whether they were depositing or removing money.

The social welfare stance of the Jewish community is reflected in an enumeration from one morning prayer. The list is not far distant from some basic "social work" functions: clothing the naked, educating the poor, providing poor girls with a dowry, providing food for Passover, caring for orphans, visiting the sick, caring for the aged, ransoming captives, and providing burials.

Judaism bases its requirements for altruism on essentially two concepts: *Tzedakah*, a mixture of charity and justice, and *Chesed*, loving kindness. In the Jewish community, historically, the giver and the recipient both needed each other. Every person has inherent dignity and should strive to live a life in the image of God. Even the poor must perform charitable acts. In regard to its basic view of humans, Judaism postulates both a force for good and a force for evil in every person. Because of these simultaneous drives, humans need the restriction, direction, and support of the commandments which enable Jews, according to tradition, to choose life and avoid death, to be supportive of humanity and justice, and not to become numb to the demands of life for oneself and for all other humans.

From our perspective today, several important themes appear in the Hebrew and Judaic culture. Social welfare became institutionalized in two important respects: in regard to expected behavior and in provision for the poor in essentially nonstigmatizing ways. Attempts were made to redistribute wealth so as to offset long-term poverty through diminishing inherited wealth. There appears to have been a universalism in services without means testing, and resources were provided as a right or entitlement, achievements which may be related to the small size of the society. Finally, a culture developed which valued enterprise but without categorizing the poor as evil or idle. On the contrary, the society and individuals in it would be judged on the degree to which they provided for the poor without demeaning them.

Greece and Rome

Beggars, scorned by Plato, could expect to be sent away from cities. They were viewed by the Greeks as being lazy and not willing to work rather than as lacking opportunity. One Spartan was quoted by Plutarch: "But if I gave to you, you would proceed to beg all the more; it was the man who gave to you in the first place who made you idle and so is responsible for your disgraceful state." Similarly, Plautus made clear the Grecian attitude: "To give to a beggar is to do him an ill service."

Aristotle in his theoretical State thought he could avoid the need for charity by making part of the land completely public, thus defraying the costs of providing common meals. Several options were available for the poor and landless. They could move to new colonies, could become mercenaries, could use contraception or abortion, or (with a high incidence of poverty) could resort to infant exposure.[31]

While according to some sources the Grecian poor could only hope for better conditions by starting anew somewhere, there are other reports that throughout Greece there were inns or resting places for strangers. Located near or at temples, these places were centers for medical relief and for the poor. Associations for the support of those in need reportedly also existed.[32]

The rejection of beggars illustrates a strong theme, more a concern with pauperism than with poverty. The issue is how to keep people from getting paid without working rather than how to alleviate poverty. This attitude pervades American society and is fundamental, as we shall see later, to the concept of less eligibility. Harassment of those on welfare continues for reasons probably close to those which motivated the exile of beggars from Greek cities. It is not the alleviation of poverty which encourages harassment of the poor; rather demeaning treatment is used against pauperism and to reduce the extent to which public funds are used to support those in need. The focus on pauperism is one that returns at a later stage as an important ingredient in Western treatment of the poor. The

---

[31] A. R. Hands, *Charities and Social Aid in Greece and Rome*, London: Thames and Hudson, 1968, pp. 65–69.
[32] "Philanthropy," *Encyclopedia Britannica*, Vol. 17, 1970, p. 823.

emphasis upon prevention of funds being given to those who are not working is a common American aim, a crucial factor in society in general and in social welfare in particular.

According to Bolkestein, in Greece and Rome, unlike in Egypt and the Jewish nation, the rich were "favourites of the gods because they were in a position to make the largest sacrifices."[33] While the Egyptians and Hebrews gave the poor special consideration, in Greece hospitality for the stranger was a relationship between nobles or merchants. Furthermore, the Romans were obliged to give hospitality "only in the case of foreigners of the same standing as the host and was seen as a means of obtaining good relations with them."[34]

By the third century A.D., 175,000 Romans were receiving free food distributions. This was in addition to the system of patrons in which everyone felt bound to someone more powerful and superior. Patrons distributed both food and money to those who were connected to them in the patronage system. During the second century, there are estimates that almost one-half of Rome's population lived on public charity. Of 1.2 million people, all but 150,000 heads of families needed to draw on public foods.[35]

In the East at Constantinople another 80,000 received free food. Requisitions and taxes supported the armies and large parts of the population. Constantine thought the poor should be maintained by the wealth of the churches and that the rich should support the needs of this world. Earlier St. Cyprian in the third century said, "The rich add properties to properties and chase the poor from their borders. Their lands extend without limit or measure."[36]

There began the development of huge country manors and, concurrently, there arose a new aristocracy. Fortified manors offered security and refuge to ruined freeholders, poor urban workers,

---

[33] Noel T. Timms, *Social Work*, London: Routledge and Kegan Paul, 1973, pp. 17–18.

[34] Timms brings into question the assertion (not made here) that the roots of social work are to be found in Greco-Roman-Christian traditions. Our exploration, not meant to be a complete history but rather an illustration of the developmental process of American social welfare, places most stress on early religious trends which are later to a large part secularized with the onset of changing Western civilization. While for comparative purposes at points we describe cultures not directly related to the American experience, we understand the development of American social welfare to have been multidimensional and a result of multifactors. We share Timms' perspective that there is no one unified source of social work or social welfare. Timms, op. cit., pp. 12–20.

[35] Jerome Carcopino, *Daily Life in Ancient Rome*, New Haven: Yale University Press, 1963, pp. 16, 65.

[36] Michael Grant, *The Climax of Rome*, London: Weidenfeld and Nicolson, 1968, p. 60.

uprooted persons from outlying regions, barbarians, vagabonds, army deserters, and escaping slaves. All of these became tenants of the large landowners. Where a person had land of his own, he might place it under complete or partial control of the large landowner in exchange for protection for which he would pay a proportion of his crop.

In late Roman times the wages of serfs were set according to those of slave laborers, their competitors. In addition, tenants were forbidden to move from place to place.

By the fourth century people were officially tied to the land. Such ties were more easily established in Grecian lands where hereditary service had been an institution. This relieved landowners of labor worries. The system was slower coming into existence in western Europe, but once instituted it was not so easily relinquished as in the East. This system which tied people to the land in exchange for support from large landowners, as we shall see, took on great importance at a later historic point and influenced our attitudes and welfare philosophy profoundly.

It is important to note that Constantine in the East eased the position of women, children, debt ridden farmers (a theme which arises frequently), prisoners, and slaves. While the western Roman Empire collapsed, the eastern Byzantine empire survived, and until the thirteenth century Constantinople was the most prosperous place in Europe.[37]

CHRISTIANITY

With the development of Christianity an important new variable entered the scene with profound implications for social welfare. Two themes were introduced which influenced social welfare for over 1500 years and remain in a minor key with us today. Charity and the near sanctification of the poor assumed great importance in societies influenced by Christian thought. A second theme derived from Christian thought was the denigration of conspicuous consumption. Until the Protestant revolution, these themes were fundamental to western social welfare practices.

Jesus, who had been a wandering preacher in the Galilee, was a healer of body and soul who cured the sick and cast out demons. Service to people is considered service to God. So it is the responsibility of Christians to take care of the poor, widows, and orphans. "Therefore love is the fulfilling of the law" (Romans 13:10).

According to Christianity, there are three abiding gifts: faith,

[37] Ibid., pp. 53, 60, pp. 62–64, 83, 99.

hope, and love, but of these love is the greatest (I Corinthians 13:13). Jesus made it clear that the outcasts of society, for example, prostitutes, were worthy of special care.

The two Christian themes of (1) charity and a sanctification of the poor and (2) a denigration of conspicuous consumption brought with them several significant social welfare themes. Very early Christians in Jerusalem pooled their possessions for relief of the poor: "They sold their possessions and their means of livelihood, so as to distribute to all as each had need" (Acts 2:44 and 4:34).[38] In Jerusalem there was a daily distribution of food to widows and perhaps to others.[39] The concept of hospitality also became institutionalized when early Christians met in homes of the members—the house church—and traveling Christians assumed they would receive hospitality, a concrete expression of Christian love.[40]

Early Christians held an ethic of poverty based on scriptural statements such as "It is easier for a camel to go through the eye of a needle than for a rich man to enter the kingdom of God" (Mark 10:25) and "Blessed are you poor for yours is the kingdom of God" (Luke 6:20). Early believers came primarily from poor groups and were rewarded with a promise that poverty, not wealth, held the key to the kingdom.[41]

Both love of Jesus and love of people were necessary for Christians. Judgment was to be on the basis of treatment of Jesus, who was considered present in those who were hungry, thirsty, strangers, unclothed, sick, or in prison. By the late first and early second centuries Christians placed an increased emphasis upon giving alms: "Almsgiving is as good as repentance from sin; fasting is better than prayer; almsgiving is better than either." By the middle of the second century, Christian charity had become organized. Voluntary offerings were collected once a week and deposited with the "president" or bishop whose responsibility it was to protect orphans, widows, those in distress, prisoners, and strangers—all who were in need.[42]

While charity and relief of the poor were Christian requisites, early Christians also held strong beliefs about the necessity of work.

[38] Jean Danielou and Henri Marrou, *The First Six Hundred Years*, New York: McGraw-Hill, 1964, pp. 14–15.
[39] Robert M. Grant, *Early Christianity and Society*, San Francisco: Harper & Row, 1977, p. 127.
[40] Abraham J. Malherbe, *Social Aspects of Early Christianity*, Baton Rouge: Louisiana State University Press, 1977, pp. 67–68.
[41] John G. Gager, *Kingdom and Community: The Social World of Early Christianity*, Englewood Cliffs, New Jersey: Prentice-Hall, 1975, p. 24.
[42] Robert M. Grant, op cit., pp. 126, 128, 131.

Three motives for work were held: (1) Christians should not be a burden to others, (2) one should obtain resources with which to help the needy, and (3) non-Christians should be favorably inpressed so as to commend the faith to them. By contrast, Greeks thought work a servile activity and Romans felt work was beneath the dignity of a citizen.[43]

By the fourth century Christians (encouraged to engage in good works) had built hospitals for the sick and established systematic charitable efforts. State, church, and voluntary social welfare functions overlapped, particularly in regard to the Roman grain dole for Roman citizens, such a widespread practice that a "steward over the grain" was appointed. Privately endowed foundations, especially in Italy, invested capital in real estate mortgages. Interest was paid to towns or to state administrators for charitable uses. By the third century oil was added to the ration of grain and eligibility for the dole was extended to noncitizens. Bread was substituted for grain by the early fourth century.

In Byzantium clergy were paid to administer portions of the grain dole distributed to Christians. Funds for this purpose were comingled with the church's general funds. Although there were some reactions from pagans, a mixed system of voluntary, religious, and state-supported social welfare had been implemented. State funds were administered by a private voluntary group for the benefit of both public and private spheres, thus anticipating a modern funding and administrative device.[44]

Later saints and ordinary Christians in some cases, for example, St. Francis of Assisi, renounced material goods and family ties and led lives of poverty, an expression of being one with the wretched of the earth and a desire to be of help to them. Such acts were viewed as imitations of the life of Jesus. Christianity expected its adherents to emulate the life of Jesus and to help those who were in need:

> For I was hungry, and you fed me,
> I was thirsty and you gave me drink,
> I was a stranger and you welcomed me,
> I was without clothes and you clothed me,
> I was in prison, and you visited me.
>
> [*Matt. 25:31–46*]

Beyond helping those who were needy, Christianity demanded that those who had excess worldly goods should share these with the underprivileged. The gift of one's property, received from God

---

[43] John G. Davies, *The Early Christian Church*, New York: Holt, Rinehart and Winston, 1965, p. 66.
[44] Grant, op cit., pp. 142–145.

through God's earth and beneficence, was a sign that one was imitating the life of Jesus. Church officials and Christians could distinguish between holy poverty, which was chosen by the person, and involuntary poverty. To an extent it was important for Christians of means to divest themselves of property to support those in need in order to show signs of one's Christian commitment. As we shall see when we examine the early Middle Ages, these Christian values influenced social welfare in important ways and had long-term effects on western European antecedents of American social welfare.

This brief excursion through nonliterate and hunting tribes, ancient cultures, and early Christianity can allow us to draw several conclusions. All cultures, in varying forms, demanded altruistic and cooperative behavior, although motives probably differed from society to society. Sometimes social welfare systems were based on economic motives and at other times on religious and social motives. It is also clear that sometimes social welfare acts were benevolent, but at other times social welfare was used as a social control. It was important to have laborers with sufficient energy available for working on canals, farming, building monuments, and the like. In addition, there is a universal quality to disasters, both natural and caused by people. At such times there were attempts to preserve life and to deal constructively with the poor, in some cases for reasons of social justice and in others to avoid violence against the established order or to make sure there was a sufficient work force in numbers and health.

In Egypt we saw how shortages of food and preparations for periods of famine led to state planning and distribution of food. Furthermore, food shortages in some locations led the authorities to forbid strangers from moving into the community. Thus early Egypt introduced residency requirements. Yet there was sharing by those who lived in the area and governmental preparations in the form of granaries to prepare for disasters.

In Egypt and China there developed feudal systems in which peasants were cared for by the landowners. When the feudal system broke down, peasants had greater independence but also additional problems. Higher authorities and the state assumed responsibility for poor persons, especially in anticipation of and in times of emergency. The care of the poor was not just an individual responsibility; there were governmental preparations to improve the distribution of food so people could live and work.

In China, to avoid starvation, resettlement programs were used in times of great stress.

In Babylonia temples served as charitable institutions and as employers of last resort. State planning also was evident in regard to control of prices and wages. Judaism introduced *Tzedakah* as religious necessity to be given without judgment. Through the utilization of the Jubilee year, as well as the seven-year cycle, Judaism introduced the radical idea of redistribution of wealth. The concept of neighborly love was acted out because of religious command. In the Judaic community, instead of residency laws which were to prohibit entry of strangers, it was incumbent on the community to accept and treat the stranger as a member.

In Greece temples served as medical centers and took care of the poor. In Rome food was distributed as a governmental act with strong political overtones. On manors it is probable that in Rome peasants were tied to the land and paid at rates similar to those paid to slaves, the lowest in the community. Tenants at one point were forbidden to move, and thus the peasant workers were in competition with slaves.

With the inception of Christianity, religious commandments and institutions supported the poor, sometimes at the insistence of the state. The spread of Christianity and its powers in the middle ages is the next major development we wish to examine.

EARLY MIDDLE AGES

During the period often referred to as the "Dark Ages," the western and eastern Roman empires developed in different ways important for the evolution of western social welfare. In Asia Minor, Syria, and Egypt, peasants, apparently, were not forced into serfdom as they were in the West. The eastern governments paid sufficient for corn so the peasants could meet their tax assessments and rents. Thus, they could meet the demands of government without being forced onto the domains of the great landowners.

While in Gaul during the Fifth century A.D., there were peasant revolts, in Syria farmers were building stone houses in villages, in the Galilee and Negev peasants were farming productively and were able to support the creation of mosaic pavements. In the Fifth century eastern monasteries, the underemployed of the towns were hired for service in the Christian church.[45]

There is a tendency to skip over the years which intervene between the collapse of the Roman empire to the later middle ages in the development of social welfare. Attention is usually paid to the role of the Church and monasteries in Europe, but otherwise little is reported from this period. It is important to recognize that social wel-

[45] Peter Brown, *The World of Late Antiquity*, London: Thames and Hudson, 1971, pp. 44, 110.

fare continued to develop in societies other than our western civilization. For instance, in Alexandria in the early Seventh century, a Byzantine welfare state had been developed in the city. There were maternity hospitals, medical facilities, and food rationing; all of which was provided from the revenues of the patriarch.[46] Thus, social welfare institutions of some sort are ubiquitous, regardless of culture or society.

When we examine the social welfare system of the early and late Middle Ages it becomes clear that later events created a tremendous disjunction in the way Western civilization viewed poor people. Because American social welfare has been influenced in so many ways by historic developments in England, it is most important to review some of the highlights of English perspectives on the poor.

During the early Middle Ages, society developed in western Europe along feudal patterns. From the king down, a hierarchy was created in which each person knew his or her place and responsibilities. The manorial system included the lord and his vassals or serfs. The lord was responsible to still higher levels, a duke or the king, and also was liable for the protection and support of the serfs and peasants who worked his land. The serf owed work and portions of agricultural produce to the lord, and the lord owed responsibility to the serf.

In addition to the responsibility of the lord of the manor to provide for those responsible to him, a number of institutions existed to take care of the poor. Canon law demanded that each parish, the ecclesiastic subdivision on the local level, provide for the poor. Poverty was not a crime. Brian Tierney has contrasted the attitudes of the English in the early Middle Ages with their views during the early twentieth century, when as late as 1909 an English royal commission assumed that every poor person was poor because of a "defect in the citizen character."[47]

In thirteenth-century society a man who garnered wealth beyond his immediate needs consistent with his status *owed* the superfluous wealth to the poor. The following are some of the canonical phrases used: "Feed the poor. If you do not feed them, you kill them." "Our superfluities belong to the poor." "Whatever you have beyond what suffices for your needs belongs to others." "A man who keeps for himself more than he needs is guilty of theft."[48]

It was the responsibility of the clergy of each parish to provide

---

[46] Ibid., p. 185.
[47] Brian Tierney, *Medieval Poor Law*, Berkeley: University of California Press, 1959, p. 12.
[48] Ibid., p. 37.

"hospitality" for travelers and other guests, but to "keep hospitality"
also meant to take care of the poor. St. Francis of Assisi is often cited
as a devotee of poverty, because he attempted to emulate the life of
Jesus. But even he made a distinction between holy poverty and
other kinds of poverty. For example, he wrote in his last testament:
"I have worked with my hands and I choose to work, and I firmly
wish that all my brothers should work at some honorable trade. And,
if they do not know how, let them learn."[49]

The only grounds for refusing to help a person who came for
assistance was the assumption that giving charity would lead the person to an idle way of life. If a person was able-bodied, he was
expected to earn his keep after a few days. While poverty was not a
crime, giving charity to those who were "willfully idle" was viewed
as squandering. Several centuries later the distinction between the
deserving poor became a more important issue. In the early Middle
Ages such distinctions apparently were poorly defined.

For our purposes, in the context of American social welfare and
our ideas about the poor, Brian Tierney has summed up how the
poor were treated in the early Middle Ages. He has concluded that
"in this particular matter, I am inclined to think that, taken all in all,
the poor were better looked after in England in the thirteenth century than in any subsequent century until the present one. The only
reservation we need make is that perhaps that is not saying much."[50]
The quality of social welfare shifts violently during the latter stages
of the Middle Ages and during the Renaissance. Since we are the
inheritors of the later and not the earlier attitudes about the poor, it
is important to note that our American perspective on the poor is not
entirely a straight line development but is tied closely to certain economic, religious, and social developments.

LATE MIDDLE AGES TO ELIZABETHAN POOR LAWS

Gradually there arose new towns, there was colonization of new
lands, and there was the growth of international trade, including
money economies. The feudal system became replaced by wages,
and the serf and the lord disconnected their allegiances and responsibilities. By the thirteenth century many English peasants were
small landholders. Land was the main source of livelihood for most
peasants. It was a time in which there was poverty, but there also
were indications of prosperity: cathedral building and the production of metal, cloth, gold, and other substances. With the demise of

[49] Ibid., p. 11.
[50] Ibid., p. 109.

the feudal system, serfdom came to a halt. With the rise of employment for wages, those on the land experienced new freedom and new degrees of self-responsibility. With the retreat of feudal society, there also arose vagrants, transients, and migrants. People were on the move from a rooted society to one in which mobility seemed demanded. From a life determined by status—the relationship of lord and serf—a new relationship was evolving, that of contract between parties to whom power had more or less to be negotiated.

To those who needed a steady and dependable labor supply, this state of affairs in which people could escape from the traditional roles and places proved unsatisfactory. Not only was their labor supply uncontrolled, but marauders also lived off the land and were dangerous to those who remained settled. The wandering poor had to be provided for.

Begging was a widespread and socially acceptable method for people to gain help. Precedents for begging were found among religious personalities and mendicant friars, and the act of giving charity was a religious obligation.[51]

In addition to the ministrations of individuals, there was the charitable work of the over 8000 parishes in medieval England. Religious monastic orders served the local poor and strangers passing through.[52] It is of interest, however, that during the Middle Ages, the percentage of monastic income devoted to charity never exceeded 5 percent.[53] Strangers were to be helped without discrimination. Even infidels and excommunicants were to be cared for. Thus, in the thirteenth century, there was little if any discrimination based upon eligibility categories or residence.

Other institutions served important roles for the poor as pre-Reformation pillars of social welfare. Given the size of the territory and population to be served, there was a massive social welfare system for the poor and needy. The guilds which were voluntary commercial and social associations of merchants and artisans were mutual aid societies and charitable organizations for their own members. They built and maintained hospitals,[54] fed the needy on feast days, distributed corn and barley annually, provided free lodgings for poor travelers, and gave other incidental help.[55]

[51] Karl de Schweinitz, *England's Road to Social Security*, New York: A. S. Barnes and Co., 1975, p. 14.
[52] Tierney, op. cit., p. 61.
[53] J. Gilchrist, *The Church and Economic Activity in the Middle Ages*, New York: Macmillan, 1969, p. 79.
[54] Roland Bainton, *The Penguin History of Christianity*, Vol. 2, Hammondsworth, Penguin Books, 1967, p. 9.
[55] DeSchweinitz, op. cit., p. 15.

Another pillar of social welfare was the private foundations created by the bequests and gifts of individual philanthropists. At the time of the Reformation there were in England at least 460 charitable foundations. As much a part of medieval life as they are today, foundations established almshouses, hospitals, and other institutions; provided money for funerals; and disbursed funds on the anniversaries of the benefactor.[56]

Hospitals of various types were established during the Middle Ages, including leper houses, orphanages, maternity homes, and institutions for the aged and the infirm. In fact, in mid-fourteenth-century England there were 600 hospitals.[57]

Tithing was a feature of life in the Middle Ages, and in England church funds secured from parishioners were divided: one-third for the maintenance of the church, one-third for the poor, and one-third for the priests.[58] There was a clear expectation that individuals on every level of society would give to the poor. King John during the thirteenth century—while he was in debt himself—continued to give alms to the poor from his revenues.[59]

Such beneficence was supported by the canon law of the church and by the experience of the preceding centuries. In addition, medieval society in its earlier stages was a simpler society, primarily agrarian, without money, and with corresponding responsibilities between lords and serfs.

The Middle Ages was a time of agreement. One historian described this period as a time when "there was practically universal agreement on the basic ideas by which men professed to live. Catholicism was not only the one Church but the primary inspiration of art, the main source of education, the accepted basis of all philosophy, science, political theory, and economic theory. Medieval men all knew the same absolute truth about the human drama, from the Creation to the Last Judgment."[60] Such a homogeneity provided people with compasses and supports, but it was also inhibiting and enslaving.

Several important factors combined to force upon the English of the late Middle Ages a very different attitude toward the poor. The movement from rural to urban settings was stimulated by the introduction of woolen manufactures. Within a relatively short period of

---

[56] Ibid.
[57] J. Gilchrist, op. cit., p. 81.
[58] DeSchweinitz, op. cit., p. 17.
[59] J. Gilchrist, op. cit., p. 79.
[60] Herbert J. Muller, *The Uses of the Past*, New York: Oxford University Press, 1952, pp. 238–239.

time the manufacture of woolen goods became in England so extensive that an export trade became established.[61]

With the growth of cities, trade, money economies, and international relations, the expiring feudal system forced large numbers of people into social chaos. Wars created a pool of wanderers who were not eager to stay in one place and who had skills for stealing. People were also displaced from their former positions physically and psychologically. The old truths were no longer valid. With the necessity for sheep grazing in order to grow wool for the textile industry, land was "enclosed," and peasants were forced from the land, dislocated, unattached, and without means of support.

Even before the middle of the fourteenth century there were difficulties finding tenants for numerous land holdings.[62] There was a poor climate for agriculture, pestilence, and continuous war in northern Europe.[63] A series of plagues decimated many parts of Europe, including England. The Black Death of 1348, however, initiated a scarcity of labor of great proportions, and a new value was awarded to the available labor because of this scarcity.

In order to deal with the new freedom of labor and with its scarcity, a series of laws was enacted. In 1349 the Statute of Labourers was passed to force those who were able-bodied and without other means of support to work for an employer in their own parish *at rates prevailing before the plague.* This is not the first time governments instituted a wage freeze (the Babylonians froze wages *and* prices), but it is obvious that the legislation was meant to protect the interests of the landowners against the freedom and bargaining power of the laborers. Those who were wandering and were unemployed outside their own parishes were whipped, branded, sent to toil in the royal galleys, or set into stocks for three days.[64]

Begging was permissible for the impotent poor, that is, those who could not possibly work. By the last years of the fifteenth century, pregnant women and extremely sick men and women were considered among the impotent. Shortly after, those poor over the age of 60 were added to the list of the impotent. The categorization of those in need was established, and the beginnings of differentiation between the "deserving" and the "undeserving" poor were initiated.

[61] DeSchweinitz, op. cit., p. 5.

[62] J. Z. Titow, *English Rural Society 1200–1350,* London: Allen and Unwin, 1972, p. 94.

[63] John B. Wolf, *The Emergence of European Civilization,* New York, Harper & Row, 1962, p. 53.

[64] Peter Archer, "The Growth of Welfare Services," *Trends in Social Welfare,* Oxford, England: Pergamon Press, 1965, p. 4.

Thus began a series of punitive laws that culminated in the Elizabethan Poor Laws of the latter part of the sixteenth century.

Meanwhile Martin Luther presaged still other changes with his momentous posting of the 95 theses upon the chapel door in Wittenburg. As a result, the foundations of Roman Catholicism were challenged, especially the notion of papal infallibility. With this one act a theological conflagration was lit and a political revolution began which weakened the Holy Roman Empire and fostered the development of the modern nation-state.

Luther defined "vocations" as a calling to do God's work. This resulted in an elevation of family and individuals in the sense that one was responsible for one's own religious fate.

Other changes were taking place as well. Early Christianity held that wealth was a danger, leads to temptations, and is morally questionable. As we have seen, this view held through the early Middle Ages when Christians were asked to give to charity their "excess" wealth. During the sixteenth century, Calvin introduced the concept that wealth, a good thing in itself, could lead to idleness and to the temptations of the world, thus distracting from the pursuit of righteous living. Calvin established a criterion for salvation: whether or not one led an upright life. Work in one's calling was for the glory of God but also served as proof of being one of those elected for salvation.

It was "not leisure and enjoyment, but only activity [which] serves to increase the glory of God. . . . Waste of time is thus the first and in principle the deadliest of sins. The span of human life is infinitely short and precious to make sure of one's own election. Loss of time through sociability, idle talk, luxury, even more sleep than is necessary for health, six to at most eight hours, is worthy of absolute moral condemnation." Work could be viewed as a chief end for life and, as St. Paul suggested, "He who will not work shall not eat."[65]

Calvin introduced new values which very much affected social welfare. Idleness of any kind was seen as the ultimate sin since people could be judged by their material achievements. Loans for interest, for example, had previously been viewed as bad; now they were seen as good in that money which belonged to a person was employed to earn more money. Avarice, which had previously been sinful, was now expected behavior, and where a person was successful at amassing wealth, this was a certain sign of election. Those who

---

[65] Max Weber, *The Protestant Ethic and the Spirit of Capitalism*, New York: Charles Scribner's Sons, 1958, pp. 157–158. "From each according to his ability, to each according to his need" has a familiar ring in this context.

were dependent were somehow "marred," and one could not be sure of the state of grace of those who were clearly the victims of disaster, because such signs were visited surely upon sinners and extra efforts might have averted them. Conspicuous consumption was still frowned on, so wealth tended to be reinvested, to become capital.

Concurrent with these many developments,

> . . . the fabric of society was being disrupted; desolate villages and the ruins of human dwellings testified to the fierceness with which the revolution raged, endangering the defenses of the country, wasting its towns, decimating its population, turning its overburdened soil into dust, harassing its people, and turning them from decent husbandmen into a mob of beggars and thieves.[66]

A new system was being created, both economic and social; people were being separated from the land and moving to the cities. Towns and cities were being enlarged for manufacture and commerce, including international commerce. Poor people were not just the victims of famines and war, but new forces came into play. Employment became variable with cycles influenced not only by local events but also by unseen international occurrences. Serfdom had provided insurance against sickness and old age, now poverty of a new kind developed.

During the Middle Ages people were poor, but those who had the greatest difficulty surviving were those we would now refer to as case poverty (widows, orphans, the old, the blind, the mutilated, and those infirm from long illnesses) in the sense that they resulted from individual tragedies. But from the fourteenth century English poverty was also of the structural type and developed from the changed economic structure of society. When living on feudal manors, a person disabled by injury could be dealt with at the local level. However, when entire industries located in cities were affected by their international markets and people were thrown out of work, the causation of the problem, the number of people affected, and the resources available for those affected were far more limited. People could not fall back upon the farmland. Previously famine could cause widespread danger; but now industry and commerce could cruelly cause poverty and do so in complex ways beyond the control of individuals.

Laboring people had been gathered together into the crowded towns and cities. The expansion of markets and the creation of new technologies in combination with many other factors gave impetus

---

[66] Polanyi, *The Great Transformation*, p. 35.

to the industrial revolution. According to one interpreter, many factors contributed to that revolution, including the rise of "factory towns, the emergence of slums, the long working hours of children, the low wages of certain categories of workers, the rise in the rate of population increase . . . the concentration of industries." All these in the view of Polanyi "were merely incidental to one basic change, the establishment of market economy."[67] But the rise of a market economy demanded certain costs. Polanyi continues, "Machine production in a commercial society involves, in effect, no less a transformation than that of the natural and human substance of society into commodities."[68]

When people are needed to strive in the "satanic mills," to produce for markets within industrializing and urbanizing societies, they become essential parts, as labor, of the grinding wheels. When this role is viewed within the context that productivity is a sign of elect standing in the world, the burden of poverty falls squarely upon the shoulders of individuals, regardless of the more complicated causation which actually creates their impoverished conditions. The message communicated was that individuals demonstrate their spiritual condition through the signs which God has provided. Poverty, then, means unworthiness and, in fact, poor people can be viewed as evil.

In an attempt to deal with the phenomenon of beggars and vagabonds, the government of England introduced the principle of governmental provision in 1531. Of great concern were the numbers of such persons, but also the fact they begin in "idleness, mother and root of all vices," and end with "continual thefts, murders and other heinous offences." But this initial act first provided for those in genuine need. Letters were given to those authorized to beg. Certification for begging was the first legal assumption by government of responsibility for care of the poor. Fines were imposed on those who would give "any harboring, money, or lodging to any beggars being strong and able in their bodies to work." An idle man was whipped and after the punishment was forced to return to the place of his birth or last dwelling place and there to "put himself to labour like as a true man oweth to do."[69]

In 1536 Henry VIII expropriated the monasteries, doing away with one of the pillars of social welfare. In that same year a statute was passed creating a comprehensive English system of relief. The statute provided that those returned after punishment to their former

[67] Ibid., p. 40.
[68] Ibid., p. 42.
[69] DeSchweinitz, op. cit., pp. 20–22.

places of residence were entitled to food and lodging for one night from the parish constable. Further loitering would be punished by whipping, cutting off the right ear, or even death. Children from 5 to 14 could be apprenticed out. Church collections were to be used to care for "the poor, impotent, lame, feeble, sick, and diseased people, being not able to work." The surplus of parishes was to be used to provide support for the poorer parishes. The collectors were to be paid "good and reasonable" wages. In addition to registration of need, licensed begging was replaced by funds derived from contributions stimulated through the force of the state and the clergy. Those who were "strong enough to labor" were given employment. Although this responsibility for providing jobs was not spelled out, the important principle of public responsibility to provide work when persons could not find it was laid down for the first time in England. Thus work relief was born in the welfare system.[70]

When the nation-state developed as a full-blown institution in society, there was a simultaneous revaluation of the role of the monolithic church. Where there had been two parallel bodies of binding law, the state began to take on many of the responsibilities that previously rested more fully with the church.

Juan Luis Vives by 1526 set forth a plan for communal care of the poor in his *De Subventione Pauperum (On the Supervision of the Poor)*. According to his plan, two senators with a secretary were to visit each institution where paupers were housed and investigate the living conditions, meanwhile counting and listing names. Those living in private homes were to be similarly registered. Those who were of a certain age and without a trade were to be taught one. Irksome tasks were to be assigned to those who dissipated their "fortunes in riotous living." Those unable to find work, including the blind, were to be assigned such work. This plan included a communal duty to care for the poor, local level inquiry into the situations of the poor so as to prioritize them, and the registration and development of different categories of the poor, particularly upon moral grounds.

There were parallel plans developed in Germany in the early 1520s, in the southern Netherlands in 1524–1525, in Venice in 1528–1529, in France in the 1530s, and in Spain after 1540.

Although references are sparse to some plans—created in some instances prior to the plan of Vives, whose efforts are most noted in American social welfare literature—it is instructive to review the Venetian plan for the sake of comparison and to acknowledge the

[70] Ibid., pp. 22–23.

international nature of the problems of poverty and the similar approaches to dealing with them.

Venice established machinery for discriminating between the worthy and the unworthy poor, developed a system of priorities for giving relief so as to eliminate "social parasites," and distinguished between paupers who were physically handicapped, able-bodied but not employed, and physically whole but ill-equipped by upbringing to do manual labor. The Venetians encouraged the greatest number of applicants to be self-supporting: they gave the able-bodied opportunities to work, and they forced those able-bodied who did not want to work to do so through corporal punishment or threat of expulsion from Venice. Beggar children were educated so as to enable them to work and be absorbed into the economic system. The impotent poor, the aged, the crippled, and others were helped through accommodation in hospitals and through distribution of charity to their homes. As a last resort they were given licenses to beg which signified their worthiness to be given charity. Paupers were the responsibility of their native communities. Native paupers had priority over strangers, and there was a municipal organization to supervise and administer poor relief.[71]

Periodically there were famines, epidemics, and wars which affected the supply of labor and the number of persons seeking poor relief. According to the Webbs, in 1572, the aged, poor, impotent, and other persons born within each county or those who had resided there for three years or more were to be "sought out, registered and assigned for their habitations and abidings." Justices of the peace were to determine weekly charges to maintain them and to tax and assess the county inhabitants. Collectors were appointed as well as overseers of the poor. Thus was started the first legislation for taxes for poor relief and the institution of overseers of the poor who were to put the able-bodied to work. Severe punishments were to be taken against "idlers, beggars, rogues, and vagabonds." These latter types were to receive funds only after the impotent poor had their needs met, and the able-bodied were to be helped only in return for their labor.

Between 1572 and 1576 several pieces of welfare legislation were enacted. Among the features of the legislation were a national system to be implemented in all parts of the kingdom. Complete and systematic maintenance was to be provided for all the indigent needing relief in the parishes to which they belonged including provision

[71] Brian Pullan, *Rich and Poor in Renaissance Venice*, Cambridge, Massachusetts: Harvard University Press, 1971, pp. 239–240.

for unemployed able-bodied. Some piecework was to be arranged for persons in their own homes to repay the charity of the local community. Penal institutions were to be used for those who refused to work or otherwise misbehaved.

Following a period of near famine from 1594 on, there had been unusual destitution and periodic disturbances, including minirebellions, and an increase in vagrancy. Legislation was enacted in 1597 that systematized earlier laws.

There was a shift at this time as more emphasis was placed upon civil power which now required appointment in each parish of overseers of the poor. It was the responsibility of the overseers and of the church wardens to take care of the various categories of poor people—able-bodied, impotent, children, aged, lame, blind, or impoverished for other reasons. There was no specific restriction to those from the particular parish. Every occupant of the parish had to pay a tax to support the poor. Parents with means were liable for their children and grandchildren. Children with means were responsible for parents and grandparents who were unable to work for their own sustenance.

Justices of the peace could send to jail those who refused to work or send to prison those who did not pay their poor tax (poor rate). If a parish was unable to support its own poor, it could levy other parishes for additional funds. In addition, a central administration was formed to ensure the execution of the laws in all parts of England.[72]

Problems of poverty on a national scale were thus met in particular ways through governmental legislation. The statute enacted in 1601 is the final codification of the English Poor Laws, which stood for almost 300 years as the basis for English and American social welfare.

The responsibility for poor relief had been shifted from the church, monasteries, foundations, guilds, and private citizens (all voluntary charities) to the local government on a national scale on the basis of legal responsibilities defined by legislation with accompanying punishments for noncompliance.[73]

Despite this shift of responsibility to the state, during the seventeenth century and later significant private charity continued alongside the public arrangements, including orphanages, hospitals,

[72] Sidney and Beatrice Webb, *English Poor Law History, Part I, The Old Poor Law*, London: Frank Case, 1963, pp. 52–66.
[73] DeSchweinitz, op. cit., p. 28.
[74] Lawrence Stone, "The Rise of the Nuclear Family in Early Modern England: The Patriarchal Stage," *The Family in History*, Charles E. Rosenberg (ed.), Philadelphia: University of Pennsylvania Press, 1975, pp. 20–21.

and almshouses for the old. Supplementary funds for poor relief existed in a significant number of villages.[74]

One emphatic and important alteration in the basic poor laws was the Law of Settlement of 1662. The statute "empowered the justices to return to his former residence any person, coming to occupy a property renting for less than ten pounds a year, who in the opinion of the overseers might at some future time become in need."[75] This power to see into the future rested, then, with the representatives of the community and essentially created a reversion to days of serfdom. By this atavistic decision it was expected by the various parishes that they would be protected from the poor who belonged elsewhere, at least back in their own parishes. Although there is no evidence that people were drifting from one jurisdiction to another and depleting their resources, the statute was obviously prepared to deal with the anxiety of the overseers. But with this enactment a strong trend toward residency requirements was united with local responsibility, a trend which has continued to our day.

It was only in 1969 (*Shapiro vs. Thompson*, U.S. Supreme Court, April 1969) that residency laws as a factor determining eligibility for public assistance were held to be unconstitutional in the United States, thus recognizing after centuries the reality that local events, at least in regard to employment, poverty, and rights to freedom of movement, were truly reflective of problems on a national scale.

Out of the remarkable sixteenth and seventeenth centuries arose expanded trade among nations, colonization, and mercantilism, the latter being the forerunner of capitalism which included government regulation of trade along with tax concessions for business. According to one interpretation, mercantilism was a system which mobilized forces for national aggrandizement. At times it used government controls. At other times it called for freedom. The essential point to recognize is that capitalism's forerunner used governmental controls when deemed appropriate. In England there were sheep and woolen manufactures. In 1571 the parliament passed a law that required the wearing of woolen hats. In 1665 the dead were required to be buried in woolen shrouds. In 1700 the government would not allow the wearing of silk apparel.

Controls extended over the lives of people which were set through the social welfare system and were related to the scarcity of manufactured goods.

> . . . they were not freely available, as was air and water in most locations. The national system seemed to need them. To make them avail-

[75] DeSchweinitz, op. cit., p. 40.

able, it was necessary to have not only land and capital but also human labor. If every human being in society could somehow be converted into an operating unit and induced to work, more manufactured goods would become available. It thus became important to emphasize the virtues of work and the evils of idleness.[76]

What began in the fourteenth century as a means of dealing with a shortage of labor for agricultural work developed by the sixteenth and seventeenth centuries into an entire philosophy which demanded controls and punitive behavior toward the poor. This change had come about because of changes in the economic, religious, and social aspects of society.

SPEENHAMLAND AND THE WORKHOUSES

The issue of subsidies to individuals and families has often focused upon the Speenhamland experiment. In 1795, meeting at the Pelican Inn at Speenhamland, the justices of the peace decided to pay subsidies to individuals and families currently employed when the cost of bread rose to one shilling. Choosing to provide the subsidy, the justices decided as well not to regulate wages. They urged farmers and others to raise laborers' wages, recommended that a few areas be set aside for the poor to grow potatoes for their own use and sale, and suggested that fuel be collected in the summer for cheap sale in the winter. The subsidy, called the "bread scale," received much publicity.

A prior history and tradition existed for supplementing inadequate wages in the parishes. The poor were put to work on the land where they were needed in a process called "going the rounds" and were given relief at what was considered an appropriate level. Such a system was open to abuse by employers and acted to depress wages.

The specific context in which the justices at Speenhamland had decided to create the subsidy is significant. In 1794 there had been a short harvest. During the severe winter of 1794–1795, it became clear the next harvest would be limited. Imports were sparse because the Baltic Sea was frozen well into Spring, thus delaying food shipments from Poland and southern Prussia. England also was at war with France, which insisted on seizing English vessels.

The pension list previously consisted of women, many widows, children, invalids, and old men. Suddenly, with the enactment of the Speenhamland system, the majority of new names were of men.

[76] Robert Boguslaw, *The New Utopians*, Englewood Cliffs, New Jersey: Prentice-Hall, 1965, pp. 132, 134.

There were certain results of the subsidy. According to one view, the subsidy as given led to ambiguity in the distinction between pauperism and independence. There was institutionalized a confusion between wage supplements and family allowances. Able-bodied persons became regular recipients of relief, and employers took advantage of the system to maintain wages at a low level.[77]

Following the implementation of the Speenhamland system in many parts of England, criticism was voiced that has a familiar ring. It was thought allowances would undermine individual responsibility, lead people to produce children recklessly, enervate the energies of the working class, foster laziness, and deplete productivity. Furthermore, such allowances, it was thought, would alter fundamentally the basic psychology of "necessary" goading and encourage freedom of choice in regard to work. Also it would cost too much. Essentially this argument derives from the belief that people must be goaded to produce. On the other hand, it is noteworthy that the burden was relieved from employers and no strictures were sent their way. From another point of view, subsidies during such a time for those in need, even the working poor, are necessary to prevent starvation and to provide a healthier family life so as to best support productivity and society in general. It is of interest to note that after the turn of the century the birth rate did not rise dramatically, and historians differ as to whether productivity actually fell or rose under the Speenhamland system.[78]

Debates on wage supplementation continue in our age, following the basic patterns established when Speenhamland was debated. So long as we operate on the theory of the economic human being, wage supplementation may demean the labor market, in the sense that employers may lower wages by taking the supplementation into

---

[77] Geoffrey W. Oxley, *Poor Relief in England and Wales 1601–1834*, London: David and Charles, 1974, p. 113.

[78] According to Steven Marcus, a fall in productivity accompanied a rise in the poor rates (taxes): Steven Marcus, "Their Brothers' Keepers: An Episode from English History," *Doing Good*, W. Gaylin, Ira Glasser, Steven Marcus, and David J. Rothman, New York: Pantheon Books, 1978, p. 49. According to Mark Blaug, however, the allowances did not encourage people to "breed recklessly," did not devitalize the working class and, after the turn of the century, there was an increase in production. Blaug suggests the allowance system was almost entirely a rural problem in particular parts of the country. The device was chosen to deal with surplus labor in a lagging sector of an expanding but underdeveloped economy, a method for dealing with problems of structural unemployment and substandard wages. According to this view, the allowance system contributed to economic expansion: Mark Blaug, "The Myth of the Old Poor Law and the Making of the New," *Journal of Economic History*, Vol. XXIII, No. 2, June 1963, pp. 151–184, and "The Poor Law Report Reexamined," *Journal of Economic History*, Vol. XXIV, No. 2, June 1964, pp. 229–245.

account. The basic problem is that of less eligibility (the belief that no person on relief should be paid as much as the lowest wage earner in the community for fear such a subsidy will impair the labor market). For those who accept the economic view of human beings, such subsidies will prove counterproductive by taking the goads away from the poor and by diminishing the motivations of those at the poverty level and those just above it.

Motivated by the Protestant ethic and the mercantilist desire to compete in the developing world economic market, in 1723 the English parliament authorized any parish to establish a workhouse. The poor were to produce goods which would earn money for the state. Typically, notice would be given to the poor that their weekly pensions were to be discontinued. Those who were unable to support themselves could apply for admission to the workhouse.

According to one contemporary quote, "A workhouse is a name that carries along with it an idea of correction and punishment and many of our poor have taken such an aversion to living in it, as all the reason and argument in the world can never overcome."[79] All categories of the poor were housed under one roof, including "fallen" women, the insane, the old, children, paupers, the sick, the disabled, and vagrants.

The problems of the workhouses were so bad that in 1762 The Act for Keeping Poor Children Alive was passed. This law required parishes to maintain records of all children admitted to the workhouses so that death rates for institutions and their caretakers could be ascertained.

Infant death in the workhouses took place within a particular historic context. With the rise of the propertyless as a proportion of the population, abandonment and infanticide were stimulated. A long history exists in western Europe of such actions. During the eighteenth century many abandoned infants were sent to parish workhouses where they died from starvation, beatings, and disease. Overseers of the poor sometimes received lump sum payments from the father or putative father if the infant was illegitimate. Sometimes murdered by their "nurses," a clear profit was made from the early death of a child. At London's Foundling Hospital during its first four years of existence (1741–1745), of the 15,000 children placed there, approximately 10,000 died. In Dublin from 1790 to 1796 of 12,600 children, almost 10,000 died. Some abandoned children were illegitimate. Others, a majority, were from couples unable to support them.[80]

[79] Norman Longmate, *The Workhouse*, London: Temple Smith, 1974, p. 24.
[80] See Lawrence Stone, *The Family, Sex and Marriage in England 1500–1800*, New York: Harper & Row, 1977, pp. 473–478.

By the nineteenth century, 4000 workhouses existed in England with approximately 100,000 residents. Despite the widespread use of the workhouse, relief of the poor in their own homes was the predominant mode of subsidy, utilizing both in-kind and monetary payments.[81]

THE POOR LAW OF 1834

Poor taxes rose rapidly, as did per capita expenditures in the latter part of the eighteenth and the beginning of the nineteenth centuries. Following the defeat of Napoleon, unemployment came, food prices fell, many small farmers faced bankruptcy, and starvation forced people to apply for relief. Parishes drove paupers out of their territories. The enactment of the Corn Law of 1815 increased the price of bread while wages remained low.

In 1832 a royal commission was established to review the poor laws. The commission was biased from the start and was supported by several ideological strands: Adam Smith and laissez-faire capitalism, Malthusian pessimism, and Benthamite efficiency and utility joined with a centralizing tendency.

In 1834 the reform Poor Law was enacted. Outdoor relief would be available for the sick and the aged, but not for the able-bodied. No relief would be given to able-bodied persons unless they were residents of the workhouse, a highly stigmatized institution. There would be a central board of control over the work of local administrators. Poor Law guardians elected by local taxpayers would be in charge of disbursement of relief locally. The principle of less eligibility and punitive stigmatization of relief recipients were basic principles of the new law.

The 1834 law was a compromise enactment in that strict Malthusians and laissez-faire economists and others had wanted a law which completely put an end to Poor Law relief. As a matter of fact, one of the motivations for the revised law was to reduce poor taxes. This did in fact occur following the enactment of the 1834 law. Good harvests and the building of railways undoubtedly had some effect on this drop. However, the trend did reverse itself and begin to climb once again, although more modestly than in the past. It is likely that voluntary charity played some part in minimizing the need for more rapidly expanding public assistance.[82] But the intent

> ... of the 1834 Law was primarily to do away with outdoor relief. Some fifteen years after the enactment of the New Law of 1834, five times as

[81] Blanche D. Coll, *Perspectives in Public Welfare*, Washington, D.C., U.S. Government Printing Office, 1969, p. 8.
[82] Ibid., pp. 14–15.

many people were relieved outside the workhouses as were being given relief inside them.[83]

Clearly, the goal of the 1834 Poor Law had not been attained.

PRINCIPLES OF THE POOR LAWS

As we have seen, the principles by which treatment of the poor was determined changed dramatically after the thirteenth century. The poor "became conspicuous as individuals unattached to the manor, 'or to any feudal superior,' and their gradual transformation into a class of free laborers was the combined result of the fierce persecution of vagrancy and the fostering of domestic industry which was powerfully helped by a continuous expansion of foreign trade."[84] The Poor Laws supported by other changing features of society, including the dissolution of the feudal system, the alteration of the churches, the emphasis on individual responsibility, and the growth of international money and trade economies all combined to ensure a market in which labor was simply another resource which must be maintained. In order to create and maintain a motivated work force, a work force available for productive employment, a series of Poor Laws was created.

The Poor Laws themselves were based upon and slowly evolved through several principles for dealing with the poor. These principles have remained with us today, sometimes in disguised form and often explicitly. Secularism was established as the basic direction of social welfare, despite the existence of a religious social welfare subsystem. Whereas during the Middle Ages there existed both a governmental and an ecclesiastic system, along with other voluntary systems, gradually social welfare became a public responsibility, that is, a secular task for the entire body politic. This development is part of the rise of nation-states with their need to care for their citizens in order to maintain morale and build the nation. It also is a result of the secularization trend, which has evolved over centuries, by which certain church functions and controls have been shifted to the public and governmental bodies. The powers of the ecclesiastic system and the demands it could make upon people diminished, while the demands of the nation-state upon its citizens increased. The provision of social welfare for the masses has become the responsibility of the taxing authority, the secular state.

The concept of risk or categories also developed as a principle;

[83] Robert H. Bremner, *"The Rediscovery of Pauperism," Current Issues in Social Work Seen In Historical Perspective*, New York, CSWE, 1962, p. 16.
[84] Polanyi, *The Great Transformation*, p. 104.

for example, the reason one was poor had taken on new and important meanings. Not only were the poor divided into categories— aged, children, lame, ill, and so forth—but these categories were further defined in moral terms: the worthy and the unworthy poor. Such definitions led to means-testing and were congenial with the view that the poor had caused their own poverty, were morally at fault, and could by sufficient motivation and willpower alter their life circumstances. As we saw in Chapter 1, such views of the poor remain with us, accompanied by punitive behavior, a remnant of philosophies centuries old. Where in the Middle Ages all poor were given assistance without consideration of the "category" they were in, now one differentiates between those who are worthy or unworthy of receiving assistance.

Another principle was the establishment of the distinction between indoor and outdoor relief. Work was demanded from the poor (a demand which had been present in the early monasteries as well); that is, some poor would have to take shelter in a public house or hospital, while others "more deserving" would be supported in their own homes. The outdoor-indoor controversy of which the workhouse is the prime example continues today in terms of community care for the mentally ill, juvenile delinquents, and others. Although it almost always costs more to have indoor relief and such relief tends to be punitive, countermoves are almost always resisted with vigor, for example, to establish foster homes for the disabled, retarded, or mentally ill or to place the poor into middle-class neighborhoods. Beneath such resistance can be found fear of differences and also the idea that the unworthy should be shunted aside and out of sight.

Residency laws, as a principle, required that laborers be tied to their lords and employers and then to their home parishes or place of birth. Binding people to places (a throwback to serfdom) served to minimize their bargaining power through restrictions on their freedom to move and thus set limits on what employers had to pay as wages. Thus residency laws served important economic purposes and had the intention of maintaining a pool of available labor for production, while at the same time implying a control over wages.

The principles of less eligibility and wage supplementation are hotly debated even today. The question of less eligibility appears to be one of the most intractable problems facing social welfare. With the establishment of this principle (the poor must not be supported at a level as high as that of the lowest employed person in the community), a problem of great difficulty was identified and a solution was suggested on the assumption that humans are economic beings, but the "solution" has proven to be unworkable. Although the original motivation for less eligibility undoubtedly rested upon the belief that the poor could be motivated only in this way, the results of following such a principle are open to question. As we saw in the case of Speenhamland, the "payoff" was really not for the employees, but actually was a use of "public means to subsidize the employers. For the main effect of the allowance system was to depress wages below the subsistence level."[85] Currently methods are being explored and tested for ways to deal with this problem, especially ways which recognize the structural nature of high unemployment and poverty in a multinational, technological economy.

Finally, the fact that the social problems of the needy were approached by and large on a case-by-case basis has supported the assumption that the problem rests with the individual or family. Such views are still subtly expressed in modern social casework when insufficient attention is paid to the structural determinants of social need and too much emphasis is paid to the "probability" that individuals are responsible for their own plight. Such views, as we shall see in Chapters 8 and 9, have far-reaching implications for social welfare and social work.

Chapter 3
Social Values and Social Welfare: The American Experience

"Did you. . . o friend, suppose democracy was only for
elections, for politics and for a party name? I say democracy is only of use there that it may pass on and come to
its flower . . . in the highest forms of interaction between
men, and their beliefs—in religion, literature, colleges,
and schools—democracy in all public and private life."

Walt Whitman, "Democratic Vistas"[1]

AMERICAN POOR LAW MENTALITY

Eight years after the compilation of the Elizabethan Poor Laws in
1601, settlements began to be established by colonists along the eastern seaboard of what was later to become the United States of America. The English Poor Laws and their underlying attitudes were
implanted early in the Atlantic coast colonies: secularism, the concept of risks and categories, indoor and outdoor relief, residency
laws, less eligibility, and approaching the poor on a case-by-case
basis.

Actually, during the early stages of settlement, clashes between
ideologies took place. The first years of the Plymouth colony were
based upon a common sharing of all property. An emphasis upon
mutual aid and socialistic organization, much like early Christian
social organization, clashed with other values. Given the need for

---

[1] James E. Miller, Jr. (ed.), *Walt Whitman, Complete Poetry and Selected Prose*, Boston: Houghton-Mifflin, 1959, pp. 474–475.

work and workers, the Protestant ethic in the form of the Poor Laws was used by the early settlers because that was the natural thing for them to do, in the sense that the laws reflected the traditions of the English founding settlers.

By 1633 the following provision was made for one of the colonialists:

> Thomas Higgens having lived an extravagant life, was placed with John Jenny for eight years, to serve him as an apprentice, during which time the said John competently to provide for him; and at the end thereof to give him double apell, 12 bushels of corn and 20 acres of land.[2]

In Massachusetts as in other parts of America, poor relief was a local responsibility. The smallest unit of government became the instrument for implementing the readily imported English Poor Law system.

By 1642 Plymouth had enacted the following law:

> . . . that every township shall make competent provision for the maintenance of their poor according as they shall find most convenient and suitable for themselves by an order and general agreement in a public town meeting. And notwithstanding the promise that all such persons as are now resident and inhabitant and within the said town shall be maintained and provided for by them.[3]

Selectmen administered aid to the poor. Almshouse care was not common until after the turn of the eighteenth century. Cases were dealt with individually and were presented to the town at a public town meeting. Settlement laws also were enacted to keep strangers out if there was an incompatibility of religious belief and/or likelihood of early public dependency.

In Fairfield, Connecticut, during the seventeenth century, according to town records, the deserving poor were maintained by the town. However, vagrant and idle persons were warned to leave town, and they and persons who harbored them were subject to prosecution. Thus two categories were again established, the worthy and unworthy poor, with the unworthy poor being warned out of the town.[4]

Children were viewed as economic assets rather than as liabilities, much as in other agricultural societies. In social welfare terms, however, children were placed with various parties by indenture;

---

[2] Robert W. Kelso, *The History of Public Poor Relief in Massachusetts 1620–1920*, Montclair: Patterson Smith, 1969, p. 95.

[3] Ibid., p. 92.

[4] Ralph E. and Muriel W. Pumphrey, *The Heritage of American Social Work*, New York: Columbia University Press, 1961, p. 24.

parents were put out to service in order to avoid public expense. If parents with children were aided by the town, they were required to set the children out to work. The poor also were boarded in private homes. Outdoor relief was given as well. Repression did accompany these early relief programs. Sometimes there were local work-relief programs, especially on projects needed by the community.

Settlement laws also played a part, as can be seen in the following example:

> Dec. 11, 1634. One Abigail Gifford, widow, being kept at the charge of the parish of Wilsden in Middlesex, near London, was sent by Mr. Ball's ship into this country, and being found to be somewhat distracted, and a very burdensome woman, the governor and assistants returned her back by warrant, 18, to the same parish, in the ship Rebecca.[5]

In the early scattered American communities (primarily rural with subsistence farming), the local community could indeed handle the few cases which were its responsibility. It was familiar with the people involved, and made what it considered appropriate provision.

As early as the seventeenth century, when America was newly settled by European colonialists and primarily an agricultural society, private and voluntary philanthropy and mutual aid both on an individual and cooperative basis developed based on religious and civic principles and traditions brought from Europe, on the views of the proper role of government, and on the limitations of resources available to governmental jurisdictions. For example, several private benefactors left bequests to Boston which when combined enabled the town to build an almshouse. As Pumphrey and Pumphrey have pointed out, this "pattern of making individual gifts or bequests to the town, rather than setting up isolated foundations, was regarded as natural. Private benevolence thus provided the capital, but the public was expected to maintain the donated facility."[6]

It is important to remember that Hernando Cortes, the Spanish conquistador, invaded Mexico and conquered the Aztecs in 1519, prior to developed settlements on the eastern seaboard. While the Spanish were exploiting the Indians, the transplanted Catholic church built in parts of what is now the United States missions, convents, monasteries, and churches and also constructed hospitals and schools. By the seventeenth century there were 3000 missionaries in New Spain, converting the unbelievers but also providing some social welfare services.[7]

[5] Ibid., p. 20.
[6] Ibid., p. 27.
[7] Albert Prago, *Strangers in Their Own Land*, New York: Four Winds Press, 1973, p. 33.

The Scots' Charitable society, first among many such nationality groups, was formed in 1657 as a mutual aid society for those of Scottish nationality.[8] Church charities, another form of voluntary social welfare, were financed by collections and gave relief to members of particular congregations.

Voluntary organizations were formed to aid special groups, for example, the Philadelphia Society for Alleviating the Miseries of Public Prisoners (1787), the Massachusetts Charitable Fire Society (1794), and the New York Society for the Relief of Poor Widows with Small Children (1798).[9] The establishment by the Ursuline Sisters in New Orleans in 1729 of a private home for mothers and children left homeless by the Indian massacres is another example of the charitable roles played by religious groups.

Noteworthy in regard to the formation of voluntary organizations was the formation in Boston of a Masonic Lodge by free blacks in 1784[10] and in 1787 of the Philadelphia Free African Society. The latter society was formed, according to the preamble, without regard to religious tenets. Persons should live "an orderly and sober life, in order to support one another in sickness, and for the benefit of their widows and fatherless children." The members of the society made insurance payments, and benefits were paid provided this necessity was "not brought on by their own imprudence." No drunkards or disorderly persons were allowed to be members. If a member became sick, he or she was exempt from payments and eligible for benefits. In addition, there were benefits for widows and children's benefits including schooling and apprenticeship.[11] Soon after the Philadelphia Society was formed, Newport, Boston, New York, and Charleston[12] formed similar associations. The intention of these mutual aid societies often was to lessen the need for benefits from public funds.

There were almost 500,000 free blacks in the United States at the outbreak of the Civil War, half in the South and many "well-to-do." The free black community created churches, literary debating societies, fraternal organizations, and other mutual aid groups to

[8] Pumphrey and Pumphrey, op. cit., p. 30.
[9] Walter A. Friedlander and Robert Z. Apte, *Introduction to Social Welfare*, Englewood Cliffs, New Jersey: Prentice-Hall, 1974, p. 62.
[10] E. Franklin Frazier, *The Free Negro Family*, Nashville: Fisk University Press, 1932, p. 16.
[11] Herbert Aptheker (ed.), *A Documentary History of the Negro People in the United States*, New York: The Citadel Press, 1951, pp. 17–18.
[12] E. Horace Fitchett, "The Tradition of the Free Negro in Charleston, South Carolina," *The Making of Black America*, August Meier and Elliott Rudwick (eds.), New York, Atheneum, 1969, pp. 206–215.

serve particular needs.[13] But even in slavery there was a system of social obligation among slaves for nonkin slaves, and there are, according to Gutman, many examples of extravagant giving in relation to available resources. Among freed slaves, indigent or helpless people were supported by relatives, parents, friends, and relief associations.[14]

In fact, Gutman has suggested that similar altruistic behavior by freed slaves over the entire South is an important reason why over the full lifetime of the Freedmen's Bureau it materially assisted only 0.5 percent of the 4 million freed slaves.[15]

Obligations to kin were transformed into larger social and communal obligations, for example, setting aside a piece of land for a community purpose or supporting free schooling for poor children. One communal value is reflected in the phrase "each putting in according to his means."

The following comments spoken by a black person regarding a school in South Carolina illustrates the mutual aid values of the black freed slave community: " . . . they were all poor, and each could do but little, but this was a work for many. . . . Should each man regard only his own children, and forget all the others? Should they leave that poor neighbor widow with her whole gang of children, and give them no chance for a free schooling."[16]

Consistently through American history there were voluntary, private aspects of social welfare. Prior to the Civil War, in New York City in 1843, the New York Association for Improving the Condition of the Poor was organized and the earlier Society for the Prevention of Pauperism in the City of New York; both linked poverty and antisocial behavior such as alcoholism and idleness. There were numerous groups concerned with utopianism, political reform, women's rights, economic reform, land reform, education, abolition of slavery, temperance, and other social issues and problems.

Following the Civil War, state boards of charities were formed in Massachusetts, Connecticut, New York, Wisconsin, Rhode Island, Pennsylvania, Michigan, Kansas, and Illinois. The first four states met in New York in 1874 and formed the Conference of Boards and Public Charities, an important beginning for the development of a national network of communication among social agencies, both public and private. This national development followed by only 11

[13] Frazier, op.cit., p. 16.
[14] Herbert G. Gutman, *The Black Family in Slavery and Freedom, 1750–1925,* New York: Pantheon Books, 1976, pp. 224–225.
[15] Ibid., pp. 224–229.
[16] Ibid., p. 229.

years the creation in Massachusetts of the first state board to supervise charitable, medical, and penal institutions.

The development of both public and private agencies was a
result in part of societal forces. Six percent of the American population lived in cities in 1800; by 1870 this had risen to 25 percent. The
problems of rapidly industrializing cities and the hordes of people
moving into them for employment could not be handled in the earlier manner; social agencies developed on the local and state level to
meet the needs of a changing society.

The inexorable secular trend toward public assumption of major
responsibility for social welfare always has been joined by a continuous involvement of private, religious, and other organizations in the
social welfare arena. By the early part of the twentieth century,
according to one major early study of American social welfare, private and public social welfare seemed to be assigned different
functions:

> The advantages of private charities over public ones are that they afford
> on the average a somewhat larger share of personal sympathy, that their
> benefits cannot logically be claimed as a right (although they often are),
> that they do not oppress the poor by increasing taxation, and that they
> are supposed to bring a somewhat smaller degree of degradation to the
> recipient of relief.
>
> The probable lines of demarcation between the field of public and
> private charity seems to lie between those dependents requiring some
> degree of control, and those that may be allowed their freedom;
> between measures for chronic dependents and those looking to preven-
> tion; between institutional care on a large scale and private aid to the
> needy in their homes. Generally speaking, private charity is best fitted
> to conditions where much personal, individual sympathy is required;
> public charity, to problems requiring large funds, equipment and con-
> trol. Finally, private charity, under the stimulus of some individual
> enthusiast, will mark out new paths which when proven may be
> adopted by the State.[17]

By the early 1930s a later student of social welfare noted that the
trend

> ... which is most important in marking the probable future develop-
> ment in social welfare is the absorption of activities as a part of public
> administration in increasing number and at accelerated rate. The gov-
> ernment's obligation to provide for certain types of dependency and
> delinquency has long been recognized; the addition of new categories
> of need requiring government support or supervision is an outstanding

---

[17] Amos G. Warner, *American Charities*, New York: Thomas Y. Crowell, 1908, pp. 393,
395.

development of the last fifteen years. . . . During the past five years the administration of relief giving has become decidedly more a function of public than of private agencies.[18]

As we shall see later, the Great Depression of the 1930s confronted the United States with problems on a scale which only could be dealt with by federal public action. But as we can see above, even relief functions had shifted to the public sphere prior to the cataclysm of the social upheaval of the 1930s.

From rural, colonial, agrarian America to the modern, industrial, and urbanized United States, private voluntary welfare, formal and informal, played an important part in meeting human needs. Informal natural helping systems always played a significant social welfare function. Extended families, friendship circles, churches, and neighborhood, ethnic, and religious groups all have contributed to individual and family welfare. Although the major trend in American society is toward formalization of social welfare functions, one should not forget that informal, spontaneous helping outside of formal channels has been and remains a most significant portion of American social welfare.[19]

THE AMERICAN FRONTIER

America existed as a physical frontier but also as a psychological frontier. It was a place where a new life was possible, where dreams of freedom or sustenance or success were possible of fulfillment.

The fact that America was a frontier land in which the horizons always beckoned influenced how people viewed themselves and how they viewed others. The frontier myth was that all things were possible; the land was open for the benefit of those who were hardy and brave enough to venture forward. Beyond the next hill, beyond the next river, or beyond the next mountain range, life would be better. One part of this frontier philosophy was the belief that riches belonged to those who dared to seek them and who were strong enough to earn their way. The other side of this myth of the frontier and the frontiersperson was that those who did not or could not venture forth or "make it" financially were suspect.

[18] Sydnor H. Walker, "Privately Supported Social Work," *Recent Social Trends in the United States*, Vol. II, New York: McGraw-Hill, 1933, p. 1222.
[19] See, for example, Alice H. Collins and Diane L. Pancoast, *Natural Helping Networks: A Strategy for Prevention*, Washington, D.C., National Association of Social Workers, 1976; and Irving M. Levine and Joseph Giordano, "Informal Coping Systems and the Family," background paper for Consultation on Strengthening American Families Through the Use of Informal Support Systems, American Jewish Committee, mimeographed, 1978.

Into the frontier land of America came waves of immigrants. At first, during the colonial period, immigrants to America were English, German, Scotch-Irish with small numbers of French Huguenots, and indentured servants and slaves sought for the development of a new country.

Later Irish, Swiss, Swedish, Danish, Italian, Portuguese, Spanish, and West Indians came to America to be followed by other groups. During the period from 1783 to 1830 some parishes in England sent paupers, paying their passage and giving them money to start with.[20] Still later immigrants came from northwestern Europe to be followed by immigrants from eastern and southern Europe.

Earlier immigrants came for political, religious, and social reasons. Later immigrants came primarily for economic reasons in order to make a living. As the various immigrant waves reached America, the earlier settlers would accuse the later settlers of depressing wages and of being the cause of various social problems. Culture conflicts abounded between the various groups and within ethnic groups. Religious differences established some conflicts. Within some groups there were conflicts as to whether the culture and language of the "home country" should be preserved or not. And there were differences of race. In addition, many immigrants came from rural homes and had to deal with urban problems in America. The experiences of the waves of immigrants coming to America created a strong "we-they" feeling and attitude. For example, Chinese immigrants who came to western America during pioneer days and during the Gold Rush were viewed as economic competitors, and by 1882 Chinese laborers had been excluded from immigration on the basis of race alone.

The existence of a "we-they" attitude was strengthened by economic competition. However, the attitudes that one person was better than another on the basis of some personal characteristic also played a part in how Americans viewed those who were different from themselves, including those who were in need of help, financial or otherwise. They somehow did not fit in. In addition, as the different waves came to America, it was always "they" who needed help. Mutual aid may have been retarded and racism and rugged individualism advanced by the notion that it was always some other ethnic group, not one's brothers and sisters, who needed help in America.

For one group, at least, immigration was not voluntary. In 1619, one year prior to the arrival of the Mayflower, 20 blacks were brought

[20] Lawrence G. Brown, *Immigration*, New York: Arno Press and *New York Times*, 1969, pp. 62–63.

to Jamestown, Virginia, by the Dutch and sold into indentured servitude. At this point in American history the treatment of white and black indentured servants did not differ. From such a relatively benign circumstance, however, a tangled web of black-white relationships and problems developed which has confronted American society continually through its history.

By 1640 different treatment for blacks and whites had been instituted, and in 1641 Massachusetts became the first colony to legally recognize slavery. After the middle of the seventeenth century, all blacks—and only blacks—came as slaves.[21] Until the onset of the Civil War and the promulgation of the Emancipation Proclamation in the nineteenth century, most blacks existed in slavery and were victimized by their white enslavers with their only security being the best interests of the slaveholders as they saw them. This reality and the fact that the United States was settled at the expense of nonwhite native Americans have produced a backdrop of racism and oppression of minorities by color for all United States history.

One ethnic group preceded European immigration, and its fate at the hands of the immigrant majority was particularly cruel. The early generosity of native Americans, commonly referred to as Indians, stands in marked contrast to the values of the early American colonists. It is a trait remarked upon by the earliest colonists both in the area which has become the southwestern part of the United States and in the eastern parts as well. They have been described as people who "at times . . . even gave their possessions away for nothing to those who asked for them."[22] This openhanded quality of Native Americans was noted by Columbus in a letter to the king and queen of Spain: "So tractable, so peaceful are these people that I swear to your majesties, there is not in the world a better nation. They love their neighbors as themselves and their discourse is ever sweet and gentle, and accompanied with a smile; and though it is true that they are naked, yet their manners are decorous and praiseworthy."[23]

The European colonists and later Americans pushed the native Americans before them, purchasing, conquering, and removing native Americans from the land, decimating them as they moved westward. In the nineteenth century a policy of assimilation developed in which native Americans were forced to forsake their reli-

[21] Thomas R. Frazier (ed.), *Afro-American History: Primary Sources*, New York: Harcourt, Brace Jovanovich, 1970, p. 29.
[22] Lewis Hanke, *The First Social Experiments in America*, Cambridge, Massachusetts: Harvard University Press, 1935, p. 30.
[23] Quoted in Dee Brown, *Bury My Heart At Wounded Knee*, New York: Holt, Rinehart and Winston, 1974, p. xiii.

gious, social, and cultural practices. Native American tribes were removed to the West in a trek described by the Cherokees as a "trail of tears." Confined to specific reservations, their game was destroyed and they became dependent upon rations and assistance. A policy of forced assimilation controlled everything from hairstyles to language. Treated as wards of the state, they were not allowed to make decisions about their own lives and were forced into a "melting pot."

While the United States through public policy was creating a dependent group—the native Americans—it also was creating many social problems among them as immigrant Americans destroyed the fabric of native American life. By contrast there is evidence, for example, that in the 1820s, left to their own social welfare devices, "there were no paupers in New Mexico at that time, nor could there be any." In the southwestern culture a poor man would go to a rich stockman and offer to assist him by herding sheep. The shepherd would give of the future increase, and wool would be contracted at the current market price. Materials from the sheep would be used to construct housing, milk and meat were used as food, and the wool was marketed as blankets, stockings, and the like. Thus the necessities of life were supplied. The observation there was no poverty made by a Mexican lawyer in 1827 was confirmed by earlier visitors.[24]

The General Allotment Act (1887), known as the Dawes Act, divided tribal land into individual 40, 80, and 160 acre shares for agricultural and grazing purposes. The native American would become a voting citizen if his residence was maintained separate from the tribe and he became a farmer. However, this value imposed by the American government was contrary to the tribal and communal property traditions and values of the native Americans. A chief result was that many lost their land.[25]

By 1934 the Indian Reorganization Act permitted tribes to reorganize their own institutions and to handle many of their own concerns. Nevertheless, the Bureau of Indian Affairs sustained for itself a veto power over most tribal decisions.

In the 1960s as part of a general claiming of ethnic identities and as part of the civil rights movement, native Americans expressed vigorously their rights to their cultures and civil rights within American society. Although it was quite late and much damage had been done, groups of native Americans set out to lay claim to their languages,

---

[24] David J. Weber (ed.), *Foreigners in Their Native Land,* Albuquerque: University of New Mexico Press, 1973, p. 38.
[25] Sar A. Levitan and Barbara Hetrick, *Big Brother's Indian Programs with Reservations,* New York: McGraw-Hill, 1971.

general culture, and a rectification of the history of broken American promises and treaties. Thus a series of court cases was instituted holding the United States liable for lands belonging to the tribes, a wealth which Americans had taken for their own while destroying in many ways the culture and lives of the native American people.

FEDERAL ROLE IN SOCIAL WELFARE

In 1854, Dorothea Dix, who worked strenuously for better treatment of the indigent insane, managed to get the Indigent Insane Bill passed by Congress to provide funds to improve the care of such people. The bill would have granted 10 million acres of public lands to the states, in proportion to their congressional representation. The states could then sell the land and use the proceeds for the perpetual care of the indigent insane. The bill was a popular one because it provided "payoffs" for both land speculators and for philanthropists. However, President Franklin Pierce vetoed the bill and was sustained by Congress, and killed a landmark in American governmental philosophy concerning social welfare.

Pierce used several arguments, including one which President James Madison had presented in an 1811 veto that the federal government could not give legal sanction to charitable governmental acts. Furthermore, if help was to be given to the indigent insane, he suggested that all the needy eventually would have to be helped. Pierce also used an argument put forth by President Andrew Jackson that lands given to the states must be used for the common good. In addition, financial expediency played a part, as Pierce claimed the lands were security for the Mexican War debt.

However, he intimated he would approve land grants to railroads. The purpose of granting lands to the railroads, as Pierce viewed it, was to enhance the value of the whole nation as a "prudent proprietor" would. The crucial assumption, however, is that property needs improvement through governmental assistance while people do not. Interestingly, Pierce had previously given land to soldiers and to railroads. One editorial interpretation at the time suggested the veto halted an erosion of states' rights. Another argument used by Pierce was based on a strict construction of the Constitution: if the Founding Fathers had wanted such programs, they would have made it explicit in the Constitution. Essentially, Pierce refused to make "the Federal government the great almoner of public charity throughout the United States."[26]

[26] Carlton Jackson, *Presidential Vetoes: 1792–1945*, Athens: University of Georgia, 1967, pp. 100–102.

And yet the federal government, so reluctant to assume a welfare role, did so in several instances. Following the Civil War and during the period of Reconstruction, the Freedmen's Bureau was created as part of the War Department. Among its functions, it furnished food and supplies to blacks and needy whites, found employment for former slaves, supervised labor contracts affecting freedmen, established freedmen on homestead lands, fixed wages and terms of employment, provided transportation to new found homes, formed settlements of blacks, and established schools.[27]

Important legacies were established by Reconstruction and the Freedmen's Bureau. But, when Reconstruction ended, most energies were directed toward separate public institutions for blacks and whites with the inferior services designated for blacks. This pattern culminated in the "separate but equal" Supreme Court ruling in 1896 which gave legal sanction to segregated facilities. Nevertheless, one authority has suggested a number of positive accomplishments arose out of public welfare efforts in the South during the period of 1865 to 80: universal public education was established, attention was given to children, agencies were created to improve health conditions, and poor relief was implemented at the local level more than at the state level.[28]

The importance of the Freedmen's Bureau for our discussion lies in its example of governmental intervention during a time of stress to assist people with their problems rather than to leave them entirely at the mercy of accidental events. Thus there was a commitment by the federal government to meet the fundamental welfare needs of people, despite the Pierce veto. Furthermore, governmental programs of a diverse nature (income maintenance, child welfare, medical care, work projects, education, and so on) provided a comprehensive series of services to deal constructively with a serious social upheaval and foreshadowed across-the-board, comprehensive programs like those of the Great Depression and the War on Poverty in the 1960s.

Even the Indian Bureau, racist and punitive to native Americans as it was, demonstrated that when other values took precedence, the federal government did administer welfare programs. These shifts in

---

[27] J. G. Randall, *The Civil War and Reconstruction*, New York, D. C. Heath, 1953, pp. 731–733. And see Victoria Olds, *The Freedmen's Bureau as a Social Agency*, unpublished doctoral dissertation, New York: Columbia University, 1966.

[28] Howard N. Rabinowitz, "From Exclusion to Segregation: Health and Welfare Services for Southern Blacks, 1865–1890," *Social Service Review*, Vol. 48, No. 3, September 1974, pp. 327–354; and John Hope Franklin, "Public Welfare in the South During the Reconstruction Era, 1865–80," *Social Service Review*, Vol. 44, No. 4, December 1970, pp. 379–392.

values and philosophy varied. Some were undoubtedly based upon political motivations. Others represented exempting certain groups from Puritan and Social Darwinist considerations.

For example, the historical treatment of veterans of wars and their families in the United States is based upon such a suspension of the Protestant ethic. Based on the veteran's sacrifice (and our guilt?) and loss of time, the veteran is seen as entitled to help even if he or she is unworthy. Following the Revolutionary War, veterans were recipients of generous grants to western lands.[29] An anonymous quote from the period following the War of 1812 makes the argument straightforwardly: "Who but the Soldier and his family should eat the bread from the Soil his own blood has enriched?"[30]

Beginning in 1776 there has been a series of pension acts that generally provided assistance to veterans who were disabled. But other types of aid also were given. The Homestead Act was passed in 1862 and made it possible for any American citizen to obtain 160 acres of unoccupied government land if he or she lived on it for five years. In 1870 special privileges were given to soldiers who had fought in the Union army. Such soldiers could count their time of service toward the five-year required period. Widows could count the full term of their husband's enlistment.[31] Following every war, various techniques are found to provide resources for veterans and their families. While in many cases the resources provided are given to those who have been disabled, at other times these rules are suspended. Following World War II, the 52-20 program provided $20 per week to each veteran for one year whether or not the veteran had been disabled and, more important, whether or not the veteran had been actually engaged in battle. The "GI bills," begun in World War II and continued following the Korean and Vietnam conflicts with variations, are examples of this type of exceptional program. The only requirements in order to receive most of the educational and other benefits were to have been in service during a certain period and not to have been disabled or to have been in a war zone.[32]

The federal government enacted such legislation out of complex motivations. However, in addition to rewarding such veterans, one important factor was the view that giving benefits to veterans and their families would have a long-term beneficial effect on the total

[29] Cortez A. M. Ewing, *American National Government,* Norman: University of Oklahoma, 1958, p. 583.

[30] Marcus Cunliffe, *Soldiers and Civilians,* New York: The Fress Press, 1973, p. 81.

[31] John D. Hicks, George E. Mowery, and Robert E. Burke, *The American Nation,* Boston: Houghton-Mifflin, 1963, p. 96.

[32] *Those Who Served. Report of the Twentieth Century Fund Task Force on Policies Toward Veterans,* New York: The Twentieth Century Fund, 1974.

society, raise the average educational and skill level, provide needed technical and other training to be used by the society, and allow greater societal and governmental future income from the improved earnings of the veterans and their families. Investments in veterans historically have been viewed as exceptions to the Protestant ethic. The eligibility rules often are not rigorous in the sense of using "means tests," and such programs are established despite the philosophical leanings of many congresspeople in other areas.

For our purposes, treatment of veterans may be seen as an example of what might be possible were we able to free ourselves from the values of Calvinism and our terror of idleness. The veterans who benefitted after World War II from receiving $20 per week for 52 weeks included the majority who used the time to seek work. But it also included some who used this "dole" to postpone decision making and to get something for nothing or who could have lived comfortably without it. Similarly, a number of veterans used educational benefits to kill time, to get a free ride, or to have paid for them what they could easily have paid for themselves. Still, the net effect of these programs was

1. to avoid a major economic depression as millions of soldiers were rapidly demobilized and thrown into a civilian economy
2. to upgrade the quality and earning power of the American work force for a generation

Thus, by forgetting about who was worthy and unworthy, about means tests and the like, a dignified welfare program benefitted the whole economy. In fact, if one takes the great cost of the GI education program following World War II and balances it against the tax revenues gained by the federal treasury due to a better educated work force attributable to the GI bills, the treasury has come out ahead, even on a dollars-and-cents basis, without even considering the avoidance of depression, crime, and the like. Thus a shift in values makes possible a shift in types of welfare programs. What might result if all Americans were deemed as worthy as veterans?

SOCIAL DARWINISM

In 1859, Charles Darwin published *The Origin of the Species*, a book which had a remarkable impact on the world. Essentially a biological study, it postulated the concepts of natural selection and evolution as its result. Around these two concepts, individualism, competition, and the "scientific" attitude coalesced. Serving a myriad of purposes, Social Darwinism was born. Earlier Adam Smith had suggested that "each man by pursuing his self interest, helps the common good."

To the Darwinian scientific interpretation of biological phenomena are added social and theological overtones. The person who is rewarded deserves the reward. Thus one interpretation of amassed wealth was that such wealth reflected God's grace upon individuals who were rich. As we have seen, this view is consistent with the Protestant ethic. From the point of view of Social Darwinism, those who become wealthy in the struggle for existence do so because they are superior people.

Admittedly a capitalist economy was the scene of struggle and competition in which morality as such did not exist. Anything and any action was permissible in the capitalist struggle. Beyond this, however, the struggle and competition were viewed as justifiable and glorifying the natural order and even God's will.

Of course, because of the theory of natural selection and evolution, the triumph of the "fit" was that they survived and prospered. This, then, was prima facie evidence of their fitness and their worthiness. All these views were justification for ruthless competition and for protection of those who had enriched themselves. Herbert Spencer, an American philosopher, sociologist, and coiner of the phrase "survival of the fittest," defended the moral aspects of individualism and laissez-faire economics. He suggested the poor "were unfit . . . and should be eliminated. The whole effort of nature is to get rid of such, to clear the world of them, and make room for better."[33]

Social Darwinism developed in a period of urbanization, industrialization, and the growth of big business. Capitalism supported such a philosophy and especially, following the Civil War, American giant industries developed rationalized in part by Social Darwinism. Predatory competition in business and industry was given a philosophical cachet.

We have reviewed the growth of individualism and scientism, the Protestant ethic, industrialism, and Social Darwinism. Given these perspectives, those who survived were "elected" to survive and prosper. Logically, the poor, ill, and disadvantaged were—from the same perspective—not able to compete and were responsible for their limitations and their poverty, perhaps through lack of God's grace but surely through their being less able and therefore not as good. This tangle of interrelated concepts led directly to victim blaming. The widow, the disabled, the orphan, the mentally ill, and

---

[33] Richard Hofstadter, *Social Darwinism in American Thought*, Boston: Beacon Press, 1967, p. 41.

the impoverished were all victims of their own personal responsibilities and actions. The way of the world was just as it should be. The status quo reflected not only human achievements and limitations but also God's will. Furthermore, social welfare efforts, however well meant, interfered with the process of natural selection and, in the long run, injured society.

THE COMING OF SOCIAL INSURANCE

Just as the early American social welfare system was influenced by Europe and the English poor laws, later American developments were influenced by the coming of social insurance in Europe, a forerunner of the Social Security Act of 1935.

In a recently united Germany during the 1870s, Social Democrats were urging the workers of a rapidly industrializing Germany to demand a republican form of government, a bill of rights, and support for the international socialist movement. In the political and industrial ferment of middle Europe, the socialists were gaining strength.

As a result in 1879 there were enacted Anti-Socialist Laws which forbade parties aimed at "overthrowing the established state or social order." Otto von Bismarck shifted from laissez-faire economics and free trade to protectionism and instituted tariffs in 1879. Since the antisocialist laws created enemies among the workers, he decided he needed to do something that would assure contented workers in a period of great industrialization.

As a result of these forces, in 1881 all workers in mines and factories whose earnings did not exceed 2000 marks per year were insured against accidents. In 1883 there was enacted a Sickness Insurance Law; in 1884, an Accident Insurance Law; and in 1887, an Old Age and Invalidity Law.

Bismarck presented a remarkable argument in his speech to the Reichstag in which he proposed social insurance in 1881: "I am not of opinion that *laissez faire, laissez aller,* 'pure Manchester policy,' 'everybody takes care of himself,' 'the weakest must go to the wall,'. . . can be practiced in a monarchically, patriarchically governed state."[34] As he presented his arguments in favor of social insurance and of governmental intervention, they amalgamated several themes. Bismarck went further to say that "an appropriate title for our enterprise would be 'Practical Christianity,' but we do not want to feed poor people with figures of speech, but with something solid.

[34] Louis L. Snyder, *Documents of German History*, New Brunswick, New Jersey: Rutgers University Press, 1958, p. 245.

Death costs nothing; but unless you will put your hands in your pockets and into the state Exchequer, you will not do much good. To saddle our industry with the whole affair—well, I don't know that it could bear the burden. All manufacturers are having hard times."[35]

By 1889 the principle of financing for these social insurances included contributions from employers, employees, and the government. Social legislation did not halt the rise of the Social Democratic Party because German workers did not trust the government's motivation and workers really wanted improved working conditions and higher wages.

Bismarck, who for the time being had taken a liberal stance in regard to the creation of social insurances, stubbornly refused legislation on working hours, woman and child labor, factory inspection, or changes in government policy regarding labor unions, which were carefully controlled. When it suited his purposes, he reverted to Manchester laissez-faire arguments. But the historic principle of contributory social insurance was institutionalized in a modern nation-state for the first time. The reverberations of this event have been felt in every modern society, and the principle of various forms of "social security" continue to be developed and refined.[36]

THREE DISCOVERIES OF POVERTY IN THE UNITED STATES

Social Darwinism did not go unchallenged during the latter part of the nineteenth century. Counter to the arguments of the social Darwinists, there existed a progressive and anti-Darwinist mood. Those who were not in the "driver's seat" had different ideas:

> Grangers, Greenbackers, Single Taxers, Knights of Labor, trade unionists, Populists, Socialists—Utopian and Marxian—all presented challenges to the existing pattern of free enterprise, demanded reforms by state action, or insisted upon a thorough remodeling of the social order.[37]

Social Darwinism was a fatalist, status quo philosophy, useful for those who were in control of industry and business. Paradoxically, such a conservative philosophy existed at a time when—because of science, technology, and progress—it was felt that human beings could do whatever they chose, including modifying the natural selection process. Lester Ward and other pioneers in sociology claimed that Social Darwinism was not scientific at all but simply

[35] Snyder, *Ibid.*, p. 247.
[36] Hajo Halborn, *A History of Modern Germany*, New York: Alfred A. Knopf, 1969, p. 292.
[37] Hofstadter, op. cit., p. 46.

descriptive. The new confidence in science and technology suggested that society could reconstruct itself as it chose. A century earlier Thomas Paine, an exponent of the doctrine of progress, argued that the United States had the potential for abolishing poverty. He thought security could be provided for the aged through the use of inheritance taxes and ground rents.[38]

The Poor Laws in England and in American communities were not primarily concerned with *poverty* and how to eliminate it. Rather they were concerned with *pauperism* and the potential claims on community funds, the danger that paupers might get by without working. In the United States prior to the 1890s, the predominant attitude was that society and the community had no real obligation to the poor. Until the last decade of the nineteenth century, reform movements in the United States did not focus on the problem of poverty or on its elimination. But the new progressives, socialists, and utopian thinkers viewed poverty as a result of the structure of society.

Communal responsibility existed for criminality, prostitution, poor housing, and intemperance. The expectation was that any remedial work should be focused on the capacity of the individual for self-improvement. In the cities there were tremendous relief problems as the major effects of industrialization and urbanization came to be felt.

During the 1880s Toynbee Hall, a settlement house in London, began to attract middle-class idealists to life among the poor. During this period as well, the Social Gospel began to be preached. There was a growing devotion to the improvement of living conditions and numerous exposés of working and living conditions. In the United States there began to be instituted some modifications of the complete laissez-faire philosophy which had been prevalent during the intense rush to industrialize America. In 1887 the Interstate Commerce Commission was formed; there were numerous exposés of business and political corruption.

The "muckrakers," journalists who exposed social ills, and the progressive movement during 1890 through 1915 focused a spotlight on the societal problems of the time, including poverty. It was during these years that the initial movement took place to enact various insurance laws, particularly unemployment and disability protection, stimulated in part by the earlier German experience. Actually, this period produced much social legislation, including antitrust laws, civil service reform, creation of the Childrens' Bureau, child

[38] Merle Curti, *The Growth of American Thought,* New York: Harper & Row, 1964, p. 165.

labor laws, health and safety laws, the income tax, direct election of senators, and other laws with direct social consequences. This progressive period marked the first "discovery" of poverty as a problem in America.

With the onset of World War I, the progressive era of legislation faded. In the United States disillusionment with and fear of left-wing philosophies, including socialism and anarchism, combined following the war to put a damper on social legislation. During the 1920s there was a return to the philosophy that government should not intervene and that the country should return to the "good old days" and thus the first discovery of poverty passed, leaving a wave of social welfare legislation in the states and on the federal level.

After a hiatus, a second illumination of the problem of poverty took place during the Great Depression of the 1930s. President Franklin Roosevelt during his second inaugural speech in 1937 spoke of the poor as "trying to live on incomes so meager that the pall of family disaster hangs over them day by day . . . under conditions labeled indecent by a so-called polite society half a century ago . . . lacking the means to buy the products of farm and factory. . . . I see one third of a nation ill-housed, ill-clad, ill-nourished."[39]

So many people were in poverty during the 1930s that the federal government was forced to act. It was no longer "they" who were poor; it was "us." Although there had been efforts to attain various types of social security in the states and on the federal level, until the Great Depression, Congress had failed to enact social insurance. Then in 1935, as part of a wave of New Deal legislation, the Social Security Act was enacted as a contributory insurance, based upon contributions by employer and employee, federally administered, and including unemployment compensation, public assistance, and services. The New Deal era was marked by an enormous variety of legislation, including rural electrification, farm legislation, a nationwide unemployment exchange system, youth programs including the Civilian Conservation Corps and the National Youth Administration, and a broader work relief program (the Works Project Administration), plus monetary, food subsidy, and banking laws among many others.

Our current social welfare programs, as explored in Chapters 6 and 7, are primarily based even now on the legislation of the 1930s, the second discovery of poverty, or focus on poverty as the problem. This discovery of poverty, highlighted by the large percentage of

[39] Max Lerner, *America as a Civilization*, Simon and Schuster, 1957, p. 335. The New Deal reform will be discussed in greater detail in Chapter 6, dealing with economic security programs.

unemployed during the 1930s, also faded during World War II, probably due to the focus on the war effort and full employment in it. The decade of the 1950s was not unlike the decade of the 1920s in the generally low-key role of social legislation in regard to social welfare.

The first American discovery of poverty in the nineteenth century came at a time when poverty had been viewed as a personal and moral fault of the poor. So many persons were in poverty during the 1930s—the second discovery period—that the systemic and structural nature of poverty was clear, and invidious moralizing necessarily was limited. However, the third discovery of poverty, coming during an affluent period, returned to a sense of victim blaming, although this time it was of a subtle and sophisticated nature.

In the late 1950s the general belief exemplified by John Kenneth Galbraith's *The Affluent Society* was that poverty as a social problem in America was past. There was still *residual* poverty, in Appalachia and other special pockets, and *case* poverty among those of low intelligence or with emotional problems. Such poverty could be reduced by having more trained social workers in welfare departments rehabilitating the poor (who were the cause of their own problems). This was the thrust of training amendments in 1962 to the Social Security Act which sought more social workers in welfare. While this was good for social workers, it ignored the social aspects of poverty. In a constant level of unemployment, every welfare client rehabilitated and put to work was replaced by another person put out of work.

Into this atmosphere came Edgar May's book *The Wasted Americans* and, most influential, Michael Harrington's *The Other America*. These books pointed out that if in the depression of 1933 one of every three Americans were poor, in 1960 one in four were still poor. And further this 25 percent was essentially constant and had not decreased since World War II. Dwight MacDonald popularized these ideas and the idea of a poverty "line" below which people should be considered poor in a series of articles in *The New Yorker* magazine. These articles caught the attention of advisors to President John Kennedy who were seeking programs to stimulate the economy. After the Kennedy assassination, these advisors brought their preliminary thinking about a "war on poverty" to President Lyndon Johnson, who liked the idea. And thus was born the Economic Opportunity Act of 1964—the so-called War on Poverty. The strategies chosen to deal with the problem did not include transfers of money directly to the poor. Instead, like the 1962 amendments to the Social Security Act, a strategy was selected which focused on services and offering opportunities for self-advancement and for further involvement in the decision-making of the society. This focus on services is subtly victim blaming in the sense that services are tied to a suggestion that one has not made it in the society because of personal shortcomings and therefore needs assistance of a service nature. The problem of inadequate income was viewed as insepara- ble from other and different kinds of problems.

The nature of the poverty war was related to the values and phi- losophies of the period. The antipoverty agencies grew from incipi- ent antidelinquency agencies which had just been funded and there- fore reflected theories on juvenile delinquency.

At one time delinquency was seen as related to certain genetic or physical characteristics of the delinquent. A more "modern" approach was to view the juvenile delinquent as psychologically dis- turbed. The sociologists then claimed that delinquent behavior rep- resented normal participation in a separate delinquent subculture. But the theory current in the late 1950s was "opportunity theory" as developed by Lloyd Ohlin and Richard Cloward.[40] The delinquent gang did not operate in a separate culture with different values and aspirations. Rather delinquents shared the same desires for a house with a picket fence and the like. It was the gap between these aspi- rations and *opportunities* available which caused delinquent behav- ior. Thus opportunity had to be opened.

Therefore it is no surprise that the War on Poverty was the Eco- nomic *Opportunity* Act and that its programs stressed access and opportunity and participation for the poor. Out of these participatory efforts grew the later demand for income transfer itself.

There is some evidence that the War on Poverty worked to a significant extent to reduce the incidence of poverty although it is hard to separate the Economic Opportunity Act and its programs from the growing income transfer programs of the 1960s and from general economic growth. OEO's specific programs are discussed in Chapter 7. Nonetheless, the 1960s focused the most attention on the problems of poverty since the 1930s. The fact that the President and the society had agreed through the enactment of legislation to attack poverty per se was a new step in the development of social welfare. It was a federal and local approach to the problem, brought resources to the task (obviously not sufficient), and defined the problem broadly.

How did the third discovery of poverty, so close to us in time, develop? Two different points of view expounded hold special inter-

---

[40] Richard A. Cloward and Lloyd E. Ohlin, *Delinquency and Opportunity: A Theory of Delinquent Gangs*. Glencoe, Ill.: The Free Press, 1960.

est because they reflect the realities of the 1960s as a period and identify the development of an entirely new feature in society. Further, they may be instructive in pointing out the directions from which reforms will come.

First, Daniel Moynihan suggested that a new phenomenon had occurred: the professionalization of reform. The question of poverty was now being dealt with, planned for, and coped with by administrators, professional organizations, doctors, teachers, social workers, and others, and special initiatives were being taken by government-employed professionals.

Moynihan's argument was that the Office of Economic Opportunity (OEO) programs were the result of this "professionalization" of reform.[41] Based upon social statistics, newly available for use, and expanded social science research, OEO included high level planning by professionals and maximum feasible participation by the poor in the development of programs. Furthermore, Moynihan argued, these programs had the effect of re-creating ethnic politico-social organizations in the big cities. According to Moynihan, for the first time in history professionals took the lead in the search for reform. They had access to information, they had expertise, and they knew where the entry points to the gates of power were located. Thus, in a way, the search for reform had taken a new turn after all prior history in that certain people (professionals), for good or bad motives, took on the responsibility of reforming society as a part of their own job definitions and responsibilities. The War on Poverty had not resulted from marches, demonstrations, or popular demand. It had evolved, as outlined in this chapter, in intellectual circles: from Galbraith, Harrington, MacDonald, and the President's advisors to a legislative program.

Second, Richard Cloward and Frances Fox Piven claimed that the War on Poverty was a response to the civil rights movement, beginning unrest in the cities, and political payoffs to poor urban constituencies to whom the Democratic Party owed a debt. Thus, in this view, OEO was the continuation of a political process which had gone before. This is in contradistinction to the Moynihan point of view, that no one was specifically "banging on the door" for a war on poverty. Where the two points of view apparently cross is in the fact that maximum feasible participation, as a principle, was invented by the professional planners but also was inherent in the political realities among the poor, a demand for greater recognition, and partici-

[41] Daniel Patrick Moynihan, "The Professionalization of Reform," *The Public Interest*, Vol. 1, Fall 1965, pp. 6–16.

pation in the political process. Both theories are correct but incomplete. There would have been no War on Poverty without the unrest Cloward and Piven describe. Yet it might not have developed when and in the way it did without the process described by Moynihan.

Following the events of the 1960s, again there was a retreat after the third discovery of poverty. During the decade of the 1970s, there was a waning of interest and initiatives in social welfare. In the early stages of the Richard Nixon presidency, there was some exploration, led by Moynihan, of a family assistance plan, a reorganization of the welfare system. Our welfare system continues to be structured essentially as it had been following the enactment of the Social Security Act in 1935.[42] It becomes constantly clearer that it does need a major overhaul. One outstanding pressure for change comes from large cities, which are hounded by immense costs of welfare. There is a strong movement for the creation of a national, federal welfare system, especially in terms of funding. States and localities have been enormously burdened by the welfare costs they have been forced to meet. Greater recognition has been given to the fact that local welfare costs are inseparable from major economic trends in our society. This recognition, plus the pressure to reduce or maintain taxes, suggests that in the near future serious attempts will be made to shift the cost of welfare to the federal level.

THE POOR LAWS TODAY

Despite the passage of time and the many changes that have taken place in our society, the Poor Law mentality remains with us. The welfare system, broadly defined, is the nexus for conflicting values — humane and punitive. In almost every sphere of life, punitive laws are interpreted to the disadvantage of the poor. Other persons as well are treated badly with the excuse that they are somehow unworthy. Nevertheless, certain changes have taken place among the basic principles of the Poor Laws.

The major trend toward secularism continues. The taxing authority of the state is so overwhelming that the secularization of welfare moves steadily along. However, a strong counterpoint exists in the voluntary welfare area, in the use of third party payments and purchase of service contracts with religious and privately sponsored social welfare agencies, and in the use of tax deductions as supports for the private and voluntary social welfare sphere.

---

[42] Two of the most important changes since 1935 are the enactment of Medicare-Medicaid and Supplemental Security Income, both of which are discussed in Chapter 6.

Risks and categories remain with us. For example, public welfare categories traditionally have favored female-headed families over male-headed families. The system as designed may create incentives for desertion.[43] In this way the laws destroy families and supplant two-parent with single-parent families. Categories of the worthy and the unworthy still exist. There is little concern about funds paid to those with physical handicaps. At the same time, pressures are exerted to drive those with "invisible handicaps" off the welfare rolls. Benefits tend to be for people who fit certain categorical requirements, as tested by individual means tests, rather than broadly inclusive.

There are few claims that indoor relief is cheaper or more productive than outdoor relief. In general, we have learned that institutionalization is more expensive than outdoor relief, both for the short and the long term. A respect for independent functioning also serves to support outdoor relief. Still institutional care remains in effect for more people who need it in ideal terms.

---

[43] Recent studies point out that while males are unlikely to desert their families for a few extra dollars a month, once a family is broken "welfare" does act as a deterrent to remarriage. Gilbert Steiner has pointed out there is no definitive evidence that the design of AFDC causes fathers to desert in order to make their families eligible for benefits. However, whatever is known or not known scientifically, there is a general belief that AFDC does have a bias against families.

Final conclusions on these issues are difficult to draw. The nature of support programs does influence, to some degree, the stability of the family and family composition. But, different variations of income guarantee programs may have different effects.

In 1978 the Seattle and Denver Income Maintenance Experiments reported that there were no "dowry" effects stimulating marriage for single householders. They did find evidence of an increased rate of marital dissolution in the experimental groups relative to the control groups. But this evidence is ambiguous in that the higher income levels do not produce the same effects on the marital dissolution rate for blacks and whites and appear to have very different effects for Chicanos, as well as producing stability rather than dissolution. Future studies may make it possible to better understand the relationships between income maintenance programs, family structure, and family life.

See: Gilbert Y. Steiner, *The State of Welfare*, Washington: The Brookings Institution, 1971, pp. 81–82. David Kershaw and Jerilyn Fair, *The New Jersey Income Maintenance Experiment*. Vol. I. *Operations, Surveys, and Administration*, New York: Academic Press, 1976, p. 21. Harold W. Watts and Albert Rees (eds.), *The New Jersey Income Maintenance Experiment*. Vol. III, *Expenditures, Health and Social Behavior; and the Quality of the Evidence*. New York: Academic Press, 1977, pp. 13–14. Robert G. Spiegelman, Lyle P. Groenveld, and Philip K. Robins. "Additional Evidence on the Work Effort and Marital Stability Effects of the Seattle and Denver Income Maintenance Experiments." Testimony before the Sub-Committee on Public Assistance of the Senate Finance Committee, November 15, 1978. Mimeo. Menlo Park, Calif.: SRI International. Roger Wilkins, "Study Finds Some Prevalent Ideas About Welfare Families Incorrect," *New York Times*, August 7, 1978, p. A11.

With greater mobility, brought about by new modes of transportation and the need for manpower in various parts of the nation for industry, residency laws are being eroded as the United States moves toward a national society. The connections between what occurs in Mississippi, for example, and what happens in major metropolitan areas of the northern or western states has increasingly become clearer as the various regions become much more aware of their interconnections. The erosion of residency laws also has been supported by court cases, calling into doubt and doing away with residency requirements which had historically been used as punitive and primitive protection devices.

The issue of less eligibility remains even today one of the most difficult and intractable problems in social welfare. Benefits for social welfare payments are typically computed on the basis of minimum level subsistence, and a percentage is usually taken then of that inadequate sum. If you are poor and working, the welfare system is designed to retain you as a public charge. This results from the fact that payments are reduced largely dollar for dollar according to the income of the recipient. Thus there is little incentive for earning a living when you are close to the public welfare level but actually working and earning an income. One particularly modern development related to less eligibility, in general a rule which continues in use, is the "notch problem." Certain people in welfare receive several types of benefits: monetary, nonmonetary, or service. When the services are computed, for example, for child care or medical care, in monetary terms, the total income for the welfare recipient may surpass that of an employed person. In this way, in part, less eligibility, too, has been modified as a universal rule. As peoples' incomes rise above a "notch" they may become ineligible for one or more of the other benefits, suffering a net loss. Thus, our fear of having people receive too much serves as a disincentive to earning more.

The treatment of poverty on a case-by-case basis has been changed primarily in the sense that our understanding has been broadened to appreciate structural components that contribute to poverty in individual cases. We better understand the relationship between public issues and private troubles. Even so, psychological counseling is the treatment of choice by many for those with private troubles, as though the "fault lies in ourselves."

Stigma remains a part of welfare today, and there is much victim blaming. Since the Poor Laws utilized stigma to control people's lives, to create a climate in which people would be punished for not working, it is reasonable to assume that today's remaining harsh attitudes also serve purposes and reinforce the Poor Laws of the modern era—laws and attitudes which continue a slow change over time but have a stubborn hold on our American minds. On the other hand, a growing sense of entitlement serves to reduce the stigma for some who receive public aid.

INDUSTRIAL SOCIETY, SOCIAL VALUES, AND MODERN VIEWS OF HUMAN NATURE

In preindustrial societies, poverty was general at many times and places, but those who were dependent were deemed worthy of assistance. In time of catastrophe, as we have seen, the larger group had the duty of providing regular basic essentials for survival. Typically, the local community was responsible for relief within its own boundaries.

Problems developed in the fourteenth century when "able-bodied" poor, the "sturdy beggars," became visible. As a result of their increased numbers and threat, there began the regulation of beggers and the development of different criteria and treatment for paupers.

In general with the development of industrial society (urbanized, specialized, and making new demands on individuals and families), it was hoped the able-bodied would be given employment through economic expansion. For the rest, self-help, mutual aid, charity, and ad hoc emergency measures would be used. Public assistance would be only for those least able to cope and for those caught up in catastrophes.

The economic human being, whose motivation was understood as being strictly economic, was a creation of the industrializing society. The object of Poor Laws was to "oil" the working of the free economy, to facilitate labor mobility, and to separate the deserving poor (whose situations could not be remedied) from all the rest of the people.[44]

The Protestant ethic served many of the same purposes. It stressed the need for visible proof of one's being elect. According to this ethic, "not leisure and enjoyment, but only activity serves to increase the glory of God, according to the manifestations of His will. Waste of time is thus the first and in principle the deadliest of sins. The span of human life is infinitely short and precious to make sure of one's own election."[45] Thus the Protestant ethic was a kind of "conspicuous assumption." If a person has worldly goods, the

---

[44] E. J. Hobsbawm, "Poverty," *International Encyclopedia of the Social Sciences*, Vol. 12, David L. Sills, (ed.), New York: Macmillan and The Free Press, 1968, pp. 398–404.
[45] Max Weber, *The Protestant Ethic and the Spirit of Capitalism*, New York: Charles Scribner's Sons, 1958, p. 157.

assumption—according to this interpretation—is that the person is of the elect of God. Of course, for those who are poor in worldly goods, the assumption is the reverse. Their poverty is a mark that they are not among the elect.

In the latter part of the nineteenth century it became clear that the "iron hand" of the self-regulating capitalist economy just might not be an iron hand. The capitalist economy might not be self-regulating. Furthermore, to the extent it was self-regulating during the industrial process, it left many by the wayside, a seemingly natural concomitant of the "self-regulating" mechanisms.

The growing influence of the working classes, of the nearly poor and the poor, resulted in the evolution of economies in which (as in Germany in the 1880s) it became important to create welfare for the vast majority of persons for the sake of productivity and for the cohesion of the society. Dealing with pauperism became a part of the problem of minimum standards for all citizens.

In the early stages of industrialization it could be argued that punitive welfare laws were necessary to maintain a pool of motivated workers. In this sense, and from this point of view, it is possible the Poor Laws were functional in that they supported the industrialization of society and thus the creation of more wealth. As welfare systems evolved, especially after the creation of social insurances, support systems for more and more people were indeed built into Western societies.

Punitive welfare laws are not needed today. The creation of the service economy (currently approximately 70 percent of the work force is in service-producing industry) has limited the number of potential jobs for those who do not have the abilities, health, and education required. Finally, the rise of technology and of a professional class has reduced the employment options for those without first-class credentials.

Yet simultaneously, fewer people are able to support more people than ever before. The possibility of creating wealth at a rate which makes possible the elimination of poverty, according to some absolute standard, is possible.

Today, through subsidized education and forced retirement, we spend billions of dollars to keep millions of people out of the labor force. Still our welfare laws are structured to "protect" society from anyone receiving benefits without working.

As we have seen, poverty is an historic problem. In every age explanations are offered for the causation of poverty. A major disjunction occurred in the explanations offered during the latter part of the Middle Ages. Following this critical period, two primary but conflicting assumptions have been offered: poverty is caused by a flaw in the moral character of an individual, or environmental factors create poverty, especially exploitation.

The utility of poverty (and of the blaming-the-victim syndrome) was that it assured cheap labor and exports at low cost while high wages would diminish productivity, raise prices, and lower exports. Either people must be kept poor or in some manner motivated and driven to produce goods. Two classes of the destitute were established, the deserving and the undeserving poor. In the latter group were vagabonds, thieves, and sturdy beggars, all of whom ostensibly could work for a living. But the brand which was used for the undeserving poor somehow also touched the others who needed assistance. From severity and punishment, the method for dealing with the poor was shifted to an examination of their sinfulness and, finally, not many years ago, to their need for treatment.

Structurally, several rationales were given for poverty's existence. Thomas Malthus postulated his "laws." The law of large numbers suggested that population expands exponentially while the necessary resources did not expand at the same or at a sufficient rate. The growth of population in and of itself implied poverty. Karl Marx, too, with his theory of economic determinism and class struggle, offered structural interpretations of the existence of poverty. However, in the United States the most prevalent understanding of poverty was in terms of "blaming the victim" and of character faults. Structural interpretations implied, however, that in a time of industrialization and high productivity, it was possible to create surpluses and to redistribute them through institutional arrangements, by controlling population growth or increasing food production or revamping the socioeconomic system. At the same time, the engines of production and urbanization were grinding people up in them. One way of dealing with these massive problems was to blame them on the individual and to offer charity, meaningful but not requiring the alteration of basic arrangements.

In the latter part of the nineteenth and in the twentieth centuries, a new possible explanation arose. Perhaps poverty was due to other causes or to many interrelated variables. Such an explanation could only arise in wealthy societies where there was high productivity, and it became clear that poverty could be reduced. Institutions in the society could be used to reduce the poverty of the present and to prevent poverty in the future. Previously when poverty was the rule in a changing society, the personal characteristics argument was useful.

The historic disjunction that occurred in the late Middle Ages and created 500 years of punitive social welfare legislation was undoubtedly connected with the many trends, ideas, and technical developments we have reviewed. But if changes of such tremendous importance could take place, there is a suggestion the future also could be different. On the basis of prudence, societies could decide to treat those in need humanely so as to avoid clashes, make human relations more peaceful, and assure that all citizens are treated with respect and are sustained.

HUMAN NATURE AND THE AMERICAN DREAM

In every society people express their values about human nature and the image of the good society. Throughout history we have seen that each society acts on its ideas through its social welfare system. In a sense, all modern societies are at the lead of long marches across time. Slowly constant historic processes have brought each society forward.

In the United States, according to the Constitution, we are to seek the "general welfare," but how shall we seek it (with what means?) and what is it? As in the beginning, we arrive at values. If people are basically good, we shall open our hands to give to them. If they are evil, we will close our hands to deprive them of their ill-gotten gains.

Despite our values, however, we have seen that other constraints enter the picture. Social welfare is intricately related to the view of humanity held by citizens, especially decision-makers, but it also reflects our view of ourselves and the society we wish to create. Even on pragmatic grounds, it appears there is much to be said for an openhanded social welfare policy, because what is sown now will be reaped in a few years.

But American values are mixed. Along with the Protestant Ethic and Social Darwinism is an impetus toward equalitarianism, democracy, and a belief in mutual aid. The American dream also calls for equal opportunity. While it does not make claims for all persons being equal, it does demand that American society strive to give all persons equal opportunity, which is to say that all persons, including those who need help from the society through public welfare, have a right to equal opportunity to health, education, and the basic necessities of life. They, too, are building America.

The ideal of equal opportunity is as yet unfulfilled. The degree to which the dream remains unfulfilled is dependent not only upon the will of our society to fulfill it, but also on its inherent difficulties. The fulfillment of the dream of equal opportunity for one individual may diminish that opportunity for other individuals; the enhancement of one group's, neighborhood's, or region's opportunity may have adverse effects upon others. The complete resolution of such dilemmas about the American dream remains before us.

Finally, the American dream includes pluralism, many groups, many life-styles, and many ethics, and this pluralism and differentiation have to be respected by the law. Social welfare, as an important institution in our society, has to deal evenhandedly with all who need help, regardless of their values or their differences. The American dream is enacted in "minute particulars," in the way each person is dealt with under the law and by the professional social worker who makes decisions about a person's future.

Chapter 4
Conceptions of Social Welfare

" . . . all collective interventions to meet certain needs of
the individual and/or to serve the wider interests of society
may now be broadly grouped into . . . categories of
welfare."[1]

WHAT IS SOCIAL WELFARE?

This is a book about social welfare. In the early chapters we discussed the history of social welfare, the impact of social values on
social welfare, and related matters. Perhaps the time has come to
stop and define our terms. Just what do we mean by social welfare?
What does the term encompass? What are its boundaries? And what
in society is not part of the social welfare system?

One can attempt to define social welfare in narrow or broad
terms. In its narrowest sense, social welfare includes those nonprofit
functions of society, public or voluntary, which are clearly aimed at
alleviating distress and poverty or at ameliorating the conditions of
the casualties of society. Just about everyone would include the public assistance program as part of the U.S. social welfare system. Similarly the food stamp program, hospital social service programs,

[1] Richard Titmuss, "The Social Division of Welfare," *Essays on the Welfare State*,
New Haven: Yale University Press, 1959, p. 42.

social service departments in homes for the aged, and the like would be seen as part of the social welfare system. These are the programs people commonly have in mind when they speak about "welfare" or social welfare.

One also may define welfare more broadly. The National Association of Social Workers (a professional group) puts it this way: "Social Welfare generally denotes the full range of organized activities of voluntary and governmental agencies that seek to prevent, alleviate, or contribute to the solution of recognized social problems, or to improve the well-being of individuals, groups, or communities. Such activities use a wide variety of professional personnel such as physicians, nurses, lawyers, educators, engineers, ministers, and social workers. . . ."[2]

Another by now classic text defines social welfare as "those formally organized and socially sponsored institutions, agencies, and programs, exclusive of the family and private enterprise, which function to maintain or improve the economic conditions, health or interpersonal competence of some parts or all of a population."[3] The quotation from the late Richard Titmuss with which this chapter opens and some of his other writings suggest that all activities of society are divisible into two basic categories.

1. Those which are conducted for profit, the market activities of society.
2. The collective interventions that are welfare oriented.

In other words, all nonmarket activities are social welfare ones.

Neither the narrow nor the broad definitions are perfect. Narrow definitions tend to exclude the most important and effective social welfare programs of society. They define social welfare in what will be defined later on as *residual* terms. Social welfare is seen as the activities directed toward helping to pick up the fallen, those casualties of a society which normally operate with the institutions of the market. For people for whom the market fails, we have something called social welfare so that they do not starve, or go without shelter.

But increasingly, social welfare needs are being met by broad programs of prevention or insurance, such as the Social Security system which covers almost everyone today or social programs for the retired to meet a broad need for leisure and recreation or Workers' Compensation for rich and poor alike. We live in a society where

---

[2] National Association of Social Workers, *Encyclopedia of Social Work*, Vol. II, New York: 1971, p. 1446.
[3] Harold L. Wilensky and Charles Lebeaux, *Industrial Society and Social Welfare*, New York: The Free Press, 1958, p. 17.

welfare is much broader than what is conjured up by the common term "welfare."

Even the broad definitions of welfare are not fully inclusive, and at the same time they suffer from being somewhat too inclusive. On the one hand, by dividing between the profit sector and the welfare sector, they appear to exclude the growing delivery of social services for profit in the context of the private sector. Private hospitals, nursing homes, day-care centers, and private practice by social workers and other helping professionals all deliver services which are definable as social services and are part of the social welfare system, and yet they are not divorced from the private sector. As we will see further on, the whole division between private and public has become increasingly blurred in the United States. One could argue that the emergence of these private forms of social welfare are ultimately financed in the vast majority of cases by money from the public sector through third party payments such as Medicare, Medicaid, or other forms of health insurance, public agencies paying for purchase of day-care services in the private sector, and the like.

We simply want to make the point here that even the broadest definitions we are familiar with may not cover everything that will come to be recognized as social welfare. Furthermore, the broad definitions tend to focus on the formal as opposed to the informal social welfare institutions. Thus a street beggar is not considered part of the social welfare system nor of consideration in social welfare as an institution. But policy-makers are becoming increasingly aware that social welfare as an institution in the United States needs to become more aware of and more connected with the informal, natural systems for helping that people use. For example, the woman in the garden apartment complex who is turned to for counseling by her neighbors, the parish priest, and the gang leader all are, in a sense, part of the helping system and need to be taken into account as part of a full appreciation of the scope of social welfare. Even individual beggary, when it becomes large enough, has an institutional framework of its own such as the carving out of certain street corners or turfs for various beggars, certain informal rules of the game which have a social system of their own on how begging is to be done, and what the police will and will not tolerate.

On the other hand, the broad definitions of social welfare also are too all encompassing by claiming to cover "all collective interventions to meet needs" or by making similar broad statements. The definition intrudes on territory that has come to be defined institutionally as belonging elsewhere. The nonmarket portion of society also covers police and fire services, education, medical care, tax policies, and the like. Are all of these subsumed under our definition of social welfare? There is a logic in such a definition, but it would make the task of a text too broad for any meaningful discussion or understanding.

What then are we to do? Shall we throw up our hands and admit defeat in an attempt to define social welfare? To an extent we must. The sophisticated student must realize that social welfare is an ambitious, changing, and blurred term. Still we generally know what we are talking about when we discuss social welfare, and it is possible to suggest a definition which will serve for working purposes. For our purposes, we will assume the following:

1. All social interventions which are intended to enhance or maintain social functioning of human beings may be defined as social welfare in the largest and broadest sense. Titmuss even goes so far as to try to break down all these interventions into three basic categories of welfare: fiscal, occupational, and social.[4]

2. As social welfare programs, services and institutions enter the mainstream of society and become more universally used and accepted; they tend to lose their identity as social welfare services. This blurring will confuse the picture, but we need to understand it. The best social welfare programs are those so accepted that they cease to be commonly defined as social welfare. Only the worst and most demeaning programs are clearly social welfare to all citizens. The kindergarten movement started as a social welfare program in settlement houses. As it became accepted as an important part of the American educational system, it moved into the public school system, and now is seen as part of the domain of education. There is no need for us to claim kindergarten or to study it in a text on social welfare, although students should be aware that, in the largest sense, kindergarten and the entire public school system is a welfare program. Social Security, too, as it has become more universally used and accepted, is another program which is less identified as social welfare than it once was. Recipients of Social Security do not think of themselves as "welfare" cases in the same way that recipients of public assistance do. Nonetheless, it is essential to study Social Security as part of the social welfare system of the United States. It is not part of any other domain. As Wilensky and Lebeaux put it: "it seems likely that distinctions between welfare and other types of social institutions will become more and more blurred . . . all institutions will be oriented toward and evaluated in terms of social welfare aims. The "welfare state" will become the "welfare society.""[5]

3. Because of the considerations mentioned above, our defini-

[4] Titmuss, op. cit., pp. 34–55.
[5] Wilensky and Lebeaux, op. cit., p. 147.

tion will tend toward the broad rather than the narrow approach to what is social welfare. In fact, we will be prepared to include interventions for the enhancement of the social functioning of human beings, even where they are in the private profit-making sector or where they are part of an informal, less clearly institutional structure.

4. For the sake of practicality, however, we will limit our consideration to those parts of the broad social welfare system which are *not* clearly the domain or territory of other fields or disciplines, such as education, medicine, and police and fire services. This, too, will pose problems, because the domains are not always clear. Health care and health insurance are part of the domain of social welfare, while medical practice is not. Similarly, there are social welfare programs and concerns related to corrections and public justice even though police science is not social welfare.

If the above definition is complex and a little fuzzy, the student needs to understand this as the necessary concomitant of a society which is mixed in its functions between market and nonmarket activities and which is specialized and multidisciplinary in its provision of services. There is no easy answer or way out. But we think that the boundaries that we have suggested will give us relative clarity in seeing what is part of our system and what is not. Briefly, everything for the enhancement of social functioning is "in," except those activities clearly part of another domain or territory.

Wilensky and Lebeaux go further in giving us some guidelines for the recognition of a social welfare institution.[6] They suggest that the characteristics or activities which fall within the range of welfare in America today are the following:

1. *Formal organization.* This would exclude the handout, individual charity, and other neighborhood, family, and related mutual aid arrangements. Our own bias is that this delineation is a bit too strict and that social welfare needs to look more carefully at the informal institutional arrangements. Nonetheless, social welfare activity may be limited to that which can be examined in terms of some form of *organization*, formal or not.

2. *Social sponsorship and accountability.* Wilensky and Lebeaux point out that socially sanctioned purposes and methods, accountability to some government agency, some board of directors, or the like are the critical elements in social welfare service, distinguishing it from the profit-making institution. Again, this characteristic needs to be modified somewhat as America continues to blur the lines between the private and the public sector. This will be discussed more fully later on, but social sponsorship, or at least

[6] Ibid., pp. 138–147.

accountability to the public, *is* a characteristic of most social welfare institutions.

3. *Absence of profit motive as dominant program purpose.* We have pointed out that, in our mixed economy, the profit motive is increasingly present in social welfare activity. Wilensky and Lebeaux suggest that where a private practitioner is subject to professional norms, the profit motive is limited. Surely the ultimate source of funds is almost always the public purse. So this may still be a reasonable, if imperfect, guideline.

4. *Functional generalization—an integrative view of human needs.* Wilensky and Lebeaux suggest that social welfare activities are those not limited to a special need or function, such as fire services, but which are general and substitute for needs formerly met by families and now unmet. While this characteristic is not true of all social welfare programs, it is generally true that it is the function of social welfare to come in and to pick up the pieces in any area of need where other institutions of the market do not do the job. Social welfare may place babies in foster homes, operate recreation programs, administer social insurance, and develop medical services in a rural community, activities which have little in common but which take on a social welfare aspect in that they are functionally generalized, attached to or performing in place of the family, education, or industry—wherever there are unmet needs. This realization helps us to exclude certain broad activities instituted for the general welfare but which are segmental and part of the domain of other specific fields, such as the school system.

5. *Direct concern with human consumption needs.* Some activities of society are primarily directed at the requisites of the society itself, such as national defense, and only indirectly and ultimately with the fate of the individual. Other activities of society are those which provide direct services to meet immediate needs of individuals and families, such as subsidized housing, counseling, and medical and hospital services. It is in this last group that what we call social welfare tends to fall.

In spite of our disagreements, in part, with these five characteristics as defining social welfare, they provide a useful guide to the student in identifying social welfare services in the United States.

SOCIAL POLICY, SOCIAL SERVICES, AND SOCIAL WORK

Before proceeding, there are a few other terms which come up frequently in social welfare and need to be defined.

1. *Social policy.* Social policy is both *the decision-making process* and *its outcomes* concerned with social welfare, social services,

and closely related spheres. It has been pointed out that policy refers both to the "practice of social decision-making by which a course of action is determined, formulated, and promoted" (policy-making) and to the "product of that process" (the resulting policy).[7]

2. *Social services.* It is probably simplest to think of social services as those conducted by social welfare institutions and which may even be called *social welfare* services. Occasionally such services will be delivered by institutions which are not recognizable as social welfare institutions and, therefore, it is helpful to think in terms of services delivered rather than simply of social welfare institutions. To the extent that an institution delivers a social service, one could argue that it is, by definition, a social welfare institution. But the distinction is helpful, because often a largely nonwelfare institution will deliver a social service, for example, social services provided by the Department of Defense or an industry. Social services include both *personal services* (services to individuals based on relationships) and more *institutional services* (income programs, housing projects, and the like). Alfred Kahn defines social services in terms of the tasks a service must meet to be defined as a social service. These are

1. To strengthen and repair family and individual functioning with reference to ongoing roles.
2. To provide new institutional outlets for socialization, development, and assistance, roles that once were but are no longer discharged by the nuclear or extended family.
3. To develop institutional forms for new activities essential to individuals, families, and groups in the complex urban society even though they are unknown in a simple society.

In other words, social services do not merely replace or seek to correct the family or earlier social forms; they also are new responses to new social situations.[8]

3. *Social work.* It is important that social work not be confused with social welfare or social services. Social work is a professionalized occupation. It operates largely in the delivery of social services and in social welfare institutions. Social welfare is the primary territory, turf, and arena in which it operates. Social services are what it performs, along with others. Social work is the major professional group in the social welfare arena. If an analogy might help, think of

[7] Irving Weissman, Curriculum Study, Council on Social Work Education, Vol. 2, *Social Welfare Policy and Services in Social Work Education,* New York: 1959, pp. 32–33.
[8] Alfred J. Kahn, *Social Policy and Social Services,* New York: Random House, 1973, p. 16.

medical doctors as the professional group in the arena of health services. While social work does not have the dominance and power in its arena that medical doctors have in health services, the analogy in terms of distinction between the professional group and the arena is accurate. Not everyone performing social services is a social worker anymore than everyone providing medical services is a medical doctor. The distinction can become very important. Headlines around the country, on one occasion, proclaimed that a "social worker" had ordered sterilization of two young black girls without parental consent. The "social worker" was not a social worker at all, but there is a tendency to use the term for people working in the social services, even when that person is not a professional. This will be discussed more fully in the chapter on social work as a profession.

EXAMINING A SOCIAL WELFARE PROGRAM[9]

What tools does a student need in order to develop some intelligent understanding of a social welfare program, some intelligent analysis of its characteristics, and some informed opinion as to its desirability?

First, a student needs to know what basic components there are in any social welfare program which he or she must look for; we will discuss four of these. The student who can apply an understanding of these four *structural* components to social welfare programs should have at least a beginning grasp and understanding of what they are all about, what they are intended to do, for whom, and at what price.

Second, the student needs to know what some of the basic issues are about alternative ways of organizing social welfare programs, alternative *characteristics* that they may possess, and we will discuss a number of those.

Finally, the student needs to know what criteria he must apply to any social welfare program in order to *evaluate* it, and we will offer several of those. Prepared with this schema for examining the structure of a welfare program, we will then apply the schema to a variety of major social welfare programs in the United States, both economic security programs and programs which are coming to be termed the "personal social services."

[9] The authors assume responsibility for the model which follows. It should be noted that it is, however, drawn from the kind of schema developed by Eveline Burns in her writings and teaching. Another similar model, also drawn from Burns, may be found in Neil Gilbert and Harry Specht, *Dimensions of Social Welfare Policy*, Englewood Cliffs, New Jersey: Prentice-Hall, 1974.

Examining a Social Welfare Program

 I. Structural components
   A. What is the form of benefit that the program produces?
   B. Who is eligible for the program?
   C. How is the program financed?
   D. What is the level of administration?
 II. Alternative program characteristics
   A. Residual, institutional, developmental
   B. Selective, universal
   C. Benefits in money, service, utilities
   D. Public, private
   E. Central, local
   F. Lay, professional
   G. Resources, or engineering as the problem
 III. Evaluating the program
   A. Adequacy
     1. Horizontal
     2. Vertical
   B. Financing
     1. Equitable
     2. Priority use of funds
     3. Efficient: cost and benefit
   C. Coherence
   D. Latent consequences

I. STRUCTURAL COMPONENTS

• *A. What is the Form of Benefit that the Program Produces?* This is simply another way of asking, "What is the output of a program?" What does the program produce? For instance, unemployment insurance produces a certain amount of cash income for a certain number of weeks. A family agency might "produce" individual or group counseling, or help in negotiating other social systems. A housing project might "produce" apartments of from one to four bedrooms at low cost. It is important, to begin with, to get a good fix on precisely what the benefits of a given program are so that the program can be understood and evaluated on its own terms. We will see that the form the benefits take is a major issue. Should they be in the form of money such as rent, of personal services such as tenant counseling, or of the provision of a new social utility such as a housing project? The question of the level of benefit in programs is crucial. Is the level of cash benefit in an economic security program adequate? Is the kind of counseling available in a personal service agency adequate or underadequate or overadequate for the task? The concept is simple enough. The first thing anyone who examines a social welfare program will want to know is what the benefits are and what form they take.

• *B. Who is Eligible for the Program?*   Another way of saying this is what risks of human existence are covered by the program? The concept of covering certain risks of living, or categorical programs, is basic to the Western social welfare system. At least since the English poor laws, and probably of necessity in any modern society, there are few agencies which simply provide "help." Even generalized multiservice centers can offer services, can provide information, and can make referral to others only for people within a given area or a certain age range. A program will not provide services to people below a certain age without parental consent, for example. And so the student must learn the categories for eligibility.

In order to receive food stamps, for example, a person needs to be poor. How poverty is defined may vary from year to year and may be debated, but the food stamp program is not simply a program which puts food on the shelf and invites people to come and help themselves as they feel the need. One needs to establish eligibility. The food stamp program covers the "risk" of being too poor to buy adequate food. To be eligible for service in a community mental health center, a person must live within a certain district; if not, the person is referred to another community mental health center. To be eligible for Medicare, a person must be above a certain age level. To be eligible for Social Security, among other things, a person must be largely retired from working for wages. To be eligible for day care, a person must be below a certain age. So along with the question of what the benefits or output of a program are, one must ask the companion question, "For whom are the benefits?" How is eligibility determined? The choices in determining eligibility raise major issues in the characteristics of social welfare programs, as we will see. But if the student knows the answer to the questions of what the benefits are, and who is eligible for the benefits (what class or classes of people are eligible), one can get a good beginning understanding of the nature of the program.

• *C. How is the Program Financed?*   Financing is a crucial component of any social welfare program, and one that is too often overlooked by social workers and others who are concerned only with the output of the program. If one can think of the social welfare program as a sort of simple mechanical device, an oven, for instance, then the benefit of the program may be seen as the cake which is baked in the oven. The financing is the equivalent of the ingredients which are put into the cake batter. No matter how skilled the baker may be at mixing ingredients and decorating cakes, the cake will not be any better than the ingredients that have gone into it. The availability of the ingredients, where they come from, and in what proportion are all crucial to the outcome. A social welfare program may be financed by any one or by a combination of sources including the following.

1. *General revenues.* At each level of government, local, state, and national, there are general tax funds collected from income taxes, sales taxes, and the like which go into a general purse. Out of this general purse the legislature will allocate monies for various social functions, defense, highways, safety services, and social services. Some social welfare programs are financed completely or partially from such general revenue monies. In discussing financial equity as part of the evaluation of a social welfare program, we will see that it can make a tremendous difference to the fairness of a program, and to its qualities in many ways whether monies come from general revenues or other sources. The private or voluntary sector often has a rough equivalent of general revenues. In most communities there is a United Way or Community Chest which raises money for the social service needs of a whole variety of local agencies such as scouts and family service agencies. These funds become a kind of general revenue source for making allocations to the various member agencies for their own general operations.

2. *Earmarked taxes.* Sometimes a locality, a state, or even the national government will develop a special tax or revenue collecting program, the money from which is earmarked in advance for a special purpose. A federal gasoline tax is an interesting example. Proceeds from this tax are kept in a special trust fund for purposes of transportation. It sometimes makes taxes more palatable to indicate to the general public that the proceeds from this tax are going to some agreed-on important purpose. A state lottery may designate its proceeds for education or the aged. Of course, there are drawbacks to this approach, too. It makes for limited flexibility. For instance, there has been much argument and litigation about using the transit trust fund referred to above for mass transit as well as for the building of highways. As our understanding of transit needs has evolved, is that a legitimate discharge of the purposes of the fund or not? Again the voluntary agencies have a roughly equivalent mechanism to the earmarked tax. In addition to the general fund-raising drive, they may have a special drive for a new building or for the local chapter

of the American Red Cross, or they may make an allocation to one of its member agencies to hire an outreach worker to teens or to offer some such specialization within its general revenue responsibilities.

3. *Employer/employee taxes.* A number of social programs are financed by taxes on employees or employers or on a combination of these. Such programs tend to be for the social insurances. They connote, in some ways, an insurance concept: that a person pays for insurance out of his or her earnings and is thus getting back what was put in when a claim is filed. We will see in our discussion of Social Security that these are not really insurances in that the person who is contributing is not buying benefits with this contribution. But they do have the advantage of creating a sense of personal possession of the right to the benefit on the part of the payee. On the other hand, as we shall discuss further under financial equity, these kinds of taxes to finance social programs tend to be regressive.[10] They put more of the burden on low-income people than do other taxes, and they have been criticized for that reason. Like other earmarked taxes, they also tend to be limited in flexibility. Social Security and Medicare, for example, are financed by a tax on employers and employees. Unemployment insurance is financed by a tax on the employer for a percentage of the payroll. The closest thing to this kind of tax in the voluntary sector is the degree to which a United Fund may suggest in its community a "fair share," a percentage of income which it recommends employees volunteer to have deducted from their pay as a contribution to the general community fund. Groups of industrialists and businesspersons also may informally tax themselves at a certain level based on their assumed ability to pay. While there are no formal sanctions that can support this form of "taxation," in communities where community traditions for voluntary giving are strong, this does have some effect.

4. *Payment by the recipient of service.* Many social welfare programs derive at least a portion of their income from the payments by recipients of the service. Often payment is on a sliding scale based on ability to pay. For example, those who are able pay for family counseling or services at a day-camp or day-care center pay at a rate

---

[10] We will be using the terms *progressive* and *regressive* in describing taxes. A progressive tax is one in which larger percentages of taxpayers' incomes are taxed as those incomes rise (such as the Federal income tax). A regressive tax is one in which a fixed fee is paid by everyone (such as an automobile use tax), or a fixed percentage of the cost of an item or income is taxed (such as sales taxes, social security tax). A fixed fee is most regressive because the poor then pay a higher percentage of their income. A fixed percentage is less regressive, although when there is a maximum taxable income (such as in social security tax), the rich finally pay a smaller percentage of their total income.

which would make the center self-supporting if everyone paid that rate. Those with less income pay progressively less. Some private services in social welfare are available only to those who can pay a regular fee for the service by themselves.

5. *Combinations.* Increasingly social welfare programs are financed through some combination of all of the above. There will be demands that a social welfare program or agency raise its own funds through fees where able. A voluntary agency receiving a general grant from its United Fund also may be receiving some special purpose or earmarked grant from some branch of government for a particular service. The complexity of financing may affect the efficiency of an agency operation. The time allotted to satisfying the accountability requirements of different grantors may be excessive. In the extreme and not uncommon case, an agency may recast its services, not in terms of the needs of its community, but in terms of the purposes for which funds are available.

An agency is often receiving a combination of funds from the different levels of government, federal, state, local, public, and private. We will be examining some of the effects of this in further discussion.

6. *Third-party payments and purchase of services.* A growing phenomenon on the American social welfare scene has been the financing of services through the purchase of services and third-party payments. This can mean different things. In its simplest form a governmental unit is mandated or decides to provide a certain social welfare service. It may decide that rather than create a new social service on its own, it may be more economical to purchase service from an existing institution or social agency or a new one created for that purpose. Thus the state agency that wishes to provide homemaker services may develop a homemaker division of its own or may purchase homemaker services for eligible clients from some voluntary or private profit-making organization. A public agency may pay the cost for placing children in day care or residential treatment rather than create a network of such centers of its own. This is what is generally meant by purchase of service. While one can see where this might be economical, it also is easy to see where it could be wasteful. It can lead to a lack of accountability (or very expensive policing procedures so that there will be accountability) and opportunities for "sweetheart deals" between private contractors and the government, with the client or recipient of service being a pawn in the middle.

Third-party payments usually refer to a more generalized form of this phenomena where there is no plan, intent, or possibility of the social welfare program providing the service directly, but where the social welfare program itself consists entirely of payment to a "vendor" or deliverer of service to a client. Thus a patient goes to a medical facility and payment may be made directly to the facility by the Medicaid program for that patient, if he or she is eligible. As an example of the popular insurance concept in American life translated into social welfare, the problems in such a program also can be best seen by comparison with insurance. Think of collision insurance for an automobile. The person having the accident pays a yearly premium. At the moment of his accident he is not likely to think in terms of the effect on his premium of an inflated bill for repairs. He is only one of a million insurees, and what he wants is the best possible repair service. The insurance company may find it less profitable to mount the policing systems necessary to keep costs down than to pay whatever the repair shop asks for and, if necessary, to simply raise its collision rates by an extra percentage point or two the following year. The repair shop, not pressed by the direct customer, has very little motivation to keep its prices down, because everything over the deductible amount is covered by insurance anyway. So in a sense no one is responsible, and costs keep escalating. This has been true in the health service system in the United States and is one of the problems that is accompanying the growth of third-party payments as a form of financing health and social welfare programs.

To study a social welfare program it is crucial to know just what the sources of funds are, in what proportions, from what levels, and in what ways. We will see in examining specific social welfare programs that this affects the outcome tremendously. On a simple yet important level, the beginning social worker should understand the agency in which he or she is employed: from where do funds come, and how stable are the sources?

• *D. What Level of Administration?* Some programs such as Social Security or Medicare are completely federal or national programs. That is, although there may be offices in each locality, the program is a single one for the entire nation, similar in its administration and its benefits. Its employees are employees of the national government, and the policies are made in Washington, D.C. Other programs are state, county, or local programs.

As with financing, there is a growing trend toward a combination. There is a peculiar American institution known as the *grant-in-aid*. In a grant-in-aid, one unit makes funds (a grant) available to another level of government or to a voluntary or private agency and allows that unit to administer the program itself, so long as it is in keeping with some general guidelines which are set by the granting agency. Some examples may help to clarify the grant-in-aid concept.

The federal government provides 50 percent of the cost of public assistance to each state that develops a public assistance program.[11] In order to receive that money, the state must comply with certain regulations which are set down by the federal government when it gives its 50 percent. It must provide the opportunity for fair hearings or appeals by clients who are found ineligible and other such obligations. Thus, if one were talking about financing, it would be mixed. In talking about administration, the public assistance program is administered on the state and county level, but to the extent that the administration must meet certain guidelines from the federal government, even administration can be viewed in combination. Similarly, some students reading this text may be receiving in their college or university scholarship assistance which is ultimately provided by the federal or state government. The scholarship program is administered by the university. It receives a grant-in-aid for its scholarship program, and its administration is colored by the necessity of meeting certain guidelines of the granting agency. That is, to receive the scholarship you may need to have been a state resident for a certain period of time, to be interested in a certain field of study, and so on.

And so in developing a basic understanding of a social welfare program, the student of such a program will want to know

1. What are the benefits of the program?
2. What are the eligibility requirements for the program?
3. How is the program financed, at what level, or from what combination of sources?
4. How is the program administered, by whom, and at what level of government or in what combination?

II. ALTERNATIVE PROGRAM CHARACTERISTICS

No matter what the basic structure of the social welfare program under study may be, the program may choose among alternative program characteristics. There are different ways in which the program may be organized and different philosophies that it may entail. Different social planners have different biases as to how programs should be geared, to the extent that choices are possible. We will examine some of the alternative program characteristics from which social welfare programs tend to choose. That is, any given social welfare program will tend to be more like one or another among the list of alternatives to follow:

[11] This discussion is based on the administrative and funding pattern of public assistance programs at the time of this writing. Alternative organizational and funding patterns are being studied, including a nationalization of the public assistance programs in the future.

• *A. Residual, Institutional, Developmental* Any social welfare program will tend in its approach to be more or less residual, institutional, or developmental. The residual-institutional dichotomy was best conceptualized by Wilensky and Lebeaux.[12] The residual concept of social welfare is based on the premise that an individual's needs should be met through the market economy and through the family. This is the normative system in society. Occasionally, however, individuals are incapable of taking advantage of the market system or the family, or there is some sort of disruption that hits the market system, such as a depression, or a family may have a crisis. In these cases the social welfare system comes into play. It is seen as a kind of necessary evil, a backup system for the market and the family, which should be the appropriate tools for operating the society. Theoretically, the social welfare system is supposed to withdraw when the normative institutions of society, the family and the market, can once again function for the particular individual. Thus we see this conception translated into people saying that if society were only properly organized, there would be no need for social work or that the goal of the public assistance system is to do away with itself—get everyone off of welfare and into the job market. No one seriously believes that this is a possibility, and yet the whole public assistance program is structured as though it were a necessary evil: it is evaluated on the basis of how many people leave the welfare roles as a sign of success and of how many come on as a sign of failure. The residual concept in social welfare leads to the kind of programs in which eligibility is based on proving a need, that is, proving the breakdown of the other normative systems that should be working.

Institutional programs imply no abnormality or stigma. From this perspective it is accepted that social welfare is a legitimate function of modern society. It is assumed, for instance, that when people become elderly they will cease working and therefore will be faced with the problem of a possible lack of income. Therefore, there is an institutional structure such as Social Security which is intended to meet that normal need. Similarly, it is assumed that in an industrial society there will be some industrial accidents. Therefore, a system such as Workers' Compensation is set up to meet the risks of working in an industrial society, so that people who are injured can get medical care and some income protection during the period of their absence from employment. This is the institutional view, seeing social welfare as regularized, permanent, necessary, and a desirable part of the social structure.

[12] Wilensky and Lebeaux, op. cit., pp. 139–140.

What we are calling the developmental conception of social welfare grows from the writings of Alfred Kahn and John Romanyshyn and moves one step beyond the institutional concept.[13] Even the institutional view assumes some social problem which a social welfare institution is set up to prevent or correct. The developmental view, however, assumes that it is possible for society to set up a social welfare institution simply to make living better and to fulfill human development, not necessarily to solve a problem. Kahn uses the word "provisional"; Romanyshyn speaks of human development or social development, but the concept is similar.

An analogy may help to clarify these concepts. If one instituted telephone service in the United States because people were getting laryngitis from shouting messages at each other across the windows of office buildings, this would be a residual concept for the development of telephone service. People with laryngitis might apply for such service, and telephone service might be supplied for as long as was necessary until they were cured or could figure out some other method for communicating with their neighbors. This would be residual. An institutional approach to the provision of telephone service might stem from a desire to be preventive, from a recognition that people might get laryngitis if they were forced to communicate by voice across office windows. Therefore telephone service would be instituted, across the board, as a permanent and desirable institution for all people so that they would not get laryngitis. On the other hand (as was the actual case), if telephone service were instituted because it was seen as a way in which communications and the quality of life itself might be improved and human potential expanded, rather than to solve or prevent the problem of laryngitis, this would be provisional or developmental. Similarly in social welfare, if day-care services are instituted because certain parents are not yet properly trained or are incapable of taking care of their children as should be the norm, this is a residual concept of day care. If it is assumed that many parents in industrial society will need to work and will need the help of day-care services, this would be the institutional concept. If on the other hand, a society simply said it would be better for the quality of life if parents going to shopping centers could have a nursery to drop their children off for an hour or

---

[13] Alfred J. Kahn, "Therapy, Prevention and Developmental Provision: A Social Work Strategy," *Public Health Concepts in Social Work Education*, New York: CSWE in cooperation with Public Health Service, Department of HEW, 1962, pp. 132–148; John Romanyshyn, *Social Welfare: Charity to Justice*, New York: Random House, 1971.

two while they were doing their shopping, and the society instituted a network of drop-in nurseries in shopping centers, this would be a developmental approach to social welfare.

The distinctions among the categories are not always that clear: there is no single on or off switch that can differentiate between residual and institutional programs. It is more a question of the attitude toward the program, the way it was conceived, and what it is intended to do. Nonetheless, this is a rather fundamental issue in social welfare and affects the question of whether people are treated humanely or whether they are stigmatized and whether a program is starved or encouraged. The distinction also represents a gradual development of our thinking in the welfare society. We have moved from a largely residual concept of social welfare to a more institutional one, and in some cases toward a developmental concept of social welfare. Different social welfare programs will be found somewhere along the spectrum from residual to developmental, and a program may be designed having the characteristics of a more or less residual, institutional, or developmental nature.

There are alternative program characteristics in a social welfare program that are similar to the residual, institutional, and developmental idea. The view of a social welfare program as a *right* versus a *charity* is one such alternative. The charity concept is very much like the residual concept. Since it is not a basic and permanent part of the system, it is something that society does for people, in a sense, out of the goodness of its heart. To the extent that social welfare is institutional or developmental, it is more like a basic social right of citizens in a given community. In the 1960s we saw the development of something called welfare *rights* organizations which tried to build on the assumption that entitlement to social welfare programs was as much a right of eligible citizens as the right to vote or to be treated without discrimination. On the other hand, the stigma associated with many welfare programs, particularly the residual ones, continues to support the notion that social welfare is a charity.

An interesting example of this problem came about in a Supreme Court ruling in 1971. A particular welfare office sent a welfare worker to the home of a client. The client refused the worker admission and was subsequently dropped from the welfare roles. The client sued, saying that her eligibility for welfare was not subject to her willingness to admit into her home a caseworker without a search warrant. That is, since public assistance was her right, she did not have to give up any of her other rights in order to receive it. The Supreme Court did not rule in the client's favor. It said that she did indeed have a right to refuse admission to anyone into her home without a search warrant, but that the locality, in turn, could refuse her public assistance unless she complied with various rules that it set up, which might include allowing a caseworker into her home. Thus the idea that public assistance was a kind of a special favor or charity of society based on conditions, rather than a fundamental human right, was enhanced.[14]

The history of seeing social welfare programs as a charity has led to evaluation of who is the worthy versus the unworthy poor, that is, of who is deserving of the benefits of these special programs. Increasingly, as programs become more institutionalized or developmental, it is difficult to enforce this concept, and the very notion begins to change. Recipients of Social Security benefits feel that this is their right and their entitlement, something that they have contributed to in their working years, just like private insurance. In fact, there are limitations on this right; there was question during the 1950s, during the height of the anticommunist frenzy, whether an avowed member of the Communist Party could receive Social Security benefits, even though he or she had been contributing to the Social Security system for the appropriate number of quarters. In the development of a welfare society, it becomes increasingly difficult to deny people their entitlements based on the charity concept, but this is part of the evolution from a residual to an institutional or developmental social welfare system.

Another closely related conceptual design is the degree to which a social welfare program is seen as *minimal* or *optimal*. That is, does it seek to provide a basic floor below which no citizen should be expected to fall, or does it try to create an institutional structure which meets the desired needs of human existence in a given area? For instance, most income maintenance plans (public assistance or other kinds) attempt to be minimal at best. They establish a floor below which it is impossible to maintain any sort of living standard, and they may bring people up to that level. Beyond that level it is expected that market mechanisms appropriately should take over and should provide for the other amenities of life. On the other hand, certain institutions, such as public parks, are more institutional or developmental in concept and therefore more optimal rather than minimal in design. It is simply decided that the social system rather than the profit-making market system should be given responsibility

[14] Prospective social workers should know that professional social workers refused to make *surprise* "raids" on clients' homes, usually intended to see if a man was living in the home of a welfare mother. With the help of the profession, a social worker, Benny Parrish, was upheld by the courts in his right to refuse this unprofessional duty. *Benny Max Parrish vs. The Civil Service Commission of the County of Alameda*, State of California. District Court of Appeal, State of California. 1 Civil No.22556. San Francisco: Pernau-Walsh Printing Co., 1965.

for providing park land in cities or national parks to optimize the quality of life in that community. It certainly goes beyond the minimal. It is also, in a sense, striving for equity in certain areas of life.

In income maintenance it is not considered necessary or even desirable that everyone should have equal incomes. What is seen as desirable for the moment is that each person should have a certain minimum income in order to survive. To the extent, though, that tax laws are made more progressive, there is an attempt to provide more equity in society between rich and poor and not simply to provide minima. To the extent that the same fire services are made available for everyone in society despite their contribution, that social welfare program is organized to provide equity rather than minima. And so any social welfare program may be designed essentially to provide a floor or minimum or to provide more equity or to optimize the quality of life in a given area. This, too, can be seen as another expression of the residual, institutional, and developmental concept.

In examining or designing social welfare programs, one needs to have a sense of one's own philosophy about this residual, institutional, and developmental continuum as it applies to the area of any particular social welfare program. This will affect how the program is structured, who is made eligible for it, the nature of the benefits, how it is financed, and so on.

● *B. Selective, Universal* A crucial question in any social welfare program is the degree to which that program is selective or universal. Here the definitions are a little more precise. A selective program is one in which eligibility is based on a determination of the individual financial means of the potential client. A universal program is a program which is open to anyone who meets a certain class or category or area criterion. Students are often confused by this definition. They may call a selective program universal because "*anybody* who is poor enough can be eligible," or they may call a universal program selective because "*only* those over 65 are eligible." This is an erroneous understanding. If a person has to prove eligibility based on financial status, that program is selective no matter how generous the provisions or how broad the coverage. If anyone who is under 3 or over 65 or is a resident of Chicago or is a veteran or has been laid off is eligible for a program without a test of individual financial means, that program is by our definition universal, no matter how limited the program may be. The difference between the two is rather crucial. Public assistance, Medicaid, and food stamps are all selective programs. Unemployment insurance, Workers' Compensation, Medicare, and Social Security are all universal programs. Somewhere in between might be those programs, such as family services and some day-care services, which are open to everyone but on a sliding scale, based on an examination of individual ability to pay.

Programs which are residual in their concept will tend to be selective. Programs which are institutional or developmental in concept are more likely to be universal. Thus, if people should not be receiving income supplementation unless they've hit a personal impasse, such as in public assistance, this is a residual concept, and the program is a selective one. Individuals have to attest to their economic need to be eligible. On the other hand, if the program is more institutionally conceived, such as the Social Security system, anyone who is over 65 and is not working may receive Social Security no matter how wealthy that person is. The program is universal. The student should be aware that residual concepts and selectivity go together and institutional concepts and universality go together, although not in perfect step.

For instance, in disasters, floods, or earthquakes, programs may be set up which are residual in nature, that is, temporary and necessary because of the breakdown of a system which ordinarily meets people's needs. But during the period of its operation it may be operated universally; that is, anyone who needs help may avail himself or herself of disaster relief without proving eligibility based on financial need. On the other hand, a program may be institutional in concept; for example, the poor of a given community may be required to have x number of seats on a community planning board as a permanent and desirable part of social welfare planning. In order to vote for those x number of members of the board, people may have to declare themselves to be poor. It is thus a selective program, although it is somewhat institutional in concept. And so these are not synonymous ideas, although the examples just cited are the exceptions rather than the rule.

Why should a program be selective or universal? What are the advantages and disadvantages of each? The most obvious advantage of the selective program is limitation on cost. Few programs or societies have all the resources or all the funds to do everything that might be desirable. Therefore, there is an almost natural tendency to try to limit a program to a specific target population, the one that is in need. Society is in no mood to "waste" money on people who do not need a particular service or financial aid. The simplest answer appears to be for a program to be limited to people who meet certain criteria of financial eligibility on an individual basis. This is the heart of the argument for selectivity.

It is also philosophical in the feeling that society should not pay for services which can be afforded privately. Sometimes no real money difference is involved. For example, if I pay $5 in taxes to help support my poor neighbor for his medical services, and I pay

$5 to my own doctor for my medical services, medical care is costing me $10. If I pay $10 to the government for medical care which will cover both me and my neighbor, I am paying the same $10. The question becomes, should only those who are unable to afford private services be subsidized by a state system and should others pay privately, or would it be better for society for a variety of other reasons to have one medical care system for all with my $10?

There are other reasons besides the basic financial one for preferring selective programs. For one, there is a fear on the part of some social planners that universal programs are "creamed" by the rich and middle class. That is, when a program is available to all, it is the wealthier and the more sophisticated who have better access to it, who hear about it, and who take advantage of it the best, leaving less for the poor. For instance, the family service agency which is kept quite busy doing individual counseling with middle-class neurotic families may never develop the impulse to do outreach services to poor clients who may not be aware of these services. The library which is kept quite busy by the middle class may not develop the kind of services that are necessary to improve the reading skills of the poor. It is this fear of creaming which causes some people to favor services specifically pinpointed and targeted at the poor. Certainly, because of our tradition as a private enterprise society with welfare as an ancillary or residual function, the majority of our social welfare resources are still given over to selective services such as public assistance.

Why, then, might one prefer universal services over selective ones, if they do tend to cost more and if there is the danger of creaming, of not having the services go to the most needy population? There are several reasons why many favor universal programs as a rule. First, universal programs limit the stigma, the sense of being demeaned that go with an examination of one's income. The idea of being a welfare client is still a frowned-on position in society. A universal program eliminates this stigma. Anyone in a given category is eligible. There is no testing involved of one's individual bank account or income.

Second, many have despaired of finding any sort of fair formula by which one can administer a selective program. For instance, let us assume that you and I each earned $10,000 a year for ten years. At the end of those ten years, both of us found ourselves without employment or other insurances and turned to welfare. You had saved $1000 a year of your salary and now had $10,000 in the bank. I had spent all my salary and had nothing. Should I be eligible for welfare and you ineligible because you had saved? Should you be penalized for your thrift? If you say no, what if you had $20,000 or

$30,000 or $40,000 in the bank? How does one develop a fair system without trying to legislate public morals? The whole selective system lends itself to a continuation of judgments being made by others of who is the worthy and who is the unworthy poor, something that we have been trying to get away from and that is deeply imbedded in the English poor law history.

Just as creaming may limit the availability of universal programs to the poor, there are other factors which limit the ability of selective programs to serve the poor. Selective programs have a limited constituency: those who are financially in need. Because they lack broader support from a broader constituency, they also tend to lack the legislative power to improve programs aimed at them. Thus, whenever money is tight, there tend to be cutbacks in welfare and concern about spending too much, even while universal programs continue to be expanded and improved because of the breadth of their constituency. Universal programs tend to be improved once they are established, even though they cost society dearly, while selective programs, even though they may save money at first, tend to get cut back to effect even greater savings at the expense of the poor.

Because of concerns about possible cheating, investigations and roadblocks are set up for selective programs such as the need to report and to have checking and rechecking done. This may lead many of the needy people who would be eligible not to apply or to be denied acceptance into the program. Thus selective programs tend to reward the aggressive poor rather than the poor per se, and because selective programs are not for everyone and are not advertised broadly and easy access is not made to them, many of the poor never find their way onto their rolls. It has been estimated that there are almost as many people eligible for welfare but who are not receiving welfare as those who are on the welfare rolls.

While scandals in public assistance have been exaggerated and have been used as a club with which to hurt welfare recipients, the truth is that any system which is based on individual testing and eligibility does inevitably result in more opportunities for cheating and corruption than a more simply administered universal program. This tendency toward corruption is another argument in favor of more universal programs.

There is also a certain amount of financial waste in selective programs. While money is not "wasted" on the rich, there is a great deal of waste which is called cost inefficiency, the proportionate cost of a program used in its administration. Selective programs demand much more administrative cost than do universal programs because there need to be procedures for determining eligibility, investigators, checks, and doublechecks. The vast universal Social Security retirement system is operated from a single computerized facility and serves its clientele with only a fraction of a percent of the total funds used for administrative purposes. Public assistance, by contrast, uses a significant amount of funds in administering its own operation. The waste in using the money allocated for a program in large measure on administration is called "cost inefficiency." The so-called waste in having large amounts of the money go to people who are not needy or not the original targets of having such a program is called "benefit inefficiency." In a large national program, the price of benefit inefficiency is likely to be a good deal greater than cost inefficiency, but the latter is not inconsiderable and does offset in part the loss in the former.

Even to the extent that universal programs serve those above the minimum target line, a good deal of the benefit may go to those who are near poor or just above the line, and many social planners would consider that not wasted or benefit inefficient at all. This is another reason why many planners favor a universal approach to social services.

Universal programs tend to be cohesive factors in American society. Selective programs tend to pit recipients against nonrecipients. So long as I am getting some benefit from a program, I am willing to pay for it, even if you are getting a little bit more benefit from that program. I am willing to see that program expand and improve. But as long as I am paying for a program for which I am ineligible and which goes only to you, I will tend to be guarded about the program. There is always the person who is ineligible for a selective program who sees his neighbor down the street who is eligible but seems to him to be no more deserving. This, for example, has tended to pit the near poor and the low and middle class against the poor and the ethnic minorities who are eligible for assistance programs. Selectivity tends to perpetuate what is only a partial myth: that to get services in the United States one needs to be very rich or very poor. For all of these reasons, the bias of the authors is clearly toward a universal approach to social welfare. However, students should be aware of the arguments for and against either system and see the applicability of each. It has been argued, for instance, that with new technology the stigma associated with selective programs can be avoided. Each American could have a health credit card, could go to a health facility for the care generally provided and have his or her card punched on the way out. The poor then would get free service, and the rich would be billed for the same service. Thus you could have a selective program without the stigma normally attached to selectivity.

This argument does not eliminate the problems of how one determines in a fair way who is eligible and who is ineligible; neither does it deal with the fantastic complexity which has grown up in the American welfare system as programs have been added. The more selectivity, the more problems associated with what has been called the "notch" effect. As people's incomes rise, they become ineligible for other kinds of selective programs so that their net positions may be worse than before. This is one of the disincentives to work which has been built into the current welfare system. For instance, if a person starts earning $2000 more than he had earned before, he might suddenly find himself ineligible for Medicaid, food stamps, subsidy for his housing, and other benefits, so that his net financial position may be worse than it was before. Universal programs eliminate this disincentive.

Finally, even in terms of cost, if one keeps in mind, as has been discussed under financing, that there is an input and an output side to the social welfare program equation, the problems of the cost of universal programs can be solved. Tax policies and tax rates can be engineered so as to recover whatever portion is deemed desirable for a welfare program for which the rich are eligible. For instance, if Social Security income were considered taxable income, then those who are very wealthy and had other income from stocks and dividends would be returning a major portion of this so-called wasted money to the tax treasuries. Other income tax policies can be engineered so that universal programs can be less benefit inefficient.

In any event, there is probably no program characteristic more crucial to social welfare in our society than the question of selectivity and universality. It is one on which the student should have a point of view and an understanding as he or she approaches social welfare programs.

• *C. Benefits in Money, Services, Utilities* Under the question of structural components, we have indicated that the nature of benefits is a crucial concern. The nature of a benefit, besides the question of *amount*, may take several forms. Benefits may come in the form of money—cash income or vouchers with which to purchase goods or services. Benefits also may come in the form of services,—concrete (such as an apartment or a medical exam) or psychological (such as counseling). Services also may take the form of utilities, also called amenities (the creation of new expressions of society's meeting our basic needs available to everyone), for example, a housing project, a health clinic, or a park. The form that a social welfare program takes in its service delivery is quite important.

During the late 1960s there was a strong push away from the

provision of services, concrete or psychological, in favor of what has been called an income strategy. The poor themselves were saying, "Stop analyzing us and trying to make us better. This is simply a sophisticated form of victim blaming or of deciding who is the worthy or unworthy poor. Give us the money and let us do with it what we decide needs to be done." This is a rather attractive philosophy in many respects. Social services do have a tradition of being judgmental. There is a kind of cleanness about the concept of giving eligible people money and then letting them go out into the market and do what they wish with it. In fact, there was an interesting similarity of views on this question between far rightists who believe in a total free enterprise society and leftists who believe in welfare rights. The former, since they had to accept some welfare program in a society that would not allow its casualties to starve, preferred to put that program in the form of cash (so that the recipients could go out into the market and function in the market) rather than to create governmental services, bureaucracies, and other forms of socialized activity. The poor themselves, upset by being "done to" by welfare bureaucracies, preferred the cleanliness of an income strategy. Thus, for instance, there was the famous separation of services and eligibility in the public assistance system. Before the late 1960s a potential client for public assistance would meet a worker in the social service system who would become his or her worker, and that worker would determine eligibility, provide the monthly checks, offer counseling, and give whatever other help was supposedly needed to help that client do better budgeting and find a way to more independent living. The objections of the poor were that poverty did not imply any inability in social functioning and that a person should be able to establish eligibility independent of whether or not he or she needed counseling; there should be no presumption that being in poverty is the equivalent of a need for counseling. The welfare system was mandated to develop this kind of separation. Thus clients would have their eligibility determined by clerks and computers. If they were eligible, they would get financial assistance and might separately request or be offered other public services, such as family planning and counseling, but one would have nothing to do with the other. This has helped to lead to a greater sense of entitlement among recipients of social service to aid as a right rather than as a charity and in that sense may have been progressive. On the other hand, other forms of service have been lost to the poor who never connect with the social service part of what the public assistance system may have to offer. Partly as a result of this, the strict separation of services and eligibility has been modified in more recent years.

There is little question now that an income strategy is needed in the United States. That is, the United States needs some form of income maintenance or basic income support such as other modern societies have instituted. But it is not necessarily true that whenever a choice is possible an income or money strategy is better than a service strategy. It has been suggested that instead of public housing there should be vouchers that may be used for housing. Instead of aid to education, the poor should be given vouchers with which to help buy education. This automatic preference is a denial of the very nature of society as a mechanism which may help people. In some cases vouchers may be desirable. In others society as a whole may do a better job of creating a social institution than giving people money and sending them into the market.

Using the marketing of soap as the paradigm for all human activity is obviously an imperfect way to proceed. We are not so assured that we have the best soap at the most competitive price so as to make this a model for all other human activity. One can give people money to buy medical services or one may create a medical clinic. In some cases one may be desirable, in some cases the other, but we would be very cautious about abandoning the concept that social services, psychological or concrete, may be the best form for some social welfare programs. This is particularly true when the social services take the form of a new utility or amenity to human life. The creation of information and referral services in each community operating out of the public libraries might be a desirable new social utility available to all that might not be duplicated by distributing among the general population the per capita cost of such a service. The same may be said of fire, park services, and other social services that are not strictly identified as social welfare. The same care and vigil should be applied with all social welfare services before becoming enamored with an income strategy as the answer to all problems. Even people with adequate incomes may need some services.

• *D. Public, Private* The history of Western social welfare, at least since the beginning of the development of nation-states, has seen a gradual shift of social welfare responsibility to the public sector, to the nation-state, as opposed to private foundations, guilds, and the church. This trend continues unabated in the contemporary United States, and it is impossible to conceive of its being sharply reversed. It is the government and particularly the federal government which alone has the resources to meet the social welfare needs of the population. Increasingly, new areas of living are being recognized as social responsibilities to be guaranteed by the government. Less than a century ago the United States guaranteed almost nothing and private charity gave financial assistance, such as it was, and other benefits. Today we have various kinds of income supports for retirement, poverty, and disability. We have family planning. We have a certain amount of responsibility for housing assumed by the state. We have programs which are at least supposed to eliminate starvation and even are moving toward greater public employment.

The transition of certain areas of living from a luxury or charity to a right or public responsibility can be seen in medical care. Not too long ago medical care was seen as something available only on the basis of being able to afford it. If doctors gave time to the poor or to clinics, this was a charitable act they performed. But the concept that every American should be guaranteed minimum medical care is one which we are only in the process of digesting; it is for this reason that various schemes for the development of health care systems are argued and under consideration. And so the growth of the public sector to operate or at least to finance social welfare programs is likely to continue unabated. However, there is a peculiar American history to the form this takes, and so there are questions related to how this public trend will work in cooperation with the private sector, the nature of the private sector, the issue of third-party payments, and other areas worth exploring.

In spite of the growth of the public sector there continues to exist a vigorous and healthy part of American society which is known as the voluntary or private voluntary sector in social welfare. These are the agencies which comprise philanthropic fund-raising efforts and services in various communities—the United Way agencies, youth service agencies, the American Red Cross, settlement houses, camps, leisure time activity clubs, senior centers, sectarian agencies, religious associations, family service and counseling agencies, voluntary hospitals and their social welfare programs, self-help movements, racial equality leagues, job counseling services, and others. As public responsibility has grown, the private sector has limited its responsibility to those areas that remain or have found new ones or have become the delivery mechanisms of services with public funds.

In one sense it is almost impossible to identify a truly "private voluntary" agency in the United States anymore. Increasingly, voluntary agencies such as those mentioned above operate with grants-in-aid, money which is given them by the federal, state, or local government to deliver some social service which is a public need but which the public does not want to operate directly, and so one gets a kind of partnership. In this model the growth of public responsibility may even cause the growth of the so-called private sector, albeit with public monies. The agency is still a private voluntary agency if it is run by its own board of directors, which bears corporate responsibility for the enterprise, rather than by an arm of the government.

Even where private agencies do not take direct support they may be giving service to people whose money for the service may be paid for by an arm of the public such as persons who go to a private physician with money from some public insurance. Even where this is not the case, private agencies are supported through exemptions from local property taxes as a rule or by having people's donations to their causes being tax exempt. At least in that sense, the federal government is sharing in the fund raising for that agency, and one might say that the agency is not completely voluntary or private. Nonetheless, the private sector does exist in the areas mentioned and others and does important work in the entire social welfare spectrum.

With the growth of these third-party payments and other government subsidies, the private sector needs to be divided in our minds into two parts: (1) the private voluntary sector which is not for profit, such as a philanthropic organization operating with a community board of directors, and (2) the private proprietary agency, an organization which is in the business of making profit but in a social welfare related area, for example, nursing homes, child care agencies, or medical service clinics. It sometimes becomes hard to distinguish between the two forms, because proprietary agencies want to be listed among the social agencies in a community and want to apply for food subsidies for their camps or other programs. How does one tell them apart? It is not by a profit balance alone, because even the proprietary agency may show no corporate profit; instead it may pay handsome salaries to its staff and officers, who also are its owners. The difference is usually in its form of accountability. If its corporate responsibility is vested in a board of directors of community members and community leaders, philanthropists, and others in a cross section of responsible people; and if its policy-makers, its board of directors, are different from its staff, then it is likely to be a true private voluntary agency. If the staff delivering the service or their families serve as officers, it is most likely a proprietary agency, even if it is not frank about stating that fact.

There are those who question whether the proprietary agency has any place in a description of social welfare programs, but so long as it is government policy to operate through the payment of fees to third parties for the delivery of services, it is unlikely that its role will ever be eliminated. Instead there will be more calls for policing to make sure that services are humane, that clients are not victimized, and that quality services are provided.

Another question might be raised: If one believes in the welfare

state, if one believes that society as a whole and through its government should provide for the general welfare through the provision of
social welfare programs, what function, if any, is there for a private
sector—even a private *voluntary* sector? In an ideal society would
there need to be a private voluntary sector, and what function would
it really play?

There are those who have argued that the private agencies are
more innovative than government agencies and that this justifies
their continued existence. Sometimes voluntary agencies can be
more innovative than governmental agencies. But in an increasingly
complex society, research and development become a government
function. It is the government alone which had the resources to
develop communication satellites, even though later patents and
rights may have been turned over to private companies for exploitation. Similarly, most of the innovations in social welfare in the last
generation have been through government agencies, in spite of
bureaucracy and lack of flexibility. Private agencies have been hard
pressed to raise the money to maintain their "bread and butter" services without being able to do much in the way of research and
development of new forms of social welfare. Should the ideal society
to which we may be moving look toward the elimination of the private sector altogether? It is our feeling that there will continue to be
a need for a private voluntary sector, at least for several important
functions:

1. It is only the private agency which can offer the kinds of services that are not yet public policy. A generation ago it was only the
private agencies which could develop and offer family planning services. Today this is accepted as a function for public agencies. But
before this became public policy, those who believed in family planning activities had a right to have a vehicle for the expression of their
beliefs, and this could only take place through private voluntary
agencies. Similarly, today there may be other kinds of services which
are legitimately offered to those who want the services but which are
not public policy. They may evolve into public policy or they may
never do so, but so long as there is an interest group that wants something done which it sees as social welfare and which is not inimical
to others, this should be possible. And this is a continuing function
of the private sector.

2. The voluntary agency is the only one which appropriately
should deliver sectarian services or services for any special ethnic or
interest group. Public services are and should be open equally to all
citizens and should not be geared toward a specific position or point
of view. On the other hand, it is quite legitimate in a plural society
for Catholics, for example, to want to instill values of Catholicism

among Catholic youth and to do this in the context of recreational or leisure time activities. It is quite legitimate for blacks to organize other blacks to appreciate their common heritage and the concept that black is beautiful. Ethnicity and cultural pluralism are one of the hallmarks of the American scene which should be nurtured and continued. And it is only the private agency which can devote itself to such causes. This will continue to be necessary in any society.

3. There is a growing recognition of the importance of self-help groups from Alcoholics Anonymous to post-mastectomy groups. These groups harness volunteer energies of citizens, save money, and provide a unique form of help, which is impossible in more bureaucratized or public systems. Although some of these groups may be faddish or even destructive, this impulse properly utilized can be an invaluable "private" social service resource.

4. The private agency may be the most appropriate or best vehicle to provide an advocacy and ombudsperson function for the sake of clients, sometimes in an adversary position with the government. What the architects of the War on Poverty found quickly in the 1960s was that there is only so far any organization will go in financing attacks on itself. If we value the role of consumer organizations such as the ones created by Ralph Nader (organizations which can, for example, criticize the lack of sensitivity of public agencies to the poor), then we must recognize that it is really only the private agency that can adopt this role. An ombudsperson and an advocacy function will always remain needs in the best of societies.

Finally, it should be emphasized that quite apart from the four legitimate functions above, the special nature of American history makes it likely that the private sector will continue to exercise a major function in the American social welfare scene, even though its activity may represent a smaller portion of the dollars which are being spent on social welfare. Funds will increasingly come from the public sector. The delivery of services will continue to be mixed, and it is even possible, at least in the short run, that the private sector will grow as the deliverer of services for government. A student of social welfare needs to understand the division between the public and private sectors and the division between private voluntary and private proprietary agencies and needs to have a point of view about what kinds of services are best delivered by which agencies, under what conditions, and with what financial support. The financial support for the public agencies clearly comes from the public treasury from the various kinds of financing described earlier. The support for the private voluntary agencies comes from their own fund raising, contributions of ordinary citizens and philanthropists, United Way fund drives, and various grants-in-aid as well as fees for service.

The funds for the private proprietary agencies come from fees for service including, of course, third-party payments whose ultimate source is the public treasury and purchase of service contracts from public sources.

• *E. Central, Local* Another program characteristic is the degree to which any social welfare program is operated or administered on a local level versus on a national or state level. What is the appropriate level of administration and control for various kinds of programs? Again the United States, because it is a federal society with a background of states rights, has a peculiar history. In most countries of the world, policies are made much more centrally, even though local offices to administer policy may exist and may even have some discretion in administering policy differentially. However, in the United States, one has a Social Security or Medicare or Veterans Administration program which is on a strictly national basis, a public assistance and Medicaid and food stamp program which is a combination of state and local benefits with national support and guidelines, housing programs and hospital programs which may be municipal or state, a correctional system on all levels, and—in general—a crazy-quilt pattern for the administration of social welfare services. What are the trends and what is the appropriate level of control for what programs?

There are two dichotomous trends which seem to be emerging simultaneously. On the one hand, the available resources and therefore the initiative for social welfare programs are increasingly in the federal government. It is from this source that basic policy decisions need to be made and programs voted. On the other hand, there is simultaneously a trend towards greater revenue sharing, getting control to individual states for their making choices within broad guidelines for the administration of social welfare programs, and a movement for community control. The rhetoric of community control is most attractive. It is argued that the bureaucrats in Washington are so far removed from the "people" that they do not know what is needed at the local level. The more layers of intervention between the people and the decision-makers, the more decisions may become confused, diluted, or sabotaged. Therefore, one finds an odd situation in which liberal radicals and activists in local communities argue for community control and conservatives argue similarly for turning control over to states and localities and away from the federal government. In fact, some of the best social welfare programs in the United States in terms of service to people and efficiency are those which are completely national, such as the Social Security system and Veterans Administration operations. A direct federal program need not have many layers between it and the people it serves. It is only when there are guidelines, grants-in-aid, working through third parties, and other complicating factors that this happens.

It also is true that greater percentages of people vote in national elections than in local elections. One may argue that there is more democracy in the decisions that are made by the Congress than by a local legislature and less opportunity for quiet corruption. This argument is enhanced by the fact that in a national society such as ours is becoming, people take their news from the national television networks, national news magazines, and major state newspapers more than from local newspapers, and so there is more exposure of national chicanery or politics than there is on the local level where corruption may go more unnoticed. Revenue sharing is a system by which the federal government makes money available through some formula to individual states to spend as those states see fit. Specialized revenue sharing is the same except that the states are enjoined to spend it for a certain general area such as education. So long as the purse and the basic decision to spend money comes from the federal government, it is hard to see how giving states a blank check increases the responsiblity or power of the people over their own decisions. The social welfare student and the social worker need to understand community input and community control as vital elements of good social programs, whatever their source. But this is not the same as suggesting that state or local administration is better than federal administration of any given program. There is much that can be said for and against community control as a movement.[15]

Certainly a revolution took place in the sixties which is vital to the future of social welfare. Before that time the very concept that the ultimate recipients of service or a local community needed to be consulted on a social welfare program that was envisioned for that community was generally not accepted. As a result of the struggles of the sixties, that principle is now clearly one of those which has found its way into legislation in all areas related to social welfare and one which all social workers need to accept. But community input is not community control. For example, community control has in other

---

[15] See Bertram Beck, "Community Control: A Distraction, Not An Answer," *Social Work*, Vol. 14, No. 4, October 1969, pp. 14–20. According to a study done by the Office of Revenue Sharing, Department of the Treasury, only 2 percent of total revenue-sharing funds went for social services by all local governments between July 1, 1973, and June 30, 1974. For city governments only during the same entitlement period, only 1 percent of such funds were used for social services. Thus local control and decision-making in the use of revenue-sharing funds appear to have a negative affect on social welfare. See Robert S. Magill, "Federalism, Grants-in-Aid, and Social Welfare Policy," *Social Casework*, Vol. 57, No. 10, December 1976, pp. 625–636.

times meant states' rights, white supremacy, and the ability of the John Birch Society to dictate what books would be permitted in local libraries. The problem is how to maintain community participation and neighborhood vitality and activity and at the same time not to suffer from "the tyranny of small decisions," which may be illustrated as follows:

When I go to work in the morning and I have to decide on whether to take the car or bus, I may take into account the cost of tolls, gasoline, parking, and perhaps if I am careful even the depreciation on my car, and weigh these against the cost of public transportation. Figured that way, taking my car might be cheaper. I can hardly be expected to figure in my calculation the fraction of a percent my decision may be contributing to the cost of roads and highways, and police protection that is necessary for traffic control or the cost of cleaning up pollution in the city to which my air exhaust contributes. Thus we have the tyranny of small decisions.[16] The decision that I make on my local level cannot begin to take the entire public need into account. Yet in the long run I am being penalized for all these costs which do not go into my calculation. Therefore, I elect legislators who represent me and who are supposed to be able to consider the larger picture in making decisions. I may recall or not reelect them if I am unhappy with their decisions, but for the moment they make their decisions while considering the larger picture.

Similarly, in social welfare it is necessary to have a body that can make the big decisions about public policy, although hopefully without ignoring the input of local communities. Most people favor drug rehabilitation programs; few people want them in their own neighborhoods. How much of an input is necessary in which kinds of programs, which programs should be controlled by the local group, and which ones should simply have input are hard decisions that have to be made, issue by issue. Which social welfare program is best administered by the state or federal government or by the local community also will vary based on the nature of the community and program, but there are no pat answers inherent in rhetoric. The community control movement of the sixties showed some of the positive values in community control. It can bring new faces and new leadership to the table and new bargaining power to people who have been dispossessed. It can produce insights which are not available to the

---

[16] See Thomas A. Schelling, "On the Ecology of Micromotives," *The Public Interest,* No. 25, Fall 1971, pp. 61–98, for an exploration of the relationship between discrete microdecisions and macroevents.

planner distant from the local scene. It can become a training ground for local figures to develop into leaders on a larger scale and on the national scene. On the other hand, it can become a bastion of feudal fiefdoms for small politicians who claim to speak for the "people." At worst it can become, in spite of radical tactics and rhetoric, the most conservative force of all because the local community control movement is not related to the kind of change which is necessary to correct the social problems in American life which are national in scope. The major social problems in America of income maintenance, housing, employment, crime and corrections, and others are not going to be solved by local self-help groups but only through major legislative changes and adjustments in priorities and funding on the national level. And unless that is the ultimate direction of one's efforts and energies, community control can become a sad diversion. It also can tend to pit local groups against each other instead of a more common enemy. Thus, when a million dollars is allocated for housing to a given city, Hispanic and black groups may vie for that million dollars rather than ally themselves against the state or national government to see that the funding is increased. Ethnic and other rivalries can be exacerbated while the real centers of power are untouched.

Perhaps the greatest genius of the late Martin Luther King, Jr., was his ability to merge local and national concerns. He operated on issues of community control and local significance such as voting in Selma, Alabama, and segregated seating on buses in Montgomery. Each of these issues were legitimate on the local level and in their own right, met peoples needs, developed local leadership, and had all the assets of community control. But each of them was an orchestrated step toward the changing of national policies on segregation and voting, which was always kept in mind as the goal and target. It is that vision which all of us in social welfare need to maintain even while we work on the local level. The level of administration and operation of services is a major consideration for each social welfare student to keep in mind as a characteristic of any given program.

• *F. Lay, Professional*   There are two major senses in which a social welfare program may have more of a lay or professional orientation. On the simplest level there is the question of who delivers the services. There does not exist as there does with engineering or medical practice, for instance, the general public acceptance of a body of hard skill which only the professional may apply. In fact, social workers themselves believe that there are important roles for citizens and paraprofessionals to play in human services. Therefore, there is some confusion and often conflict as to the appropriate division of labor between lay and professional involvement in social service programs. What kinds of tasks demand professional work skills, what kinds of tasks demand the skills of other allied disciplines, and what kinds of tasks can be performed by community leaders, volunteers, and untrained workers? How these questions are answered will affect the quality, the cost, and the legitimacy of a given program. There are times when for a specific purpose such as maintaining contact with an indigenous community which may be hostile to a particular social service program there may be more reliance placed on lay people, while for other kinds of situations more emphasis may be placed on professional skills.

In another sense the question of lay versus professional is the question of control, policy, and decision-making. What are the decisions that are legitimately the "people's" decisions in social welfare? What are the decisions that are decisions of professional judgment? For instance, no community board should tell a medical doctor what medicine to prescribe for a certain illness. However, medical doctors ought not make the decision as to what kind of national health insurance plan the nation should have. Similarly in social welfare there are professional judgments which social workers should make and other policy decisions which should be the decision of community advisory groups or boards of directors. What the borderlines are between these areas is sometimes a subject for confrontation and conflict. How well a program confronts these issues will often determine its success or failure.

• *G. Resources, Engineering* To what extent is a program designed with the concept that the problem in achieving success is a problem of investing adequate resources in a program? And to what extent is it designed with the thought that the central problem is one of good social engineering? This issue is real, not simply theoretical. Is the apparent resistance of social problems to solution (whether they be in housing, corrections, income maintenance, or whatever), a function of society's lack of commitment of resources to their solution or due to the fact that we have not yet found the designs or the engineering to solve them no matter what the resources? Social welfare planners are fond of using the analogy of the social policy decision made at the beginning of the 1960s to land a human being on the moon by 1970 whatever the cost. In the course of implementing that decision, there was a great deal of waste and of expense and lives were lost, but the moon was reached in the summer of 1969. It is often felt that if the same sense of commitment were applied to the eradication of poverty or other social problems similar results could be attained. Other social planners have been particularly impressed by the intractability of poverty and other social problems in spite of the resources invested in their elimination.[17]

Some have suggested that the War on Poverty was not more of a success because we did not know how to fight poverty, how to use adequately the funds which were allocated. Others feel that the War on Poverty did not achieve more because it was only a skirmish in terms of the resources invested and that had an adequate investment been made it might have succeeded more dramatically. In any social welfare program one needs to examine the degree to which success is built on design and engineering and how much it is built on providing the resources to guarantee success. Neither can really succeed without the other. The most carefully engineered program can be undermined by underfunding, and the most well-funded program can be sabotaged by foolish policies, spending, and design of the program. Both aspects have to be looked at carefully in the development of a social welfare program.

III. EVALUATING THE PROGRAM

Let us now assume that a social welfare student has the basic tools for understanding any social welfare program. She understands the nature of the program in terms of its four basic structural components discussed above. She also understands the program characteristics, whether it tends to be more residual and selective or more universal and institutional, the degree to which its services are seen as a right or as a charity, the lay-professional division, the nature of the social engineering, the level of administration, and all the other characteristics that have been discussed above. The student has an opinion as to which would be most appropriate for that kind of program. Finally, how will the student evaluate whether the program is a good program or a poor program, one that needs to be improved, and in what ways? On the basis of an understanding of all of the above, the following are some of the questions which need to be asked about any program in its evaluation:

• **A. Adequacy** Is the program adequate to meet the problem for which it was set up? Adequacy has to be judged on two levels, which we will call horizontal and vertical. On the horizontal level we want to know whether the program reaches the target population. Let us assume that we are setting up a program on family planning for a city of 300,000 people. The services which the family planning program

[17] Nathan Glazer, "The Limits of Social Policy," *Commentary*, Vol. 52, No. 3, September 1971, pp. 51–58.

may offer may be magnificent in their quality, may change people's lives dramatically. But if it is only geared to serving 10,000 people, if information about its availability does not reach the rest of the population, or if there are long waiting lists which develop, then the program is horizontally inadequate. It cannot meet the problem for which it was set up. So one basic question we must ask of any program is whether it has the coverage, the capacity, the will, the resources, and the means for access so that it can cover its target population. The allocations for many programs are based on the assumption that a major percentage of those who might be eligible will not hear of it, apply for it, or actually go on the rolls.

One needs to ask how vertically adequate the program is. Is each recipient covered adequately? For example, a family planning program may "reach" in a sense an entire city of 300,000, but its services may consist only of a mailed brochure to each of those 300,000 people. In this case the coverage for each person served is not adequate and is not of sufficient depth and substance to affect major change to deal with people's problems and lives. The program is horizontally adequate but vertically inadequate. Every program needs to be weighed in terms of its adequacy, horizontal and vertical, to see whether it is doing the job it was set up to do. How many are served? How well is each served?

• **B. Financing** There are a number of questions about *financing* which need to be addressed in the evaluation of every program.

1. Is the program equitably financed? The Social Security system may be a relatively excellent program in terms of the benefits it provides to people, the needs and risks which it covers and the universality and neatness of its operation. But if it continues to be financed by a regressive tax which draws more heavily on the poor than on the wealthy, this is a serious shortcoming in the program. One needs to look not only at the output side but at the input side in order to evaluate a program. There is little point in redistributing income to the poor on the output side of the program if this is done by taking money from the poor on the input side of the program. And so the student needs to evaluate how a program is financed and how this needs to be changed to be made more fair if necessary.

2. Does this program represent a priority use of funds? If resources were infinite, this question would not need to be asked. But since resources are finite, every time a dollar is spent on one program there is an opportunity cost: the loss of the opportunity to spend that dollar on some other program. Does the particular social welfare program have a high priority in terms of the needs of the

community or nation and of the agency in which the social worker is working compared to other programs that the agency might be engaged in? These are the kinds of questions about financing which the student needs to ask.

3. How cost or benefit efficient is the program? In our earlier discussion we pointed out that all programs lose some resources one way or another. Administrative costs of operating a program will take away some portion of every dollar spent for the program. Money spent on service to others than the target population also can be seen as a kind of waste or benefit inefficiency. If a program is set up to distribute funds, for example, but uses 30 percent of the funds for the staff needs to distribute them, this is severely cost inefficient. If a program is set up to do family counseling but 30 percent of its funds goes for rental of facilities, this is cost inefficient. On the other hand, if a program is set up to serve a particular need of a particular group and members of other groups use up 30 percent of the service, this is benefit inefficient. Every program needs to be evaluated in terms of whether its dollar is being spent as well as possible in the delivery of the services to the target population for which the program was set up. It is almost impossible for this to be 100 percent efficient, but the degree of inefficiency that can be tolerated needs to be part of the evaluation. Universal programs, as has been mentioned, tend to be much more cost efficient because they do not get involved in investigatory bureaucracy. Selective programs may be more benefit efficient in that they limit their eligible beneficiaries more stringently.

• *C. Coherence* In evaluating a program a student needs to ask the question, is this *program coherent* with other social policies and programs? When former President Richard Nixon wanted to stimulate the economy in the face of a recession, he removed certain taxes on automobiles to encourage more purchases of cars. One might argue that this social policy to combat recession was not coherent with a social policy to combat pollution. Very often certain social policies may operate at cross purposes and undermine other social policies and programs. Programs to aid the working poor have to meet the objection of those who are afraid of the destruction of work incentives, unrealistic as this attitude may be. Many social planners have advocated that the United States have a children's allowance as does just about all the other Western industrialized countries of the world. However, one of the criticisms of a children's allowance is that it would encourage greater fertility, something which population controllers feel would be bad policy. Studies indicate that a children's allowance does *not* encourage such greater fertility. But a question which needs to be answered in the implementation of any social policy is whether the policy is compatible with other social policies and program.

• *D. Latent Consequences* Programs never exist in a vacuum. As a result of one program other things happen. Sometimes effects are anticipated and intended, sometimes they are unintentional and actually undermine the program itself. We will see examples of this as we discuss the various social welfare programs. For instance, a jobs creation program is often seen as a way of stimulating more jobs. As a certain number of people are put back on payrolls and earn incomes they purchase more, creating the opportunity for still more jobs and a rising economic cycle. This is called a "multiplier effect," a way in which a small investment in a social program can have consequences which will multiply its effects in the direction desired. On the other hand, sometimes a latent consequence of a program undermines its very purpose. For example, in the unemployment insurance program which will be discussed further on, an incentive was given to employers not to lay off workers. If they fired fewer workers, the insurance rates they paid for unemployment insurance would go down, thus saving them money. It was intended that this would keep employment higher. However, one of the latent consequences was that some employers were reluctant to hire new workers when they were not sure that these people could be kept on. Rather than take the chance of having to fire them later and have their insurance rates go up, the employers did not hire them in the first place. Thus the program had the precise opposite effect to what was intended, as a latent consequence. Sometimes latent consequences are neither multipliers of the program's intent or saboteurs of the program's intent but create new and different problems. When Medicare was instituted it opened up a whole new market for medical services and created a run on hospital beds which had not been properly prepared for. It took a number of years before hospital bed capacity was able to catch up to the demand in the United States which had been created by the institution of Medicare and Medicaid. Therefore programs have to be evaluated in terms of their potential and real outcomes for consequences which may multiply their intended effects, sabotage their intended effects, and create new and unanticipated problems which may throw into question the value of the original program.

The above are some of the points the intelligent student will consider in evaluating any social welfare program. Prepared with this schema of analysis for understanding and evaluation, it should be possible to look at a number of social welfare programs—both the economic security programs and the personal social services—and to understand them much more clearly and to be able to identify their values, drawbacks, and weaknesses. We shall do precisely this in the coming chapters.

Chapter 5
The Welfare Society and Its Clients

"It's no shame to be poor, but it's no great honor either."
Fiddler on the Roof

"Wealth is well known to be a great comforter."
Plato, *The Republic*, Book I

WHO IS A CLIENT OF SOCIAL WELFARE?

As discussed in the previous chapter, definitions of social welfare differ. Given a very narrow definition one could conclude that only those who are public assistance recipients are on "welfare." Given broader definitions of social welfare and looking at the many non-market functions which serve most citizens, we must conclude that we are all clients of the welfare system.

For example, John and Jane Citizen are married and have two children. Following World War II, John, a veteran, attended college and graduate school with assistance from the GI Bill. Married and prepared in his profession, he and his wife bought a house using a Veterans Administration mortgage loan guarantee. Over the years the family has deducted taxes and interest paid on the mortgage from their taxable income on federal income tax returns. When the children were in the publicly funded public school, they ate lunches which were subsidized by federal funds and the family used the local library which was partially supported by federal funds. In an emergency they used the local hospital which was built with federal funds. When the first child was ready for higher education, she received a student loan from the college, most of which was forgiven under a government program because she became a teacher. John died suddenly, and his Social Security benefits helped to support Jane and the younger child.

Social welfare is pervasive throughout the breadth of the "welfare" society. According to Richard Titmuss,

> . . . considered as a whole, all collective interventions to meet certain needs of the individual and/or to serve the wider interests of society may now be broadly grouped into three major categories of welfare: social welfare, fiscal welfare, and occupational welfare. When we examine them in turn, it emerges that this division is not based on any fundamental difference in the functions of the three systems . . . or their declared aims.[1]

Welfare then may be found in diverse locations, including tax deductions, subsidized hospital and educational programs, social security, health insurances and other socialized risks, family planning, and unemployment insurance, among others.

The income tax system serves as one major vehicle through which the government develops social welfare programs. Whether the government gives a person money or permits a person not to pay money due to the government, the effect is the same: a transfer of funds from government to people for some socially determined good purpose. Contributions to voluntary social agencies, for instance, are tax deductible. Such support is really another method for the government to support social welfare programs. But there are other ways in which the Internal Revenue system serves as a welfare system. When a corporation or individual deducts given sums from taxes owed, these sums—since they are not to be paid and are retained by the taxpayer or corporation—are in reality "tax expenditures." That is, the retained monies are really payments to the persons or corporations.

Some observers have suggested that in the United States we have capitalism for the poor and socialism for the rich.[2] Just as social welfare guarantees against certain risks, there are many guarantees for business against risks which confront them. Michael Harrington, for example, suggests that society has been more ready to socialize risks for large businesses than for individuals. The larger the busi-

---

[1] Richard M. Titmuss, *Essays on the Welfare State*, Boston: Beacon Press, 1969, p. 42.
[2] This is a theme in Michael Harrington's *Toward a Democratic Left*, Baltimore: Penguin Books, 1969.

ness, the greater the protection afforded. Big businesses may be able to write off losses or be bailed out through government guarantees. Direct and indirect subsidies have helped large business. In this way risks have been socialized with greater generosity to the business enterprises than to salaried employees, who ultimately depend in many cases on their social insurances and public assistance.

All of the social welfare services described in this book, both economic security programs and personal social services, are forms of welfare. Many of these services (from parks to mental health programs) serve Americans of all classes.

Titmuss' final category is that of occupational welfare, or welfare associated with having employment. For example, if you have employment, you and your family may be the recipients of insurance benefits which cover health and hospital care, disability, retirement, dental work, and perhaps legal bills. In a few industries you may be entitled to guaranteed annual income. In this way, to varying degrees, employment and occupations serve also as means for distributing welfare benefits.

We can see that social, fiscal, and occupational welfare systems are widespread throughout our society. Most people, if not all, are served by these different but functionally similar systems. We are all "welfare clients" in the welfare society. The issues are simply who benefits and to what degree from each program.

Still our concern here is primarily with the poor and the disadvantaged, and so we want to focus in large measure on the programs for alleviation of poverty in the United States, even while we recognize the universal nature of welfare in its several guises.

A DESCRIPTION OF THE POOR

When you are poor in the United States, you are poor in one of the wealthiest nations on earth. Poverty in the United States is often hidden from the eyes of the middle and upper classes. But wealth and luxury are not hidden from the eyes of the poor, who see in movies and on television how the "good life" is lived. The expectation is that adequate people should be able to find adequate income.

As Table 5-1 shows, in 1977 there were 24,720,000 poor persons in the United States or approximately 12 percent of all Americans. The poverty threshold for a four-person, nonfarm family was $6,191. By comparison, the median family income in the United States for the same year was $16,010. While there was a significant decline in the percentage of persons in poverty from 1959 (22.4 percent) to 1969 (12.1 percent), since 1969 the percentage of the population in poverty has risen and declined generally within a narrow range.

Of the approximately 25,000,000 poor in 1977, 16,416,000 were

Table 5-1 THE NUMBER OF POOR PERSONS, FAMILIES, AND
UNRELATED INDIVIDUALS—1977

CHARACTERISTIC	1977 (THOUSANDS)
All persons	24,720
White	16,416
Black	7,726
Spanish origin[a]	2,700
Under 65 years	21,543
65 years and over	3,177
Related children under 18 years	10,028
Related children 5 to 17 years	7,249
North and West	14,471
South	10,249
Inside metropolitan areas	14,859
Inside central cities	9,203
Outside central cities	5,656
Outside metropolitan areas	9,861
All families	5,311
Husband-wife	2,524
Male householder, no wife present	177
Female householder, no husband present	2,610
All unrelated individuals	5,216
Male	1,797
Female	3,419

SOURCE: U.S. Bureau of the Census, "Money Income and Poverty Status of Families
and Persons in the United States: 1977," *Current Population Reports*, Series P-60, No.
116, Washington, D.C.: U.S. Government Printing Office, 1978, p. 3.
[a] Persons of Spanish origin may be of any race.

white, 7,726,000 were black, 2,700,000 were of Spanish origin, 21,-
543,000 were under 65 years of age, 3,177,000 were 65 or older, and
10,028,000 were poor children under 18 years of age. Of 5,311,000
poor families, 2,610,000 were headed by females. Seven percent of
all white families were poor (3,540,000) and 28 percent of all black
families were poor (1,637,000).[3]

[3] U.S. Bureau of the Census, "Money Income and Poverty Status of Families and Persons in the United States: 1977," *Current Population Reports*, Series P-60, No. 116,
Washington, D.C.: U.S. Government Printing Office, 1978, pp. 1, 3, 20, 21, and 29.
Minority group members and women suffer from significant inequalities in education,
unemployment and occupations, income and poverty, and housing. U.S. Commission
on Civil Rights. *Social Indicators of Equality for Minorities and Women*, Washington,
D.C.: U.S. Government Printing Office, 1978.

Table 5-2 PERCENTAGE OF POOR IN TOTAL POPULATION IN 1977

	PERCENTAGE OF THE POOR	PERCENTAGE OF TOTAL POPULATION
Blacks	31	12
Spanish-speaking origin	11	6
65 years or older	13	11
Related children under 18	41	29
Female householders with no husband present	37	12

One can observe in Table 5-2 that 31 percent of the poor persons in the United States in 1977 were black, while blacks comprised only 12 percent of the total population. Eleven percent of those of Spanish-speaking origin were poor (6 percent of the population), the elderly were 13 percent (11 percent of the population), those living in families with a female householder and no husband present were 37 percent of the poor but only 12 percent of the population.[4] The groups overrepresented among the poor are blacks, those of Spanish-speaking origin, the elderly, persons in families with a female householder, and children under 18 years of age.[5] See Figure 5-1 for a graphic portrayal of similar statistics.

Your chances of being poor differ not only by your personal characteristics (such as race, age, sex, and educational level) but also by the region of the nation in which you live. For example, 41 percent of the nation's poor live in the South, although that region has only 30 percent of the total population.[6] In addition, the Southern Regional Council estimated that two-thirds of the southern poor are not reached by any form of public assistance.[7]

In 1977 there were 177,000 poor families with male householders and no wife present, but there were 2,610,000 female householders with no husband present. Men working year round full time had median earnings of $14,630 in 1977. Median earnings for women working in the same pattern were $8,620.[8] Median earnings for women working full time in 1956 fell from 63 percent of men's to 57 percent in 1974.[9] Figure 5-2 shows the proportion of all poor persons

[4] *Money Income and Poverty Status of Families and Persons in the United States: 1977*, p. 3.
[5] U.S. Bureau of the Census, "Characteristics of the Population Below the Poverty Level: 1976," *Current Population Reports*, Series P-60, No. 115, Washington, D.C.: U.S. Government Printing Office, 1978, p. 3.
[6] Ibid., p. 5.
[7] Wayne King, "Poverty and Disease in Carolina Low Country Belie the New South Boom," *New York Times*, April 1, 1977, p. 11.
[8] See "Money Income and Poverty Status," op. cit., pp. 2–3.
[9] Peter Kihss, "Women's Wages Fall Even Farther Behind," *New York Times*, April 3, 1977, p. 35.

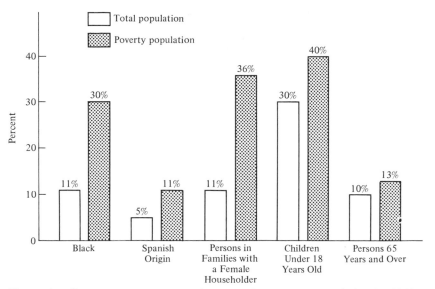

Figure 1.   Groups overrepresented among the poverty population in 1976.
(Source: From U.S. Bureau of the Census, "Characteristics of the
Population Below the Poverty Level: 1976," *Current Population Reports,*
Series P-60, No. 115, Washington, D.C.: U.S. Government Printing Office,
1978, p. 3.)

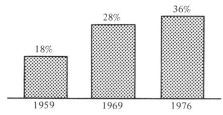

Figure 2.   Proportion of poor persons living in families with a female
householder, no husband present. (Source: From U.S. Bureau of the
Census, "Characteristics of the Population Below the Poverty Level: 1976,"
Current Population Reports, Series P-60, No. 115, Washington, D.C.: U.S.
Government Printing Office, 1978, p. 4.)

living in families with a female householder and no husband to be
18 percent in 1959, 28 percent 1969 and 36 percent 1976.[10]

As Figure 5-3 indicates, between 1959 and 1976 the proportion
of poor children under 18 years of age living in families with a female
householder and no husband present increased in this pattern: 24
percent 1959, 45 percent 1969, and 55 percent 1976. Between 1960
and 1974, the number of children in female-headed poor families

[10] "Characteristics of the Population Below the Poverty Level: 1976," op. cit., p. 4.

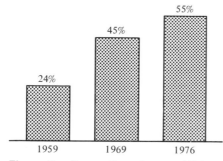

Figure 3.   Proportion of poor children under 18 years old living in families with a female householder, no husband present. (Source: From U.S. Bureau of the Census, "Characteristics of the Population Below the Poverty Level: 1976," *Current Population Reports,* Series P-60, No. 115, Washington, D.C.: U.S. Government Printing Office, 1978, p. 4.)

increased by a third,[11] and in 1976 more than a majority of poor children were in families headed by women with no husband present. Poor children are increasingly found in families with a female householder. The number of poor blacks living in such families increased from 2.4 million (1959) to 4.4 million (1976) or from one-fourth of the black poor in 1959 to 60 percent of the black poor in 1976.[12]

Employment and the lack of it play important parts in contributing to the poverty of Americans, particularly minority group members. For instance, average unemployment in the United States during 1977 was 7.3 percent. Average black unemployment was 13 percent with that of 16 to 19-year-old blacks ranging up to 40 percent.[13] Furthermore, while blacks are 12 percent of the working age population, they are 22 percent of the nation's unemployed. Those of Spanish-speaking origin are 4.6 percent of the working age population and account for 6.4 percent of total unemployment.[14]

But poverty is not simply a matter of unemployment. In 1976, 1,654,000 males and 891,000 female householders (family heads) worked full time year round and were below the poverty line.[15] The Secretary of Health, Education, and Welfare has called attention to the characteristics of the poor, including the working poor:

[11] U.S. Bureau of the Census, "A Statistical Portrait of Women in the U.S.," *Current Population Reports,* Washington, D.C.: U.S. Government Printing Office, 1976, p. 46.
[12] "Characteristics of the Population Below the Poverty Level: op. cit., 1976," p. 5.
[13] *Economic Report of the President,* Washington, D.C.: U.S. Government Printing Office, 1978, p. 292, Table B-30.
[14] *Employment and Training Report of the President,* Washington, D.C.: U.S. Government Printing Office, 1978, pp. 26–27.
[15] U.S. Bureau of the Census, *Statistical Abstract of the United States: 1977,* Washington, D.C.: 1977, p. 453, Table No. 734.

71 percent of the poor in this country, many of whom are on welfare, are people a civilized society does not normally ask to work—children and young people under 16, the aged, the severely disabled, students and mothers with children under six. Nearly a fifth of the poor work either full- or part-time, but do not earn enough to take themselves out of poverty. Some eight percent are women with family responsibilities. Only two percent even resemble the stereotype—able-bodies males under 65 who do not work. Census figures indicate that most of this group is between 62 and 64 and is ill or looking for work.[16]

While most poor persons are white, clearly disproportionate numbers of persons from minority group backgrounds are found in the poverty group. From 1955 to 1973, the earnings of black full-time, full-year workers shifted from 56 to 66 percent of the earnings of white full-time, full-year workers. Black females in the same period went from 56 to 86 percent of full-time, full-year white workers' earnings. Black family incomes as a percentage of white family income rose between 1947 and 1973 only from 51 to 60 percent.

Poverty is differential among minority groups. Hispanic families, for example, in 1969 had incomes 58 percent of the average white family's income. At the same time, black families had an income equal to 63 percent of the average white family. By 1973 the average black family income had dropped to 60 percent of the average white family income. But the average Hispanic family had increased its income to 69 percent of the average white family. Much of the gain is attributable to the success of Cubans, Central and South Americans, and Spanish segments of this population whose increase went from 65 to 89 percent of white family income. Chicanos (Mexican-Americans) increased their share of income from 56 to 67 percent of white family income.

Median native American family income in 1969 was $3300, ranging from $1000 on several reservations to $15,000 on one reservation. Their median income as a group was approximately one-third that of white family income.[17]

A large portion of the poor population is accounted for by those on public assistance, although there are more poor people who do not receive public assistance than there are who do. In 1978 there were 3,555,205 families receiving Aid to Families with Dependent Children (AFDC), the major public assistance program. There were 10,927,320 recipients in these families of whom 7,684,000 were chil-

[16] Joseph A. Califano, Jr. "Putting the Public Into Public Policy Development," *The Journal of the Institute for Socioeconomic Studies*, Vol. III, No. 2, Summer 1978, p. 3.
[17] Lester Thurow, "Not Making It in America: The Economic Progress of Minority Groups," *Social Policy*, Vol. 16, No. 5, March/April, 1976, pp. 5–11.

dren. The average size of such families was 3.3 persons residing in cities. Slightly over 50 percent of the families receiving AFDC were white, while blacks constituted just over 44 percent, and Hispanics (including white persons) were 12 percent. Eighty percent of these families were headed by women.[18]

As we have seen, one serious misconception about the poor is the belief that they do not work, a "blaming" of the victim. In fact, the poor work more than they are generally given credit for. In 1974, 16.6 percent of the heads of poor families worked full-time all year and an additional 35.6 percent worked for some of the time. Of the heads of the poor families who did not work at all, 16 percent were either ill or disabled.[19] Perhaps most important is the fact that every public jobs program in the past generation has been swamped with applicants—the poor work or want to work.

Race, age of head of household, sex, years of schooling of the head of the household, geographic region of residence, center city, and suburban or nonmetropolitan residence are factors associated with poverty. When these factors are taken multiply, the risk of poverty soars. Consider that

> . . . some 10 percent of all families are poor, 22 percent of families with seven or more members are poor, 28 percent of black families are poor, and 32 percent of female headed families are poor. Taking two characteristics at a time, we find that 53 percent of black female headed families are poor and that 66 percent of female headed families with seven or more members are poor. Considering all three characteristics together, we find that 73 percent of black female headed families with seven or more members are poor.[20]

Many of those in poverty are victims of our industrial and complex society and the normal course of events. One estimate of the number of handicapped persons in the United States has suggested 40 million handicapped or more. There are 11.7 million physically disabled, 12.5 million temporarily injured; 2.4 million deaf, 11 million hearing impaired, 1.3 million blind, 8.2 million visually

[18] See *Social Security Bulletin*, February 1978, p. 81, Table M-35, and Howard Oberheu, "Studies of the Characteristics of AFDC Recipients," *Social Security Bulletin*, September 1977, Vol. 40, No. 9, pp. 15–20.
[19] U.S. Department of Commerce, Office of Federal Statistical Policy and Standards, Bureau of the Census, *Social Indicators, 1976*, Washington, D.C.: U.S. Government Printing Office, December 1977, p. 468, Table 9/19.
[20] John B. Williamson *et al., Strategies Against Poverty in America.* New York: Schenkman Publishing Co., 1975, p. 12.

impaired, 6.8 million mentally disabled, 1.7 million homebound, and 2.1 million institutionalized. Even accounting for overlap where persons fall into more than one category, the disabled are a very significant proportion of the potentially poor.[21] In one program alone (OASDI) Social Security for those permanently disabled, as of December 31, 1972, there were 3,271,000 beneficiaries in disabled worker families.[22]

All of the above numbers raise as many questions as they answer. How, for instance, do we know when we make progress in combating poverty? When there is a dramatic change, such as from 22 percent of the population in 1959 to 12 percent in 1969 in poverty, we know that there has been progress. The discussion then shifts to what the key elements were in the progress. But when change is more gradual, economists and statisticians may argue over whether it is significant at all.

For instance, if black family income rises from 58 to 60 percent of median white family income, this might appear to be modest progress. But if in that period income rose generally, the dollar gap between black and white income might have actually increased. To illustrate: if I earn $50 and you earn $100, my income is 50 percent of yours. If my income rises to $120 while yours rises to $200, my income is now 60 percent of yours. But the dollar difference between our incomes has increased from $50 to $80. This is what has occurred in the "progress" of black income vis-à-vis white, and this often causes argument as to whether there has been progress at all.

Poverty can be approached from another perspective. One can examine the total income of the nation and see how much of it went to the poorest 10 or 20 percent of the population and how much went to the richest 10 or 20 percent. Thus we can see if there is progress in sharing the wealth more equitably.

Inequality in the United States has remained fairly stable over the past decades. In 1956 the lowest fifth of families received 5 percent of the income. In 1976 the lowest fifth received 5.4 percent. The second fifth received 12.5 percent in 1956 and 11.8 percent in 1976, while the middle fifth went from 17.9 to 17.6 percent. The fourth fifth received 23.6 percent in 1956 and 24.1 percent in 1976. The highest fifth received 41 percent in 1956 and 41.1 percent in 1976.

---

[21] "Uncertainty in the Figures," *New York Times*, February 13, 1977, p. E8.
[22] Congress of the United States, *Studies in Public Welfare. Paper No. 20, Handbook of Public Income Transfer Programs: 1975, Subcommittee on Fiscal Policy of the Joint Economic Committee*, Washington, D.C.: U.S. Government Printing Office, 1974, p. 23.

The top 5 percent received 16.4 percent in 1956 and 15.6 percent in 1976.[23]

Not income alone, but wealth is an important factor:

> The richest 10 percent of the population receive 29% of personal income but own 56% of national wealth. And that wealth is largely income producing, while the 44% in the hands of others who are less wealthy more heavily represents homes, cars and appliances.... In 1970, owners of wealth received $82 billion in interest, dividends, and rent. (Capital gains are not included in the figure.) The total amount spent for public assistance and other noncontributory welfare programs was $16 billion. So the distribution, setting wages and salaries apart, ran five to one in favor of advantaged people.[24]

Lester Thurow cites two studies of wealth separated by almost a decade which throw light on this subject in the United States, data about which is sparse. According to one study conducted by the Federal Reserve Board in 1962, the poorest 25 percent of the population has no net assets. The top 18.7 percent of the population has 76.2 percent of total wealth. The top half of 1 percent (0.5 percent) owns 25.8 percent of all the privately owned physical assets in the United States. A later study conducted in 1969 reached essentially the same conclusions. According to this latter study, the top 7.4 percent of our population owns almost 60 percent of all United States wealth. The wealthiest 8 percent of the top 7.4 percent (0.6 percent of the population) owns 25 percent of all the assets of the entire population.[25]

Thus we see that progress in reducing inequality seems minimal. But here, too, there is room for interpretation. The quintile, or 20 percent of the population, at the lowest end did not have the same characteristics in 1976 as in 1956. Persons in families have become slightly more concentrated in the upper quintiles. Also the lowest fifth of families in 1976 had a smaller percent of earners and the highest quintile had a larger percent of earners than in 1956.[26] With the increase in life span and in single parent families, more of that population was aged or single, groups where poverty has been more prevalent. So when one corrects the statistics to control for these

[23] U.S. Bureau of the Census, "Money Income in 1976 of Families and Persons in the United States," *Current Population Reports*, Series P-60, No. 114, Washington, D.C.: U.S. Government Printing Office, 1978, p. 11, and U.S. Bureau of the Census, *Statistical Abstract of the United States: 1977*, Washington, D.C.: 1977, p. 443, Table 713.
[24] Alvin L. Schorr, "Fair Shares," *Jubilee for our Times*. New York: Columbia University Press, 1977, p. 8.
[25] Lester C. Thurow, *Generating Inequality: Mechanisms of Distribution in the U.S. Economy*, New York: Basic Books, 1975, pp. 14–15.
[26] "Money Income in 1976 of Families and Persons in the United States," op. cit., p. 10.

characteristics, progress against inequality may seem to have been more significant. And for all its problems our society offers more mobility than any other. One of every ten sons born into families of manual workers achieves elite status.[27]

But looking at the lowest fifth illuminates another issue. The income at the upper limit of the lowest fifth of incomes for families in 1972 was $5612, not very much above the poverty level for a family of four.[28] A major problem in America is that of the "near poor," those who are employed and earning only slightly more than is received by those who are assisted with one or more public programs.

People are helped out of poverty by governmental income transfer programs. In 1976, 68 percent of major government income transfer payments consisted of social insurance program expenditures such as Social Security, government pensions, and unemployment insurance designed to replace reduced income. Cash assistance (AFDC) and Supplemental Security Income (SSI) accounted for 10 percent of income transfer payments; in-kind transfers (food stamps, Medicare, Medicaid, veterans' programs, health care, and aid to education) accounted for 23 percent. Such transfer income amounted in 1976 to 14.7 percent of total income.

One can observe in Table 5-3 that 27 percent of all families and unrelated individuals (approximately one in every four families) were below the poverty line in 1976 pretax and pretransfer of income. After social insurance income is accounted for the percentage of families and unrelated individuals in poverty dropped to 15.7. Cash assistance further reduced the percentage to 11.3. If one then accounts for in-kind transfer programs the percentage in poverty drops to 8.1.

Table 5-4 shows that almost 25 percent of white families were in poverty pretax and pretransfer of income. After all transfers have been made—social insurance, cash assistance, and in-kind transfers—this figure drops to 7.1 percent. For nonwhites, 43.8 percent of

---

[27] S. M. Miller and P. Roby, "Poverty: Changing Social Stratification," *On Understanding Poverty,* Daniel P. Moynihan (ed.), New York: Basic Books, 1969, p. 72. Regardless of the degree of mobility in our society, there are significant numbers of poor. As we have seen poverty has its relationships with many facets of our society and serves some purposes in accordance with our dominant values. Herbert J. Gans has suggested in "The Positive Functions of Poverty" that the poor perform many functions in society, ranging from making sure "dirty work" is done and supplying labor to absorbing the economic and political costs of change and growth (*American Journal of Sociology,* Vol. 78, No. 2, pp. 275–289).

[28] Alvin L. Schorr, "Fair Shares," *Jubilee for our Times,* New York: Columbia University Press, 1977, p. 4.

Table 5-3 FAMILIES[a] BELOW THE POVERTY LEVEL UNDER ALTERNATIVE INCOME DEFINITIONS, FISCAL YEAR 1976

FAMILIES IN POVERTY	PRE-TAX/ PRE-TRANSFER INCOME	PRE-TAX/ POST-SOCIAL INSURANCE INCOME	PRE-TAX/ POST-MONEY TRANSFER INCOME	PRE-TAX POST-IN-KIND TRANSFER INCOME[b]		POST-TAX/ POST TOTAL TRANSFER INCOME[b]	
				I	II	I	II
Number in thousands	21,436	12,454	10,716	8,978	6,441	9,165	6,597
Percent of all families	27.0	15.7	13.5	11.3	8.1	11.5	8.3

SOURCE: Congress of the United States, Congressional Budget Office, *Poverty Status of Families Under Alternative Definitions of Income.* Background Paper No. 17, Washington, D.C.: U.S. Government Printing Office, 1977, p. xv.
[a]Families are defined to include unrelated individuals as one-person families.
[b]Column I excludes medicare and medicaid benefits received by families participating in those programs; Column II includes medicare and medicaid benefits.

Table 5-4 FAMILIES BY RACE BELOW THE POVERTY LEVEL UNDER ALTERNATIVE INCOME DEFINITIONS, FISCAL YEAR 1976

FAMILIES IN POVERTY	PRE-TAX/PRE-TRANSFER INCOME	PRE-TAX/POST-SOCIAL INSURANCE INCOME	PRE-TAX/POST-MONEY TRANSFER INCOME	PRE-TAX/POST-IN-KIND TRANSFER INCOME[a]		POST-TAX POST-TOTAL TRANSFER INCOME[a]	
				I	II	I	II
A. White							
Number in thousands	17,330	9,305	8,006	6,053	4,948	7,013	5,091
Percent of white	24.7	13.3	11.4	9.8	7.1	10.0	7.3
B. Nonwhite							
Number in thousands	4,106	3,148	2,709	2,126	1,492	2,152	1,506
Percent of nonwhite	43.8	33.6	28.9	22.7	15.9	23.0	16.1

[a] Column I excludes medicare and medicaid benefits received by families participating in those programs; Column II includes medicare and medicaid benefits.

SOURCE: Congress of the United States, Congressional Budget Office, *Poverty Status of Families Under Alternative Definitions of Income.* Background Paper No. 17, Washington, D.C.: U.S. Government Printing Office, 1977, p. 11.

families were below the poverty level prior to taxes or transfer of income. After accounting for social insurance, cash assistance, and in-kind transfers, 15.9 percent of nonwhite families remained below the poverty level. Startling is the fact presented in Table 5-5 that almost 60 percent (more than one in every two) of those 65 years of age and older were in poverty pretransfer programs (1976), but after all transfers this percentage was reduced to 6.1. Without Medicare and Medicaid about 14.1 percent of aged families would be counted as poor.[29]

Transfer programs are powerful forces to bring people out of poverty. However, as we have seen above, the working poor account for large numbers of those in poverty (one in six of the heads of poor families worked full time year round). The interrelation of poverty, employment, wage levels, and income security programs is clear, and the reduction of poverty cannot be accomplished by only income transfer devices; obviously other interventions will be required.

The poverty line itself is an arbitrary division. Although it has been adjusted to account for inflation since the mid-1960s, it does not take into account the rising expectations or the norm of American living. Therefore, the gap between the official poverty line and comfortable living may be growing greater, and a large army of "near poor" and nominally lower middle-class people are really poor and feel discriminated against: women, children, racial minorities, prisoners, and the working poor. One can almost say that almost everyone in our society is discriminated against in one way or another. While major attention has and should be paid to the plight of those who are most embedded in poverty, Michael Novak has pointed out "the great majority of high school dropouts are not from among the poor but from the working class, white and black." And "forty percent of lower-middle-class husbands and wives both work. Even adding their salaries together, their median income is $10,700.[30] The poverty problems of women, children, the aging, and racial minorities are clearly disproportionate, but it is important to note the problem of poverty is endemic to our society and not confined to any one group. It is widespread, and every group has a share in the burden, although some carry undue loads. But the problem of poverty cannot be understood or approached without considering the groups whose income is just slightly more than those in poverty.

At different times, different groups have been most discrimi-

[29] Congress of the United States, Congressional Budget Office, *Poverty Status of Families under Alternative Definitions of Income*, Background Paper No. 17, Washington, D.C.: U.S. Government Printing Office, 1977.
[30] Michael Novak, *The Rise of the Unmeltable Ethnics*, New York: Macmillan, 1972, pp. 21–22.

Table 5-5   FAMILIES BY AGE BELOW THE POVERTY LEVEL UNDER ALTERNATIVE INCOME DEFINITIONS, FISCAL YEAR 1976

FAMILIES IN POVERTY	PRE-TAX/PRE-TRANSFER INCOME	PRE-TAX/POST-SOCIAL INSURANCE INCOME	PRE-TAX/POST-MONEY TRANSFER INCOME	PRE-TAX/POST-IN-KIND TRANSFER INCOME[a]		POST-TAX/POST-TOTAL TRANSFER INCOME[a]	
				I	II	I	II
A. Under 65							
Number in thousands	11,789	8,994	8,029	6,710	5,463	6,886	5,615
Percent of under 65	18.6	14.2	12.7	10.6	8.6	10.9	8.9
B. 65 and Over							
Number in thousands	9,647	3,459	2,686	2,268	977	2,279	982
Percent of 65 and over	59.9	21.5	16.7	14.1	6.1	14.1	6.1

[a] Column I excludes medicare and medicaid benefits received by families participating in those programs; Column II includes medicare and medicaid benefits.

SOURCE: Congress of the United States, Congressional Budget Office, *Poverty Status of Families Under Alternative Definitions of Income.* Background Paper No. 17, Washington, D.C.: U.S. Government Printing Office, 1977, p. 12.

nated against. Usually the latest wave of immigrants took the brunt of the oppression. For whites, the major force of such oppression may end, while for blacks, Mexican-Americans, and native Americans there has been a continuity to the discrimination aimed at them and their poverty has persisted even in the best of economic times.

Those who are in poverty are besieged by their difficulties. It is natural that one group or another should claim that the oppression aimed at them is the most difficult, the most trying. Programs aimed selectively at particular groups hold a certain fascination and promise easier success while they often have accompanying costs. What is needed is equal access to opportunities. Separatism and local control have been praised as necessary by both left and right politicians, who argue for local decision-making and control. Bayard Rustin has placed this call within perspective:

> Another current axiom of black self-determination is the necessity for community control. Questions of ideology aside, black community control is as futile a program as black capitalism. Assuming that there were a cohesive, clearly identifiable black community . . . and assuming that the community were empowered to control the ghetto, it would still find itself without the money needed in order to be socially creative. The ghetto would still be faced with the same poverty, deteriorated housing, unemployment, terrible health services, and inferior schools— and this time perhaps with the exacerbation of their being entailed in local struggles for power. . . . For in a complex technological society there is no such thing as an autonomous community within a large metropolitan area.[31]

Implied in Rustin's argument is the need for universal services which offer equal access to opportunity for all groups. Universal coverage in a welfare society would meet basic needs and provide for the development of individuals, families, and communities. Kahn has pointed out that universal services are quality services and must meet the general community standards, not just those for the poor. Kahn also raises a question about the use of universal services in particular contexts.[32] A major argument against universal services was made by Miller and Roby when they argued "universalistic policies that are aimed at simultaneously improving the conditions of all in society do not reduce the distance between those at the top and those at the bottom."[33] This, too, can be questioned. More people are

[31] Bayard Rustin, "The Failure of Black Separatism," *Down the Line*, Chicago: Quadrangle Books, 1971, p. 297.
[32] Alfred J. Kahn, *Social Policy and Social Services*, New York: Random House, 1973, p. 79.
[33] S. M. Miller and Pamela A. Roby, *The Future of Inequality*, New York: Basic Books, 1970, p. 220.

transferred out of poverty by the universalistic Social Security system than by selective public assistance programs.

WHAT IS POVERTY?

In spite of all programs and progress, widespread poverty and near poverty persists. If poverty is to be combatted successfully, it must be understood. But there even exist very different ideas about what poverty is.

We can understand poverty easily as the result of individual failure, the traditional blaming the victim theory of causation. But if one adopts the idea that structural causes have the greatest impact on the incidence of poverty in our society, then more investigation is necessary. For instance, Rustin has pointed out that

> . . . in the period immediately following the war [World War II] black unemployment dropped dramatically to 4.1 percent in 1953, a figure lower than at any time before or after. The jobs filled by these black migrants, however, were almost entirely in the unskilled and semi-skilled categories, those areas of the economy most susceptible to the ravages of automation and advanced technology.[34]

Rein and Heclo found an increase in female-headed, one-parent families in the United States, Great Britain, and Sweden. While one could seek to explain this fact by changes in moral standards, the breakdown of married life, or individual focused causation, Rein hypothesized that the proportion of women marrying has increased, the proportion of women bearing one child has increased, there is a greater tendency than in the past for a mother to form a separate household and to take welfare benefits, and women find themselves discriminated against in the labor market.[35] Thus structural changes in the acceptable institutional patterns can explain much of the rise in those who live in such families and need the assistance of society. And although it is believed that large numbers of American black women have used the AFDC program (they are in the program disproportionate to their percentage of the population in general), between 1961 and 1971, blacks as a percentage of AFDC families increased only from 40 to 43 percent.

Rashi Fein has demonstrated how white Americans have attained particular levels of health, education, and income decades before black Americans. When the blacks have caught up, whites

[34] Bayard Rustin. *Strategies for Freedom: The Changing Patterns of Black Protest,* New York: Columbia University Press, 1976, p. 59.
[35] Martin Rein and Hugh Heclo, "What Welfare Crisis? A Comparison Among the United States, Britain, and Sweden," *The Public Interest,* No. 33, Fall 1973, p. 78.

have moved still further to new attainments.[36] The only convincing explanation of such lags is that discrimination is structured into our society. But we are all losers in many ways because of such institutionalized discrimination. As early as 1970, Wilbur Cohen (former Secretary of Health, Education, and Welfare) suggested "the elimination of racial discrimination would increase incomes by some $15 billion a year and would aid in the reduction of poverty and the increase in productivity and in the enhancement of individual dignity and self-reliance."[37]

Automation, discrimination, and other institutional factors need to be examined in order to understand poverty. We seek to look next at the major definitions of poverty itself. This may seem overly simple at first. We all "know" what poor means. And yet there are significantly different explanations of what constitutes poverty, and the differences have profound implications for what should be done to end it.

1. Below an Established Minimum

One way of defining poverty is to draw a neat poverty line, a dollar figure, and suggest that everyone below the line is in poverty and everyone who has more is above the poverty level. For example, in 1974 the poverty threshold for a nonfarm family of four persons was $5038. Using that figure, 24.3 million persons were below the poverty level in 1974—12 percent of the U.S. population.[38] By 1976 the total number of persons in poverty had risen to 24,975,000 but remained at 12 percent of the U.S. population.[39]

The poverty standard which is most used is the index used by the Social Security Administration based on the Department of Agriculture's estimate of the cost of a temporary, low-budget, nutritious diet for households of different sizes. Through the use of these estimates a figure is reached which is needed to buy a subsistence level of goods and services.

[36] Rashi Fein, "An Economic and Social Profile of the Negro American," *The Negro American*, Talcott Parsons and Kenneth B. Clark (eds.), Boston: Beacon Press, 1967. pp. 102–133.

[37] Wilbur Cohen, "Social Welfare Priorities for the 1970s," *The Social Welfare Forum, 1970*, New York: Columbia University Press, 1970, pp. 4–5. Current direct and indirect losses to the economy from discrimination are estimated to be in the tens of billions of dollars per year. See Bradley R. Schiller, *The Economics of Poverty and Discrmination*, Englewood Cliffs, New Jersey: Prentice-Hall, 1976, pp. 133–135.

[38] *Current Population Reports, Consumer Income, Characteristics of the Population Below the Poverty Level: 1974*, Washington, D.C.: U.S. Government Printing Office, 1976, p. 1.

[39] "Characteristics of the Population Below the Poverty Level: 1976," op. cit., p. 6.

The efficiency of such standards makes possible comparisons over time. If we state, for example, that 22.4 percent of the population was in poverty in 1959 and today approximately 12 percent are in poverty, we have a clear picture (given acceptance of the definition of poverty) over a period of time.

Even if we argue that the poverty line, as defined, is inadequate, there is a certain neatness in the concept of defining poverty as being anything below x dollars of income per year.

One limitation of such an income-based poverty level is that it includes insurance payments such as Social Security and unemployment compensation and cash assistance programs but does not include in-kind assistance such as Medicaid. According to one estimate using in-kind assistance as well as cash payments, there were 9.5 million American families in poverty in 1965 and only 5.4 million families (6.9 percent) in 1977.[40]

Second, poverty lines exclude the near poor as discussed above and may give a deceptive picture of the population. Another limitation is that income definitions do not include wealth or assets. There is a vast difference between two elderly people, each receiving $300 monthly in Social Security benefits, if one owns a home free and clear while the other does not.

Finally, needs may differ in various ways and are based upon assumptions about the poor, such as that the poor have knowledge of nutrition and marketing and are extremely resourceful. The current poverty line distinguishes only between farm and nonfarm families.

Some leaders in welfare rights organizations postulate that the only problem of those in poverty is the lack of money. They suggest that no theories or social workers are needed, just an adequate annual income. In 1970 they recommended a minimum of $5500 for a family of four. But no matter what is established in any society as the floor, there will still be relative inequality. The new floor becomes the poverty line, a never-ending dilemma. Still, defining poverty as some amount under x dollars per year gives us a handle on poverty and suggests ways of fighting it, specifically with income supplementation.

2. Relative Inequality

According to Michael Harrington and others, the problem is basically one of rising expectations which are in infinite acceleration. The standard of living has gone up, and so have expectations over time. An automobile was an unusual thing to own in the 1930s. By

[40] David E. Rosenbaum, "Budget Office Finds that Welfare Reduced Poverty Rate 60 Percent," *New York Times*, January 18, 1977, p. 10.

1970 it was practically impossible in most parts of the United States to work or live without one. Television, which was unusual in the early 1950s, by 1970 had been accepted as a typical, if not necessary, part of a home. Similarly, the gap between the poverty line and median family income today is greater. Relative inequality is thus greater. It is this perception of relative inequality which is at the bottom of the most difficult problem of poverty, because relative poverty is an inescapable concomitant of poverty. When the government establishes a poverty line, it suggests it is responsible up to a point and has no responsibility beyond that minimum income; it is stating that governmental responsibility is for the establishment of an income floor no one shall fall below. But this still does not remedy the fact there always will be richer and poorer persons regardless of what the standard for poverty might become.

In addition, definitions of the expected services of a society alter over time. At one time in the United States there was an expectation generally held that people might complete the eighth grade. Today it is widely accepted that almost everyone will complete education through secondary level. Health care was a privilege, and today it is coming to be judged a right. In France and several other nations, women with families are provided with vacations from home. While this service is not provided by the government in the United States, it is not farfetched to imagine such a benefit being provided in the future. Thus evolving rights also serve to alter the perception by those in poverty of what their situation means to them and changes the definition of poverty.

Poverty may be defined as a standard of living less than the expectation of a society or as an unfair gap between one's resources and that of others. On one level this definition could become ludicrous. Is the ultimate goal the elimination of all difference, of all inequality? Of course not. And therefore the sociologist Robert Nisbet challenges proponents of equality to define how much equality they really seek; without such a clear definition, he dismisses the argument.[41]

It is not necessary to be trapped into such absurd arguments. The answer to how much equality is wanted can be the same as Samuel Gompers' answer to the question of what the American labor movement wanted: "more."

The rich have the infinite capacity to invent new luxuries as yesterday's luxuries become today's necessities for all. Absolute equality is not achievable or even desirable. But the feeling that people live in one society which fairly allocates the necessities of life is one

[41] Robert Nisbet, "The New Despotism," *Commentary*, Vol. 59, No. 6, June 1975, pp. 31–43.

key definition of nonpoverty. Titmuss pointed out that in wartime, when rich and poor lined up for rationed food, no one felt poor. It is the lack of something which others have and to which one feels entitled which defines poverty. Inequality is a less exact definition of poverty than an absolute definition, but it may be more realistic. Accepting this as the key to poverty suggests transfers of resources as the key antipoverty weapon whether through income redistribution or through amenities equally available to all.

3. Lack of Power, Access, and Inclusion

Titmuss has suggested that "command over resources" is a new measure of wealth and thus, by implication, poverty is the lack of "command over resources." Paradoxically, as certain benefits become available to categories of people, they create benefits for those who command them but relative inequality for those who do not have such access. He has suggested that welfare actually is delivered in three ways: fiscal welfare in which benefits are distributed through the tax system, as in the example with which we began this section; occupational welfare in which welfare benefits are associated with and tied to the job one has; and the more well known and identified social welfare.

Credentials and entitlements have become a major form of wealth in our society.[42] These entitlements vary. They include seniority and tenure, licenses and franchises, academic degrees and union membership, and many others. Each has a certain value translatable to tangible wealth, and some (New York City taxicab medallions, for instance) are even transferable or may be inherited. The value of many credentials and entitlements is compounded to the degree that they serve as a form of capital rather than simply as a form of consumable wealth. An acre of land has an immediate market value or may produce a certain amount of grain. The same acre of land also can be used as collateral for additional purchases or can serve as the base for a high-rise apartment building. Similarly, a credential, an entitlement, can be a building block for the development of additional wealth. A college graduate has the option not only of working and earning money as a result of having a degree, but of "investing" that degree in an advanced degree to bring still better returns in the future.

In the past certain groups have been denied a fair share of, and access to, traditional forms of wealth. Now demands for greater equity are worldwide, and each society to some degree redistributes

---

[42] This theme is developed by Charles Reich in "The New Property," *The Public Interest*, Vol. I, No. 3, 1966, pp. 57–89.

and transfers income. But as this "new property" grows more important, it becomes the focus of attempts to achieve greater equality. Without greater access to this new form of wealth, the poor are doomed to continuing poverty or dependence.

Not only do the economically deprived have less access to credentials, but there exist fewer safeguards for the protection of those credentials. In the long struggle for more economic opportunity and equality, certain gains have been made. If a person works for wages and does not receive them, he or she has access to the courts. But the credential system still exists largely in self-regulating and self-determining programs not subject to the legal safeguards which have developed around the marketplace. Diplomas and licenses are often awarded or withheld with broad discretionary powers. If a man is a communist, this fact does not allow individuals or governments to walk into his home and to steal his tangible property. It may, however, permit the state to strip him of Social Security benefits or of some other entitlement. Not all hearings of government regulatory agencies are subject to the same safeguards and restraints as are present in the legal tradition.

Privilege and aspects of an industrial and technological society combine so the poor have less power and curtailed access to resources. In large part the poverty of many people is the result of the opportunity structure of our society. To what extent is it possible for our society to create sufficient jobs for all potential workers on the basis of an unregulated labor market? Given a willingness to create jobs, to what extent can these jobs be productively targeted at those who are the least able and least trained and who are ill-equipped to do tasks which require high levels of skill? To what extent is the job situation open to upward mobility for those who enter at very low levels of employment?

Racism, agism, and sexism are all forms of denial of access. If a person is denied access to jobs, to entitlements, to respect, and to knowledge about where to go for service, that person may be defined as poor.

While few would argue that lack of power to affect the political system or discrimination is a complete definition of poverty, it can hardly be ignored as a factor. A whole variety of inclusionary strategies are needed if one sees this as a key factor in poverty.

4. The Culture of Poverty

Poverty consists of economic inequality and also of noneconomic features. In a nation in which social honor, prestige, and self-respect as well as quality of life are important, poor persons are viewed as lacking in such honor and prestige and deriving their self-image from society's view of them. They may victimize themselves to some extent by internalizing society's view. To a degree their sense of aspiration is battered and the gap between early aspiration and opportunities grows large resulting in behavior which assumes "making it" is impossible.

According to one point of view, perhaps best articulated by Oscar Lewis in *La Vida*,[43] which has become identified as the "culture of poverty" thesis, poor persons have particular behavioral characteristics, *and* these characteristics are transmitted from one generation to another. Among the attributes suggested are inability to defer gratification, a present orientation with less emphasis upon the future, lack of aspiration for upward mobility, female centered families, alienation, a freer sexual code, and less investment in child rearing.

While these characteristics, which are open to debate, are entitled the "culture of poverty," they are curiously very much like a description of the "jet set." Missing from the description are those characteristics typically associated with the upwardly mobile, future-oriented middle class. But it may be that once one has reached a point of affluence and discovered there are no magic answers to life's mysteries, one can become prey to alienation. Perhaps there is not much difference between those in the affluent culture and those in the "culture of poverty" in this respect.

Is there a group of behaviors specific to the poor? Peter Rossi and Zahava Blum set out to answer the question: How different are the poor? On the basis of a review of social science literature published since the end of World War II they concluded

> ... in almost every case it is clear that the alleged "special" characteristics of the poor are ones that they share generally with the "working-class" or "blue-collar" component of the labor force. In other words, the poor *are* different, but the difference appears mainly to be a matter of *degree* rather than of kind.[44]

Not only do Rossi and Blum question the first half of the culture of poverty thesis that the poor are different, but they go on to raise a serious question about the second half of the "culture of poverty" argument, that is, the transmission of characteristics from one gen-

---

[43] Lewis stated that "the culture of poverty, however, is not only an adaptation to a set of objective conditions of the larger society. Once it comes into existence it tends to perpetuate itself from generation to generation because of its effect on the children." (*La Vida*, New York: Random House, 1966, p. XIV.)

[44] Peter H. Rossi and Zahava D. Blum, "Class, Status, and Poverty," *On Understanding Poverty*, Daniel Moynihan (ed.), New York: Basic Books, 1969, p. 39.

eration to the next. They argue that a review of the literature does not

> ... support the idea of a culture of poverty in which the poor are dis-
> tinctively different from other layers of society. Nor does the evidence
> from intergenerational mobility studies support the idea of a culture of
> poverty in the sense of the poor being composed largely of persons
> themselves coming from families living in poverty.[45]

When viewed from this perspective (the life-style of the poor differs only in degree from the groups above their socioeconomic level and their lifestyles are not necessarily transmitted from generation to generation), one can state certain facts. The lower the socioeconomic level, the higher the incidence of family disorganization, the greater the sense of alienation from the larger society, the higher the incidence of symptoms of mental disorder, the less competence with standard English, the higher the rate of mortality and the incidence of physical disorders, the lower the "need for achievement," the less likely parents will socialize their children through the use of explanations for obedience to rules, the higher the crime and delinquency rates based on arrests and convictions (but there is evidence poor people are treated more harshly than others), and the more likely one is to be liberal on economic issues but less liberal regarding civil liberties or political deviants. But these are differences of degree, not of kind.

Unemployment and poverty have a startling impact upon people, and the impact is not limited to those who live in poverty. The human impact of a 1.4 percent rise in unemployment during 1970 was studied through 1975. The effects associated with the rise in unemployment were a 5.7 percent rise in suicides, a 4.7 percent rise in state mental hospital admissions, a 5.6 percent rise in state prison admission, an 8 percent rise in homicides, a 2.7 percent rise in cirrhosis of the liver, a 2.7 percent rise in cardiovascular-renal disease mortality, and a 2.7 percent rise in total mortality. The financial impact and economic losses accompanying the 1.4 percent rise in unemployment were also traced. The economic losses are in the billions. Thus living in poverty does take its toll on human lives.[46]

[45] Ibid., p. 43.
[46] "PACE Points to Unemployment/Health Correlations in Get-Out-The-Vote Effort," *NASW News*, Vol. 22, No. 1, January 1977, p. 10, and Harvey Brenner, *Estimating the Social Costs of National Economic Policy: Implications for Mental and Physical Health, and Criminal Aggression;* Joint Economic Committee, Congress of the United States, "Paper No. 5: Achieving the Goals of the Employment Act of 1946," *Thirtieth Anniversary Review*, Washington, D.C.: U.S. Government Printing Office, 1976.

Nevertheless, we are apt to blame the victim for his or her victimization and attribute to the person characteristics which may be more or our own making than inbred. This, then, is the key: it would be foolish to ignore that poverty creates certain behavior. What is crucial is that if the poverty is removed, the behavior tends to change. It is not true that the "culture of poverty" becomes a self-perpetuating force, continuing over generations. If this were true, the poor could not be helped without massive rehabilitation efforts aimed at the psyches of the poor.

For those who are tempted to believe that contemporary poverty groups are truly different in culture, the following excerpt may be instructive:

> Today there is an enormous alien population in our larger cities which is breeding crime and disease at a rate all the more dangerous because it is more or less hidden and insidious. . . . it is my fear and belief that within five years the alien population of the country, or rather cities, will constitute a downright peril.[47]

The author was talking about Jews and assumes some intrinsic cultural failure among Jews similar to things said about blacks or Hispanics today. But today Jews (and Japanese) are generally believed to be among America's most upward-striving minorities.

The concept is useful, however, in examining specific families or groups. At any given time there are people technically not in economic poverty or receiving resources who nonetheless are among the "poor" in that they adopt or maintain the life-style described above. Similarly there are economically poor people who are unidentified as such because they maintain a self-reliant life-style. In this sense the culture of poverty concept can be helpful.

STRATEGIES FOR FIGHTING POVERTY

Rein and Miller have classified approaches to dealing with poverty into six types of programs: amenities, investment in human capital, transfers, rehabilitation, participation, and aggregative and selective economic measures.[48] Each of these approaches has to be considered within the context of rationality, political feasibility, and value preferences. Each approach rests upon particular assumptions about the

[47] Allon Schoener (ed.), *Portal to America: The Lower East Side 1870–1925*, New York: Holt, Rinehart and Winston, 1967, p. 26.
[48] Martin Rein and S. M. Miller, "Poverty, Policy, and Purpose: The Dilemmas of Choice," *Economic Progress and Social Welfare*, Leonard Goodman (ed.), New York: Columbia University Press, 1966, pp. 20–64.

definition or cause of poverty. Each has both positive and negative or functional and dysfunctional aspects. In a word, social programs directed against poverty are usually mixed in the sense they require trade-offs of certain gains against other losses.

Amenities

These are services which contribute to strengthening and enriching the quality of life. Alfred Kahn has used the term "social utilities" for these programs. Access to birth control methods, family planning, or health services is in effect a transfer of money to the poor. Where our society makes available $1000 worth of medical care for a poor family, we are providing outside of the market an equivalent of income for that family. Other examples are parks, free education, police or fire services, universal day care, employment information, and public housing. This is one approach to fighting poverty. Some persons oppose social utilities and amenities because they require government planning and bureaucracy. One variation is to provide poor persons with vouchers worth a certain amount of money which they then can spend on food, education, or housing. In this latter case, vouchers support the free market and may or may not give the poor person more options, depending upon the terms of the voucher. The great advantage of amenities or social utilities is availability. Typically social utilities are nonstigmatized services because the community recognizes the necessity for particular services in an industrial and changing society, and they become available to all.

Vouchers run the danger of enriching purveyors of service without equalizing services. Universal amenities are a form of income transfer (if one believes poverty means having less than a minimum) and a form of reducing inequality. Those who see lack of access as the key to poverty also may favor the development of utilities as a strategy.

Investment in Human Capital

This approach to poverty attempts to improve the capabilities of the poor by investing in them through education, health, job training, and the like. Just as investment in capital such as machinery and new plants increases productivity, so does investment in the quality of the work force.

One of the important contributors to American growth has been its world leadership in universal free public education, a form of investment in human capital. Farmers in the United States who are literate have read pamphlets and journals and utilized new methods, while farmers in some other countries farmed traditionally, producing less. Public school education in America had this effect upon farmers and consequently upon the agricultural production of the United States. Essentially, this strategy is an indirect service strategy through education, labor manpower, and casework and other services.

Perhaps the best example of investment in human capital is the GI Bill which followed World War II. During the war unemployment was erased. But economists feared a return of massive unemployment after the rapid demobilization of millions of servicepeople. Two factors prevented this. First, people had savings and money in their pockets as a result of the war effort, high employment, and the shortage of consumer goods. There was a backlog of demand which created jobs. Second, millions of discharged servicepeople took advantage of the educational opportunities made possible through the GI Bill, deferring entry to the job market and eventually improving the quality of the labor force. One payoff for the United States has been higher tax revenues from those who took advantage of the opportunity. Several million people paying taxes through their lifetimes on incomes generated by a college education, rather than on income generated by a high school education, has more than repaid the government for its investment in education. Other payoffs have been less crime, higher morale, new inventions, social stability, and a more productive society. Consider the alternative if 11 million returning veterans had not been absorbed either into the labor market or given other options. Even when returning veterans took part in the 52-20 clubs ($20 per week for 52 weeks), there were no means tests; the program was universal and served to cushion their adjustment to civilian life.

One negative aspect of training is that in static economies, higher education and credentials as a result of human investment programs simply produce rearrangements within the line of people seeking work. Higher education then is taken mainly as a defensive ploy to get ahead or to hold one's employment level. Conversely, in a growing economy there is more opportunity for moving up. A growth economy is a precondition for some of these human investment situations to work well.

Investment in human capital—training programs and the like— is one way of bringing poor and disadvantaged groups into the system and therefore a way of combatting poverty for specific target groups at any time for all in a period of growth.

The development of community colleges since 1950 has been a

new social utility and a great investment in human capital described as "the bluing of America": the advanced technical or preprofessional training of the children of the blue-collar workers.

Income Transfers

Transfer systems take money from one population group and redirect it to another. Such transfers can be made from middle-aged persons to the elderly, from the employed to the unemployed, and from the rich to the poor. There are two ways in which such redistributions can be made. Either money is redistributed vertically in the sense that those who have more channel their money through a tax system to those who have less. Or redistribution can be made horizontally in that those who have, say, fewer dependents (including children) contribute through the tax system to those who have more dependents. The essential assumption of income transfers is that poverty is equivalent to a deficit of income. While this is a main factor in poverty, as we have seen earlier, this is not the complete definition of poverty.

It is now clear that the United States could eliminate poverty, at least in an absolute sense. The expenditures of the recent Vietnam War on an annual basis would—if directed at poverty individuals and families—probably come quite close to complete elimination of people below the absolute poverty line in our society.

However, a very strong taboo in American culture stands in the way of making such a commitment. There is something abhorrent in the American value system about giving money directly to both the "worthy" and the "unworthy" or able-bodied poor. Such an abhorrence seems ingrained in some Americans. While programs such as public assistance, social insurance, family allowances, and negative income taxes all have their potential uses in an attempt to do away with poverty, the essential questions are not about technology, the ways in which poverty could be overcome most effectively or efficiently, but instead are fundamental questions about values. For example, to what extent do Americans want to redistribute income to do away with poverty? Who would support whom? What are the benefits in such a move? And what are the losses such as high tax rates which supposedly would minimize investment in capital goods? However, such questions do not ask whether or not it could be done. They are all questions directed at the intentions, the trade-offs, which would have to be made and the identification of who would pay at what price. None of the above denies that problems in social engineering exist in devising appropriate income transfer programs.

But additional transfer in some form probably will need to be an essential part of any strategy to eliminate poverty.

Rehabilitation

This strategy is aimed at changing people through psychological and sociopsychological methods to restore and enhance social functioning. The underlying assumption of some approaches to guidance, social casework, and psychotherapy is that the fault lies within the person or the family, and it is consistent with the "blaming the victim" syndrome. The assumption is made that people who are poor have problems for which they need help, that is, problems other than lack of money.

Such programs are aimed at helping persons find means for holding a job, managing their emotional and interpersonal problems to a sufficient extent for them to be successfully employed. Such programs tend to be limited in scope and their capacity to affect poverty. This has been a traditional major approach to the issue of poverty. The Social Security Act amendments of 1962 actually suggested that more trained labor power—social workers and others—would result in lower welfare rolls. If sufficient numbers of trained social workers, for example, were prepared, they could be expected to rehabilitate so many welfare recipients that this would serve as a means of eliminating poverty. Actually, the results were opposite to what was expected. More social workers were able to do a better job of finding people who rightfully belonged on the welfare rolls.[49] However, the basic fallacy in such an approach is that it substitutes personal and familial causation for structural causation. The economic cycles of the nation much more determine the rate of growth or decline of poverty than does the pool of trained social workers.

Rehabilitation tends to see the victim as the problem and to offer sociopsychological supports for the person or family to be self-sustaining as the key element in help. Nevertheless, rehabilitation has legitimacy because there are people who will have emotional problems even in the best of worlds. Some people have special

---

[49] Generally there is a tendency to confuse welfare rolls with poverty. As Cloward and Piven have pointed out in *Regulating The Poor* (Frances Fox Piven and Richard A. Cloward, *Regulating the Poor: The Functions of Public Welfare*, New York: Vintage Books, 1971) in times of poverty there may be fewer people on welfare. The 1960s were relatively affluent times, but an explosion took place in the welfare rolls. This was part of a political change in which people took advantage of entitlements. But poverty and eligibility for welfare are two independent factors.

needs as situational crises occur, and they will be driven into poverty or be unable to drag themselves out of poverty without rehabilitation. Rehabilitation cannot be used as an effective, and certainly not as an efficient, means of eliminating poverty, but it is one of the legitimate ways of coping with *some* poor people as it is with helping some people of every class.

Aggregative and Selective Economic Measures

Aggregative economic measures are those which purport to help the poor at the bottom of the economic scene through economic growth resulting from tax reductions, and incentives meant to increase hiring and production. A growth economy seems required if we want to do away with poverty. When we have the kind of economy which is healthy and growing and employment is high, this makes the greatest contribution to defeating poverty. A healthy economy in which labor is in demand and productivity and consumption are high may do more than specific poverty programs to lessen the brunt of poverty.

The U.S. Congress in 1946 passed the Employment Act creating the Council of Economic Advisors. A commitment to stimulate high employment was reaffirmed in the passage of the Humphrey-Hawkins Full Employment Act in 1978. But a commitment to a full employment policy in which government provides jobs as the employer of last resort has never been seriously implemented. As a result, the coincidental phases of American economic cycles have done more to create poverty or to do away with it than the employment policies of the government.

Selective economic measures are designed to "bubble up" from poverty those poor who could benefit from job creation, minimum wages, and other programs for the poor. While these strategies seem attractive, 95 percent of those receiving welfare are women and children. The redesign of jobs and the creation of jobs will not in themselves move all women and children off welfare. However, where there is economic uncertainty such as unemployment and underemployment, family instability is sure to follow. For this reason job creation is often targetted at specific groups of males as a prevention of family breakup and dependency. Construction workers and workers in the durable goods sector of manufacturing were hard hit during the recession of the early and mid-1970s. Men in the young adult range from 16 to 24, especially minority males, needed opportunities for governmentally provided full-time work at a living wage.

The minimum wage is a two-edged sword in that it raises the

income of most employees through wage raises at the minimum level and through a chain of events, including union contracts, which then raise other levels of salaries upward. The negative consequence of such a raise, however, is that jobs in marginal industries and businesses are then cut back, further reducing the real supply of jobs which would be available for persons who are semiskilled or without skill or work experience.

Growth in the gross national product, that is, the total value of all goods and services produced, is a key ingredient in any program to reduce poverty. Growth is needed. During World War II there was practically no unemployment and poverty was reduced through means associated with the war effort. A bigger pie means potentially more for everyone, including the poor who may be recipients of redistributive efforts made possible by rising tax revenues which result from an expanding economy. Growth per se does not guarantee a reduction in poverty. Most people who seek to eliminate poverty are not satisfied that enough benefits will automatically trickle down to the poor. Other strategies are needed. But economic growth appears to be a precondition for other efforts to succeed or often even to be tried.

Participation

These programs are intended to promote social inclusion and to reduce problems among the poor by providing them with a stake in society. Whether there is a culture of poverty or problems of access or lack of power, or whether the key is discrimination, one of the strategies to be used is bringing people into the mainstream. Such programs are meant to raise the self-esteem of poor persons, to raise the honor and prestige they are awarded in society by enhancing their political power. They also try to provide access to "the new property." Such programs involve antidiscrimination laws, bilingual schools for Spanish-speaking children, zoning rules, access to municipal contracts and jobs, "new careers"-type programs for climbing the job ladder, access to the political process, voting, and direct engagement in political decision-making. The community action programs are devoted to the theory and policy of inclusion.

The 1960s' War on Poverty and the concomitant civil rights movement focused broadly on strategies of inclusion. They managed to develop successes in many local situations. They also raised expectations by giving people a sense of entitlement even faster than they could deliver results. Some feel this is an inevitable problem with such approaches.

SUMMARY

In our view the growth of the economy with its concomitant options for use of growing revenues is essential to combatting poverty. These options must be used toward a degree of redistribution, both through income transfers and creation of social utilities. Rehabilitation for some also is needed. These fundamental programs joined with inclusion, antidiscrimination laws, and investment in human capital add up to a program which could make poverty a thing of the past and cause the United States to become one of the first major nations in modern times to do away with poverty.

Chapter 6
Current Social Welfare
Programs—Part One

"The public services in the modern democratic 'Welfare State,' or . . . 'Welfare Society,' in which all citizens are potentially both givers and receivers, are administered by people who are, constitutionally, the servants of those they serve, and responsible to them. Representative democracy has taken on the character of a mutual aid society."[1]

This chapter and the next will show that there is no comprehensive and unified social welfare system in the United States. The American "system" has developed incrementally in a crazy quilt pattern. In reality, the American social welfare institution is a series of systems rather than one system, although they are sometimes more or less interrelated.

The scope of social welfare programs and services in the United States is so broad and complex that it is not possible to review all the social welfare programs in depth here. While we will not review every program, we will describe and examine the major facets of the main social welfare programs. Because change is so rapid, we will not describe programmatic fine details such as benefit levels.

It is important for social workers and all citizens to know about the various social welfare programs, their aims, for whom they are intended, benefits, funding, and administration because these facts

[1] T. H. Marshall, *Social Policy in the Twentieth Century*. London: Hutchinson University Library, 1967, p. 173.

affect all our lives. In Chapter 4 we presented a paradigm for the description and analysis of social welfare programs. This section is an exercise in the use of the analytical tools presented earlier. We will use the paradigm and analytical tools again in this chapter and in Chapter 11 when we consider alternative social welfare programs for three important areas: economic security, aging, and health. As one reads this chapter, it will be helpful independently to analyze in turn each of the programs as they are described so that you can compare your own conclusions with the analysis provided.

WORKERS' COMPENSATION

Who Is Eligible?

Workmen's Compensation, recently renamed Workers' Compensation (WC), is designed to provide benefits to victims of work-related accidents and illnesses regardless of fault. However, it must be demonstrated that the injury or the death is or was related to the victim's employment.

One problem of the industrial era is the loss of income because of job-related injury, sickness, or death. In a wage economy workers are dependent upon wages. Simplistic as it may sound, "out of work" means "out of wages." It is this risk which Workers' Compensation seeks to insure people against. Workers' Compensation became in 1902 one of the earliest social insurances in the United States when Maryland enacted the first state compensation law in which benefits were paid without proof of fault. In 1908 a program was enacted for federal civil service workers who were employed in hazardous work. By 1948 all states had enacted Workers' Compensation laws.

Previously, employee injuries (or death) were viewed as the responsibility of the employer. In practice, however, the worker had to prove injuries were due to employer negligence. In such a system workers were at a disadvantage because of the expense and other resources needed to challenge the employer.

It is easy to see why Workers' Compensation was the first system of social insurance in England, and even earlier in Bismarck Germany as well as in the United States. The earlier anarchic system meant that the worker was never sure of receiving compensation for work-related injury and, even if he or she did, this would come after long litigation. Thus the worker was not covered during the crisis period, and a good deal of the cost of the system went to pay attorneys. Even the employer had to live with an uncertainty principle because eventually there could be a very large liability settlement that could be injurious to him as well. Therefore both parties could see benefit in a no-fault insurance system, which is what Workers' Compensation is.

Many states exclude agricultural workers (some cover farm workers when power technology is used), domestic workers, and casual employment. Most states permit employees in exempt classes to be covered through voluntary action by the employer, sometimes with the required agreement of the workers. There is a trend toward inclusion of smaller firms, and most states do not exclude firms on the basis of size, increasing the numbers of eligible workers.

Injuries must not have arisen from the employees' gross negligence, willful misconduct, or intoxication. The worker who is disabled or, in the case of death, the worker's survivors, are eligible for benefits. There is no income or assets test. There is no responsibility by relatives in the situation.

Form of the Benefit

In order to compensate for economic loss suffered, loss of earnings, and expenses related to the injury and recovery, several types of benefits are provided. Cash benefits through periodic payments during the period of disability are paid to the injured worker or, in the case of death, payments are made to survivors including burial expenses.

Injuries result in combinations of temporary or permanent disabilities which are partial or total. A short waiting period for eligibility is often used to eliminate short duration cases and serves to decrease the cost of the program. It is assumed that sick leave or savings can cover the average worker through short crises.

Cash benefits are limited either by time or amount and the differences between permanent and temporary disabilities. Many states pay temporary total disability for as long as the worker is disabled. Some states have a maximum number of weeks for benefits which range from 206 to 500 for temporary disabilities. Some have maximum total payments which range from $10,750 to $65,000. For permanent total disability payments are made in 70 percent of the states for life. In other states payments are made for 300 to 650 weeks or up to $21,000 to $35,000. Survivors' benefits are provided to spouses until remarriage and the children reach particular ages.

Benefit amounts are based on the wage at the time of the accident or the onset of illness. Temporary total disability is usually compensated at two-thirds of the wage, up to a limited maximum. In some cases there may be duplication of benefits with OASDI (Old Age, Survivors, and Disability Insurance).

Medical services as needed both as to time and to amount of care also are provided as benefits. However, some states have limits on such care which can be extended under certain circumstances. Rehabilitation services also are provided in some states as well as maintenance payments during the rehabilitation period.

How Is the Program Financed?

The funding of Workers' Compensation is almost entirely borne by employers. In a few states employees contribute to medical care, and in some states contributions are made from general revenues to the Workers' Compensation fund. Several states have exclusive state Workers' Compensation insurance funds to which employers pay. About a dozen states have state insurance funds and private insurance funds, and employers select their preference. In most states there is no state fund, and employers are simply mandated to contribute to some private insurance fund.

In most states there is a penalty if an employer does not have insurance. In states where employers have the option, some large firms are self-insured. There is no federal government trust fund, and Workers' Compensation is dominated by private and self-insurances. Premiums are based on the size of the firm and the nature of the risk involved in the work. Firms are assigned experience ratings on the basis of the use of insurance funds by their employees. This rating is an attempt to introduce a degree of equity into the programs.

Level of Administration

Workers' Compensation is enacted through state laws and is state administered through state departments of labor or independent Workers' Compensation boards.

The national Occupational Safety and Health Act of 1970 was intended to provide workers with safe and healthy work conditions by setting standards and is thereby preventive. The act authorized a national commission on Workers' Compensation laws to evaluate the situation and to report findings and make recommendations.[2] As a result, the commission recommended compulsory coverage, no exemptions for small firms and governmental employees, coverage of all types of workers, coverage of all work-related diseases, and weekly cash payments at two-thirds of the gross wage up to a maximum weekly benefit equal to 100 percent of the average weekly wage in the state. In addition the commission recommended no limits for permanent total disability benefits or for medical services and

[2] Donald E. Chambers, "Reform of Workmen's Compensation," *Social Work*, Vol. 20, No. 4 (July 1975), pp. 259–265.

physical rehabilitation. These recommendations are indicative of a probably increased federal role in the Workers' Compensation system.

Analysis

As one can see, the Workers' Compensation system is a universal form of social insurance. There is no means or eligibility test based on the worker's income. It is viewed as an insurance and as a right by the injured worker. It represents an institutional kind of social service program, recognizing that some degree of injury is inevitable in an industrial system and seeks to provide a simple and equitable compensation for that eventuality. There are several principles that are illustrated by the Workers' Compensation system.

First, it is a basic no-fault system. No-fault has become very popular in recent years in auto insurance and is being discussed as a possible solution to medical malpractice and other areas where costs escalate. The no-fault concept can be understood as against the alternative: the liability concept. In the liability concept the person or institution which caused the injury or accident has to be determined. If there is *fault* or *liability*, then the faulty or liable party must pay damages to the injured party. In addition to paying for all the costs of the injury and making up for the loss, there also may be punitive damages for having been at fault. This is seen as an incentive for safety. In the no-fault system there is no attempt made to assess liability. The insurance simply covers the injury and its related costs, and there are no punitive damages. The advantages of no-fault insurance are immense. It eliminates a waiting period and uncertainty. It omits legal fees and litigation. It avoids massive punitive damages which may destroy a somewhat innocent party who was responsible for the accident.

The same arguments are made in auto insurance and the other areas mentioned. However, there are civil liberties purists and others who feel that the no-fault system and Workers' Compensation are unfair, that they deprive the citizen of a constitutional right to sue for damages. It also is argued that since the original enactment of Workers' Compensation, there are now public assistance and other vehicles by which the injured party can get temporary relief while waiting to go through the courts. Finally, some see no-fault as injurious to incentives to maintain safety. However, the majority view would seem to be that the current insurance system represents a dignified approach which serves the interests of the American industrial system best, and there is no major movement to change its basic form.

Another principle that is illustrated by Workers' Compensation is that when a system is financed completely by the employer, as is the case in most states, rather than by employer-employee contributors or by general tax funds, the employers (since they are the contributors) tend to have controlling interests in the regulatory boards and state commissions which govern Workers' Compensation. This has acted, according to workers' groups, to prevent the improvement of the Workers' Compensation system, has caused narrow definitions of what constitutes a work-related versus a nonwork-related injury, and so on. It is easy to understand why unions often support employer-employee contributions to systems, even though it costs the worker money: it gives the workers "a piece of the action."

If one may borrow phraseology from community mental health, it is possible to see the evolution of systems for workers' safety in the following ways. The original system of suing for liability is a tertiary kind of care for the injured party, giving rehabilitative relief well after the fact. Workers' Compensation represents a secondary level of care which is prompt, universal and more adequate. The Occupational Safety and Health Administration (OSHA) attempts primary prevention by creating the kinds of conditions in the industrial society where accidents are less likely to occur. OSHA has been criticized for focusing on petty matters rather than on major safety issues and on not fulfilling the original promise of the agency, but the concept of society's working to guarantee safe conditions has been challenged only by a few unreconstructed free enterprise purists who believe that the government should stay out of this area completely.

The major criticism directed against the Workers' Compensation system is its still incomplete horizontal adequacy. This gradually gets corrected as coverage broadens state by state. The system is also criticized on the level of vertical inadequacy. The maximums are now seen as too low in many states—hence the calls for maximums up to average weekly wage levels or other such formulas. There is some cost inefficiency in the determination of whether an injury is work related or not. This would be eliminated in a national health insurance plan which covered all medical care regardless of cause. Apart from such a development it is hard to see how this cost inefficiency can be eliminated. The total coverage of medical care makes it possible for doctors to prescribe whatever is necessary rather than to direct care to particular expensive or inexpensive areas. On the whole, Workers' Compensation is one of the least criticized social insurance systems in American life and one which has found broad acceptance, although the total medical coverage in a society which does not have this for other situations can lead to individual cases of abuse and exploitation of the system.

Workers' Compensation also is a good example of a state welfare system as opposed to a federal one, with all the problems and benefits therein. The problems come from great variations among states, with workers sometimes being unaware of what benefits they actually have, particularly if they move, and the lack of a large federal insurance pool. On the other hand, the fact that there are state variations has allowed progressive states to move faster than the nation might have moved as a whole.

UNEMPLOYMENT INSURANCE

Who Is Eligible?

Unemployment insurance is designed to provide regular cash benefits to normally employed workers for a limited period of involuntary unemployment. The first governmental unemployment insurance program created in Wisconsin in 1932 was the forerunner for inclusion of unemployment insurance in the Social Security Act of 1935. By 1937 all states, Alaska, Hawaii, and the District of Columbia had enacted programs, and Puerto Rico joined in the 1950s.

In 1972 almost 85 percent of wage and salaried employees were covered by unemployment insurance laws. An unemployed worker with prior wages in covered employment who earned a specified amount of wages or worked for a certain period of time in a "base" period is eligible. Other requirements are that the worker must be able to work, available for work, and free of any disqualification (such as voluntary separation from work, fired because of willful misconduct, or refusal of suitable work). Most states also restrict benefits for students, pregnant women, and individuals unemployed because of marital or family obligations. The question of benefits during unemployment due to a labor conflict is at issue in some states.

There is no assets test, and income from rents, dividends, or earnings of other family members are not used to determine eligibility. It is an insurance benefit available to all who qualify, regardless of their wealth: if you are laid off, seeking work, and unable to find it, you qualify for unemployment insurance. Unemployment insurance staff members in various states at various times vary in how much proof they demand of unemployed workers to demonstrate their having sought work each week.

Form of the Benefit

Cash benefits are provided on a variable basis dependent on a worker's wages earned during a "base" period with certain minima and maxima. Payments—qualified by the maximum and minimum amounts—usually are 50 percent of the worker's former weekly wage up to the maximum. The maximum duration of benefits is usually 20 to 36 weeks. During periods of high unemployment states may pay benefits to those who exhaust these basic entitlements. In such high unemployment periods, a federal-state program adds 13 weeks and then an additional period can be added, up to half the number of weeks of the regular benefit period (e.g., $\frac{1}{2} \times 20$ weeks = 10 more weeks). Some states pay small allowances for dependents, inserting an element of need into the benefit package. Most states regularly recompute benefit amounts based upon average wages paid in the state.

Several states have added a small tax to cover temporary disability which is not work related as well. This has been one of the "cracks" between social insurances through which some people fall, and this "crack" is covered by a very small tax. Additional benefits are made available in the form of free placement and counseling services for use by employers, veterans, and employees. Work training and retraining programs also may be available.

How Is the Program Financed?

Employers pay a tax on their total payroll. The federal share of the tax is earmarked for federal and state expenses for administering the program, for the federal share of a federal-state extended unemployment compensation program, and for repayable noninterest advances to the states when they run out of funds to pay the benefits. States receive back from the federal government the major portion, which is used for the payment of benefits. The tax is collected and deposited in the federal treasury in the U.S. Employment Trust Fund and invested, and each state is credited with its share of the interest. States draw as necessary for payment of benefits.

"Experience rating" was introduced to discourage "layoffs." Employers with good records, those who do not discharge workers, are given the benefit of lower tax rates on their payroll.

Level at Which the Program Is Administered

The unemployment insurance program is administered through the Manpower Administration of the United States Department of Labor. The collection of taxes is the responsibility of the U.S. Department of the Treasury. But states each administer their own benefit programs which vary somewhat by state.

Analysis

Unemployment insurance is a classic example of the grant-in-aid described in Chapter 4. The federal government never formally forced states to adopt unemployment insurance programs. The federal government simply legislated a payroll tax on employers throughout the nation. If the state wanted to get the bulk of those taxes back into the state, it had to follow the guidelines for receiving that rebate, namely, setting up a state unemployment insurance system. State programs vary in maximum benefits, number of weeks covered, and so on, but all must meet certain basic guidelines of the federal legislation. This is the grant-in-aid principle: money and guidelines come from one higher level, and the administration and some local initiative remains at the lower level. The incentive to get the grant-in-aid and not to lose the money for the state was so great that within two years of the establishment of the Social Security Act all states had enacted programs.

Unemployment insurance also may be seen as an example of the problems which arise when a program designed to accomplish one purpose is used for another purpose. Unemployment insurance is meant as a universal and institutional program of society to meet the reality that in such a society there will be temporary dislocation due to shifting market needs, new locations, and changes in the industrial system. Thus in the best of all economies some businesses should close, change, and move locations, and some workers therefore will be dislocated. Unemployment insurance is to give this small number of workers breathing space so that the labor market is not degraded and they are not forced to take the first available job at a lower level of skill. It protects the worker, allowing time to seek employment at his or her level. The worker, in reporting to the unemployment insurance office, must demonstrate the fact that he or she has sought work but cannot be forced to accept work in another area from that of prior employment.

The unemployment insurance reserves tend to build up in periods of high employment when there is little call on them by unemployed workers. Thus in the mid-1960s most liberal economists felt that the benefits should be raised considerably because the reserves were building up unnecessarily. However, with the rise in unemployment since 1970 unemployment funds have been drained, and the unemployment insurance system is being used as a quasi-welfare system. The public assistance program is so degrading with its means test and has such a stigma attached to it that there is great pressure on Congress to extend the benefits of unemployment insurance for longer periods of time when many normally nonwelfare people need this kind of help. But the unemployment insurance system was never set up to meet this massive need, and thus we find a great strain on the system today.

The unemployment insurance system also is a classic example of what is called a "countercyclical program." This term refers to the normal business cycle in capitalist or "free enterprise" economies. Normally economic activity moves up and down like a wave every few years, through periods of high economic activity (high employment and the danger of inflation) to periods of low economic activity (high unemployment and the danger of depression). The government sees its role as trying to reduce these waves, to take steps which will counter the normal business cycle, deflating the economy in times of boom and pumping up the economy in times of recession. Programs which automatically have this effect are called countercyclical. One such program is unemployment insurance. Some other social welfare programs also have the same effect. During a time of high employment, when there is an economic boom, little money is paid out of the unemployment insurance system since there is little unemployment; more money is squirreled away in reserve funds since more people are working and there are more payroll taxes to be collected. This taking of money out of the economy is a deflating move, flattening out the tendency for economic boom. On the other hand, when unemployment is high in times of recession or depression, the unemployment insurance system is collecting less funds since less people are employed and is pumping more funds back into the economy in the form of unemployment insurance benefits since more people are collecting. This money added to the economy serves to generate more economic activity. Thus the unemployment insurance system is seen as countercyclical.

Two principles are illustrated by the concept of experience rating, described above. Experience rating is a way of rewarding the "good" employer who does not lay off workers. This is supposed to serve as an incentive to keep employees on the job. However, it shows the strains in every insurance program between the insurance principle and the incentive principle. The whole concept of insurance is too pool or "socialize" a risk. For example, if there are 40 people in a class and the odds are that 1 person will break a leg during the year, each of the 40 contributes something so that whoever breaks a leg will have adequate compensation. However, if an analysis is made of the likelihood of each person's breaking a leg and the amount each person contributes is based on that, we no longer have a true insurance system but a system where each person is paying for his or her own care. Thus in health insurance, in auto insurance, and in the social insurances, experience ratings of specialized groups by age, sex, geographic location, race, prior experience, and the like tend to break down the whole concept of pooled risk. On the other hand, some people feel that if one were not to reward safe drivers and good employers, for example, with financial benefits, one would take away the incentives. There is no "right" answer to this balance. The trade-offs are constantly argued by economists and social welfare experts.

But experence rating is also an example of how latent or unanticipated consequences may undo the purpose of a program. As explained, experience rating was initiated to keep employers from laying off workers in order to maintain their lower insurance rates. However, it also may work in reverse. The concerned employer may not take on new employees or may lay them off before they have worked long enough to become eligible for unemployment insurance just to protect an experience rating. Thus the experience rating may produce just the opposite effect from that originally intended.

Those who evaluate the unemployment insurance program tend to give it high marks for its universalism and simplicity of administration. However, many feel that, as in the case in certain western European countries, the American unemployment insurance system should be tied more clearly to retraining and laborpower programs. After a certain number of weeks a worker should be eligible for continued unemployment insurance, perhaps even at higher rates, if he or she is willing to retrain in a new skill which is more needed by society than the one that produced the unemployment. West Germany has been particularly successful in using this approach to keep down unemployment. The United States lags behind most industrial societies in such programs for the unemployed, having opted in recent years for simply providing a limited number of jobs for the unemployed primarily in the public or not-for-profit sector. In fact, becoming a full-time student is "evidence" that the worker is not available for work and therefore ineligible for unemployment insurance.

SOCIAL SECURITY (OASDI)

Who Is Eligible?

The Social Security Act of 1935 was a watershed piece of legislation establishing several assistance and insurance programs, but when people refer to "Social Security," usually they mean Old-Age, Survivors, and Disability Insurance. Other programs have been added since. OASDI, which we will examine here, originally enacted in 1935 as old age insurance, is to replace some income which is lost to workers and their dependents when a worker retires because of old age, has a permanent or total disability which prevents substantial earnings from employment, or dies.

Over 90 percent of the nation's employed persons contribute to the OASDI program, and over 90 percent of the elderly either get monthly benefits or will be eligible for them when they or their spouses retire. Ninety-five percent of young children and surviving parents are eligible for payments. About 80 percent of persons 21 to 64 years of age are protected in the event of a breadwinner's long-term disability.

Details of the OASDI program, both in eligibility, benefits, and financing, have undergone numerous changes in recent years and continue to face changes. Some options are discussed in Chapter 11. Therefore, it is more necessary here than elsewhere to focus on the skeletal structure of OASDI rather than on specifics which may be obsolete by the time they are read.

To be eligible for retirement benefits a worker must be 62 years old or over with the required number of quarters of covered employment. If one retires before age 65, reduced payments are received. For disability coverage a person must be permanently unable to work, younger than 65 years, and (except for the blind) meet certain employment longevity requirements. Survivors must be dependents of dead workers who were insured at the time of death, a spouse age 62 or older, an unmarried child to 18, an unmarried child 18 to 22 who is a full-time student, an unmarried child over 18 if continuously disabled before reaching age 22, or a spouse at any age caring for a child under 18 or disabled.

Eligibility for benefits is universal and not related to wealth, assets, or unearned income. But since this is a benefit for those not working or those unable to work, there is a loss of benefits beyond a certain level of earned income. That is, a person can be eligible for full Social Security benefits if he or she earns up to a certain maximum per year. Beyond that maximum Social Security benefits are reduced $1 for each $2 earned. Congress has considered eliminating this limitation (and has for those over 70).

Form of the Benefit

Benefits are in the form of a monthly check. The amount ranges from a certain minimum to a maximum depending on how much the worker has contributed over a period of years. The formula has changed from time to time, but OASDI benefits have remained somewhat related to contributions. Beginning in July 1975 monthly payments have been increased on an annual basis whenever the consumer price index increased by 3 percent or more. This increase is automatic except where there has been enacted a general benefit increase in the current or prior year. Recently revisions have been made to create equity between husbands and wives if the spouse dies or retires.

How is the Program Financed?

OASDI is financed by a tax on wages paid by covered employees, by employers, and by the self-employed. This tax always has been a fixed percentage of the wage, up to a certain maximum. Serious questions about the financing have been raised for years and are discussed below, and in Chapter 11.

Level of Administration

The OASDI program is administered by the Social Security Administration of the Department of Health, Education, and Welfare. Organized on a federal basis, there are approximately 1250 offices located in various parts of the United States with a central record office in Baltimore, Maryland. Claims are reviewed in regional centers. The Treasury Department collects taxes, prepares checks, and maintains trust funds. Disability determinations are made by state agencies and reviewed by the Social Security Administration. The Social Security system is among our most cost-efficient programs, lacking a means test and administered centrally.

Analysis

The OASDI program is clearly a national and an institutional social welfare program. There is no means test, and everyone in the category is eligible for assistance. It is seen as a necessary and desirable element in society to provide some support for people who have retired or who have become totally disabled or for the dependent families of breadwinners who have died. It is viewed as a right by those who receive it and does not bear the stigma attached to public assistance and some other social welfare programs. Central to this psychology of acceptance of Social Security has been its contributory nature—that is, those who ultimately are to receive benefits are those who have, to some degree, made contributions to the system. Thus it has a feeling very much akin to private insurance, and beneficiaries feel that they are entitled to receive the benefits—that they are in a sense being repaid their own money. All of this has contributed to making Social Security our largest income transfer program and the bedrock of social insurance in the United States. At the same time it has led to some problems and a good deal of confusion, which the student should be able to dispel. The very word "insurance" can be confusing. We speak of a social insurance, meaning a welfare program designed to insure against a certain risk. But when most people speak of insurance, they mean some program with the characteristics of private insurance where one pays into the gradual building up of reserves and where benefits may then accrue from those reserves. OASDI is in some ways like an insurance program and in other ways very much unlike one. It is like an insurance program in that

1. It is contributory, that is, it is true that in order to receive benefits, one must contribute to the program.
2. Benefits are to some degree related to contributions—that is, people who pay very little get less in benefits than those who pay the maximum, and benefits are graduated along the scale from a very small minimal amount to the maximum contribution.

So Social Security is like insurance in that the more you pay, the more you get. However, in at least three equally (or perhaps more important) ways Social Security is not like private insurance and should not be confused with private insurance.

1. Benefits are not *exactly* related to contributions. Although benefits will increase for those who contribute more, it is not in a direct relationship. Because Social Security is a welfare program and an income program, benefits are skewed toward the bottom end; that is, people who pay very little, let us say 10 percent of those who are paying maximum, get a lot more than 10 percent of the benefit of one getting maximum. The person who's at the top of the heap in contributions does not get ten times as much in benefits. So that while benefits increase with contributions they do not increase in a way that would be "fair" in private insurance.

2. Social Security is not like private insurance in that the benefits are not due one by contract at the time of entering the program. The benefits are based on whatever the current legislation is and not on any insurance "right." This can work both to the detriment and to the benefit of the recipient. In the 1950s, during the height of the Joseph McCarthyite anticommunist hysteria, courts ruled that an avowed communist might be deemed ineligible for receiving Social Security benefits, even though he or she had contributed. At the same time, most Americans receive much more in benefits than they were originally promised when they began contributing, as legislation has changed and benefit levels have gone up. Thus one's benefits under Social Security are dependent on current legislation rather

than on contributed funds. In order to make this possible, it is necessary for there to be the third and most important difference between Social Security and private insurance.

3. Benefits are paid essentially from current funds received rather than from reserves. In a private insurance system the company may set aside a reserve fund to get started, but eventually the funds collected from contributors must be calculated to be sufficient to pay benefits as they are claimed by beneficiaries. Not so with Social Security. Funds contributed in the past by those now collecting Social Security would be insufficient to meet the current benefit levels. While there is a small reserve fund which helps to meet sudden emergencies and fluctuations, essentially the benefits that are being paid to current recipients are the receipts from those who are *now* paying Social Security taxes. When those now paying Social Security taxes are eligible for Social Security they will depend for their benefits on legislation which will be forcing those *then* working to contribute to the system. It is only in this way that benefits could have increased as they have, but the fact of not having a massive insurance reserve does frighten some people when they think of Social Security in terms of private insurance. In order to make Social Security work that way it would demand such a massive reserve as to drain vast amounts of money from the American economy. The backing of the Social Security system, however, is not weak—it is the legislative power of the U.S. Congress, the power to tax, whether that tax is euphemistically called a contribution to an insurance system or one that goes to the general revenues.

A continuing argument about Social Security has to do with the concept of minimal versus optimal levels. Social Security was never intended as a full retirement system; it was seen as a way of supplementing people's savings, private insurance, and union pension plans. Increasingly current retirees do have other assets to draw on, but there remain many elderly who have no other insurance program, and the minimum level of Social Security benefit is too low to maintain adequate living standards for most people. To improve the minimum benefits to the point of adequacy would seem burdensome to taxpayers who resist having massive amounts of money spent for universal programs, because some of this would go to the rich who have other forms of income and do not need this higher minimum. However, not to improve it condemns many elderly to unrelieved poverty. The compromise has been to supplement Social Security minimums, where there is no other income, with a means test program, formerly called Old Age Assistance and since the 1970s known as Supplemental Security Income, which is discussed below. Thus the problem of vertical adequacy, at least at the minimum level, is somewhat covered. With the improvements in Social Security coverage since its inception in 1935, horizontal adequacy is good and almost all workers are covered today.

The most serious argument in recent years has been over Social Security's form of financing. Social Security, as we have pointed out, is not really an insurance program. The contributory form has been very valuable in affording it dignity and giving people a sense of right of entitlement to benefits, which may be incalculable in value but has been high in price. It also has meant that the Social Security system is in reality a social welfare program financed by a most regressive tax. To recapitulate, the OASDI program is financed by a fixed percentage tax on the wages of employees, by a similar tax on employers of their employees' wages, and by a tax of approximately 1½ times this amount on the self-employed. All of this is up to a fixed maximum, which has been raised from time to time over the years. However, these two components—a fixed percentage tax and a tax only up to a maximum—have added up to regressive taxation. So long as the person earning $3000 per year and the person earning $20,000 per year are both paying, let us say, a 6 percent tax for Social Security contributions, this is regressive, since 6 percent of the poorer person's tax is much harder for him to afford than 6 percent of the higher income worker's tax.

A progressive tax, as explained in Chapter 4, is one in which the percentage of contribution goes up with income. However, the second feature makes the tax even more regressive. If the maximum taxed income is, let us say, $25,000 per year, then someone earning $100,000 per year is paying the same total tax to Social Security as the person earning $25,000. This compounds the regressivity of the Social Security system. So long as the system is contributory and so long as benefits are related to contributions, some regressivity seems inevitable. To raise the level of contribution to an unlimited amount would make it necessary also to raise benefits exceedingly, beyond the intent of the Social Security system for the higher income person. Numerous ways around this problem have been suggested, from raising the maximum base of amount taxed for the employer share only, so that benefits for the workers do not have to be raised, to infusing the Social Security system with some partial relief from general revenues which would make it more progressive, even while keeping the contributory system as a base. This is discussed further in the options in Chapter 11, and laws are changing so rapidly that by the time the student reads this book the system may have changed dramatically. But the basic question of the equitable financing of the Social Security system is likely to continue to be an issue whenever the student reads this material, and so the factors should be clear.

Another problem with the Social Security system is its coherence with other social policies. If we are moving toward an age of automation, then we might want to be pushing for earlier retirement benefits. On the other hand, if we need all the laborpower we can get, then the availability of retirement at age 62 and at full funding at age 65 might be incompatible with this policy. Social Security policy has to be related to our approach to employment. When a law is passed raising the age at which mandatory retirement is legal or laws are passed making any mandatory retirement illegal, this has an impact on the Social Security system.

Latent Consequences

Social Security is another one of those social welfare programs which have countercyclical consequences. That is, in times of high employment fewer people will be retiring so that less benefits will be pumped into the economy and more Social Security taxes will be taken out of the economy from working people. When unemployment is high more people will retire and therefore more benefits will be paid out while less money comes in.

The advent of Social Security also has had tremendous consequences for the development of leisure time activities, the culture of retirement. The fact that the benefits are national rather than local has led to the possibility of retirement communities. For example, if I am in a state system, I may have to stay in the state, but if the benefits are mine wherever I go, then I can move to warmer states or to places where living costs are lower. This mobility has been a consequence of the Social Security system. In fact the availability of benefits no matter where the beneficiary goes has led a number of people to emigrate after retirement to countries where the cost of living is lower. Social Security has contributed to helping older people form perhaps the most powerful lobby in the nation and to establish a political system where Social Security is almost sacrosanct in terms of the levels of benefits. This is the most dramatic example we have of the degree to which universal social welfare systems tend to be improved even while selective ones may be cut.

PUBLIC ASSISTANCE

To this point we have examined programs which are "insurances," but there are a number of means-test economic security programs as well. In this section we will review public assistance programs, commonly called "welfare."

Aid to Families with Dependent Children (AFDC)

WHO IS ELIGIBLE?

AFDC is designed to encourage the care of dependent children in their own homes or in homes of relatives by enabling states to provide financial assistance, rehabilitation, and other services to dependents in need and to the parents or relatives with whom they are living.

Given impetus by the 1909 White House Conference on the Care of Dependent Children, mothers' pensions to enable widows and deserted women to care for their children were first enacted statewide in 1911 by Illinois and spread quickly to 19 states by 1913. Aid to Dependent Children (the original title) was enacted in 1935 as part of the Social Security Act to provide financial assistance to needy children under 16 years of age who were deprived of parental support because of the death, incapacity, or absence of a parent.

Today children must be either under 18 or under 21 and attending school, lacking parental support, and needy. Some states provide benefits when the father is unemployed (AFDC-UP). Some states provide emergency assistance to needy families.

There are income and assets tests, exempting the value of food stamp coupons, commodity distributions, relocation assistance, and undergraduate grants and loans. Recipients must register for labor-power services, training, and employment as required by the U.S. Department of Labor. Earned income less a certain amount (for example, the first $30 of a household's earned income and one-third of such income over $30) is not counted to determine the amount of the cash benefit. Incentive payments, portions of child support payments, and work expenses may be disregarded. But essentially people need to be devoid of both income and assets to be eligible for AFDC support.

FORM OF THE BENEFIT

Benefits include cash payments varied by family size and the need for employment training and placement and public service employment, day care for children of work incentive program participants, family planning services, establishing paternity and securing support from parents, reuniting families, improving housing and money management, protective services for children, and foster care, health, consumer education, rehabilitation, and legal services. Food stamps are available, as is Medicaid.

Benefit levels may vary extensively from state to state, depending on how much money the state will put toward a federal match.

HOW IS THE PROGRAM FINANCED?

States match funds, with local participation optional, on the basis of formulas: the federal grants may range from 50 to 65 percent based upon the relation of average per capita income in the state to the average per capita income of the United States with maximum amounts on the federal share. These funds come from the general revenues.

LEVEL AT WHICH THE PROGRAM IS ADMINISTERED

Based upon the concept of local responsibility for the destitute, states have developed general assistance programs for persons with emergency needs and/or persons ineligible for federally subsidized programs, such as Aid to Families with Dependent Children (AFDC) and Supplemental Security Income (SSI) for the Aged, Blind, and Disabled. The basic eligibility requirement is need, which varies in definition by state and even within some states by particular governmental jurisdiction. These programs are means tested, and there is no income which is disregarded; many states require registration with the employment service. Most states have relative responsibility rules, mainly husbands for wives or vice versa and parents for minors. Some states also consider adult children responsible for their parents and make siblings and grandparents and grandchildren responsible. A number of states have residency requirements.

FORM OF THE BENEFIT

The Social and Rehabilitation Service of the Department of Health, Education, and Welfare administers grants to the states. Some states administer the programs through state agencies with district and county offices. Other states administer the programs through local agencies which the states supervise. This is a grant-in-aid under which the state receives the money from the federal government if it matches the grant by the necessary percentage and meets certain guidelines (for example, having family planning services, having procedures for appeals or fair hearings, and trying to locate fathers who have deserted).

General Assistance

WHO IS ELIGIBLE?

Benefits range from cash payments to free groceries and shelter in emergency situations. Some states set maximum amounts which can be given to those assisted; sometimes these limits are based upon the availability of funds. Medical care may be provided. Transportation may be offered to return a person to place of residence; burial is provided for indigents. Food stamps and commodities are usually benefits tied to this program.

HOW IS THE PROGRAM FINANCED?

Using general tax revenues, the general assistance programs are financed by state funds, combinations of local and state funds, and in some locations only local funds support these programs.

LEVEL AT WHICH THE PROGRAM IS ADMINISTERED

General assistance programs are administered by state public assistance departments on a local level, by local governmental jurisdictions supervised by the state, or by local governments alone. Most common is administration on a county basis. There also are combinations of county and city administrative organizations.

Supplemental Security Income for the Aged, Blind, and Disabled

WHO IS ELIGIBLE?

The SSI program enacted in 1972 and implemented in 1974 established a national program for the aged, blind, and disabled which replaced state-administered, federally reimbursed programs for the aged (OAA), aid to the permanently and totally disabled (APTD), and aid to the blind (AB), formerly part of the grant-in-aid public assistance program. There are means and assets tests, although there are exclusions; that is, it is possible to be eligible in spite of some limited assets or income, and both earned and unearned income are considered as well as the income of other family members. There is no work requirement. There is no provision for relative responsibility, except for an ineligible spouse or parent of a child beneficiary residing in the home with the recipient.

FORM OF THE BENEFIT

Cash benefits are paid on a monthly basis. Automatic benefit increases are provided when Social Security cost-of-living increases are put into effect. Vocational rehabilitation services are available for blind and disabled recipients under age 65. Drug addicts or alcoholics are referred for treatment when it is available. Referrals are made to other social agencies where indicated. SSI beneficiaries are also eligible for Medicaid in almost all states. With few exceptions, the states make SSI recipients eligible for food stamps.

When SSI began the national level of support was higher than most state benefits for OAA, AB, and AD. However, several states were paying higher benefits than the SSI national level. To prevent reduction of income when persons were transferred from state programs to this national program, states were encouraged to supplement SSI payments. For new and old beneficiaries the intention was to make benefits comparable to those paid in the states by the earlier public assistance programs. Several states still supplement SSI payments, but it is combined administratively to one check for the recipient.

HOW IS THE PROGRAM FINANCED?
All costs of the benefits and administration of the federal SSI programs are funded through monies from general federal revenues.

LEVEL AT WHICH THE PROGRAM IS ADMINISTERED
The Bureau of Supplemental Security Income of the Social Security Administration manages the SSI program through regional and district offices located in many parts of the nation. The Social Security Administration may contract for state or local agencies to administer SSI operations for it.

Analysis

The public assistance program is at the heart of what is commonly referred to as "welfare" or the "welfare problem" or the "welfare mess." Society often is depicted as needing to protect itself against a horde of unwed mothers and other "cheats" striving to live off the public dole. This kind of image is probably inevitable given the kind of program that public assistance is. Interestingly enough, Aid to Dependent Children started in 1935 as a method of keeping mothers in the home to prevent family breakup and to spare mothers from the necessity of having to work. Today, except for very young children, a major component of the program is to encourage mothers to go to work and to get off the public dole. Thus the same program has altered to meet changing values and priorities in society.

There is probably no way in which the stigma and the ugliness can be completely removed from a massive means test program such as AFDC. If there were more social insurances, such as children's allowances or family allowances or less unemployment or other means by which the rolls could be reduced dramatically, it might be possible to develop a more humane system, but this is not an immediate prospect. If the program became very humane and benefit levels were generous, then critics might be correct in saying a point could be reached where this would be destructive to work incentives.[3] On the other hand, the alternative is the principle of least

[3] David Macarov concluded after a review of the literature on the effects of unearned income that no one knows currently exactly which factors lead some persons to become hard workers and other not. David Macarov, "Work Without Pay: Work Incentives and Patterns in a Salaryless Environment," *International Journal of Social Economics*, Vol. 2, No. 2, 1975, pp. 106–114.

eligibility, discussed in Chapter 2—that people on public assistance should not do as well or better than the least eligible, lowest paid working person. The problem is that the person working for a minimum wage may not be supporting a large family while some welfare mothers are.[4] Separation of the wage system from the need system is necessary to make a welfare program humane, but this is impossible with the current means test program.

In Chapter 4 we began to discuss the issue of the separation of services and eligibility determination. Up to the 1960s, the idea was that when one sought public assistance one would be deemed to be needing social services and this would be handled by the same worker who handled the determination of one's eligibility for financial assistance. This concept was eliminated. Welfare recipient organizations did not want their financial need criteria to be interpreted as proving emotional or other disabilities, nor should it be. However, in the course of separation, services tended to become denigrated or lost altogether, and the separation of the two today is not as strict as it was in the 1960s.

Some states allow the working poor to get public assistance supplementation, but again the principles of the program make for impossible situations. For instance, in one state workers may have been on strike. During the course of that time some people may have become so destitute as to be eligible for public assistance. When the strike is over and they go back to work, people on public assistance, because of the formula of disregarding the first part of income and then disregarding parts of additional income, might still be eligible for public assistance. At the same time, other workers who never became eligible for public assistance, earning the same salary and in the same family situation, are not eligible.

General assistance to some degree and in some form probably will be necessary in the best of societies. No matter how tightly one tries to develop a social insurance system, there are likely to be emergency situations and people needing temporary assistance who fall between the cracks of the system. Perhaps because it is handled on the local level, general assistance is very often inadequate. But to some degree it will always be with us.

SSI is an interesting forerunner of what may become a federalized public assistance program. In the early 1970s there was a move toward a national assistance plan, a little bit like a negative income

---

[4] Martin Rein has pointed out the necessity of coordinating income support programs, economic policy, and labor market conditions, particularly the nature of the low-wage job market. "Equality and Social Policy," *Social Service Review*, Vol. 51, No. 4, December 1977, pp. 565–587.

tax. When this proposal failed, Congress was able to take the less controversial parts of public assistance—the categorical sections of aid to the aged, disabled, and blind—and to federalize this program. This occurred because there is not the same kind of pejorative picture of these categories as there is of welfare mothers nor are those categories so large in size. With the blind, the disabled, and the aged, society seems to be more willing to accept the fact that continued public support at some level will be necessary.

In any event, SSI is a good forerunner of what welfare would be like if AFDC were federalized as well. The level of aid is higher than it was in the average state, although not as high as the highest states were paying. SSI's more humane and reasonable approach permits people to have some minimal assets before becoming eligible, but fundamentally it is simply public assistance on a federal level rather than on a state one. This makes little difference to the client and to the benefit of society but relieves states of a major burden and transfers this burden to the federal government. This might be the major impact of a federalized public assistance program for AFDC as well. In any event, AFDC benefits are often inadequate both horizontally and vertically, and yet in the states where AFDC is very low there is little inclination by society to raise benefits significantly. On the horizontal side, there are large numbers of potentially eligible people who never reach AFDC because of shame, ignorance, or roadblocks put in the way of their applying. The government is very concerned and has many programs to reduce the number of persons ineligible enrolled but does not have an equally firm program to bring onto the rolls all those who are eligible. AFDC is the classic example of cost inefficiency because of the massive problem of means testing and the administrative cost and effort that this entails. It is financed as equitably as possible under our tax system and is a highly necessary program, with all its faults. But the consequences of this primitive form of welfare and the absence of family allowances are stigma, cheating, indignities, wasted money, and a growing permanent welfare class.

Something needs to be said about the extent of welfare cheating. The system does, as has been said above, promote this kind of activity, and yet in the popular press and in the minds of most Americans, cheating is much more widespread than in reality. Before the 1970s numerous surveys and spot checks always found the rate of cheating somewhat under 4 percent, which is as low as one can expect in such a massive program and probably a lot less than the amount of cheating that is done on income tax returns and other forms of middle- and upper-class illegal advantage-taking of governments. But there has been a feeling that with the rise of welfare rights and the growing awareness by citizens of their entitlements that people have been more willing to take advantage of the system and that the number of persons ineligible is much higher as well. There probably has been some rise, but again the evidence is that it is much less than popular accounts would suggest. In the first half of 1977 a quality control survey of the New York City system, supposedly one of the worst areas for cheating, found that 8.6 percent of AFDC cases were ineligible, 21.1 percent were overpaid, and 12.3 percent were underpaid—high, but not astronomical. But even these figures are misleading, because much of the ineligibility and overpayment is "categorical" and "technical" rather than substantive. For example, if a supposedly absent parent is found living with the AFDC recipient, the case is marked ineligible for AFDC, but in reality if the man is not working the family is still eligible for public assistance under the general assistance program. Similarly, if the youngest child in the case is over 6 years and the mother has not registered with the State Department of Labor for possible work, the case is marked as an overpayment, but if the woman does register to work the likelihood of her finding it is infinitesimal and she would receive the same benefit.

If we exclude these categorical and technical errors we find that only 4.8 percent of the AFDC recipients are actually ineligible for any public assistance and 13.6 percent are overpaid, not much more than those who are underpaid. All told, these percentages are probably a lot lower than the percentage of eligibles in the population who never find their way to public assistance. The myth of millions of able-bodied men on the public assistance rolls is simply that—a myth.[5]

Nonetheless, it is true that the acceptance of cases as eligible seems to be related to political and social trends as much as to economics. A point made by Piven and Cloward in *Regulating the Poor*[6] is that in the 1950s when there were two major recessions and massive migration of blacks from the South to the North the welfare rolls rose minimally. In the 1960s when the economic situation was vastly improved and unemployment was down and the migration had tapered off, the welfare rolls exploded and rose astronomically. This was part of the new spirit of entitlement and welfare rights and of

[5] The above figures come from "A Report on Welfare—New York City" prepared by Herb Rosensweig, deputy administrator for income maintenance, and Martin Burdick, assistant deputy administrator for income maintenance, New York City Human Resources Administration, November 1977, mimeographed.
[6] Frances F. Piven and Richard A. Cloward, *Regulating the Poor: The Functions of Public Welfare*, New York: Vintage Books, 1971, pp. 190–191.

the politics of unrest which together produced a public response and a sense of responsibility (or some might call it political payoff) which the Democratic Party felt toward its major constituency, the urban centers in the United States. It has been pointed out that the rate of applications for welfare might remain constant over a period and the only thing that would change the welfare rolls would be the rate of acceptances which would vary with the political winds. And so, while a massive depression will swell the welfare rolls, public assistance may vary as much with political climate as with economics and, in fact, sometimes in good economic periods the public may be more willing to share its bounty with the poor than in periods of fiscal tightness.

The point has been made by some that SSI could be removed from public assistance altogether instead of simply being federalized if (1) the money spent on this program were contributed from general revenues to the Social Security system and (2) the Social Security minimum simply became the SSI minimum. The problem with this is that Social Security, being universal, would also give this minimum to people who had other income. However, most of the people on the minimum level of Social Security are people who are generally poor and who do not have other sources of income—the same people who are applying for SSI. The only massive group which makes this alteration impractical is civil service system employees who have their own pensions after 20 to 25 years and then "double dip" by working for a minimum period in other employment and becoming eligible for Social Security benefits in addition. If these public employees' pension systems were merged with Social Security, the SSI level could probably become the Social Security minimum, eliminating a means test program and probably costing the taxpayer not much more than at present.

MEDICARE

Who Is Eligible?

In the mid-1960s two massive economic security programs related to health were introduced: Medicare and Medicaid. The Medicare program originated to cover some hospital and medical expenses of the aged. In 1972 disability insurance beneficiaries and patients with chronic renal (kidney) disease were included as eligible. There is no income or assets test. When one reaches 65 years, one is eligible for Medicare hospital insurance. If one elects to contribute to it, one then also is eligible for Medicare medical insurance.

Form of the Benefit

Under Medicare–Hospital Insurance (HI), hospital and post hospital services are provided. Payment is made to the providers of the service: hospitals, health maintenance organizations, skilled nursing homes, and home health providers. Inpatient hospital care is provided up to 90 days, and a beneficiary becomes re-eligible for an additional 90 days following a period of 60 days during which no hospital services were received.

Medicare–Supplemental Medical Insurance (SMI) provides benefits such as health services from physicians, certain supplies, outpatient hospital services, home health services, diagnostic tests, and prosthetic devices. Payment is made to the beneficiary or to the provider for 80 percent of the excess of a "reasonable" charge for a particular service, beyond a deductible amount.

How Is the Program Financed?

Medicare (HI) is financed by an earmarked payroll tax paid half by the employer and half by the employee. Self-employed persons pay a tax on their earnings. Some persons who reached 65 years before 1975 and were not fully entitled to Social Security are served and financed out of general federal revenues. Others can enroll by paying a monthly premium, recomputed annually. The basic payroll tax is integrated with the Social Security tax and, in fact, the full title of Social Security is now OASDHI, Old Age, Survivors, Disability, and *Health* Insurance.

Medicare (SMI) is financed half by monthly premiums paid by those in the program and half by general federal revenues. The premium usually is deducted automatically from Social Security benefits. Participation is voluntary.

Level at Which the Program Is Administered

The Social Security Administration of the Department of Health, Education, and Welfare administers Medicare (HI) with the assistance of other federal and state agencies and intermediaries such as Blue Cross and private insurance firms which determine the amount of payments and process claims. Medicare (SMI) also is administered by the Social Security Administration with the assistance of "carriers" such as Blue Shield plans, commercial insurance companies, and group practice prepayment plans.

MEDICAID[7]

Who Is Eligible?

Medicaid serves needy families with dependent children and persons who are aged, blind, or permanently and totally disabled. States which choose to offer this program must provide Medicaid for AFDC, SSI recipients, and selected other persons (for example, children under 21 in foster homes or institutions for whom public agencies provide some financial support). The program is means tested, although asset limits may be higher for those who are medically needy than for those who are categorically needy. Only spouses of the person needing medical care or the parent of the individual (if the person needing medical services is under 21 or is permanently and totally disabled) are held responsible.

Form of the Benefit

There are no cash benefits for beneficiaries; payments are made to the providers of services. The benefits are in-kind medical care services, and individual need determines the amount of service which will be provided. Rehabilitation services to attain or retain independence or self-care also are provided. Amount or level of benefits vary from state to state.

How Is the Program Financed?

From general federal revenue funds, monies are provided on an open-ended basis to the participating states. The federal government pays a certain percentage of the amount spent by the states as Medicaid, based on a formula which considers state per capita income. The federal government also funds a percentage of the cost of paying and training professional medical personnel and program support staff, facility inspectors, management information systems, and other administrative needs. The states pay the difference in cost between federal outlays and total program costs.

Level at Which the Program Is Administered

The Social and Rehabilitation Service of the Department of Health, Education, and Welfare administers grants provided to the states of

[7] Because Medicaid is operated on a state level, certain variations in the title exist, such as Medi-Cal in California.

from 50 to 83 percent of the cost. In almost all states the same agency administers public assistance and Medicaid, and the state must pay the balance of the cost. In several states the department of health is responsible for the program administration, and one state has a Medicaid commission.

ANALYSIS

It is important for students to understand the differences between Medicare and Medicaid, and Table 6-1 may help.

The problems with Medicare and Medicaid and their adequacy are the classic problems of selective and universal programs. Medicare, which is universal, has excellent horizontal adequacy for the aged, at least in the automatic hospital insurance portion, but its benefits are limited and often run out for the elderly, forcing them to use up their limited assets until they become eligible for Medicaid. Medicaid is vertically more adequate, at least technically, because just about all kinds of medical care and services are covered, but it is not as adequate horizontally since it is means tested and one has to prove poverty in order to be eligible. Even the vertical adequacy of Medicaid is affected by the degree to which all programs for the indigent become "poor programs" and in the degree to which the poor are provided sloppy or mass-produced medical care. It is also related to the form of the delivery of health care and payment for health services in the third-party payment system as described below.

The equity of funding of the two systems is also similar to the

Table 6-1 DIFFERENCES BETWEEN MEDICARE AND MEDICAID

	MEDICARE	MEDICAID
Who is eligible	All aged for hospital insurance. All aged who contributed for medical insurance	All needy, as per means test.
Form of benefit	Partial hospital and medical service.	All medical services.
Funding	Payroll tax on employers, employees, and self-employers for hospital coverage. General revenues match voluntary contribution for medical insurance.	General revenues from the federal government with a share of the cost from the general revenues of the states.
Administered	National, using various insurers to process claims.	Grant-in-aid; federal guidelines, state variations, and administration.

differences between Social Security, which is universal but is funded by a regressive tax, and public assistance, which is selective but is funded from more progressive general revenues. Medicare and Social Security have each had one instance where general revenues have contributed to the so-called insurance: in Social Security this happened when people over 72 years were blanketed into minimal Social Security coverage whether they had contributed or not; and in Medicare this occurred when people over 65 years were blanketed in who had not been covered by Social Security taxes. Health insurance is certainly a high priority item of the use of social welfare dollars. Whether it is being spent in the most logical or organized form is a matter of great concern.

Latent Consequences

The latent consequences of this system are many and were not all anticipated. When Medicare first came into being there was a great rush to build hospital beds to alleviate what was then a major shortage. This was because Medicare paid for inpatient services and not for outpatient services—itself a strange phenomenon. The final result is an "overbedding" of the hospital system in many parts of the United States which is very hard now to contract because there are so many vested interests in maintaining hospitals once they are built. Any kind of limited health coverage will have as a latent consequence a run on that kind of coverage. For example, if you were given a choice of buying insurance for bandages or for catastrophic illness, you would tend to buy insurance for catastrophic illness and assume that you will cover the bandages yourself. But then if you become ill, you and your physician will tend to have you treated in the way in which you are insured, which may be the catastrophic way rather than the bandage way, thus causing a run on the most expensive services of all and increasing health costs. Another latent consequence which led to the escalation of health costs is in the third-party payment system described in Chapter 4. For all of these reasons, Medicare and Medicaid are now evaluated as critical stopgaps in meeting health needs but as inadequate to a rational system of health insurance for the nation, and alternatives are discussed in Chapter 11.

Chapter 7
Current Social Welfare
Programs—Part Two

"Social welfare looks to a society where each individual
has available to him the means of satisfying his needs and
a framework of community in which each member supports
and aids the other in achieving their individual and
collective goals."[1]

It is impossible to describe all the public programs in social welfare.
A listing of the federal programs alone covers several pages. This
listing for 1977 is included as an appendix at the end of this chapter
to give the reader a sense of the vast range. Here we describe briefly
some important additional programs beyond those discussed in
Chapter 6.

FOOD STAMPS

Who Is Eligible?

This program was enacted in 1964 to alleviate hunger and malnutrition in low-income households and to replace a surplus foods distribution program. It replaced a program set up not so much to meet

[1] Elizabeth Wickenden, "Developing Social Policy in Conditions of Rapid Change:
The Role of Social Welfare," *Developing Social Policy in Conditions of Rapid
Change*, New York: International Council on Social Welfare, 1973, p. 20.

the problem of hunger as to support farm prices. It has grown to become a major economic security program since then. There is an income and assets test. Eligibility is based on income. Public assistance families are eligible and other families on the basis of their assets, monthly net income, and size. Food stamps are given without charge to victims of general or individual disasters such as the destruction of a home. Able-bodied family members from 18 to 64 years of age must be registered for work at the state employment service office and must accept suitable job offers.

Form of the Benefit

Low-income persons receive food stamp coupons of specified amounts. They then use the coupons like cash to purchase most foods from participating stores. Alcohol or tobacco products may not be purchased. Housebound persons can use coupons for Meals-on-Wheels. Plants and seeds can be purchased in order to grow food. Unemployed recipients of food stamps also receive employment services when they are registered for them.

How Is the Program Financed?

The entire cost of benefit payments is met by the federal government from general revenues. Administrative expenses are met through the federal share of 50 percent, and the remainder is financed by state and local governments. Indirect payments are made to vendors of coupons and to food outlets.

Level of Administration

The Food and Nutrition Service of the U.S. Department of Agriculture administers the program through the states and the counties in the states. State welfare departments administer the program with overall supervision by the U.S. Department of Agriculture. Until 1973 it was optional for counties to participate. Now all areas must participate unless it is impossible or impractical to do so.

Analysis

The food stamp program is a good example of a program not particularly favored by social welfare experts which becomes harder to eliminate as it grows. To begin with almost all social welfare planners would have preferred to use the money involved in financing the food stamp program to increase general welfare benefits in one way or another. This is seen as more dignified and without the administrative expenses involved in setting up a food stamp operation. However, as the program grew each year and as more poor people came to depend on it, it became harder for people concerned with the poor to oppose the food stamp program because it seemed to be a choice between food stamps or nothing. Thus many welfare programs get locked into the system, although to begin with they may not be the most logical way of helping. Food stamps offer the kind of selective program which not only lacks fairness and dignity intrinsically but which forces the recipient to parade dependency in stores and wherever a purchase is made. The food stamp program lends itself to all the abuses inherent in eligibility rules. During the early years of the program, college students often took advantage of the food stamp program in spite of having parental resources. They simply established an independent residence and became eligible for food stamps. Current work requirements have tightened eligibility requirements, and the cheating in food stamps, as in other welfare programs, has been exaggerated by the media. Still food stamps remain a major and troublesome program, and from time to time schemes are projected to "cash out" the value of the food stamp program in other forms of welfare benefits for the poor.

Food stamps are only the largest of a plethora of government-assisted food programs, including lunch programs in the schools, nutrition programs for the elderly, and food programs in summer camps. There are so many special programs related to food that there is a whole field of expertise in writing government grants for food programs, coordinating food programs, picking up the overhead for food programs, and the like. There also have been some scandals connected with the private vendors who have been the purveyors of various food programs. These programs are among the areas, such as nursing homes for the elderly, where the private sector has insinuated itself as a go-between between the government and the needy, and this compounds some of the problems.

HOUSING

Who Is Eligible?

A number of public programs are designed to provide housing for low-income families and to assist in the purchase or rental of housing. Among these programs are Low-Rent Public Housing, Home Ownership Assistance for Low-Income Families, the Rent Supplement Program, Interest Reduction Payments, Lower Income Housing Assistance, Low to Moderate Income Housing Loans, Rural

Rental Housing Loans, Farm Labor Housing Loans and Grants, the Indian Housing Improvement Program, and Housing Repair Assistance for Low-Income Families. All the above are means- or income-tested programs. In addition, there is housing assistance for veterans which is not means tested, and guaranteed mortgage loans, which have made it possible for millions of middle class people to purchase homes.

Form of the Benefits

Among the benefits of the various programs are the following: low rental charges through federal assistance to local housing authorities; insured mortgages and monthly interest subsidies to the mortgage lender on behalf of lower income families; rent supplement payments equal to the difference between fair market value rental for particular housing and a percentage of the family income; low-cost rentals subsidized through low-interest mortgages; payments to owners in order to assure rentals at particular levels; insuring loans to families to buy, build, improve, or relocate homes; insured loans to farmers and associations of farmers to provide adequate housing at reasonable rents; and grants to native Americans to repair, renovate existing housing, or provide new housing. Counseling and technical assistance are sometimes available.

How Are the Programs Financed?

These housing programs are financed from federal general revenues, special insurance funds, closed-end appropriations, rental excesses over costs deposited to special funds, loans, a revolving rural housing insurance fund, and the like.

Level of Administration

Several housing programs are administered by the Department of Housing and Urban Development through area offices and local public housing authorities. The U.S. Department of Agriculture through the Farmers Home Administration administers housing programs for rural families and domestic farm laborers through state and county government and with county committees appointed by the Secretary of Agriculture. The Bureau of Indian Affairs of the U.S. Department of the Interior through area offices administers the Indian Housing Improvement Program. The Veterans Administration housing program is administered through regional offices of the Department of Veterans Benefits.

Analysis

Among those who believe that housing is an appropriate social welfare area, there is a continuing debate between those who favor vouchers or other systems to make private housing and the open market available to the poor and those who believe in public housing, housing developments, and similar projects. The former argue that major housing developments have tended to re-create slums, and to resegregate people and are expensive to maintain and that it is a lot simpler simply to provide dollars for the poor to make them eligible to live in decent housing. Although these arguments are persuasive, the voucher forms or rent supplements are not without problems either. Their existence tends to drive up housing rentals so that their benefits can be wiped out, and it has been very hard to develop ways of administering such programs without various forms of corruption. Actually, the record of housing developments in "projects" is mixed, and some have been quite successful while most publicity goes to the major big-city, high-rise public housing projects which re-create slum conditions. It is important to remember that the major effort in housing social welfare has been the effort which has helped the middle class through mortgage guarantees and loans to move into private housing and the federal government has expended much more on this over the past 30 years than it has on public housing.

SERVICES OF THE VETERANS ADMINISTRATION

The Veterans Administration operates a vast array of social welfare programs for veterans and their dependents. Veterans are entitled to a limited income maintenance program based on need, a kind of public assistance program besides the public assistance program. Many have suggested that this particular veterans' benefit became anachronistic as public assistance programs improved, but they still are available to many. Hundreds of thousands of veterans have taken advantage of special low-interest loans in order to secure mortgages to buy houses. Life insurance programs are available to veterans at low rates as well. But the two most massive and well-known veterans' programs are the educational programs, commonly known as "the GI Bill," and the health programs and hospitals administered by the Veterans Administration. Congress changes the educational benefits under the GI Bill from time to time, and therefore we will not provide details about them here. Fundamentally, the program simply provides reimbursement and some general support for the veteran for a given amount of time after service in the armed forces in order to improve vocational possibilities. A variety of educational programs are permitted. As discussed earlier in this book, after World War II the GI Bill was one of the major factors in the upgrading of the American work force and the prevention of a disruptive depression upon the discharge of millions of veterans in 1945 and 1946. In recent years veterans' benefits have become less adequate compared to the cost of tuition and maintenance, and some have argued for their improvement. Others have said that there is no reason why special benefits should be limited to veterans if, as seems to be the case, this has benefited the American economy so greatly.

The Veterans Administration operates a network of hospitals throughout the country. All veterans are eligible for completely free and comprehensive health benefits for any service-connected disability. For any health problem which is not service connected, or for health problems of dependents of veterans, these medical services are also available, but only upon a statement of financial need. What is interesting is that in contrast to the rest of the American health system, the Veterans Administration medicine is a true form of socialized medicine. There are no third-party payments or the like. Doctors and other staff are salaried, and all medical care is available for the eligible veteran. Evaluations of this system differ. They can hardly be compared to a socialized system because the salaries have to be affected by what the going rate is in the private sector. While Veterans Administration facilities have been criticized for a variety of defects, on the whole the hospitals are not considered to be less adequate or poorer than other medical systems in the United States, and the system has been of great benefit to thousands of people. If the United States moves to national health insurance, the question of how veterans' medicine would be integrated in such a plan is a major one.

Veterans are also eligible for a variety of other benefits from free burial to special appliances based on disability. The astute social worker always will want to know if the client needing help or a member of the family is a veteran because, depending upon the period during which the person served, the benefits might be worth looking into and might prove helpful.

EMPLOYMENT PROGRAMS

The employment services connected with unemployment insurance were referred to earlier. Apart from these, there has been a developing series of what used to be called manpower programs and increasingly are being called programs for human resources. The War on Poverty in the 1960s saw the development of the Job Corps and Neighborhood Youth Corps and some employment programs administered by the business sector. There have been increasing attempts to put the various employment programs under one umbrella, and at this writing most public service employment or publicly funded employment is under the umbrella of CETA, the Comprehensive Employment and Training Act. Through a formula allocated to states and then to communities CETA provides federal funding for hiring unemployed workers for positions in government or in nonprofit, voluntary agencies to perform a public service. This, as so many welfare programs, was originally seen as temporary, with people phasing out of that employment after about 12 months, but the nation has become increasingly dependent on some public service employment programs for the support of the public services and as an aid in reducing unemployment. Although the titles and varieties may change, it seems likely that public service employment of one kind or another will continue to be a major social welfare program. Other smaller employment programs continue to exist side by side, such as federally funded work-study programs for needy college students.

A little publicized but important employment-related program, which is operated through the states with federal funding, is vocational rehabilitation. Under this program, people with various disabilities are eligible for support and educational benefits for education and training programs which are calculated to make them more likely to be self-supporting and to develop career lines. There is some discretion in the definition of disability: during the 1960s people who were culturally or educationally disadvantaged were often included among those eligible for relatively generous vocational and rehabilitation benefits. The eligibility requirements have tightened since then, but vocational rehabilitation is still an important welfare program of which social workers should be aware.

The federal government also provides limited support for training programs and for students in a number of occupations, including social work.

CIVIL SERVICE RETIREMENT PROGRAMS

The United States Civil Service Commission Bureau of Retirement administers a federal civil service retirement system. This is funded by employer and employee contributions, and cash benefits are paid to retirees due to age or disability and to survivors under certain conditions. The federal government in 1934 mandated a similar system based on the Railroad Retirement Act for railroad employees. In 1974 some integration of this program with the Social Security program was developed by Congress and includes some contribution from federal general revenues. However, a major problem in reforming the Social Security system is the fact that beneficiaries of the civil service retirement program may engage in "double dipping," that is, they may retire from civil service after the required number of years while still relatively young; they may then put in a minimum period under Social Security-covered employment and on retirement collect both the Social Security minimum and their civil service pensions. Reform plans for the Social Security Administration often suggest integrating these two programs. The Department of Defense administers a similar military retirement program for the armed forces, as do many local and state public employee systems.

The above material can only discuss the major programs and can only mention a sampling of the hundreds of publicly assisted programs in all the areas mentioned. Catalogues are constantly written and changed to help people stay abreast of social welfare entitlements. In the absence of a single unitary system, programs crisscross, overlap, or are unknown to potential beneficiaries. Specialists use these manuals to assist clients and to help various organizations and agencies seek funding, under grant or contract programs, for some of the entitlements. From education to disaster relief, from housing to food programs, the social welfare system today is a very large business enterprise.

PERSONAL SOCIAL SERVICES

Historically five major social welfare or human service systems have been identified: education, income maintenance, health, housing, and employment/laborpower. Recent comparative international studies have led to the identification of a sixth system—the personal social services—with a long tradition but which now appears to be coalescing into a coherent system to meet the normal anticipated social needs which arise in modern industrial nations.

According to Alfred Kahn and Sheila Kamerman,[2] the personal social services are available outside of the market based on need, demographic category, or status, not on the ability or lack of ability to purchase the service. The functions of the system are contributing to socialization and development, facilitating information and access to services and entitlements, assuring basic levels of social care, counseling and guidance, supporting mutual aid and self-help efforts, and integrating and coordinating services for maximum effectiveness.

[2] Alfred J. Kahn and Sheila B. Kamerman have been most active and influential in defining the personal social service system in international perspective. The following discussion is based on their book *Social Services in the United States*, Philadelphia: Temple University Press, 1976.

In order to integrate the Kahn-Kamerman schema with what has been presented above, we should point out that of the five major social welfare systems outside of the personal services identified, this volume has excluded a discussion of the educational system. Although it is part of the broadest definition of social welfare, discussed in Chapter 4, we have not discussed it because it is in another functional and professional domain. Income maintenance, health, housing, and employment programs have all been discussed above, and some people would consider them all part of the economic security program system as opposed to the personal service system, although this is actually too sharp a distinction. As we now look at the personal social services the point must be made that some of them are integrated into some of the above systems, that is, counseling or employment programs may be tied to public assistance. We also will discuss mental health, although in another sense it is part of the health system.

Form of the Benefit

Among the benefits provided within the personal social services are information and access to services and entitlements, social care (practical help such as personal care and hygiene for those unable to perform particular care for themselves, home health care, homemaker services, shopping and escort services, friendly visiting, and telephone reassurance services), counseling and guidance, self-help and mutual aid services, and maximized effectiveness of services for citizens through integration and coordination. Other benefits include family planning, information and referral, family counseling, adoption and foster care, child guidance, nursing and other residential care, rehabilitation of the handicapped, probation, group socialization services, certain mental health services, education and medical or industrial social services. Generally benefits may be grouped as for child care and other child welfare, family counseling and mental health, services to the aging, and generalized information and referral.

Who Is Eligible?

Some personal social services are available on a universal basis and do not require a means test. For example, protective services against child abuse are available to all. Community or senior citizen center programs may be available to all who seek them. Title XX of the 1974 amended Social Security Act defines limits of eligibility for various benefits. A struggle was waged and won so that older people who joined senior citizens centers funded by Title XX need not go through an individual means test. However, the locations of the centers are supposed to show concern for meeting the needs of the poor. Other personal social services require a diagnostic, assessment, or other determination of need and eligibility. This latter group includes such services as medical or psychiatric treatment and child guidance.

Fees may be charged for consumers of the service on the basis of income or may be available free to all who have a particular status, for example, use of the library or an information and referral service by residents of the town.

Title XX, now the largest single source of funding for personal social services, does define income ceilings for eligibility for most services. These ceilings are higher than ceilings for welfare eligibility and therefore move the personal services beyond income maintenance in their availability. Still, the selective concept remains.

How Is the Program Financed?

Different means of funding support the personal social services. In the public sphere, services are supported by tax funds with— depending on the particular program level—money provided by the federal, state, or local government or in combination from two or more levels in the form of grants. In the private sphere sources of income include membership and user fees, grants, bequests, purchases of service, third-party payments, and donations which are tax deductible. Title XX of the Social Security Act, Title III of the Older American Act, and various titles under mental health provide most federal funding. The overwhelming majority of social welfare funds, even in personal social services, comes from the public sector.

Level at Which the Program Is Administered

There is no central coordinating organization to give direction to the personal social services. There is overlap between types of services within the system, public or private auspices, funding patterns, and the like. Services may be administered locally and relatively autonomously or by the state, or in combinations of national, state, regional, and local authorities through umbrella organizations. Title XX mandates an annual state plan for the personal social services offered. Increasingly, states and localities purchase services from voluntary social agencies or private vendors.

Because their domains and categories are somewhat unclear, we offer a brief description of mental health and correction services.

MENTAL HEALTH SERVICES

Who Is Eligible?

Mental health services are designed to promote and maintain mental health, prevent mental illness, and treat and rehabilitate mentally ill persons. Mental health problems range from severe impairments which require hospitalization through behavior which is mildly impairing to the search for personal self-fulfillment.

Mental health facilities include hospitals, both public and private. One can either voluntarily commit oneself or be involuntarily committed for treatment on the basis of a court order. Thus some mental health patients choose to enter hospitals while others are coerced into treatment or custody. Upon discharge from a hospital, aftercare is often provided for discharged patients in a local community facility.

Half-way houses and other outpatient services are provided for those who are reentering the community or need less than total hospitalization. Community mental health clinics, both public and private, provide a variety of services, including emergency services, diagnosis, treatment, referral, and community education and coordination.

In 1963 the Mental Retardation Facilities and Community Mental Health Centers and Construction Act created federally funded community mental health centers.

Some people are served by specialized mental health facilities for child guidance, married couples, persons with drug and alcohol problems, senior citizens, and the mentally retarded. Schools provide mental health services for students both typical and untypical including persons with developmental disabilities, the emotionally disturbed, and those with learning disorders.

Form of the Benefit

The benefits received in mental health programs are diagnosis, treatment in the hospital or the community, long-term or emergency consultation, professional care, and educational services in the community.

How Is the Program Financed?

Nationally mental health services are funded by the Health Services and Mental Health Administration (HSMHA) through the National Institute of Mental Health (NIMH), both of which are components of the U.S. Department of Health, Education, and Welfare. Funds are provided to subsidize local mental health services, especially community mental health centers. State departments of mental health or health operate statewide networks of mental health services, sometimes purchasing services from private facilities within their own state or others where necessary. Mental health services are sometimes financed by state departments of education through special education programs. User fees also provide some funds, often on a means-test basis and with sliding scales for clients or patients based on income.

Federal funds are available through formula-matching grants for building public community mental health centers, improving hospital patient care, increasing the effectiveness of mental hospital staffs, rehabilitating narcotic addicts, defraying costs of professional and technical personnel in new or expanded services, conducting research, and developing laborpower programs. Many health insurance plans do not include or provide minimal benefits for mental illness or mental health services. The community mental health centers have been funded in an eight-year pattern during which federal support is supposed to phase down and state and local funds are supposed to pick up the slack. In some states this has occurred; other centers have sought new special grants from Washington, D.C., or have cut services along with declines in federal support.

Level at Which the Program Is Administered

The Health Services and Mental Health Administration administers funds federally through NIMH for mental health services, often in grants of aid to states and localities. Other mental health programs are supported by the U.S. Department of Housing and Urban Development, the Law Enforcement Assistance Administration, the Veterans Administration, the Office of Vocational Rehabilitation, and the Department of Defense, among others. A large number of professional associations are involved in mental health services on both national and local levels, as well as organizations such as the National Association of Mental Health, a voluntary organization. In addition to the federal scope of programs administered by the above public agencies, state and local governments administer mental health systems in every state.

CORRECTIONS

Who Is Eligible?

The Massachusetts Bay Colony built a jail in Boston in 1632, adding a correctional alternative to fines, lashing, branding, and mutilation. By 1655 every county in the colony was ordered to erect a correctional house for drunkards and petty offenders. Correctional facilities have a long history in the United States. Today youth and adults become eligible for correctional services by being convicted of violating federal, state, county, or city laws or being found to be in need of supervision.

Form of the Benefit

Ostensibly correctional services have the intention of rehabilitation of the offender. However, in reality, rehabilitation is not the major thrust of the correctional system today so much as incarceration and punishment. Some say rehabilitation as a goal has proven to be an illusion and should be discarded in favor of crime deterrence. Others claim that rehabilitation has never really been given an adequate trial. Nevertheless, there are correctional services which aim at rehabilitation. Probation is a service in which offenders are investigated to enable the court to make a disposition of the case on an informed, individualized basis. Probation also includes treatment while final action in regard to an offender is suspended. The offender remains in the community under conditions imposed by the court, under the supervision of a probation worker. Probation workers use the resources of the community to assist the offender to become rehabilitated.

Parole is for offenders who have served some time in a correctional facility but who are released into the community under supervision and treatment by a parole officer.

Jails are county custodial institutions where violators are held for sentences less than a year for a misdemeanor or for short periods of detention. Prisons are correctional institutions where persons are detained for longer than a year and are state or federal institutions.

Community correctional services include release programs, treatment centers to reintegrate offenders into the community, work release programs, halfway houses, diagnostic parole (offenders screened routinely for eligibility for parole soon after court sentencing), therapy, counseling, and assistance with training, employment, housing, and other life problems.

Some jails and prisons offer services such as basic adult education, vocational training, alcohol and drug addiction programs, group and individual counseling, job development, and placement services.

Certain juvenile delinquency programs sponsored by the Social Rehabilitation Service of the Department of Health, Education, and Welfare provide diagnosis, treatment, rehabilitation, and prevention services to delinquent and predelinquent youth and develop community-based alternatives to imprisonment.

While sociologists and writers have lately despaired of rehabilitation as a goal of corrections, most people are agreed that jails tend to reinforce criminal attitudes. Therefore, the tendency is to support the idea of incarceration only for the "hardened" criminal as both a deterrent and as a protection to society and to use various community-based programs (such as probation, parole, and the others mentioned above) for the "nonhardened" criminal. Therefore the social welfare system is likely to continue to interact with corrections in a growing way in the coming years.

How Is the Program Financed?

The federal Bureau of Prisons and Board of Parole funded by general revenues is part of the Department of Justice. State and local correctional programs are funded by state and local jurisdictions from general revenues and from federal funds. The Law Enforcement Assistance Administration (LEAA) created by the Omnibus Crime Control and Safe Streets Act (1968) provides funds for recruitment and training of corrections personnel, improvement of correctional facilities, and programs for the rehabilitation of offenders. State and local governments provide matching funds under various formulas. Thus there is a mix of funds from several governmental levels in state and local programs. Funds are also available under the Juvenile Justice and Delinquency Prevention Act (1974) to prevent juvenile delinquency, to divert juveniles from the traditional correctional system, and to provide community-based alternatives to juvenile detention and correctional institutions. Block grants are based on each state's child population.

Although not precisely part of the correctional system, the Social Security Act also provides funds for programs for Persons in Need of Supervision (PINS) and children in need of supervision (CHINS)— people who have committed acts which are not illegal for adults but are offenses for children such as truancy and not accepting parental control.

Level at Which the Program Is Administered

The Office of Law Enforcement Programs, which administers the grant program on a federal level and assists state and local authorities in the correctional field, and the Board of Parole and Bureau of Prisons administer federal programs. The Department of Defense also administers a correctional facility program.

State and local governments operate their own facilities and programs. There is no overall coordination of the several levels of correctional programs, and facilities and combinations of state and local correctional programs take many forms.

Summary

General trends in the past decade can be discerned in the personal social services, as summarized by Neil Gilbert.[3] Increasingly the provisions of the benefits have moved from being intangible and limited to concrete, defined, and rather diversified services. Similarly there is a drift toward contracting with the private sector with public monies. There also is a trend in financing from the application for individual grants by various agencies and localities to the availability of funds on the basis of a formula by state or other population entity, and planning tends to be more decentralized than centralized. These last two trends are very much related to the development of revenue sharing under the Nixon Administration and the availability by formula of blocks of money to states and localities for local planning. Whether this has been good or bad for the social services is very much a debatable question[4]—whether it applies to the issues and decentralized versus centralized planning discussed in Chapter 4, or to the question of whether a fair formula can be found and monies can be granted to states without getting diverted to other than social services. Gilbert also sees a trend from the selective to the universal. While the provisions of Title XX certainly raised the maximums for eligibility, it is very much in question whether the War on Poverty and tighter eligibility for Medicaid, and Food Stamps do not signal the reverse. Certainly in policy discussion there has been a trend away from talking about universal children's and family allowances to more selective income maintenance programs.

PRIVATE PROGRAMS

Who Is Eligible?

Private, voluntary social welfare agencies provide services for people who have experienced almost every human risk: loss of job, poor mental or physical health, low income, or inadequate housing. They provide preventive, rehabilitative, and fulfillment services. Private agencies are sponsored under both sectarian (religious) and nonsectarian auspices. They offer services based on the needs of the local

---

[3] Neil Gilbert, "The Transformation of Social Services," *Social Service Review*, Vol. 51, No. 4, 1977, pp. 624–641.

[4] Robert S. Magill has pointed out in "Federalism Grants-in-Aid, and Social Welfare Policy" (*Social Casework*, Vol. 57, No. 10, December 1976, pp. 625–636) the negative effect on social welfare of local control and decision-making. From July 1, 1973, to June 30, 1974, all local governments ($N = 34, 487$) spent 2 percent of total revenue-sharing funds for social services. Of cities reporting for the same entitlement period ($N = 16, 763$), only 1 percent of revenue-sharing funds went for social services.

community and neighborhood services directed at particular groups (such as blacks, Catholics, Jews, women, or the retarded). Services are dependent upon the context and history of the community and the agency itself Programs often are offered on a fee-for-service basis on a sliding scale according to income or on membership or user fees. Some private services, such as American Red Cross disaster relief or Salvation Army services, are offered on demand without fee. Increasingly, as private agencies administer public programs, the public regulations for eligibility apply. In business and industrial settings, social welfare services are available for the employees and sometimes for spouses and children.

Form of the Benefit

The total range of social welfare is present among private, voluntary agencies, and a significant number and type of benefits are distributed in relation to the workplace. Pensions of varying natures are provided by many business and industrial concerns so that long-term economic security is provided in the work arena as well as in the public sphere. Private pensions and union pensions are a significant economic force, and the federal government has established rules to protect the rights of contributors. In addition, benefits found in workplaces are health, medical, and hospital insurance; food, recreation, library, and other facilities; counseling, referral, and mental health services; drug abuse and alcohol treatment; day care; and physical health services. Blue Cross and Blue Shield are the giants among private health care systems. Other health plans provide not just reimbursement but also prepaid comprehensive health care.

Voluntary agencies emphasize, to a greater extent than public agencies, services for social development such as youth services and recreation. On the other hand, voluntary agencies since the Great Depression are involved to a much lesser degree than public agencies in economic security, being limited generally to short-term emergencies or supplementing public funds in special situations.

Voluntary agencies directly or as vendors of publicly mandated services provide food (hot lunches), housing (nursing homes and homes for the aging), homemaker and home help services, rehabilitation, mental health services, child welfare services, and a host of other benefits such as services for military personnel and their families (Red Cross), rehabilitation (Good Will Industries), skills training (Lighthouse for the Blind), family planning (Planned Parenthood), general services to merchant mariners (United Seaman's Service), and emergency aid (Salvation Army).

Community centers and settlement houses provide multiservices including community development, adult education, socialization, and recreation. Hospitals and ancillary organizations provide a range of medical and health care services. Health and welfare councils coordinate voluntary agencies and their services in a community. The United Way or similar organizations raise money for distribution to the social agencies in a city or region.

Industrial concerns may hire social welfare personnel to deal with problems of alcoholism among executives, or general social services, hiring the disabled or retarded or former prisoners. Unions may support social services under their auspices.

One form of benefit in private agencies is the role of the volunteers who give to the agencies but also receive benefits (although not money) from their roles as decision-makers at several levels and as service-providers, fund-raisers, advisers, and the like.

Nader-type consumer organizations police and criticize the government in the social welfare area or help to make clients aware of entitlements.

Fraternal organizations, religious organizations, business groups, unions, hometown associations (*landsmanshaften*), foundations, and other social groups often provide welfare services of various kinds to their members and to communities from the local to the national level. There is a growing recognition of the need to support the "natural helping systems" in a community—from the value of self-help groups like Alcoholics Anonymous to training bartenders in the diagnosis of depression and the referral of depressed persons.

Financing

Private, voluntary social agencies are funded in several ways: private contributions, memberships and fees for service, funds from private central organizations (for example, the United Way or the Federation of Social Agencies), and sometimes payments from governmental sources in the form of subsidies, goods, purchases of service, third-party payments, and grants. Contributions to private welfare agencies are tax deductible, a factor which supports the diversity of voluntary agencies and services. Local affiliates of national organizations help through dues or other fees to support their national umbrella organizations such as the YMCA, Boy Scouts, Girl Scouts, Jewish Community Centers, Catholic Charities, Family Service Association of America, and the Child Welfare League.[5]

[5] According to one estimate the assets of the private social welfare sector—nonprofit organizations—in 1973 were approximately $578 billion or about 15 percent of the U.S. private national wealth. See Burton A. Weisbrod, "Some Collective Good Aspects of Non-Government Activities: Not-For-Profit Organizations," Madison, Wisconsin; Institute for Research on Poverty. Reprint Series. No. 312, 1978, p. 168.

Administration

There is no overall organization which administers or coordinates private social welfare agencies, although the national private agencies do act in concert to protect their interests. Organizations can be established on the local, state, regional, and national scene; national or lower level organizations may be formed of local agencies. There are various degrees of autonomy for social agencies ranging from rather complete autonomy (with the exception of responsibility and accountability to the state through incorporation and guidelines). to control by a council or national organization. Apart from their incorporation by state authorities, some local organizations are influenced strongly by their national leadership organization, others—much greater in number—have much autonomy in relationship to their national organizations, and the relationships are more subtle. In each case at every governmental level, private social welfare agencies are legally responsible to a governmental body and therefore never entirely free agents. In fact, the administrative ties between public and private agencies have become ever more complicated as new funding patterns have complicated the sense of autonomy which once existed in voluntary agencies.

THE WAR ON POVERTY

As suggested in Chapter 3, what we now call the War on Poverty of the 1960s was in fact the third war on poverty in American history. However, because it is recent, and because there is so much controversy about its effects, it is worth a separate discussion here at least in terms of the specific social programs or movements which were spun off by it.

The War on Poverty and its leaders in community action programs around the country adopted many of the tactics and slogans of a radical tide in America at the time. There were confrontations, sit-ins, and demonstrations. However, if by radical we mean a fundamental restructuring of the social order and by conservative we mean leaving the social order alone, then the War on Poverty was an essentially conservative program. It mandated no fundamental new income maintenance programs. Our social welfare structure is still based on the Social Security Act and the second war on poverty in the 1930s rather than on any new developments in the 1960s. In fact, one may argue that by focusing on local issues, the War on Poverty deflected from a true radical perspective. The biggest change in the social welfare system in the 1960s came through the adoption of Medicare and Medicaid, which were outside of the War on Poverty.

Expectation and Delivery

If there is one criticism of the War on Poverty on which most analysts agree, it is that the expectations engendered by the promises were far beyond anything the program had the capacity to deliver.[6] Some people see this as not all bad, because it created a sense of entitlement which has carried over and expanded the welfare state beyond the 1960s. On the other hand, that gap between expectation and delivery may have been in part responsible, along with the Vietnam War, for some of the violence characteristic of American society in the late 1960s. Perhaps Aaron Wildavsky has put it best:

> A recipe for violence: promise a lot; deliver a little. Lead people to believe they will be much better off but let there be no dramatic improvement. Try a variety of small programs, each interesting but marginal in impact and severely underfinanced. Avoid any attempt at solution remotely comparable in size to the dimensions of the problem you are trying to solve. Have middle class civil servants hire upper class student radicals to use lower class Negroes as a battering ram against the existing local political systems; then complain that people are going around disrupting things and chastise local politicians for not cooperating with those out to do them in. Get some poor people involved in local decision making only to discover that there is not enough at stake to be worth bothering about. Feel guilty about what has happened to black people; tell them you are surprised they have not revolted before; express shock and dismay when they follow your advice. . . . Alternate with a little suppression. Mix well, apply a match and run.[7]

Nonetheless, poverty did decline from the early sixties to the mid-1970s and expenditures for social welfare did rise dramatically. One can argue about how much the War on Poverty was responsible

[6] Robert J. Lampman has pointed out the escalation of goals which accompanied the War on Poverty: " . . . even the successes have been called failures by reference to newer and higher goals which have tended to emerge almost before the ink is dry on the old ones. Eliminating income poverty is not enough; income inequality must be modified. Improving expenditures for goods and services going to the poor is not enough; they must be effective, efficiently managed, and equitable. Allowing the poor to participate in decisions about how to allocate a small part of the nation's anti-poverty budget is not enough; they must be assured full participation in all matters that affect them, and rivals for leadership of the poor must have a chance to be heard. . . . some of this escalation of goals is evidence not of failure but of the problems of success. But some part of this tendency may be put down to failure to make the goals more specific and limited at the outset." From "What Does It Do for the Poor?—A New Test for National Policy," *The Public Interest,* No. 34, Winter 1974, pp. 66–82.
[7] Aaron Wildavsky, quoted in Daniel P. Moynihan, *Maximum Feasible Misunderstanding,* New York: The Free Press, 1969, inside cover page.

for these developments.[8] But there were at least seven developments out of the War on Poverty which may be seen as permanent legacies to the social welfare system of that activity and movement.

1. Involving the community in decision-making. "Maximum feasible participation" was a phrase little understood by Congress when it voted for the Economic Opportunity Act, the basis for the War on Poverty, but it is a dramatic illustration of the power of practitioners, guideline writers, and bureaucrats. They were able to give to this phrase dramatic meaning by demanding the participation of the poor in the governance of community action programs. Out of this has come a concept of community involvement which is so much part of social welfare today that the younger student will find it hard to imagine the degree of change. Before the mid-1960s it simply would not occur to social welfare planners to ask residents or local leaders if a new hospital or center should be placed in their community. The degree of community control over such decisions which is desirable is debatable, and we discussed this in Chapter 4, but most people agree today there should be some community input and involvement. This general acceptance was something which grew directly from the activities of the War on Poverty and its successor programs, all of which have made some demand for community involvement and input on decisions affecting clients.

A latent consequence of the involvement of local people in community affairs for the War on Poverty was the training and emergence of indigenous leadership which has grown beyond the locality. There are governmental leaders in Washington, D.C., and elsewhere whose training came on the local level from the civil rights movement and the War on Poverty during the 1960s.

2. Similarly, the client's right to know and to gain access to information grew dramatically with the War on Poverty. Before the War on Poverty, welfare organizations would have to plant "spies" on the staffs of social service organizations to photocopy pages of welfare manuals so that clients could learn of their entitlements.

[8] Robert Haveman in a review of poverty and social policy in the 1960s and 1970s concluded that "while planned antipoverty policies have been responsible for some increase in the productivity and earnings of the poor, other changes also contributed to poverty reduction. . . . Given the remarkable increase in social welfare spending, the income-conditioning of numerous public programs, and the reduction in the incidence of income poverty over the decade, the hypothesis that the full impact of the war on poverty is no larger than its direct effect on the incomes of the poor seems unacceptable." Robert H. Haveman, "Introduction: Poverty and Social Policy in the 1960s and 1970s—An Overview and Some Speculations," *A Decade of Federal Antipoverty Programs: Achievements, Failures, and Lessons,* Robert H. Haveman (ed.), New York; Academic Press, 1977, pp. 8–9.

Today the right of access to information is taken for granted, as well as the legitimacy of client brokerage and advocacy as a social service.

3. Through the Head Start program, with all its failures, has come a great impetus for increasing day care availability and, secondarily, as a latent consequence it contributed to the development in the women's movement of the concept of women's right to work. Another latent consequence of the Head Start program was a vast improvement in preventive dental care, which was legislated as part of that program.

4. There has been a major change in the concept of legal services which grew out of one of the programs of the War on Poverty. Previously legal services for the poor tended to be seen as defensive only. That is, if a poor person was being sued or tried on a criminal charge, legal services meant the availability of a defense. But out of the War on Poverty came the idea of offensive action or class action by lawyers on behalf of the poor and underprivileged, who could take the initiative in demanding certain rights and entitlements and call for changes in regulations through the courts. Although legal services go through ebbs and flows of greater or lesser activism and legislation has limited its role from the active one in the late 1960s, a broadened concept of legal services for the poor is now an accepted fact.

5. Through the Job Corps and other job-creation programs, the War on Poverty helped to develop an acceptance upon the part of the American people and a consciousness that public service employment is probably for the foreseeable future a necessary part of the American economy.

6. Through the Vista Corps, which followed up on the previously successful Peace Corps under John F. Kennedy, the War on Poverty established the fact that there is a human reservoir of idealism and a willingness for vountary action that could be mobilized on behalf of social issues.

7. The New Careers movement encouraged the use of paraprofessionals, and indigenous members of the community served as workers in human services. Career ladders were established, and ties were made to community colleges for many of the poor. The concepts are still part of social welfare planning.

For all of the above reasons, the War on Poverty, in spite of its lack of a major legislative landmark which has become a permanent part of the American social welfare system or of any other restructuring, has made a series of important contributions to social welfare in America and to its services.

This and the previous chapter have acquainted the reader with a broad range of social welfare programs in the United States and an understanding of them based on the concepts of social welfare presented in Chapter 4. From here on we will look at social work as a profession in the institution of social welfare. Then in Chapter 10 we will examine some of the trends in American society which are likely to affect social welfare in the future. Finally, in Chapter 11 we will consider suggested alternatives to some of our current social welfare programs so that the reader can apply analytic capacities to the elements of choice and decision-making.

The following appendix is described in the opening paragraph of this chapter.

APPENDIX TO CHAPTERS 6 AND 7 FEDERAL TRANSFER PROGRAMS— 1977

CONSOLIDATED LIST OF PROGRAMS AND OUTLAYS BY AGENCY[1]

	MILLIONS OF DOLLARS
ACTION	
Foster Grandparent Program	40
Senior Companion Program	9
Volunteers in Service to America	23
Total	72
AGRICULTURE, DEPARTMENT OF	
Agricultural Stabilization and Conservation Service	
Cotton Production Stabilization Payments	108
Dairy and Beekeeper Indemnity Payments	4
Federal Crop Insurance	67
Feed Grain Production Stabilization Payments	228
Rice Production Stabilization Payments	135
Wheat Production Stabilization Payments	111
Wool and Mohair Payments	8
	661

[1] This list of programs and outlays by agency is taken from William J. Lawrence and Stephen Leeds, *An Inventory of Federal Income Transfer Programs: Fiscal Year 1977.* White Plains: The Institute for Socioeconomic Studies, 1978, pp. 207–214. By permission.

MILLIONS
OF DOLLARS

Farmers Home Administration
Emergency Loans	0
Farm Labor Housing	7
Farm Operating Loans	0
Farm Ownership Loans	0
Low to Moderate Income Rural Housing Loans	0
Rural Rental Housing Loans	0
Rural Self-Help Housing Technical Assistance	6
Very Low-Income Housing Repair Loans	5
	18

Food and Nutrition Service
Child Care Food Program		115
Food Donations		28
Food Stamps		5,474
National School Lunch Program		2,204
School Breakfast Program		191
School Milk Program		177
Special Supplemental Food Program (WIC)		248
Summer Food Program		195
		8,632
	Total	9,311

CIVIL SERVICE COMMISSION
Civil Service Disability Pensions		1,694
Civil Service Retirement Pensions		6,370
Civil Service Survivors Pensions		1,205
Federal Employment for Disadvantaged Youth		105
Retired Federal Employees Health Benefits		433
	Total	9,807

COMMERCE, DEPARTMENT OF
Economic Development Administration
Economic Adjustment Assistance		30
Economic Development—Public Works		171
Local Public Works Employment Program		520
	Total	721

COMMUNITY SERVICES ADMINISTRATION
Community Action		346
Community Economic Development		50
Community Food and Nutrition		29
Emergency Energy Conservation Services		242
Senior Opportunities and Services		11
	Total	678

DEFENSE, DEPARTMENT OF
Military Disability Retirement		980
Military Nondisability Retirement		7,233
Military Survivors Benefits		120
	Total	8,333

	MILLIONS OF DOLLARS
HEALTH, EDUCATION, AND WELFARE, DEPARTMENT OF	
Alcohol, Drug Abuse, and Mental Health Administration	
Alcohol Community Service Programs	56
Community Mental Health Centers	79
Comprehensive Services Support	132
Drug Abuse Community Service Programs	159
Mental Health—Children's Services	18
	444
Health Resources Administration	
Health Professions—Student Loans	20
Nursing Student Loans	23
	43
Health Services Administration	
Community Health Centers	229
Comprehensive Public Health Services—Formula Grants	95
Crippled Children's Services	98
Family Planning Projects	121
Health Maintenance Organization Development	39
Indian Health Services	245
Indian Sanitation Facilities	35
Maternal and Child Health Services	241
Migrant Health Grants	32
National Health Service Corps	26
	1,161
Office of Education	
Basic Educational Opportunity Grants	1,461
Educational Opportunity Centers	3
Higher Education Act Insured Loans	484
Higher Education Work-Study	250
Incentive Grants for State Scholarships	32
National Direct Student Loans	12
Special Services for Disadvantaged Students	20
Talent Search	5
Upward Bound	39
	2,306
Office of Human Development	
Developmental Disabilities—Basic Support	32
Head Start	468
Native American Programs	42
Nutrition Programs for the Elderly	209
Rehabilitation Services and Facilities— Basic Support	733
State and Community Planning and Services for the Aging	140
Vocational Rehabilitation for Social Security Beneficiaries	93
	1,717

MILLIONS
OF DOLLARS

Social and Rehabilitation Service
  Aid to the Aged, Blind and Disabled 5
  Aid to Families with Dependent Children 5,718
  Aid to Families with Dependent Children—
      Unemployed Father 400
  Cuban Refugee Assistance 68
  Emergency Assistance to Needy Families with
      Children 60
  Indochinese Refugee Assistance 95
  Medical Assistance (Medicaid) 9,859
  Social Services 2,645
  Work Incentive Program 365
                                                                 19,215

Social Security Administration
  Disabled Coal Mine Workers Benefits and
      Compensation 935
  Medicare—Hospital Insurance 15,314
  Medicare—Supplementary Medical Insurance 6,330
  Social Security—Disability Insurance 11,625
  Social Security—Retirement Insurance 52,364
  Social Security—Survivors Insurance 18,888
  Special Benefits for Persons Age 72 and Over 236
  Supplemental Security Income 5,299
                                                                 110,991
                                                      Total   135,877

HOUSING AND URBAN DEVELOPMENT,
    DEPARTMENT OF
Community Planning and Development
    Housing Rehabilitation Loans 34
Federal Disaster Assistance Administration
    Disaster Assistance 387
Federal Housing Administration Fund
    FHA Mortgage Insurance 647
Federal Insurance Administration
    Crime/Riot Insurance 2
    Flood Insurance 178

                                                                 180
Housing for the Elderly and Handicapped 262
Housing Production and Mortgage Credit
    Homeownership Assistance and Payments 148
    Lower Income Housing Assistance Payments 362
    Public Low-Income Housing 1,112
    Rent Supplements 245
    Rental Housing Assistance and Payments 527
                                                                 2,394
                                                      Total   3,904

INTERIOR, DEPARTMENT OF THE
  Bureau of Indian Affairs
    Indian Credit Program 18

		MILLIONS OF DOLLARS
Indian Employment Assistance		36
Indian General Assistance		64
Indian Housing Improvement		14
Indian Social Services—Counseling		9
	Total	141

LABOR, DEPARTMENT OF

Bureau of International Labor Affairs		
Trade Adjustment Assistance—Workers		254
Employment Standards Administration		
Disabled Coal Mine Workers Benefits and Compensation		a
Federal Employees Compensation Benefits		589
Longshoremen's and Harbor Workers' Compensation		6
		595
Employment and Training Administration		
Comprehensive Manpower and Training Services		1,414
Employment Service		614
Federal-State Unemployment Insurance		13,490
Job Corps		230
Public Service Employment		3,159
Senior Community Service Employment		74
Special Unemployment Assistance		691
Summer Youth Employment		595
Unemployment Compensation for Federal Civilian Employees and Ex-Servicemen		712
Work Incentive Program		b
		20,979
	Total	21,828

LEGAL SERVICES CORPORATION

Legal Services for the Poor	Total	125

RAILROAD RETIREMENT BOARD

Railroad Disability Insurance		551
Railroad Retirement Insurance		2,250
Railroad Survivors Insurance		1,026
Railroad Unemployment Insurance		183
	Total	4,010

SMALL BUSINESS ADMINISTRATION

Economic Opportunity Loans		50
Handicapped Assistance Loans		13
Management Assistance to Disadvantaged Businessmen		7
Physical Disaster Loans		86
	Total	156

TRANSPORTATION, DEPARTMENT OF

Coast Guard		
Military Disability Retirement		c
Military Nondisability Retirement		c
Military Survivors Benefits		c

	MILLIONS OF DOLLARS
TREASURY, DEPARTMENT OF THE*	
Internal Revenue Service	
Additional Exemption for the Aged	1,220
Additional Exemption for the Blind	20
Credit for Child and Dependent Care Expenses	840
Credit for the Elderly	495
Deductibility of Casualty Losses	345
Deductibility of Medical Expenses	2,585
Earned Income Credit	1,070
Excess of Percentage Standard Deduction Over Low-Income Allowance	1,285
Exclusion from Capital Gains on Home Sales by the Elderly	40
Exclusion of Employer Contributions to Accident Insurance Premiums	70
Exclusion of Employer Contributions to Group Term Life Insurance Premiums	800
Exclusion of Employer Contributions to Medical Insurance Premiums	5,195
Exclusion of Employer Contributions to Pension and Profit-Sharing Plans	8,715
Exclusion of Employer Contributions to Supplementary Unemployment Insurance Trusts	10
Exclusion of Employer-Furnished Meals and Lodging	330
Exclusion of Interest on Life Insurance Savings	1,815
Exclusion of Military Disability Pensions	105
Exclusion of Public Assistance Benefits	100
Exclusion of Railroad Retirement Benefits	200
Exclusion of Scholarships and Fellowships	250
Exclusion of Sick Pay for the Disabled	50
Exclusion of Social Security Benefits	4,240
Exclusion of Special Benefits for Disabled Coal Miners	50
Exclusion of Unemployment Insurance Benefits	2,745
Exclusion of Veterans Educational Assistance	255
Exclusion of Veterans Pensions and Disability Compensation	685
Exclusion of Worker's Compensation Benefits	705
Exemption for Children Who Are Over Age 18 and Students	750
Total	34,970
VETERANS ADMINISTRATION	
Department of Medicine and Surgery	
Blind Veterans Rehabilitation Centers	3
Civilian Health and Medical Program—VA	29
Community Nursing Home Care	75
Veterans Contract Hospitalization	55
Veterans Domiciliary Care	69
Veterans Grants for State Home Care	36
Veterans Hospitalization	2,862
Veterans Nursing Home Care	147
Veterans Outpatient Care	872

	MILLIONS OF DOLLARS
Veterans Prescription Service	12
Veterans Prosthetic Appliances	50
Veterans Rehabilitation—Alcohol and Drug Dependence	107
	4,317
Department of Veterans Benefits	
Automobiles and Adaptive Equipment—Disabled Veterans	14
Burial Allowance for Veterans	150
Specially Adapted Housing for Disabled Veterans	14
Survivors Compensation for Service-Connected Deaths	1,067
Veterans Compensation for Service-Connected Disabilities	4,796
Veterans Dependents Educational Assistance	210
Veterans Educational Assistance	3,683
Veterans Housing—Direct Loans	0
Veterans Housing—Guaranteed and Insured Loans	27
Veterans Life Insurance	648
Veterans Pensions for Non-Service-Connected Disabilities	1,870
Veterans Survivors Pensions	1,322
Vocational Rehabilitation for Disabled Veterans	104
	13,905
Total	18,222
GRAND TOTAL OF ALL PROGRAM OUTLAYS	248,155

[a] See listing under Health, Education, and Welfare, Social Security Administration, for program outlays.
[b] See listing under Health, Education, and Welfare, Social and Rehabilitation Service, for program outlays.
[c] See listing under Health, Education and Welfare, Department of Defense for program outlays.
* It has been pointed out earlier that exempting people from having to pay a tax is as much a welfare benefit as giving them money directly.

Chapter 8
Social Work: The
Emergence of a Profession

" . . . the good we secure for ourselves is precarious and
uncertain, is floating in mid-air, until it is secured for all
of us and incorporated into our common life."

Jane Addams[1]

Depending upon who is doing the "name calling," social workers
are referred to in many ways: do-gooders, bleeding hearts, radicals
intent on changing our society, captives of and apologists for "the
establishment," organizers of the poor, and servers of the middle
class. All these are ways in which people stereotype social workers
and the functions they perform in society.

Societies have always provided various forms of social welfare.
The social institution of social welfare through which society
enhances and maintains the social functioning of human beings has
evolved through a lengthy process, and today the term "welfare
state" has entered our vocabulary. But social work as a professionalized occupation started its evolution at a much later stage, gaining
momentum as a result of the industrial revolution.

In this chapter and the next we will explore the profession of
social work within the context of social welfare and try to understand

[1] Christopher Lasch (ed.), *The Social Thought of Jane Addams*, New York: Bobbs-
Merrill, 1965, p. 33.

the realities behind the stereotypes used to describe all social workers. We will review various historical antecedents of modern social workers and the creation of the profession, describe the functions of social work and the arenas in which social workers perform their functions, and examine a number of current issues that confront the profession.

As our discussion in Chapter 4 illustrated, the definition of social welfare is a complicated matter. However, for our purposes here, it is only important to recognize that social welfare is a social institution organized to meet important social needs or functions. Social services, which may be called social welfare services, are simply those services produced by social welfare, ranging from economic support to counseling.

Social work too is defined in Chapter 4 and briefly is a professionalized occupation which delivers social services largely in the social welfare institution. Social work is the major professional group in the social welfare institution, but social workers are by no means limited to delivering services in the social welfare arena, nor are all services in social welfare delivered by social workers.

THE WORKERS OF "GOOD WORKS"

Many antecedents of social work as a profession are found among people who served through the ages to provide social welfare services. Such services were provided in many forms by individuals, religious charities, public communal services, and revered religious personages as well as little-known "good samaritans." Prior to the advent of industrialization, for example, it has been suggested that Father Vincent de Paul, a seventeenth-century Roman Catholic clergyman who established hospitals, orphanages, and foundling homes, also began the primitive training of social workers. When he founded the Daughters of Charity in 1633 he took young peasant women who wanted to devote themselves to charitable work and trained them especially for nursing the poor. According to this view, these young women were among the forerunners of the modern social workers.[2] However, Karl deSchweinitz has pointed out that a century earlier Vives' system in Ypres required that good persons "remember that the burden of their neighbor's calamities must be relieved not only

---

[2] Walter A. Friedlander and Robert Z. Apte, *Introduction to Social Welfare*, Englewood Cliffs, N.J.: Prentice-Hall, 1974, p. 12. We do not mean to imply they were early social workers. Social work is a creation of the latter part of the nineteenth century. However, these forerunners established a climate of functions, many of which coalesced into the functions of modern social workers.

with alms but also with their presence in visiting, comforting, helping, and in executing the deeds of pity."[3]

The above are just two examples of the fact that formally and
informally people have always reached out to help other people.
Family, church, and other institutions often have tried to institution-
alize this helping function. Historians differ on the degree to which
earlier antecedents led directly to modern social work. What is clear
is that the modern social worker is a creation of the industrial era in
the latter part of the nineteenth century.

It was particularly during the nineteenth century that more
definitive antecedents of social work as a profession were established. The coming of industrialization and accelerated movement
from rural to urban locations produced great social problems. Urban
living created social needs and social problems which were beyond
the coping powers of individual families. Along with modernization,
specialization developed so that functions which would have been
performed traditionally by family members soon became the tasks of
specialists. For example, rather than milking one's own cows, one
obtains milk provided by dairy farmers, dairies, distributors, truck-
ers, and grocers. And the retarded child who was cared for entirely
at home is now transported to a child development center for education and training by specialists. In our society many functions
which were once performed by relatives or friends today must be—
in many cases—performed by specialists.

Society also has become secularized over the past few centuries.
This has meant a diminution of concern with the sacred, with tradi-
tionalism, and with the supernatural. In their place, more value has
been placed on utilitarian and rational values. The scientific method
replaces custom, democratic values replace authority, and rational
understanding casts doubt on religious dogma.

Along with humanism, rationalism, and scientific inquiry, the
nation-state has developed as a central idea in the modern era. Not
only has the number of nation-states grown, but the responsibilities
assumed by the state have increased as well. That which was the
province of the individual or family has become the domain of the
state. One part of this overall secular nation-state trend is the growth
of the social welfare responsibilities of the state and the accompanying need for persons to implement the social welfare purposes.

Specialization developed in regard to many facets of American
life, including specializations dealing with pauperism and poverty.
Following the War of 1812, the year of 1816 was extremely cold and

---

[3] Karl deSchweinitz, *England's Road to Social Security*, New York: A. S. Barnes, 1975,
pp. 35–36.

there was a short harvest. Shortly after there followed the 1817–1821 postwar depression. John Griscom in New York organized the Society for the Prevention of Pauperism. The society aimed to investigate the circumstances and habits of the poor, to devise means of improving the situation of the poor both morally and physically, to suggest plans by which the poor could help themselves, and to encourage economy and saving. Among the remedies utilized were house-to-house visitation of the poor and the flow of charities into one distribution channel in order to prevent deception.[4] Thomas Chalmers, a minister and philosopher in England,[5] believed that his parishioners (the poor included) could provide for themselves through their own resources, the kindness of relatives, and the sympathy of the wealthier members of the community. Taking over a Glasgow parish, he implemented a new plan from 1819 to 1823. All local parish church collections would be left with the parish rather than transmitted to a central fund. These funds could be used at his discretion to provide for the people of the parish but would not be used for new families moving into the area.

The parish of 8000 people was divided into 25 districts. The office of deacon was reintroduced and made responsible for providing for all new applications for public assistance. There would be no transfers from private to public funds so that, if successful, the parish would support its own needy. Deacons were given general instructions and individual supervision and advice.

For approximately four years Chalmers supervised the program for relief in St. John's parish. During the period only 20 new applications were accepted. The parish took over the care of individuals previously under the care of the town hospital, and some money was left for the parish school.

At a time when workhouses were used cruelly and indiscriminately, Chalmers created a system of personal influence and individualization outside the framework of the Poor Laws. Investigation and district assignments were systematic techniques. While Chalmers believed in an ethic of "noblesse oblige" by the wealthy for the poor,

[4] Robert H. Bremner, "The Rediscovery of Pauperism," *Current Issues in Social Work Seen in Historical Perspective*, New York: Council on Social Work Education, 1962, p. 13.

[5] Stressing the need for caution when tracing the history of social work and social welfare organizations, Noel Timms has suggested there is no direct connection between Chalmers and his work and the creation of the English Charity Organization Society. However, there can be no doubt that in the United States earlier organizations for dealing with pauperism and poverty were known to exist. While they did not cause the creation of American Charity Organization Societies, they undoubtedly influenced the development of later organizations. Noel Timms, *Social Work*, London: Routledge and Kegan Paul, 1973, pp. 12–15.

nevertheless he created an administrative plan and trained persons to implement it, based on the belief that personal factors cause poverty and that the effort of "helping" people could help bring them out of poverty. The investigation of individual situations, regardless of the understanding brought to the assessment, was a factor in the creation of the concept of *casework* by which we mean that each person or case is unique. Thus benefits were related to the individual diagnosis.[6]

Among the social work precursors in the United States were the volunteers of the New York Society for the Prevention of Pauperism formed as a result of the 1819 Depression. The New York Association for Improving the Condition of the Poor, organized in 1843 to repress pauperism and aid the worthy poor through the use of volunteers, was not staffed entirely by volunteers. Instead, employed staff members, primarily missionaries to begin with, were used to do administrative work for districts and to train and supervise the volunteer visitors. Families were investigated by the volunteer visitors but the family conditions were reviewed by the paid agents serving as district secretaries. By 1866 the district secretaries were dismissed and the NYAICP returned to an almost entirely volunteer effort. Paid visitors were once again employed starting in the 1870s. These paid district secretaries, formerly preachers of doctrines of salvation and reform, were the forerunners of the later social workers, and the AICP structure served as a model for the later developed New York Charity Organization Society.[7]

Still other forerunners of modern social workers were members of the U.S. Sanitary Commission, a federation of voluntary organizations which helped to serve the needs of Union troops during the Civil War through supplying bandages, clothing, and food and by establishing lodging places for soldiers on leave, meals while in transit, and assistance with pay claims.[8]

The workers in the Freedmen's Bureau for former slaves created in March 1865 implemented a comprehensive program including temporary relief, food, clothing, hospitals, schools, orphan asylums, homes for the aged and the infirm, lease of lands, job finding, supervising labor contracts, housing and transportation for job-seekers, courts, and legal counsel as to rights.

According to Victoria Olds, the Freedmen's Bureau was family centered and provided unfragmented services. Designed to mini-

[6] DeSchweinitz, op. cit., pp. 100–113.
[7] Dorothy G. Becker, "The Visitor to the New York City Poor, 1843–1920," *Social Service Review*, Vol. 35, No. 4, December 1961, pp. 382–396.
[8] Robert H. Bremner, *From the Depths* (New York: New York University Press, 1967), p. 43.

mize the social upheaval of the war and the stressful emancipation of slaves, the Freedmen's Bureau offered—in our current terms—child welfare services, income maintenance, medical care, work projects, government housing, provision for the aged and infirm, employment counseling, family location, marriage counseling, legal aid, assistance with resettlement, protective services, and education.[9]

By the middle of the nineteenth century the New York Association for Improving the Conditions of the Poor (AICP) was organized and provided health, housing, and child welfare services. Later the AICP, after setting a model for following private agencies, merged with the New York Charity Organization Society to form the eminent Community Service Society of New York. It was during the mid-nineteenth century as well that the Children's Aid Society of New York, under the leadership of Charles Loring Brace, used foster home programs in an early attempt to deal with the problem of juvenile delinquency.

Philosophies and techniques continued to evolve. In the United States, for example, when Franklin B. Sanborn, a New England intellectual associated with John Brown, became the executive secretary of the Massachusetts State Board of Charities in 1863, he encouraged the use of homes for delinquent and nondelinquent children. He initiated the use of foster homes for the harmless insane on the basis of observations made in Scotland, Belgium, and France. He also recruited local volunteers, for the most part women, to serve as visitors. These "friendly visitors" were essentially middle- and upper-class women who had time and wanted to do good. They would visit the poor and try to teach them to be better citizens and parents, to budget, and to practice sobriety in all matters. The expectation was that through moral instruction one could learn how not to be poor.[10]

A major economic depression in 1873, one of many during the nineteenth century, created severe unemployment problems. It became clear that agencies, programs, and resources were not equal to the tasks they were called upon to perform.[11] As a result, during this period an English invention—the Charity Organization Society (COS)—caught the imagination of a number of American communities. Starting in Buffalo, New York, in 1877 the COS developed rapidly in a series of cities including New Haven, Philadelphia, Boston,

[9] Victoria Olds, "The Freedman's Bureau: A Nineteenth Century Federal Welfare Agency," *Social Casework*, Vol. 44, No. 5, May 1963, pp. 247–254.

[10] Frank J. Bruno, *Trends in Social Work*, New York: Columbia University Press, 1948, p. 11.

[11] Nathan E. Cohen, *Social Work in the American Tradition*, New York: Dryden Press, 1958, p. 66.

Brooklyn, Cincinnati, and New York. It was hoped that charity organizations could meet the pressing social problems of the cities—unemployment, orphans, tramps, beggars, the ill, and others—and clarify the interrelations of private and public relief agencies which had overlapping functions and different policies. Thus these new organizations were to assume two different roles: (1) direct service to individuals and families, and in this respect they were the immediate forerunners of social casework and of the family service agencies, and (2) planning and coordinating efforts which preceded the development of community organization and social planning. Implicit in the creation of these new agencies were two different functions, reflecting the two tracks of cause and function, to be discussed further in Chapter 9.

The general principles upon which the charity organizations operated were detailed investigation of the applicant, a central system of registration to avoid duplication, cooperation between the various relief agencies, and extensive use of volunteer friendly visitors. Investigative and administrative responsibilities belonged to the paid staff. However, the major treatment and helping roles rested with the friendly visitors who as volunteers had the role of directly helping those in difficulty.

Lubove reports that work was viewed at this time as the panacea for all problem families. When persons came for assistance, the Conference of the Boston Associated Charities, for example, "boasted that when the poor first called for assistance, they requested 'clothing, money, etc., etc.,' but were refused anything except work."[12] Thus there is an amazing consistency in attitude and approach to the poor in England and America from the thirteenth century until the latter part of the nineteenth century.

During these early stages of the development of social work, the views of persons in need held by those who were to help them were chiefly of a moral nature. Reverend S. Humphrey Gurteen, who had been associated with the London Charity Organization Society, when establishing the Buffalo Charity Organization suggested "by far the larger percentage of all the confirmed paupers in the country have hung for a time on . . . the borderline of involuntary poverty, and only by the sheer neglect, or still oftener through the misdirected charity of benevolent people have they been dragged down to the lowest depths of confirmed pauperism."[13]

To further illustrate the incipient social work roles and tasks

[12] Roy Lubove, *The Professional Altruist,* New York: Atheneum, 1971, p. 8.
[13] *The Heritage of American Social Work,* Ralph E. Pumphrey and Muriel W. Pumphrey (eds.), New York: Columbia University Press, 1965, p. 170.

about the same time, a *Manual for Visitors Among the Poor* was developed by the Philadelphia Society for Organizing Charitable Relief and Repressing Mendicancy. The suggestions for visitors are instructive: sympathy and encouragement are more important than money; women are the best "friendly visitors"; help, if urgently needed, may be obtained from neighbors; personal assistance should take the form of employment; cultivate the habit of looking below the surface of things; poverty is associated with disease and a consequent lack of vitality; know the sanitary laws; the poor have not learned thrift, and so on. The thrust of these instructions places the responsibility on the person or family involved. The effort to make change is marked by "moral suasion."[14]

Thus we reach a point in the development of social work in which volunteers are primarily motivated to change people as "doers of good works." It was through social investigation and attempts to understand family situations that social work began to gestate as a profession. The time and effort required to deal with many cases led to making comparisons among situations and searches for underlying causation. Although there was a strong sense of moral judgment involved, friendly visitors and charity organizations had moved toward understanding and taken a major step on the road to professionalization.

To the contemporary mind, all these early forerunners of casework will stand out for their judgmental and patronizing qualities and the tendency to blame the victim for his or her problems. While these factors were present, it is important to note that these movements were also progressive in another respect and planted one of the basic principles of all contemporary social work practice: that each person is different and has to be understood in individual terms.

Concurrently, settlement houses also were being instituted in the United States following the establishment of Toynbee Hall in 1884 in London. A group of people from the middle and upper classes would live in a poor neighborhood so they could experience firsthand the realities of life and search simultaneously for ways to improve conditions in cooperation with the residents of the neighborhood. The "friendly visitor" came for a longer stay with a different philosophy. Many of the early American settlement house workers were daughters of ministers. Just like colonialists, they wanted to teach the residents how to be good, in a way an extension of the missionary movement: poor people had to be uplifted.

[14] Ibid., pp. 176–181.

Settlement houses played important roles in cities, especially in immigrant communities. Their focus was on improving housing, health, and general living conditions; finding jobs; teaching English, occupational skills, and hygiene; and attempting to change the environmental surroundings through cooperative efforts. Social casework started in charity organization work; social group work, community organization, social action, and the environmental emphasis were stressed by the settlement houses and their staff members.

In addition to dealing with local problems by taking local action, settlement houses played important roles in gathering facts, promulgating them, preparing legislation, and collecting forces to influence social policy and legislation. Many of the key legislative enactments of the reform era had their inception in the work of the settlement houses. The settlements learned what the realities of life in slum communities were and, fortunately, had staff members who were influential on the national scene, through personal and familial connections as well as through social action pressures.

Settlement houses placed their emphasis upon reform through environmental changes, but "they continued to struggle to teach the poor the prevailing middle-class values of work, thrift, and abstinence as the keys to success."[15] One difference between the work of the charity organizations and the work of the settlement houses, which influenced both their philosophies and their methods, was the difference in the degree to which they stressed self-help.

Jane Addams of Hull House in Chicago thought that the residents of settlement houses could eventually help slum-dwellers to "express themselves and make articulate their desires."[16] By changing neighborhoods, they would change the communities; and through changing communities, they would alter the nation.

According to Mary McDowell, settlements in 1896 worked from within the neighborhood and among the people, sharing the fate of the slum-dwellers while the charity organization visitors came from without and returned to the outside after the visit. They differed in methodology but complemented each other's efforts doing together what neither could do entirely as separate agencies.[17]

According to Jane Addams, settlement houses had specific missions: to interpret democracy in social terms, to aid in the race progress, and to offer a Christian movement toward humanitarianism.

[15] Dorothy G. Becker, "Social Welfare Leaders as Spokesmen for the Poor," *Social Casework*, Vol. XLIX, No. 2, February 1968, p. 85.
[16] Clarke A. Chambers, *Seedtime of Reform*, Minneapolis: University of Minnesota Press, 1963, p. 15.
[17] Cohen, op. cit., p. 71.

When she summarized what a settlement house was, she suggested the following:

> The Settlement, then, is an experimental effort to aid in the solution of the social and industrial problems which are engendered by the modern conditions of life in a great city.

The residents of settlement houses must be

> . . . content to live quietly side by side with their neighbors, until they grow into a sense of relationship and mutual interests. . . . They are bound to see the needs of their neighborhoods as a whole, to furnish data for legislation, and to use their influence to secure it. In short, residents are pledged to devote themselves to the duties of good citizenship and to the arousing of the social energies which too largely lie dormant in every neighborhood given over to industrialism.[18]

By the end of the nineteenth century the two major tracks which would feed the development of professional social work had emerged. Future developments would be dramatically influenced by the different natures of the two tracks and by their confluence within the major stream of social work.

THE PROCESS OF PROFESSIONALIZATION

Modern society requires specialization which in turn requires particular knowledge. Traditionally only a few occupations were considered professions, including medicine, law, and theology, but even these professions have developed slowly over time. A little over a century ago, the profession of physician had not completed sorting itself out from among apothecaries, chemists, and others who performed "medical" healing.

The concept of professionalization provides an important perspective for examining social work, among all other professions. Professionalization suggests that

> . . . many, if not all, occupations may be placed somewhere on a continuum between the ideal-type "profession" at one end and completely unorganized occupational categories, or "non-professions," at the other end. Professionalization is a process, then, that may affect any occupation to a greater or lesser degree.[19]

---

[18] Jane Addams, *Twenty Years of Hull House*, New York: Macmillan, 1959, Original publication 1910, pp. 125–126.
[19] Howard M. Vollmer and Donald L. Mills, (eds.), *Professionalization*, Englewood Cliffs, New Jersey: Prentice-Hall, 1966, p. 2.

The attributes of the ideal-type profession were enumerated by Greenwood when he examined social work as a profession. The five he specified are (1) possession of systematic theory, (2) authority recognized by the clientele, (3) sanction of the community to operate, (4) a code of ethics for client and colleague relationships, and (5) a professional culture.[20]

Many students of professions have examined various occupations against this list of elements or attributes to determine whether a group is truly a profession. According to this view, the assumption is made that professionalization, for individuals and total professions, is something like an electric light switch. The light is either on or off. While there may be an afterglow for electric lights, there is no preglow, and thus one is either a professional or not. This view, however, ignores the reality of the evolution of all professions and the process by which they became defined as professions.

Others, including sociologists of the professions, maintain as above that the *process* of professionalization is most important. Caplow identified four sequential steps through which occupational groups progress: (1) establishment of a professional association, (2) assertion of a monopoly over some area of service, (3) development of a code of ethics, and (4) political agitation for certification and licensing. Two concurrent steps accompany this sequential process: gaining control of training facilities and the development of working relationships with other groups.[21] Wilensky traced the growth of eighteen professions, and all follow the same pattern: (1) a substantial number of people begin doing full time some activity that needs doing, (2) a training school is established, (3) a professional association is formed, (4) the association engages in political agitation to win the support of law for the protection of the group, and (5) a code of ethics is developed.[22]

The developmental pattern in the professionalization process for social work is clear. When charity organization societies received contracts to administer relief funds, they began to hire people as executive secretaries to organize volunteers properly and had to establish accounting procedures to show accountability for the money received from the city. These paid executive secretaries began meeting in conferences and, perhaps, were the first paid social

[20] Ernest Greenwood, "Attributes of a Profession," *Social Work*, Vol. 2, No. 3, July 1957, pp. 44–55.

[21] Donald Feldstein, "Do We Need Professions in Our Society? Professionalization versus Consumerism," *Social Work*, Vol. 16, No. 4, October 1971, pp. 5–11.

[22] Ronald M. Pavalko, *Sociology of Occupations and Professions*, Itasca: F. E. Peacock Publishers, 1971, p. 29.

workers. As a result of an inevitable process in professionalization, they needed to establish standards and training courses. In the summer of 1898 a training course was offered for charity workers by the New York Charity Organization Society. By 1904 a one-year program was offered by the newly formed New York School of Philanthropy, and by 1919 fifteen schools had organized the Association of Training Schools for Professional Social Work.[23] The American Association of Social Workers was formed as a professional association in 1921 following a vain effort to form an association several years earlier. It was not until 1960 that an official code of ethics was prepared.

Social work as a profession, then, is a development of the modern era, although it has antecedents in several forms in earlier ages. Some additional points related to the professionalization process need to be introduced to complete our perspective.

Bucher and Strauss focus attention on an implied attribute of professions. They consider professions in process "as loose amalgamations of segments pursuing different objectives in different manners, and more or less delicately held together under a common name, at a particular period in history."[24]

The rate of professionalization in our society has supported the rapid strides social work has made as a profession, telescoping into several decades processes which took centuries for other professions. In 1870 in the United States there were 859 professional persons per 100,000 population. This number had grown by 1961 to 4353 professionals per 100,000 citizens.[25]

An additional structural component of our society reinforces the role of social workers. When the United States emerged from World War II more workers were employed producing goods than were producing services. During the following decades service-producing industries moved ahead of the goods-producing industries. In 1978 service-producing industries comprised 70 percent of all jobs in the United States.[26]

Social work thus collapsed an evolutionary process into a short span of time. In a society in which individual and group fulfillment are important values and goals, the trend toward professionalization and the growth of services provide structural supports for the social

---

[23] Werner Boehm, "Education for Social Work," *Encyclopedia of Social Work*, Vol. 1, Robert Morris, (ed.), New York: National Association of Social Workers, 1971, p. 258.
[24] Vollmer and Mills, op. cit., p. 186.
[25] William Goode, "The Librarian: From Occupation to Profession?" *The Library Quarterly*, Vol. 31, No. 4, 1961, pp. 306–320.
[26] *Employment and Earnings: July 1978*, Bureau of Labor Statistics, U.S. Department of Labor, Vol. 25, No. 7, p. 73.

work profession, all of which derive from industrialization, urbanization, and specialization.

Mary Richmond, one of the eminent founders of social work and active in charity organization efforts, could say in 1890 that "only two things are necessary in order to do good work amongst the poor; one is much good will, and the other is a little tact."[27] By 1922 she was defining social casework as "those processes which develop personality through adjustments consciously effected, individual by individual, between men and their social environment."[28]

Richard Cabot introduced medical social work into Massachusetts General Hospital in 1905. Soon social workers were employed in schools, child guidance clinics, courts, and other settings. Building upon the investigatory and "friendly visiting" functions by charity organization volunteers and paid staff, social casework methodologies continued to develop. Initially based upon moral categories, the work of the caseworker was to help through persuasion and example. As knowledge developed based upon practical experience and as new knowledge became available from psychology, sociology, and psychiatry, the efforts of social caseworkers led to greater understanding of the interaction of individuals and environment. A diagnosis would be formulated and strengths and limitations identified for use in the helping process. Typically, early efforts to make change were educational and persuasive.

However, it was recognized that there are limits beyond which the individual is not responsible for the world and his or her situation and that society has a reciprocal responsibility for collective action which influences the lives of individuals.

The experience of the settlement house confirmed this view through action. Jane Addams reported:

> We early found ourselves spending many hours in efforts to secure support for deserted women, insurance for bewildered widows, damages for injured operators, furniture from the clutches of the installment store. The Settlement is valuable as an information and interpretation bureau. It constantly acts between the various institutions of the city and the people for whose benefit these institutions were erected.[29]

Not only were early social workers brokers, but they were also advocates, interested not alone in techniques and personal change, but also in altering society. This societal change perspective was cogently put by Florence Kelley, a consumer advocate, in 1905:

[27] Lubove, op. cit., p. 46.
[28] Lubove, op. cit., p. 48.
[29] Jane Addams, op. cit., (1910) p. 167.

A government which finds it possible, for instance, to take care of the health of young lobsters on the coast of Maine, would seem to have ingenuity enough at a pinch to enable it to make some sort of provision for the orphan children of skilled and unskilled workmen. It may take a long time. It has taken a long time to learn to take care of the lobsters.[30]

An event of some importance took place in 1915 when Abraham Flexner, an important critic of medical education, turned his attention to social work in a presentation at the National Conference of Charities and Corrections. Training programs had been developed, beginning with a summer training course sponsored by the New York Charity Organization Society in 1898. The creation of a scientific method for social work had been advanced, and yet Flexner raised a question as to whether social work was a profession or not. His answer was equivocal and suggested that "if social work fails to conform to some professional criteria, it very readily satisfies others. . . . In the long run, the first, main, and indispensable criterion of a profession will be the possession of professional spirit, and that test social work may, if it will, fully satisfy." Flexner was strenuous in his criticism, stating that social work lacked a specific skill for a specific function and, insofar as this was true, could not become a profession.[31]

Regardless of the criticism of social work, several events followed shortly after which energized the continued professionalization of social work. Training schools were formed, a professional association was created, and a major book was published. Within two years after Flexner's presentation, Mary Richmond published *Social Diagnosis* (1917), a work which organized a theory and methodology for social work. She formulated a common body of knowledge for casework based on collecting information and understanding the meaning of the information. The book was important for the development of the profession because it expounded an orderly professional process consisting of study, diagnosis, prognosis, and treatment planning. The focus was on an individual situation to determine what was wrong, what could be done, and how the worker should intervene.

With the advent of medical social work, psychiatric social work, the mental hygiene movement, Freudian and Meyerian psychology, and the search for a defined professional methodology, social work

---

[30] *Proceedings of the National Conference of Charities and Corrections* (Press of Fred J. Heer, 1905), p. 577.
[31] Pumphrey and Pumphrey, op. cit., p. 306.

also searched for professional status, and an emphasis was placed upon the development of professional knowledge and skills.[32] From the latter years of the nineteenth century until approximately 1915, there had developed an alteration of casework from a reform movement on a one-by-one basis to a method with beginning scientific underpinnings. The "cause" nature of the profession which had set out to change the world was changed to focus more upon the functions of the social worker and the skills and knowledge which support those functions.

Approximately two years following the publication of *Social Diagnosis,* Mary Jarrett, a psychiatric caseworker, rediagnosed the cases presented in Richmond's book and concluded that at least 50 percent included psychiatric problems.[33]

Social workers became employed in a broad diversity of specialized settings. Each social worker identified to a significant extent with particular settings so that professional roles, identities, and functions experienced a centrifugal expansion. Beyond the development of social work in psychiatric settings, including child guidance clinics, much of social work became infused with psychiatric knowledge and was especially influenced by psychoanalytic thought, both Freudian and Rankian. Jane Addams helps to place this influx of psychoanalytic thought and emphasis on individual psyche, technique, and method in perspective. She points out that the veering away from social reform can be viewed within the context of the times in that

> Throughout the decade (The Twenties) this fear of change, this tendency to play safe was registered most conspicuously in the field of politics, but it spread over into other fields as well. There is little doubt that social workers exhibited many symptoms of this panic and with a kind of protective instinct carefully avoided any identification with the phraseology of social reform.[34]

Many social workers thought of themselves as therapists, or at least believed that there were therapeutic emphases within their

[32] Nathan Cohen has suggested the search for method came at a time when the profession was eagerly trying to rebut the criticisms of Flexner and at the same time that psychoanalytic thought was making inroads into American culture.

[33] Scott Briar, "Social Casework and Social Group Work: Historical Foundations," *Encyclopedia of Social Work,* Vol. II, New York: National Association of Social Workers, 1971, p. 1239.

[34] Jane Addams, *The Second Twenty Years at Hull House,* New York: Macmillan, 1930, p. 155.

social work practice.[35] Social work continued to proliferate in health, school, family, and psychiatric settings. During the 1920s there also existed concern about the specialized nature of social work in many settings, and a systematic study was undertaken to determine what the generic elements of the profession were. A series of meetings was held from 1923 to 1929 to identify the general knowledge shared by all social workers regardless of setting. The work group became known as "The Milford Conference." In 1929 the work group consisting of executives and board members reported that generic social casework, that is, casework in all potential settings, was viewed as having these common aspects:

1. Knowledge of typical deviations from accepted standards of social life.
2. The use of norms of human life and human relationships.
3. The significance of social history as the basis of particularizing the human being in need.
4. Established methods of study and treatment of human beings in need.
5. The use of established community resources in social treatment.
6. The adaptation of scientific knowledge and formulations of experience to the requirements of social case work.
7. The consciousness of a philosophy which determines the purpose, ethics, and obligations of social case work.
8. The blending of the foregoing into social treatment.[36]

A human being with a problem (viewed in terms of deviance from accepted standards) is to be studied and treated, using relationships and community resources on the basis of knowledge and ethics

[35] The rise of psychoanalytically oriented casework at this time parallels a movement away from social reform, although it was not the cause of such a retreat. The climate of the times militated against reform efforts. But psychoanalytic thought did help veer social work's understanding of people in difficulty from a lack of character to psychological illness. See Herman Borenzweig, "Social Work and Psychoanalytic Theory: An Historical Analysis", *Social Work*, Vol. 16, No. 1, January 1971, pp. 7–16. Leslie B. Alexander has suggested that Freudian theory was not known to social workers and had an influence limited to the professional elite rather than the major part of the profession. Alexander suggests social workers used a more sociological than psychoanalytical approach during the 1920s and also that social reform debates and demands continued in relation to women's rights, child welfare, unemployment, housing reform, and the need for federal action on welfare and social insurance. Because of the nature of the times, major social reforms had to await the 1930s. Leslie B. Alexander, "Social Work's Freudian Deluge: Myth or Reality?" *Social Service Review*, Vol. 46, No. 4, December 1972, pp. 517–538.

[36] *Social Casework: Generic and Specific*, New York: American Association of Social Workers, 1929. Classic Series. Washington: National Association of Social Workers, 1974, p. 15.

in a process of social treatment. Soon after the Milford Conference Report on generic social casework, the Great Depression started.

Now derived from a scientific base, the philosophy of social casework remained focused upon the person and the psyche. Although the Great Depression had several major impacts upon social work, the social casework stream in the social work profession clung to an individual-centered and personality-focused social work.

Meanwhile the overwhelming nature and scope of human need created by the Great Depression caused social policy shifts to social welfare. Everyone was affected; so many persons were unemployed. It clearly was not the result of personal responsibility: systemic and structural factors were at work. The society and government searched for new security, and new roles for government were accompanied by new social planning trends. These new trends were supported by general agreement that government should help people, a new assumption in American life.

A myriad of New Deal programs responded to the need for national governmental entry into social welfare provision on a comprehensive basis. There were calls for social-work prepared personnel to be trained for expanding public social services. By the end of World War II, approximately ten years later, there were reports at the National Conference of Social Work that professional social work schools had made only limited impressions on the personnel in public assistance programs.[37]

One issue which arose during the years of the Great Depression was centered on the role of social work in an expanding welfare state. Integral to this issue were questions about theories of causation, both personal and societal, and about the roles of social workers in institutional services for normal but disadvantaged persons. Social work had been primarily a residual function for the abnormal.

A second issue was the occasion of an intense struggle which over the decades has proven less fundamental than thought at the time: the vying between two schools of thought, diagnostic and functional social work. The two schools share a social casework based upon psychiatry but differing on underpinning theories of personality. The diagnostic school, also known as the psychosocial (the "person-in-situation") school, was based on Freudian thought and laid stress upon the importance of diagnosis and of a person's past for treatment. The functional school, based on a psychology of growth, placed greater stress upon the function of the social agency and the impact of the agency purpose upon the casework-helping

---

[37] Frank J. Bruno, op. cit., pp. 318–319.

process, with a great emphasis upon the relationship between the social worker and the client.[38]

Paradoxically, a psychologically biased casework preoccupied with individuals remained the major trend in social casework while the economy was crumbling around people. There is some explanation for this curious persistence. The psychological casework had become the professional tool of social workers, developed over decades. A psychiatric emphasis also was supported by the Great Depression itself. Social welfare agencies, especially private social welfare ones, sought new roles as public welfare assumed the responsibility for income maintenance, a task completely beyond the ability of private philanthropy. An emphasis on psychologically oriented case work was an answer to the professional nature of social work and the changing functions of private social welfare agencies.

Simultaneously, social workers affected social legislation and social planning, which developed as part of the New Deal. Among the social workers playing important parts in the "cause" efforts of the 1930s were Harry Hopkins, Frances Dorothy Kahn, and Bertha Reynolds. They were active and influential in determining governmental policy and the administration of expanded social welfare.

World War II was a time when social work continued to emphasize the psychiatric aspects of treatment in a period of family disruption, problems of relocation, and the needs of military personnel at home and abroad.

Following the war, social work continued to be mainly influenced by psychodynamic psychiatry, but the social sciences began to be introduced to a greater extent in schools of social work. There was an emphasis upon seeking out the hard to reach, working with delinquent youth and multiproblem families, and initiating private social work practice. The commonalities and differences between social casework and psychotherapy were debated.

In the 1960s social workers were active in the civil rights struggle, housing and racial discrimination, juvenile delinquency control programs, neighborhood organization and multiservice centers, draft resistance and anti-Vietnam war efforts, the National Welfare Rights Organization, the search for economic security programs such as a negative income tax and guaranteed annual income, and the flowering of minority group organizations of many kinds.

Meanwhile there had been developing some of the components

[38] Ruth E. Smalley and Tybel Bloom, "Social Casework: The Functional Approach," *Encyclopedia of Social Work*, Vol. 2, Washington: National Association of Social Workers, 1977, pp. 1280–1290; Florence Hollis, "Social Casework: The Psychosocial Approach," ibid., pp. 1300–1308.

of professionalization referred to earlier and new streams of practice which contributed to the social work we know now.

Developments in schools of social work and in community practice both contributed to the creation of many new kinds of social work during the 1960s and 1970s. Social work practice entered new fields, including work such as social work in relationship to the women's movement, legal work, industrial and business settings, and the gay community.[39] In social work education, both graduate and undergraduate, a diversity of practice models had been developed including focus on social problems (such as addictions and poverty), methods (casework, group work, community organization, generic, and integrated), target population (the Chicano, black, and Asian-American), fields of practice (aging, youth, family, and psychiatric), and societal institutions relating to the family, justice, and health.

DEVELOPMENT OF THE PROFESSIONAL ASSOCIATION

Beginning in 1874 the National Conference of Charities and Correction provided an opportunity for social agency employees to meet together on a national basis. Various clubs and social work organizations were formed on a local basis. The National Social Workers Exchange operated in 1917 for job placement in social work positions.

By 1918 there had been an attempt to organize a national association of social workers, but the effort failed partly because of lack of agreement on membership qualifications. In 1921 the American Association of Social Workers was formed and grew until 1955. Meanwhile social workers from specialized settings formed national organizations, including the American Association of Medical Social Workers (1918), the National Association of School Social Workers (1919), the American Association of Psychiatric Social Workers (1926), the American Association of Group Workers (Study Group, 1936; Association, 1946), the Association for the Study of Community Organization (1946), and the Social Work Research Group (1949). In 1955 these specialized associations combined to form the National Association of Social Workers (NASW), the national professional association which now represents the full range of professional social workers.[40]

---

[39] See *Social Work Practice*, Bernard Ross and S. K. Khinduka, (eds.), Washington, D.C.: National Association of Social Workers, 1976.
[40] Ernest F. Witte, "Profession of Social Work: Professional Associations," *Encyclopedia of Social Work*, Vol. 11, 1971, p. 976.

From 1956 to 1976 the membership of the professional association more than tripled in number to approximately 70,000 persons.[41] Membership is open to baccalaureate graduates of accredited social work programs as well as master's graduates from accredited schools and holders of doctorates in social work or social welfare.

The professional association provides a wide variety of services including insurance, retirement funds, legal defense, and employment and plays an active political action role. Concerned with professional competence, NASW provides continuing education efforts and is engaged in women's issues, minority affairs, peace, social welfare, and issues relating to specialization, personnel policies in employing agencies, ethics, the aging, gay rights, mental health deinstitutionalization, and other timely and important social welfare matters. In addition, the professional association prepares and implements examinations and publications and offers other services.[42]

A number of smaller offshoots have developed, for example, the National Association of Black Social Workers, the Puerto Rican Social Service Workers, Christians in Social Work, Societies for Clinical Social Work, the Society for Hospital Social Work Directors, and others. This burgeoning of splinter groups reflects the pluralism in our society, the difficulty of having a major organization to satisfy all segments of the profession, and efforts by particular groups to enhance their own legitimate goals.

The National Association of Social Workers has evolved into a major organization with a substantial membership. By comparison, the memberships of other organizations are medical, 179,900; nurses, 198,000; architects, 25,442; lawyers, 210,000; and psychologists, 40,000.[43] The social work professional organization has strength in itself which is expressed politically, but in coalition with other organizations it becomes potentially quite formidable.

SOCIAL GROUP WORK

Social group work, an integral part of social work, developed from several different sources and from roots different than those of social casework. An outgrowth of the social reform era during the first

[41] *Encyclopedia of Social Work*, Vol. 11, Washington, D.C., National Association of Social Workers, 1977, p. 1670.

[42] Bertram M. Beck, "Professional Association: National Association of Social Workers," *Encyclopedia of Social Work*, 1977, pp. 1084–1093.

[43] Margaret Fish, et al. (eds.), *Encyclopedia of Associations*, Vol. I, *National Organizations of the United States*, Detroit: Gale Research, 1977.

decade of this century, settlement houses focused in part on group services, including cultural and art groups, recreational groups, education, and physical health and education experiences in groups. There was a focus on the importance of mutual aid and cooperation and on recreation and informal education.

Settlement houses emphasized social participation and association, democratic processes, learning and growth, the encouragement of interaction among persons of different backgrounds, the impact of the environment on persons, and the potential impact of persons on the environment.

As settlement houses declined, probably because of changes in the political context and because of limited immigration preceding the Great Depression, leisure time agencies grew in number such as YMCAs and Girl Scouts.

In group service agencies of many kinds, there was the belief that the road to democracy was through democratic participation at every level of society. Group service agencies would foster such participation at every level—from children to adults and from the group itself to the greater society. Support for the evolving methodology came from sociology and from progressive education as expounded by John Dewey.

The first course on group work in a school of social work was taught by Clara Kaiser in 1923 at Western Reserve University in Cleveland. The University of Pittsburgh and the New York School (later to become the Columbia University School of Social Work) instituted programs in the 1930s with other schools later offering group work courses.

By 1936 the American Association for Study of Group Work was formed. Noteworthy was the great increase in the use of groups in psychiatric settings during World War II, in part created by the need for a few trained persons working with large numbers of persons affected by the war experience. In 1946 the National Conference of Social Work recognized social group work as a part of the social work profession.[44]

Early social group work evolved several major goals: (1) democratic experiences, (2) cooperative problem-solving and mutual support, (3) improvement of society, and (4) character development. While there was hesitancy about the place of social group work in the social work profession as early as the Milford Conference report, the fundamental techniques of social work in 1929 were "recognized as social case work, community organization, group work, social

[44] Scott Briar, op. cit., pp. 1237–1245.

research, and since social work is almost invariably carried on through the medium of organizations, we may add the technique of administration."[45] Thus the elite group which prepared the Milford Conference report viewed group work as an intrinsic part of social work.

Today there appears to be a growing relationship between work with groups and social casework, and work with groups is very much in vogue in all types of institutions and treatment agencies. The creation of generic social work, micromethods (individuals, families, and small groups), and integrated social work methods have led in the past few years to a simultaneous inclusion of group methods into the broader social work and perhaps a diminishing of traditional social group work.

Three fundamental models of social group work vied for leadership among social workers. Beulah Rothman and Catherine Papell have identified three major streams of social group work: the social goals model, the remedial model, and the reciprocal model. In brief, the social goals model is concerned with social consciousness and social responsibility, the creation of an informed and able democratic citizenry. The remedial model is greatly congenial to the mode in the social work profession in that it focuses upon the treatment of individuals as the primary function of group work. The reciprocal model has a dual focus: society and the individual which meet in the group as a mutual aid system. Thus the reciprocal model is a helping process aimed at serving both individuals and society with an emphasis on the enabling process. The focus is on interdependence: mediating the interdependent actors and nourishing social functioning of both individuals and society. The group is central and is viewed as a cooperative effort by the individual members.[46]

Reflective of recent theoretical developments, by the mid-1970s work with groups had been conceptualized in four models

1. The behavioral model views social group work in terms of behavior change through a focus on immediate antecedents or consequences of specific behavior efforts to achieve acquisition of behavior or to strengthen, maintain, or eliminate it.[47]

2. The developmental approach is concerned with the enhancement of social functioning through restoration, prevention, or devel-

[45] *Social Case Work: Generic and Specific,* op. cit., p. 78.
[46] Beulah Rothman and Catherine Papell, "Social Group Work Models: Possession and Heritage," *Journal of Education for Social Work.* Vol. 2, No. 2, Fall 1966, pp. 66–77.
[47] Edwin J. Thomas, "Social Casework and Social Group Work: The Behavioral Model Approach," *Encyclopedia of Social Work,* Vol. II, Washington, D.C.: National Association of Social Workers, 1977, pp. 1309–1321.

opment toward optimal functioning. It is focused on function-
ality rather than pathology, abnormality, or illness, and on self-
actualization rather than cure. Focused on current group and
individual behavior rather than on prior personality diagnosis, the
developmental model stresses the common human condition and the
group worker within a communal perspective. The emphasis is on
the here and now in groups focused on common goals.[48]

3. The interactionist model (a further development of the reciprocal model) suggests that "a self-realizing, energy producing client
with certain tasks to perform and a professional with a specific function to carry out engage each other as interdependent actors in an
organic system."[49]

4. Finally, the organization and environmental approach aims
to help individuals to maximize their own social functioning, giving
priority to settings related to social problems and poverty, mental
illness, malperformance in educational settings, crime and delinquency, and so on. The focus is on the individual in the context of
the group and the social environment. It is provided in organizations
and intends to interrelate the individual, group, and environmental
strategies in an attempt to serve individuals and to bring about the
kind of organization required to maximize effective practice.[50]

Social group work which started with a focus on work with children and youth in settlement houses and youth groups and in adult
education and social action has become practiced in a great variety
of settings. From groups in administration to treatment groups, from
informal education to social action groups, and from consciousness-
raising to socialization, social group work has become an integral
part of social work practice used for many different purposes in many
different settings.

COMMUNITY ORGANIZATION AND SOCIAL PLANNING

Community organization and social planning have their roots in the
reform efforts of the latter part of the nineteenth century. The Charity Organization Society sought to develop cooperative planning and
coordination among local charities and worked for reforms in housing codes, antituberculosis associations, legislation in support of

[48] Emanuel Tropp, "Social Group Work: The Developmental Approach," ibid., pp. 1321–1328.
[49] William Schwartz, "Social Group Work: An Interactionist Approach," ibid., pp. 1328–1337.
[50] Paul H. Glasser and Charles D. Garvin, "Social Group Work: The Organizational and Environmental Approach," ibid., pp. 1338.

juvenile courts and probation, programs for the care of dependent children, cooperation with the police in regard to beggars and vagrants, and legislation to require absent fathers to support their children. As we have seen earlier, settlement houses were active in organizing neighborhoods, studying social problems, making program and policy proposals, forming pressure groups, and conducting campaigns.[51]

Social workers such as Jane Addams and Lillian Wald were very much involved in efforts to improve the quality of life in the United States. Following Jane Addams' election as president of the National Conference of Charities and Corrections in 1909 a committee was appointed to undertake a study of "certain minimum requirements of well being" in an industrial society. In 1911 Florence Kelley, activist and general secretary of the National Consumers League, chaired the committee, followed by Owen Lovejoy, secretary of the National Child Labor Committee, in 1912.

It is interesting to note the minimum platform which was created in "Social Standards for Industry": the eight-hour workday, the six-day week, abolition of tenement manufacture, improvement of housing conditions, prohibition of child labor under 16 years, regulation of employment for women, and a federal system of accident, old age, and unemployment insurance.[52]

From these early beginnings until the mid-1930s, community organization efforts were made by voluntary agencies such as community chests and health and welfare councils. During the Great Depression there was a shift from private to public auspices, including continued mutual aid and cooperatives among farmers.

In 1939 the *Lane Report* prepared by Robert P. Lane emphasized community organization as a social work method and suggested that local welfare councils and other coordinating bodies all shared the purposes of local planning and coordination in order to seek the congruence of community social welfare resources and needs.

During World War II one part of the massive war effort was community organization, especially through the U.S. Office of Civilian Defense and the Office of Defense, Health, and Welfare Services to coordinate health and welfare services, public and private, for defense-impacted localities. Following World War II, in 1947, *Community Organization: It's Nature and Setting* was published empha-

---

[51] Fred M. Cox and Charles Garvin, "The Relation of Social Forces to the Emergence of Community Organization Practice: 1865–1968," *Strategies of Community Organization*, Fred M. Cox et al. (eds.), Itasca, Ill.: F. E. Peacock Publishers, 1970, p. 41.
[52] Allen F. Davis, *Spearheads for Reform: The Social Settlements and the Progressive Movement: 1890–1914*, New York: Oxford University Press, 1967, p. 196.

sizing integrative efforts, consensus, and process-oriented models to increase the capacity to cooperate within the society.[53]

Generally, community organization was a method which for a long time featured attention to cooperative efforts to rationalize the social services in a community. The basic methodology was consensual in which conflict was minimized and the attempt was made—as in intergroup work—to utilize a process which led to understanding and cooperation. The process was intended to be productive in that rivalrous entities could be helped to identify common goals and through cooperative efforts attain a better society and their own goals. Community organization thus was based primarily on enabler roles.

By 1962 the Committee on Community Organization of the National Association of Social Workers published "Defining Community Organization Practice" based upon several years of discussions to clarify terms, roles, and methods. At the same time the Council on Social Work Education issued a curriculum policy statement identifying community organization as a third major social work method.

During the 1960s our society was in ferment with a change in important dimensions taking place. Community organization was an important contributor to efforts to overcome juvenile delinquency and to attain civil rights and made contributions to community development and improvement through the War on Poverty and the model cities programs. A major emphasis during this decade was on grass roots organizing and community participation and action.

Various models or combinations of community organization models are utilized by practitioners. (1) The intergroup model is used, for example, in councils where representatives of groups come together for cooperative planning such as is done by health and welfare councils. A potential limitation of such efforts is the possibility of their operating as closed systems in which particular groups of individuals maintain control. (2) The enabler model places emphasis upon the democratic process, and the effort of the community organizer is to assist the organization to attain its goals. (3) The advocacy model unites an organization and worker with a common agenda in which they join their efforts to attain the shared goal. (4) The planning model stresses the social worker's expertise, often while using the above three models, in engineering and designing solutions to social problems.

Today community organization plays many roles, including pro-

[53] Donald S. Howard, (ed.), *Community Organization: Its Nature and Setting.* New York: American Association of Social Workers, 1947.

gram development, political and social action, planning, interorganizational work, community development, coordination, and self-help, and has begun community organization and social planning roles in both voluntary and public areas within the social welfare sphere and in other social institutions.[54]

The focus here on the historic major methods of casework, group work, and community organization should not blind us to the fact that social workers and social work educational programs continue to be involved in a variety of other ways as well. They are involved in specific fields of practice such as aging or child welfare, on settings such as community mental health centers or settlements, and on other divisions of social work such as micro- and macro systems. In addition to roles in the administration of social service programs and in social policy and social planning, another role of social workers is in the sphere of social action. Social work has a powerful tradition of social action ranging from the highly successful efforts of early social workers in both Charity Organization Societies and settlement houses, as well as in their citizen capacities, to attain legislation which significantly altered our society. Social workers were in the forefront on child labor, health and safety legislation, social insurances, and on many issues were in the vanguard of new national social welfare ideas.

Throughout their history, social workers have been active in social causes as individuals, in groups, and as participants in coalitions. More recently, social workers played important roles in the Civil Rights movement of the 1960s, the peace movement of the latter years of the 1960s and the early 1970s. Also in the early 1970s, ELAN (Educational Legislative Action Network) was organized by the professional association to maintain contact and communication with congressional representatives. PACE (Political Action for Candidate Election) played an active role in the 1976 presidential campaign and election.[55]

TOWARD A UNIFIED PROFESSION

Modern social casework which has remained the major professional stream has evolved into a plethora of models and approaches to

[54] For further detail, see Robert Perlman, "Social Planning and Community Organization," *Encyclopedia of Social Work,* Vol. II, Washington, D.C.: National Association of Social Workers, 1977, pp. 1404–1412; Neil Gilbert and Harry Specht, "Social Planning and Community Organization: Approaches," ibid., pp. 1412–1425; and Irving A. Spergel, "Social Planning and Community Organization: Community Development," ibid., pp. 1425–1433.

[55] Bertram Beck, "Professional Associations: NASW," *Encyclopedia of Social Work.* John B. Turner, et al., (eds.), Washington: National Association of Social Workers, 1977, pp. 1084–1093.

working with people. For example, the recent volume *Social Work Treatment* exemplifies, despite the criticisms of the 1960s, an emphasis upon the treatment aspects of social casework; therapy is primary and remains transcendent. A listing of the book's chapter titles suggests the wide range of social casework theories and methodologies today: psychoanalytic theory, ego psychology, psychosocial therapy, problem-solving theory, functional theory, client-centered system, cognitive theory, existential social work, role theory, general systems theory, communication concepts and principles, behavior modification, crisis theory, and family therapy.[56]

The need to define a common core and common methodologies continues unabated in social work. Increasingly there is concern about this issue within the profession; at the same time there continues to develop diverse types of social work practice. The types of concentration increase but, simultaneously, there is a strong sense of concern that a generic core should be maintained for all social workers.[57] In regard to professional practice methodologies, increasingly a part of training is the provision by social work educational programs of generic methods or multimethods. This type of educational emphasis is generally accepted among baccalaureate level programs, and—on the graduate level—in 1976 forty-five percent of master's degree first year students were enrolled in such programs and one in eight second-year students (13 percent) was being similarly educated. In both instances, first- and second-year graduate students, increases in the number of students in generic or multi-method tracks from 1975 to 1976 continued a trend of some years.[58]

In the professionalization process, social work has created training programs, a professional association, and a code of ethics; is increasingly licensed by governmental bodies; and has created a knowledge base. Nevertheless, social work is an insecure profession because of its developmental status and because of its perceived limitations, despite a very rapid growth. The human service professions, in general, as deliverers of "software" services, are sensitive to criticism both from within and external to their own associations.

Despite the internal debates of the social work profession and criticisms which were sharply made during the Nixon Administra-

[56] Francis J. Turner (ed.), *Social Work Treatment*, New York: The Free Press, 1974, table of contents.
[57] For extended discussions of this issue see Lilian Ripple, *Report to the Task Force on Structure and Quality in Social Work Education*, New York: Council on Social Work Education, 1974, and Ralph Dolgoff, *Report to the Task Force on Social Work Practice and Education*, New York: Council on Social Work Practice and Education, 1974.
[58] Ann W. Shyne and G. Robert Whitcomb, *Statistics on Social Work Education in the United States: 1976*, New York: Council on Social Work Education, 1977, p. 25.

tion years, by 1978 there were approximately 78,000 members of the professional association and over 330,000 social workers employed in the United States. As of September 1977 social work was licensed in 22 states.[59] So social work in all respects seems to have very much completed the professionalization process. While some will disagree with this assessment, even within the profession itself, society through regulating sanctions seems to be moving forward in its recognition of social work as a profession.

[59] "Oregon Passes Title Protection Law; 22 States Now Regulate Social Work," *NASW News,* Vol. 22, September 1977, p. 10.

Chapter 9
Social Work: Functions, Context, and Issues

" . . . the negative policy of relieving destitution, or even
the more generous one of preventing it, is giving way to
the positive idea of raising life to its highest value."

Jane Addams[1]

According to Werner Boehm, "The functions of social work, if it is to
achieve its goals of self-actualization and social functioning, are
habilitation, rehabilitation, resource provision, and prevention of
dysfunctioning."[2] One of the terms used above is not commonly met
in social work literature: by habilitation is meant helping people live
effectively, people who are not defective emotionally or psychologically or lacking in social resources but who for a variety of reasons
may lack the competence to live effectively at a particular time without help.

The National Association of Social Workers adopted a definition
of social work in 1970, a definition inclusive of the broad variety of
interventions and services which social workers provide in their
actual practice:

> Social work is the professional activity of helping individuals, groups,
> or communities enhance or restore their capacity for social functioning

[1] *Jane Addams: A Centennial Reader,* New York: Macmillan, 1960, p. 85.
[2] Werner W. Boehm, "Common and Specific Learnings for a Graduate of a School of
Social Work," *Journal of Education for Social Work.* Vol. 4, No. 2, Fall 1968, p. 17.

and creating societal conditions favorable to this goal. Social work practice consists of the professional application of social work values, principles, and techniques to one or more of the following ends: helping people obtain tangible services; counseling and psychotherapy with individuals, families, and groups; helping communities or groups provide or improve social and health services; and participating in relevant legislative processes.[3]

Social workers in order to achieve the goals of the profession are employed in health, education, and welfare settings; in the justice system, and in industry and business work locations. They are employed under public and private auspices on the local, state, regional, and national levels. Some social workers are self-employed private practitioners.

Using social work methodologies in work with individuals, families, groups, organizations, neighborhoods, and communities, social workers assist persons, groups, and communities to deal constructively with drug and alcohol addiction, deal with adult education, aging, child welfare (adoptions, foster care, day care, institutional care, and treatment), civil rights and liberties, crime and delinquency, disabilities and handicaps, family life education, sex education, services to families with problems, immigration, genetic counseling, health care, homemaker services, housing, illegitimacy, economic security, services for adults, intergroup relations, human resources development, legal services, mental health, problems of migrants, protective services, recreation and informal education, social planning and development, social action and policy, and socialization efforts for different groups.[4]

The tasks needed to implement the aims of social work include an array of activities ranging from counseling to research, from organizing to administering, and from planning to influencing a group in favor of legislation.

Several short examples may give a sense of social workers in action. Suppose a person has encountered a series of social and psychological setbacks, including loss of job, serious illness in the family, depleted funds, and conflicts within the family which seem to derive from stress. A social worker employed by a family service agency would attempt to partialize the problems and to solve them in order of priority with the person(s) involved. This could mean

---

[3] *Standards for Social Service Manpower*, Washington, D.C.: National Association of Social Workers, 1974, pp. 4–5.
[4] This listing is based on the index of the *Encyclopedia of Social Work, 1971*. It could be expanded to include even more categories.

assistance in finding work, in dealing with hospital or medical personnel, and in assisting the family with its interpersonal problems through social work counseling.

A social worker employed by a health and welfare council, a neighborhood council, or a settlement house may discover a large number of young adult males and females in the community between 16 and 24 years of age who do not have jobs. Because of much time on their hands, frustration, and resultant anger, they are involved in a series of destructive acts, both against themselves and society. Social workers may intervene with governmental and other bodies toward the creation of the necessary resources, jobs, training, reentry into schools, and other needed resources. A social worker may help to form groups of such young people in order to develop better their own productive actions.

Social workers in a community may organize services for aging persons who live isolated and lonely lives, have difficulty shopping, and eat poorly. They may help by arranging homemaker services, organizing a volunteer group which visits with isolated persons and renders simple assistance, establishing a meals-on-wheels program for those unable to prepare hot meals for themselves, or organizing a recreational program in a nursing home to stave off loneliness, to prevent further physical and mental disabilities, and generally to support motivation and life involvement.

THE PROFESSIONAL WITHIN THE ORGANIZATIONAL CONTEXT

Social workers are employed primarily in public or private social agencies. There are certain effects which working in bureaucracies have upon both the professional social worker and the services which can be performed with or for the client. The goals, roles, and actions of a social worker are in major part determined by his or her position in the organization, and the functions which he or she can carry out are heavily influenced by the policies and structure of the organization. There are limitations upon the worker's actions which result from working within a bureaucracy, and there are strengths for social service which derive from the organizational setting for social work practice.

The Nature of Bureaucracies

The classic bureaucracy is the Weberian monolithic and rational model of complex organization. According to the Weberian model, these are the criteria for individual officials within rational bureaucracies:

1. They are personally free and subject to authority only with respect to their impersonal official obligations.
2. They are organized in a clearly defined hierarchy of offices.
3. Each office has a clearly defined sphere of competence in the legal sense.
4. The office is filled by a free contractual relationship. Thus, in principle, there is free selection.
5. Candidates are selected on the basis of technical qualifications.
6. They are remunerated by fixed salaries in money, for the most part with a right to pensions.
7. The office is treated as the sole, or at least the primary, occupation of the incumbent.
8. It constitutes a career.
9. The official works entirely separated from ownership of the means of administration and without appropriation of his position.
10. He is subject to strict and systematic discipline and control in the conduct of his office.[5]

The word *bureaucracy* and even less charged words such as *formal organization* or *complex organization,* are code words which conjure up images in our society. We envision a desolate land in which nothing can end well and behold a punitive image of the "welfare" caseworker. The connotations of bureaucracy and "bureaucratic" behavior are so widespread that none of us is immune to the negative images and stereotypes we base upon them. Bureaucracies exert pressures on their employees to be "methodical, prudent, disciplined."[6] While such words often may convey positive attributes, for the most part within our society they are associated pejoratively with the thought that bureaucrats are unsympathetic, do not treat persons in humane ways, are uncreative, follow the rules of the system scrupulously, and do not challenge the policies of the particular bureaucracy.[7]

---

[5] Max Weber, "The Essentials of Bureaucratic Organization," *Reader in Bureaucracy,* Robert K. Merton et al. (eds.), New York: The Free Press, 1967, pp. 21–22.
[6] Robert K. Merton, "Bureaucratic Structure and Personality," ibid., p. 365.
[7] One study which challenges this view of bureaucrats is Melvin L. Kohn's "Bureaucratic Man," *New Society,* No. 474, October 28, 1971, pp. 820–824. On the basis of a study he conducted comparing bureaucrats and nonbureaucrats, Kohn reported that "even with education statistically controlled, bureaucrats are found to value self-direction more highly than do non-bureaucrats, to have more personally demanding moral standards, to be more receptive to change, to be intellectually more flexible (especially in dealing with ideational problems), and to spend their leisure time in more intellectually demanding activities."

Professionals in Bureaucracies

Nevertheless, bureaucracies are not all bad. As our society becomes more complex and interdependent, as business and other organizations grow in size, there has been more employment within bureaucracies, even by professions which in the past have been noted for their "free" stances. Subliminally we recognize the change that has taken place in employment, but the image of "professionals" remains one of independent operators. However, sociologists of professions have pointed out this increased bureaucratic employment by professionals:

> Physicians are now affiliated in larger numbers with hospitals and clinics; attorneys with law firms and, in increasing numbers with industrial corporations; scientists and engineers also with industry, government, large independent research organizations, and a collection of institutes and departments in academic institutions.... No profession has escaped the advancing tide of bureaucratization.[8]

Problems in Bureaucracies

While professions and bureaucracies are intricately tied, there are real problems for social workers as professionals as they function within these complicated human networks. Essentially these problems can be categorized into two areas: (1) the relationship between bureaucratic structure and professional culture and (2) the structure of authority.

Bureaucracies and Professional Culture

In a discussion on access to service, Alfred Kahn has suggested that

> Organizational factors and bureaucratic realities may supersede professional ethics. No one professional is a social service generalist. He is child welfare worker, psychiatrist, family service worker, child guidance staff member, school personnel officer, and so on. His specialization and competence demand of him that he have a special perspective. Yet professional and organizational perspectives do affect the ways in which a problem is perceived and structured, the values that are held supreme, the priorities given to components of and the sequences in a solution to a family's difficulties, the "costs" to be tolerated for given outcomes or "benefits."[9]

[8] Howard M. Vollmer and Donald M. Mills, *Professionalization*, Englewood Cliffs, N.J.: Prentice-Hall, 1966, p. 264.
[9] Alfred J. Kahn, "Perspectives on Access to Social Services," *Social Work*, Vol. 15, No. 2, April 1970, pp. 95–101.

Thus there are problems of congruency between the professional's culture and the demands of organizational life.

But the effects of professional identity within a bureaucracy include issues equally subtle. For example, Robert Vinter suggested that when

> ... professionals are present in large numbers and assume elite positions, dependence on them brings with it limiting commitment to particular ideologies and strategies of change. Alternative approaches are thus denied the organization except as these are mediated through the profession. The risk is that the approaches defined by one or another profession may not be sufficient for achievement of treatment goals, yet the organization is no longer as free to pursue alternative means.[10]

Bureaucracies and Authority

Professional identity and perspectives cause the selection of particular interventive strategies. Generalized professional knowledge and identity, however, are expressed in the individual case. It is here that individual professionals may enter areas of potential conflict with their superiors in the hierarchical arrangements in the bureaucracy. Etzioni has suggested that a basic administrative principle is thus put in jeopardy because

> ... knowledge is largely an individual property; unlike other organization means, it cannot be transferred from one person to another by decree. Creativity is basically individual and can only to a very limited degree be ordered and coordinated by the superior in rank. Even the application of knowledge is basically an individual act, at least in the sense that the individual professional has the ultimate responsibility for his professional decision. . . . Only if immune from ordinary social pressures and free to innovate, to experiment, to take risks without the usual social repercussions of failure, can a professional carry out his work effectively.[11]

But these are demands which cannot be admitted by a bureaucratic organization, not only because of internal accountability but because of accountability to the wider community. Peer support for professional experimentation or decision-making is one thing, but administrative responsibility and accountability run counter to such freedoms.

The longer the training and the greater the professional orien-

[10] Robert D. Vinter, "Analysis of Treatment Organizations," *Social Work*, July 1963, pp. 3–15.
[11] Amitai Etzioni, *Modern Organizations*, Englewood Cliff, N.J.: Prentice-Hall, 1964, p. 76.

tation, the greater the tendency to take as one's reference group the profession rather than the agency.[12] This, too, runs counter to a demand of bureaucracies. One method in social agencies or other organizations to standardize the discretionary component in the work is to make rules. Another method is by reducing the number of written rules and by buying personnel who have complex rules built into them. We generally call these people "professionals."[13]

Thus social agencies hire social workers as professionals to ensure high standards and quality service delivery. But the fact of being professional in itself runs counter to bureaucratic demands while it meets the need for the ability to narrow the outer limits of discretion through professional training.

These are issues of autonomy. The dichotomy for professionals of autonomy and nonautonomy has been questioned as a result of the intricate interrelationships which now exist for professionals with organizations of all kinds. Nina Toren has suggested that rather than label professionals in relation to their autonomy, it might be better to ask: "Which aspects of the professional's daily conduct are controlled by whom, and how? If this is specified, the description of any profession becomes more complex and realistic and less idealtypical."[14]

The Role of the Profession

Toren is speaking of description, a relatively simple thing to do. The more difficult problem is to reconcile professional autonomy with bureaucratic demands. Willard Richan pondered this question and focused upon "the social work profession as a corporate entity in its relation to social welfare as an institutional complex ... for the behavior of the individual social worker within an organization will be influenced by the posture the profession assumes at large; and that posture, in turn, will be modified as the constituency of professional employees find a particular stance more or less consistent with the demands of the work setting."[15]

Richan's argument places the dilemma in a different context: the

[12] Etzioni, *op. cit.*, p. 88.

[13] Charles Perrow, *Complex Organizations*, Glenview, Illinois: Scott, Foresman, 1972, p. 27.

[14] Nina Toren, "Semi-Professionalism and Social Work: A Theoretical Perspective," *The Semi-Professions and Their Organization*, Amitai Etzioni (ed.), New York: The Free Press, 1969, p. 155.

[15] Willard C. Richan, "The Social Work Profession and Organized Social Welfare," *Shaping the New Social Work*, Alfred J. Kahn, (ed.), New York: Columbia University Press, 1973, pp. 147–148.

individual worker must be viewed within the context not only of the agency and the profession, but the agency and worker must be viewed within the context of the profession within the social welfare institution. The power of the social work profession, according to Richan, depends upon the cohesion of the profession. He suggests "the issues of professional autonomy and professional cohesion are closely related. To achieve the former, the organized social work profession must demonstrate the latter; that is, its ability to speak for the social work community. And both of these depend, in turn, on effective control over social work practice and the social work education process."[16]

Paradoxically, as Richan continues his argument, the attainment of greater autonomy for social workers is tied to greater controls. The regulation of practice, control over who practices and the conditions for practice, and licensing and "enforceable expectations"—that is, greater regulation of social workers—is the means he suggests for achieving greater autonomy. So in regard to the problem we have come full circle.

At bottom the issue which revolves around the question of autonomy is social reform and social work's role in it. Social reform is one part of the social work tradition. However, as Kathleen Woodroofe has stated, the struggle to gain

> . . . professional acceptance in the community has accentuated some of the stresses within social work itself. Some of these stresses spring from attempts to fix rightful boundaries to its domain; others from efforts to define its function in new areas and settings. Some spring from limitations of its knowledge and experience; others arise from the nature of its own activity. But perhaps the most serious source of stress has been the attempt to reconcile the caution of professionalism with social work's traditional commitment to reform[17]

There are certain more pedestrian problems and dysfunctions of bureaucracies. For example, the specialization of social workers within a bureaucracy means task specialization. Such specialization increases the quality and quantity of work, but it also may lead to discrete responsibilities and areas of service. When this occurs, it is often accompanied by disjunctions among the several services available, and people who need service may fall through the cracks.

Work within bureaucracies is accompanied by frustration, lack of congruency between individual and organizational needs, skewed time perspectives, rivalry, and conflict. To the extent these attitudi-

---

[16] Richan, ibid., p. 164.
[17] Kathleen Woodroofe, *From Charity to Social Work in England and the United States*, Toronto, Canada: University of Toronto Press, 1974, pp. 224–225.

nal effects carry over into work with clients, members, and others who come for service, they may be dysfunctional in regard to services.

Supervision as frequently conducted in social agencies also plays a part in the professional's self-image, and not entirely as a negative factor. For example, it has been suggested that close supervision, especially where it is therapeutically focused, may allow "caseworkers to maintain their conception of themselves as professionals in a manner not possible under the more direct control attempts associated with the bureaucratic approach."[18] It may be that social workers who accept the therapeutic function for the profession and experience it in their practice (and perhaps in their supervision) may be less critical and more accepting of the structure of the organizations in which they work. Both professionalism, in this case therapeutic focus, and practice in bureaucracies may lead to an acceptance of the structure of the organization because of a deflection of ascribed motivations from "structural" considerations to personal and individual ones.

Alternatives

Much emphasis and a growing literature has been aimed at understanding bureaucratic settings and developing ways of operating successfully within them. The range of options available include less active and dramatic roles for the social workers to conscious and planned efforts to alter the agencies in order to improve service.[19]

Still another perspective on how to reduce the friction between professionals and bureaucracies can be found in the work of Warren Bennis, exponent of *ad hocracy*. In his view, "organizations, if they are to survive, must become decentralized, practice participative management, and be adaptive and responsive to their members."[20]

From permanent and enduring administrative forms, there has been a movement to temporary and transient changing forms. In har-

---

[18] W. Richard Scott, "Professional Employees in a Bureaucratic Structure," *The Semi-Professions and their Organization*, p. 110.

[19] Some examples of this literature are Willard C. Richan and Allan R. Mendelsohn, *Social Work: The Unloved Profession*, New York: New Viewpoints, 1973, pp. 201–220; Rino J. Patti and Herman Resnick, "Changing the Agency from Within," *Social Work*, Vol. 17, No. 4, July 1972, pp. 48–57; Robert Pruger, "The Good Bureaucrat," *Social Work*, Vol. 18, No. 4, July 1973, pp. 26–32; Harry Wasserman, "The Professional Social Worker in a Bureaucracy," *Social Work*, Vol. 16, No. 1, January 1971, pp. 89–95; and Harold H. Weissman, *Overcoming Mismanagement in the Human Service Professions*, San Francisco: Jossey-Bass Publishers, 1973.

[20] Perrow, op. cit., p. 172.

ried and pressed bureaucracies, "with no time for decisions to wend their leisurely way up and down the hierarchy, 'advisors' stop merely advising and begin to make decisions themselves."[21] These alterations in the traditional model of bureaucracy support the autonomy and professional self-expression of professionals, albeit within the context of accountability.

An untypical form of private practice has been suggested as another way to overcome the dysfunctions of bureaucracy. Warren Hagstrom has suggested that the poor be organized and with minimal financial investments from each poor individual large sums could be made available from the mass of the poor. If social workers were employed by the poor under such conditions, a new configuration of power and bureaucratic functioning could result.[22]

According to some social workers, the trend toward private practice is a key mechanism to offset the forces of bureaucracy upon social workers. Irving Piliavin, for example, has suggested that social workers can serve their clients truly only if they accept and use the entrepreneurial model. He thinks social workers are trapped by their roles in social agencies and must conform to the rules and practices of the agencies to the detriment of their clients.[23] The private practice of social work in the marketplace is, indeed, an important feature of today's social work. However, when that choice becomes true for much of or the entire profession, a question can be raised about the social commitment and philosophy of the profession.

The quest for professional status by social workers has often led them to identify themselves with entrepreneurial models of professions, such as medicine and law which are predominantly conducted in the United States by "independent" practitioners. To the extent that social workers become private practitioners they delimit the communal (societal) sanction they receive through social welfare and other sponsoring organizations. Social sponsorship and commitment have been important factors in the development of social work's professional identity. For better or worse, an emphasis on private practitioner models of professional activity serves to limit the socially sponsored, communal aspects of social work as a profession. According to some observers, tendencies away from the social commitment of the profession lead to a deemphasis on social action,

[21] Alvin Toffler, *Future Shock*, New York: Bantam Books, 1972, p. 140.
[22] Warren C. Hagstrom, "Can the Poor Transform the World?" *Readings in Community Organization Practice*, Ralph M. Kramer and Harry Specht (eds.), Englewood Cliffs, N.J.: Prentice-Hall, 1969, pp. 301–314.
[23] Irving Piliavin, "Restructuring the Provision of Social Services," *Social Work*, Vol. 13, No. 1, January 1968, pp. 27–35.

acceptance of the role of technician-implementer in contrast to policy change, and a lessening of the ideological gap between social workers' ideas and those of the dominant groups in society.[24] Thus, bureaucratic organizations, although subject to criticism, may be better settings for social workers to engage in social change and social action than some of the alternatives offered.

SOCIETY, THE FUNCTIONS OF SOCIAL WORK, AND SERVICES FOR PEOPLE

Social work enacts particular roles within the social welfare territory. The society in which social work functions sets certain demands and limits upon the profession. Nevertheless, the functions of social work have been vigorously debated within the social work community. Essentially, the question is "How many kinds of social work should there be: repair, prevention, human rights, or social justice functions?" The major functions expected of social work determine how many different kinds of social workers must be prepared to implement them. From one perspective, all roles performed by social work can be viewed as deriving from two basic societal functions, social control and social change.

Society assigns the functions of social welfare, and therefore for social work, in formal and informal ways. Various sanctioning bodies provide that social welfare agencies will perform specific functions, and they typically determine how these functions will be implemented. These sanctions derive not only from consumer demand but also from legislation, funding, and other formal and informal devices. The roles and functions of social workers are dependent upon the priorities set by society through various control mechanisms. While every profession, including social work, would like to think of itself as an independent variable, it only partially chooses its own roles and functions. Professions, to varying extents, are dependent variables whose limits are set by powers external to them. Social work is not alone in this characteristic, although the degree to which each profession is controlled will differ.

Social agencies exert control in several ways, including the selection of populations to be served, selection procedures, and methods of service. Thomas Szasz stated:

> In the United States, state or local governments or private philanthropic agencies (supported by the upper classes) employ social service work-

[24] Herbert Bisno, "How Social Will Social Work Be?" *Social Work.* Vol. 2, No. 2 April 1956, pp. 12–18.

ers. Without wishing to deny the benefits that often accrue to social work clients, this arrangement clearly empowers the employers to exert a measure of social control—in this case, over members of the lower classes.[25]

Not only are social control mechanisms operating manifestly through social agencies which wish to socialize clients to dominant societal values, but more subtle controls are expressed through functions which are latent in the choice of methods and technologies.

Limitations, however, are placed upon the change functions of social work. These limitations were dramatically enacted during the 1960s. Mobilization for Youth, a New York City War on Poverty multifaceted social service program, began seriously to test its theoretical base, opportunity theory, and found it had to make interventions which challenged the status quo of socioeconomic arrangements. As soon as the serious nature of the challenge became known, influential factors in the New York political scene began to act to buffer the interventions of the staff and citizen participants.[26]

Limitations also exist for social work's social change role because of the limitations of knowledge implicit in the state of knowledge itself in the social sciences. According to some, these limitations lead to certain consequences within the profession. One observer has suggested the real lack of knowledge is masked by the promotion of a mystique of expertise, that the lack is not sufficiently acknowledged because to do so would threaten professional authority and standing and would undermine the ability of social workers to market their skills while the very survival of the organizations for which they work would be threatened.[27]

Finally, both on philosophical and empirical grounds, there are social workers who suggest that any profession which focuses primarily upon individual change cannot be truly focused upon social change. According to this view, individual change is simply inconsistent with the demands of social change and, in reality, such an approach is more consistent with social control. To this group, the fact that social work maintains its clinical, one-to-one focus suggests not social change but social control as the higher professional value.

[25] Thomas A. Szasz, *The Myth of Mental Illness,* London: Secker and Warburg, 1961, p. 68. Szasz did not limit his criticism to social service but viewed psychiatry as a social control, stating "coercion and deceit are rampant in the legal and social uses of psychiatry."

[26] See Peter Marris and Martin Rein, *Dilemmas of Social Reform,* New York: Atherton Press, 1969, pp. 177–181.

[27] Dorothy M. Jones, "The Mystique of Expertise in Social Services: An Alaska Example," *Journal of Sociology and Social Welfare,* Vol. III, No. 3, January 1976, p. 344.

The "Bottom Line"

Social work is not a "free agent" which can choose completely whether it wishes to be predominantly a profession of social control or social change. Regardless of whether the profession operates within bureaucratic settings or as an entrepreneurial service, it is dependent upon the sanctions of society. Social workers enact their roles and work within society. In addition to whatever limitations exist as to knowledge needed for social change or the choices of interventions, social work can only make choices within certain limits. Societies do not hire "social change" agents, but they do hire persons who can perform important functions which in the ways they are performed have the potential of changing parts of society as well.

CAUSE AND FUNCTION

An historic tension has existed between two tracks of social work which have lived in an uneasy alliance, yet the relationship has continued so long that one can suspect a functional basis for the continuation. These two streams have been described variously as "cause" and "function" and as the social reform and case service tracks. Almost from the inception of social work the two tracks came to be associated with particular persons and institutions. The case service track which developed from the work of Thomas Chalmers translated to America is ordinarily associated with the charity organization societies' friendly visitors who culminated in the social casework track. The social reform track associated with the settlement houses and social workers involved in seeking better environmental conditions through legislation and other means also included charity organization persons as well.

Beginning with settlement houses, the efforts of the charity organization societies with the second track of social reform were influenced by muckraking journalists and liberals during the progressive era. The first track is best represented in the United States by Mary Richmond, who developed early casework theory and techniques, and the second track by Jane Addams who as a settlement house founder and director was active in social reform and in enacting legislation.

These two tracks reflect separate and different conceptions, and yet the social work profession hangs together. Why this is the case is an important question for our consideration. Historically the dichotomy—the two tracks—arises in different forms and under different names.

During the 1890s there had been hostility toward settlement

houses and their workers at the National Conference on Charities and Corrections. Originally formed by volunteers who created neighborhood service centers in the midst of poverty neighborhoods, the settlement houses and their leadership (exemplified by Jane Addams of Hull House in Chicago) focused not only on services to individuals, families, and neighborhoods, but also on changing society and the world in which the poor existed. They were not confident of their acceptance by others in the field of social welfare. In 1897 Jane Addams apologized for being at the national conference because "settlements are accused of doing their charity work very badly."[28]

In her thought and work Jane Addams expressed the social reform track in social work. On the basis of her experiences, she recognized a multicausation for social ills, a fact which suggested multifocused action to alter life conditions. In regard to this multicausation in life she stated:

> The settlements have often been accused of scattering their forces; as institutions they are both philanthropic and educational; in their approach to social problems they call now upon the sociologist, now upon the psychiatrist; they seek the services of artists, economists, gymnasts, case-workers, dramatists, trained nurses . . . the first time I heard a sociologist use the phrase, "vortex causation"; the universities were at last defining the situation and it was possible that they would later enter this inter-related field of personal difficulties, bewildering legal requirements, ill health and conflicting cultures which the settlements find so baffling.[29]

Representative of the case service track in social work, Mary Ellen Richmond was employed in charity organization societies in Baltimore and Philadelphia, formulated the first global statements of the principles of social casework, taught at the New York School of Philanthropy, and was the author of *Social Diagnosis*, the first formulation of the theory and method of social diagnosis.[30]

Charity organization society workers were investigating each needy person and family in detail, attempting to avoid duplication of benefits of any kind, seeking cooperation among agencies, and fostering the use of friendly visitors.

Very early in its development the case service track had an indi-

[28] Allen F. Davis, *Spearheads for Reform: The Social Settlements and the Progressive Movement 1890–1914*, New York: Oxford University Press, 1967, p. 195.

[29] Christopher Lasch (ed.), *The Social Thought of Jane Addams*, New York: Bobbs-Merrill, 1965, p. 216.

[30] D. G. Becker, "Mary Ellen Richmond", *Encyclopedia of Social Work*, Vol. II, Robert Morris (ed.), New York: National Association of Social Workers, 1971, pp. 1135–1136.

vidual and family focus, based on the character of the individual, the relationship with the people to be helped, and a search for technique. The social reform track, while serving individuals, families, and neighborhoods, also stressed more global change through political action, publicity of social problems, legislation, and a greater emphasis on the surroundings in which people lived. This stream of social workers was doing the preliminary work to attain workers' compensation, health insurances, and mothers' pensions and generally worked to prepare for the financial protection of workers and their families.[31]

Thus, in its early stages, social work contained several different kinds of social workers. They were employed or served as volunteers in a wide variety of situations. They were based in settlement houses and focused on societal changes. They were employed as administrators and friendly visitors in charity organization societies, constructing a method for helping individuals and families. They were framing and lobbying for the preliminary social insurances and for other social legislation.

Despite the differences in emphasis, spokespersons for the two tracks (social reform and case services) agreed there were commonalities between the two tracks, and each had need for the complementary actions of the other. For example, in *Social Diagnosis* (1917), Mary Richmond concluded that the majority of social workers were in casework: "in work, that is, which has for its immediate aim the betterment of individuals or families, one by one, as distinguished from their betterment in the mass. Mass betterment and individual betterment are interdependent, however, social reform and social case work of necessity progressing together."[32]

In 1929 Porter R. Lee, director of the New York School of Philanthropy, in his presidential address to the National Conference of Social Work provided a perspective on the tensions which existed between the social reform and the case service aspects of the profession. He suggested that social work was *both cause and function.* (A cause is fighting for certain goals, a crusade to attain certain objectives. A function is a collection of technical skills.) He defined cause as a "movement directed toward the elimination of an intrenched evil," a function he viewed as an "organized effort incorporated into the machinery of community life in the discharge of which the acqui-

[31] Roy Lubove, *The Struggle for Social Security 1900–1935,* Cambridge: Harvard University Press, 1968.
[32] Mary E. Richmond, *Social Diagnosis,* New York: Russell Sage Foundation, 1917, p. 25.

escence at least, and ultimately the support, of the entire community is assumed."[33]

Lee defined these two aspects of social work as overlapping and symbiotic; they were also parts of an historic process through which society and social work both change. According to this view,

> . . . social work, however, is cause as well as function. Much of what we do in social work we do because, on the whole, we prefer a civilization in which such things are done to one in which they are not. Some values are beyond measurement.
>
> That new causes need to be initiated every social worker is painfully aware. Efficient social work everywhere means the constant discovery of new evils, of ancient evils in new forms which are taking their toll of men. Good social work creates the necessity for more social work.[34]

In a catchy phrase, Clarke A. Chambers offered another way of viewing these two social work tracks. He called them the "retail" and the "wholesale" services; not only do they differ in regard to cause and function, but they also differ in regard to the size of the population unit to which they give emphasis and in regard to the roles their professionals play. He suggested that

> . . . the two overlapping phases of social work continue to exist, not always harmoniously, but certainly in interdependence—the one focused on the individual and his welfare, strongly influenced by the psychological disciplines, introspective dealing in personalized retail services; the other concerned with reform, with reconstruction, informed primarily by the social sciences, extroverted, dealing in group or community or wholesale services.[35]

Chambers went further and suggested the two tracks of social work require two different major roles: priest and prophet. The priest is a "shepherd, he serves, he counsels, he comforts, he reconciles, he listens, he accepts, he judges not, he plays out a ritualistic role, he bears witness to a transcendent concern." The prophet, however, "holds up absolute standards against which the sins of man and the shortcomings of the world may be measured and judged; his cry is less for charity and compassion than for justice; he is not content

[33] Porter R. Lee, *Social Work as Cause and Function*, New York: Columbia University Press, 1937, pp. 3, 5.

[34] Lee, op. cit., pp. 19, 21.

[35] Clarke A. Chambers, "An Historical Perspective in Political Action vs. Individualized Treatment," *Current Issues in Social Work Seen in Historical Perspective*, New York: Council on Social Work Education, 1962, p. 53.

merely to stand and serve; repentance and reform or doom is his prophecy."[36]

But the argument as to cause and function, case services, or social reform has been dismissed by at least one author who suggests that the different methodologies of social work are all conservative, social control forces, the only differentiation being which level of society is addressed for intervention. Jeffrey Galper in *The Politics of Social Services* has suggested that casework operates on a sociopsychological view insufficiently related to the societal roots of peoples' dilemmas and therefore cannot develop strategies equal to making social change. Furthermore, he suggests that community organization—even through the more radical of its historic interventions—also serves as a conservative force in that whatever changes it accomplishes do not lead to change in the basic structures of society.[37]

This latter argument suggests changes in social work methodologies but also, in fact, calls for the politicization of social work as a profession. The early social workers of the progressive era took political stands and affected party platforms and legislation to significant extents. Still later, other social workers influenced decision-makers and legislation. Over the years, however, as Daniel Moynihan has suggested, there has arisen the "professionalization of reform." The professionalization of reform implies a certain objectivity and attention to professional expertise rather than investment in the movement aspects of the professional aims and their achievement. Ideology can be a resource and lead social workers toward the achievement of social reform or help to veer social work into new professional paths. It is possible that more radical professional stances, including alliances with particular political parties, could serve to create new roles for social workers as their functions changed. This might be one method of combining the cause and function dichotomies into unique new professional configurations. However, the alliance with particular political parties or ideologies also will cause losses. Given the existence of a democratic United States in which parties move in and out of power, it appears more likely that on balance social work will not choose to become overly identified with one party, or to cut off its links with any party or ideology which has the possibility of potential power and for helping create better services for people.

[36] Ibid., p. 63.
[37] Jeffrey H. Galper, *The Politics of Social Services*, Englewood Cliffs, N.J.: Prentice-Hall, 1975, pp. 111–130.

Today the historic argument continues. On the one hand there are social work proponents of social action and societal change to create a just society; on the other hand there are social workers who emphasize the clinical case service track who want to help people on a case basis.

Some social workers have attempted to create ways out of the two-track dilemma through the creation of new methods and new types of professionalism. Others have attempted to reconcile the differences through redefining traditional methods so the connections between the two tracks stand out.

William Schwartz in attempting to reconcile the two tracks reminds us that certain human issues seem always with us: mass or individual betterment, process or goals, and individual or state freedom or discipline. The emphasis is always on the choice—either one or the other. But, as he suggests, the choices once made seem incomplete. Schwartz joins private troubles and public issues through the mediating role of the social worker. The mediating process between individuals and society—the engagements of people with their systems—are real struggles in which both can change. The professional role of social workers is to help change the nature of individuals and of the society through these engagements, thus tying societal and individual change (cause and function) together.[38]

Another effort to resolve the dilemma was made by Martin Rein, who postulated four types of social work creeds and interventions: traditional casework, radical casework, community sociotherapy, and radical social policy. Faulting social work for its "professional doctrine that emphasizes therapeutic solutions," he recommended a casework practice which would "challenge the standards of society by showing that they are irrelevant or have hurtful consequences, that valid and relevant standards are not implemented, or that the standards men live by are faulty."[39]

Social work can contribute, according to Rein, by helping to improve the "quality of urban life, humanizing institutions, and altering the priority of social values," by dealing directly with "relevant people and institutions contributing to persons' difficulties," by encouraging "individuals to alter their external circumstances—seek to change the framework of expectation and level of provision," by emphasizing "skill in practicing casework in a hostile environment," and by using "casework not to encourage conformity but to marshal

---

[38] William Schwartz, "Private Troubles and Public Issues: One Social Work Job or Two?" *Perspectives on Social Welfare*, Paul Weinberger (ed.), New York: Macmillan, 1974, pp. 346–362.

[39] Martin Rein, "Social Work in Search of a Radical Profession," *Social Work*, Vol. 15, No. 2, April 1970, pp. 13–28.

resources of clients to challenge reality." Rein chooses radical social work because it combines the element of cause with the element of function. Social workers are employed to perform certain functions using professional skills. This baseline function may be the starting place for societal change, because employers do not ordinarily fill functional job slots with "world-changers."

Some years ago Porter Lee tried to tie the two tracks together suggesting that "the capacity of the social worker, whatever his rank to administer a routine functional responsibility in the spirit of the servant in a cause lies the explanation of the great service of social work."[40]

In a more recent discussion of this question, Roy Lubove also has suggested why the disparate elements within the profession hold together. Casework, that is, case services, was a key to "a knowledge base and helping technique more 'scientific' and hence more professional." However, "if social work could claim any distinctive function in an atomized urban society with serious problems of group communication and mass deprivation, it was not individual therapy but liaison between groups and the stimulation of social legislation and institutional change"[41] which offers that unique function. Agreeing with Flexner that social work's unique feature is its "traffic cop" function, Lubove (like Rein) suggests that the clinical case services offer social work a baseline for practice while reform gives the profession its uniqueness, and the two—cause and function, social reform and case services—together form a team which provides a profession for a territory, the arena of social welfare. The functional specialty is needed to give social work a professional image and base, and social work needs the element of cause to give it uniqueness and difference from the other therapeutic or helping professions.

GENERIC-SPECIFIC SOCIAL WORK

Even within the relatively homogeneous case services stream of social work, there were problems of generic skills, knowledge, and attitudes applicable to a broad variety of practice settings while—at the same time—there are counterforces for specific training for specific agencies and fields of practice. Lubove identifies some of the consequences of this situation:

The functional generalization in casework, which contributed so much

[40] Lee, op. cit., p. 24.
[41] Roy Lubove, *The Professional Altruist: The Emergence of Social Work as a Career,* 1880–1930, New York: Atheneum, 1969, pp. 210–211.

to the absorption of social workers in problems of skill and technique, also created obstacles to the attainment of a group identity. . . . Until it became clear that social work was more than a series of occupational specialties there could be no group identity and no subculture. Mary Richmond's *Social Diagnosis,* the first systematic effort to formulate the principles of casework, addressed itself specifically to the problem of unity despite diversity of settings. She sought to define casework practice in terms of social investigation and the use of social evidence.[42]

Social work contained tensions between generic and specific qualities just as it did between cause and function. The price of functional diffusion and generic qualities, seemingly, was a limited sense of identification by workers as to themselves as social workers and a limited sense of the totality of the profession as social work. Constant, in addition, was the early identified problem of educating workers equally prepared for work in several fields.

In the 1929 monograph *Social Casework: Generic and Specific* these issues again moved to the fore. A work group struggled with the generic and specific aspects and the issues which underlay the concepts. Their work had commenced from

. . . a recognition of the importance of the problems of division of labor among case work agencies. This, again, was not a new question. It has furnished material for discussion for a generation. After a generation's discussion, however, it seemed to the group that dividing lines between the specific fields of social case work were still lacking, as well as the fundamental principles underlying the practical working divisions among the case work agencies of the community.[43]

But it is not simply a question of division of labor. The different philosophies (for example, cause or function) and different methodologies (specialization or generic) raise bothersome but important questions. In 1936 Sophonisba P. Breckenridge, a professor at the University of Chicago, reported the problem and drew attention to its importance. In an article on professional education for social work she remarked:

Another subject on which agreement has been slowly developing is the generalized, as over against the specialized, nature of the desirable curriculum. Some schools, possibly because of the nature of their origin, provided instruction in family welfare, in child welfare, and in group work, organizing the instruction in fields quite distinct from the others.

[42] Ibid., pp. 119–120.
[43] *Social Casework: Generic and Specific,* New York: American Association of Social Workers, 1929, Classic Series, Washington, D.C.: National Association of Social Workers, 1974, p. 4.

On the other hand, some schools have taken the position from the beginning that their responsibility was the education of persons who should enter a field of social work, thus recognizing the probability of a worker's passing from one area in the field to another.[44]

With a social worker's passage from one field of service to another or entry into new settings, the profession became functionally diffuse (social workers function in many settings with many different sets of skills to meet many different kinds of needs). This fact, on the one hand, creates problems for the profession, mainly relating to issues of education and professional identification: What are the commonalities of social workers trained in diversity who practice in even more diverse settings?

On the other hand, the fact the profession is functionally diffuse and of a generalized nature allows for the entry of social workers into many different types of employment and service settings. The functionally generalized nature of the profession also makes it possible for it to bring knowledge and skills when the society alters its major concerns or new problems arise. Social work has been quite successful at entering new fields and making contributions. This flexibility is the positive side of the functionally diffuse nature of the profession, a trait shared with other professions as well.

While some view the diversity of social work as a drawback, it can be viewed as an important strength or, even more, as an unplanned strategy related to the achievement of widespread social services. The fact that the profession plays an important intermediary role among different institutions makes it possible for the profession to help people meet needs of diverse kinds since every social institution a priori cannot meet all the needs of people related even to its own area.

Another positive attribute derives from functional diffusion. It has been suggested that specialized roles in organizations allow professionals to carry out their activities with a greater degree of freedom than would be the case where substructures and roles would be more generalized. The autonomy of a professional in an organization is supported by the differentiation of roles and consequent specialization.[45] By analogy, the social work profession also may function in this manner. Specialization tends to support the autonomy of separate divisions of the profession. However, problems of communication, influence, and cooperation may be created because of the lack

---

[44] Sophonisba P. Breckenridge, "The New Horizons of Professional Education for Social Work," *Social Service Review*, Vol. X, No. 3, September 1936, pp. 434–444.
[45] Bernard Barber, "Some Problems in the Sociology of the Professions," *Daedelus*, Vol. 92, Fall 1963, pp. 669–688.

of a common language and the resistance of different camps to accept the views of others.

The question can be raised as to whether a profession can have too many specializations. The diversity of specializations sometimes can be a detriment in that licensing and sanctioning bodies may have difficulty in distinguishing those in the profession who have particular skills. This also can be a difficulty in relationship to the potential receipt of third-party payments.

Despite the difficulties of diversity and functional diffusion, and despite the problems related to professional identity, over the past decades it is clear that the development of the profession and services for people have been encouraged by this feature of the profession. While there are difficulties which arise, they seem on balance to be outweighed by the gains for society and for the profession.

One study has concluded that the controversy of clinical, that is, case service, versus social goals for social work is neither real nor important for practicing social workers.[46] Dichotomizing social workers into those with a "clinical" orientation (predominant belief in the efficacy of individual treatment to improve social functioning and solve social problems) and "social" orientation (predominant belief in the necessity for directing social change), this study concluded that the clinical-social division found in social work literature does not characterize the attitudes of professional social workers toward their field.

The authors offered two explanations. Perhaps a coordinated view of casework and social reform reflects the reality of most social workers' practice, and they coordinate both functions in their daily work. Or such dichotomies of thought may reflect existing practice theories which need to be reformulated. Although the authors of this one study explain away such dichotomies, it is clear empirically that social workers continue to maintain two camps. However, if caseworkers assume that their clinical orientations provide social change of a broad significant nature, it is possible that the wrong questions have been asked or that fundamental differences remain between the two groups in regard to what is meant by social reform. From the point of view of the social reform wing of the profession, clinical practice simply cannot be viewed as social reform. Insofar as social work practice is clinical, and most of it is of that nature, this fact would minimize the potential—in the view of the social reformists—of social work's contribution to social change. In fact, most social

[46] Merlin A. Taber and Anthony J. Vattano, "Clinical and Social Orientations in Social Work: An Empirical Study," *Social Service Review*, Vol. 44, No. 1, March 1970, pp. 37, 42.

reformists would view clinical practice as an enhancement of the social control functions of the profession.

In the 1970s a growing literature began to be developed in an attempt to create generic methods. The emphasis in baccalaureate social work education was upon the education of "generalist" social workers. This aim was achieved through the utilization of generic methods per se or through the integration of traditional methods: casework, group work, and community organization. There was some indication the profession would assign generalist preparation to baccalaureate programs and build specializations in depth at graduate level.[47] The complications of such curricula development are involved and problematic. While such structural solutions may be faulty, there is, nonetheless, a continued trend developing toward the creation of ever-improved generic methods, and generations of social workers are now being trained in their use.

PROFESSIONALS, PARAPROFESSIONALS, AND VOLUNTEERS

Social work is organized formally with two entry points to the profession: the bachelor of social work and the master of social work. There are differences of opinion as to whether the two levels of personnel should be prepared for differences of kind in function or differences of degree. Despite a long and divisive debate, the issue of baccalaureate social work per se has been settled by the NASW as a result of a 1969 referendum of its membership which resulted in a vote favorable to the bachelor's program. The professional association's decision is reflective of the reality of federal legislation supportive of the use of baccalaureate social work personnel.

Many social work educators and practitioners are wrestling with how to rationalize the bachelor's, master's, and doctor's programs in a continuum. Among the issues which arise in a consideration of this question are

1. Should generalists be prepared (analogous to a general practitioner physician) at the bachelor's level and at the graduate level? If desired, what are the feasible and preferred parameters for each?
2. Are or should the differences between the bachelor's and

[47] The House of Delegates of the Council on Social Work Education approved a policy statement in 1976 stating, "Graduate degree (candidacy) programs in social work shall consist of advanced specialized education that requires and is built upon the core of social work knowledge, skills, and attitudes and content in basic supporting disciplines." *Policy Statements on Social Work Practice and Education and Structure and Quality in Social Work Education,* Adopted by the House of Delegates, March 1976.

master's programs be defined by varying degrees of sophistication of skills in the same configuration?

3. Or should the bachelor's and master's programs be different in kind: two qualitative preparations different in natures?
4. If differences of kind are desirable, what should they be?

The result of research, discussions, and thought on these issues remains to be worked out for everyday professional decisions at the two levels in practice and education and for those who employ and educate social workers.

Approximately 330,000 persons were employed with the title of social worker in 1976, two-thirds of them women with an equal percentage employed by state, county, and city governments. A small number of social workers are employed by the federal government. Other social workers are employed by voluntary and private agencies with a small number involved in international service as teachers and consultants.[48]

In addition, in 1976 there were approximately 100,000 social service aides, 80 percent of whom were women, largely employed in government service in inner city areas. These aides provide important helping functions in the delivery of social services by supplementing the work of professional social workers, especially in assisting to link people to required services and to deliver "concrete" services such as assistance traveling to and from an agency and assistance at home.[49]

Social service aides may hold an associate degree in social welfare or human services or have even less formal education. (According to the NASW, a person with a BA in a field other than social work who is employed in a social work position is also called a social service aide.) The professional association recognizes the importance of associate degree level social welfare personnel, whose preparation was given major impetus by the Manpower Development and Training Act (1962), the Economic Opportunity Act (1964) and the Social Security amendments of 1967.

As one can note by the discrepancy between the number of members of the professional association (78,000) and the number of persons employed in 1976 in social work positions (330,000), large numbers of persons employed in social work positions as defined by employers are untrained in social work prior to their employment. Implications of the discrepancy are that social work as a profession

[48] *Occupational Outlook Handbook 1978–79*, Bureau of Labor Statistics, U.S. Department of Labor, Washington, D.C.: U.S. Government Printing Office, 1978, pp. 562–565.

[49] Ibid., pp. 560–562.

has not been in a position as yet to control sufficiently the use of the professional title and designation or to prepare sufficient numbers of trained personnel.

Finally, volunteers occupy an extremely important position in the social welfare arena. In 1974 there were 37 million volunteers (50 percent in religious groups, 15 percent education and health, 11 percent recreation, 12 percent civic work, and 7 percent social and welfare organizations, with the remainder in other types of organizations). Depending upon how one defines social and welfare organizations, as well as the others above, the 2.5 million social and welfare volunteers are undoubtedly low figures for such volunteer involvement. In a 1974 study the United Way of America studying only that organization and its member agencies found volunteers contributed *2.4 billion* person-hours per year. The dollar value of volunteer services was set at $67.8 billion for 1974. Volunteers are involved in direct service programs (83 percent), fund-raising (12 percent), and (5 percent) policy-setting through boards and committees.[50]

Task differentiation among professional social workers (bachelor's and master's), paraprofessionals, untrained persons employed in social work positions, and volunteers is a relatively undefined but important area of concern in social welfare. The entire issue of who may do what is somewhat ambiguous and unsettled. Even the value of voluntarism itself is subject to objections from unions and women's groups which want to enhance employment opportunities and which view voluntarism as undermining the goal of paid work. And yet the development of citizen leadership (voluntarism) is a basic goal of social work practice.[51]

Questions about the areas of competency of professionals and of lay persons confound many professions. Which social policy decisions should be decided by lay persons and which only by social workers (or by physicians, engineers, etc.)? Some questions about health insurance or public assistance programs may rest in the broader citizen sphere, while questions of specialized particular competency (such as to operate or not or to place in a foster home or not) belong in the professional judgment sphere. Yet some social welfare policy questions are ambiguous so that it is difficult to differ-

[50] Violet M. Sieder and Doris L. Kirshbaum, "Volunteers," *Encyclopedia of Social Work*, Vol. II, John B. Turner (ed.), New York: National Association of Social Workers, 1977, pp. 1582–1591.
[51] One estimate in 1973 suggested that 6 billion hours of labor were volunteered in the nonprofit sector of the economy—the equivalent of 3 million full-time workers. Burton A. Weisbrod, "The Forgotten Economic Sector: Private But Nonprofit," Institute for Research on Poverty, Reprint Series, No. 309, Madison, Wisconsin, 1978, p. 34.

entiate the dividing line between professional and lay or citizen decision-making.[52]

RACISM, SEXISM, AND A PLURAL SOCIETY

The profession of social work has made efforts to deal constructively with racism and sexism within its professional ranks and in society. While the efforts so far need to be continued, social work as a profession has done well compared to other groups. Nonetheless, problems remain.

The membership of the NASW in 1975 was 63 percent female[53]; 71 percent of the students enrolled in master's degree programs in 1977 were female.[54] Fourteen percent of the professional association members are minority group members;[55] 18 percent of master's degree students are ethnic minorities. Faculty members in graduate schools of social work are 49 percent women and 21 percent ethnic minorities.[56]

Of full-time students enrolled in undergraduate programs in 1977 about 80 percent were female and almost 30 percent were members of ethnic minority groups. Of those faculty members teaching only in undergraduate programs, 50 percent were female and 26 percent were of ethnic minority backgrounds.[57]

Between 1970, when strenuous efforts began, and 1976 the national leadership of the professional association (elected and appointed) has been changed from 75 percent male and 86 percent white to 50 percent male and 70 percent white in terms of gender, and racial balance.[58] Estimates of the proportion of females and minority group persons in administrative positions in general social work practice are far below the proportions of such persons who are professionally trained. For example, in 1976 of 84 deans or directors of graduate schools of social work, 12 (14 percent) were female.[59]

At one level all people are the same and have "common human

[52] Donald Feldstein, "Do We Need Professions in Our Society? Professionalization versus Consumerism," *Social Work*, Vol. 16, No. 4, October 1971, pp. 5–11.
[53] Rosemary Sarri, "Administration in Social Welfare," *Encyclopedia of Social Work*, Vol. II, 1977, p. 48.
[54] Allen Rubin and G. Robert Whitcomb, *Statistics on Social Work Education in the United States: 1977*, p. 37.
[55] Sarri, op. cit., p. 48.
[56] Rubin and Whitcomb, op. cit., p. 37.
[57] Ibid., pp. 6, 24.
[58] Maryann Mahaffey, "Sexism and Social Work," *Social Work*, Vol. 21, No. 6, November 1976, p. 419.
[59] *Schools of Social Work with Accredited Master's Degree Programs, July, 1976*, New York: Council on Social Work Education, 1976.

needs," but at another level, we are all different. One way we deal with differences in our society is by discrimination. As a result, there is a need for affirmative action programs in social work and social welfare, at least for the foreseeable future. One major reason for the necessity of inclusion is the need that all groups have for role models to identify with in terms of sex, race, and ethnicity. But this rationale must not be taken too far and argue that only blacks can work with blacks or blind with blind or those who have been addicted to work with those who are addicted.

Social work is struggling with this problem. For example, it is legitimate that a social service in a Chicano neighborhood ask that all workers speak Spanish and be familiar with Chicano culture, but to ask that all workers also be Chicanos may be going to an extreme.

Race and ethnicity are factors in U.S. culture, and social work recognizing this has influenced recruitment, admissions, hiring, and promotion patterns. Similar decisions regarding women are being made relative to promotion to leadership positions. These trends are not just personal professional career decisions affecting individuals but have an impact upon the delivery of social services, resource allocation, and community conflict and consensus. Race, ethnicity, and women's issues are important areas for social work and social welfare in which significant strides have been made. Continued efforts will remain needed in order to attain an equitable plural society.

For all its weaknesses and ambiguities, the profession of social work is strong, growing, and a fundamental part of contemporary society.

Chapter 10
Social Trends Affecting
Social Welfare

"Is it possible to make sense of what is going on in the world, to set oneself for the future? Of course we cannot predict the sudden storms of history. But history is more than storms; it is also a great Gulf Stream, carrying us along on its broad currents."[1]

Robert L. Heilbroner

Knowledge about the future has always been sought by people. Seers such as Tiresias or the Delphic oracle were present in many cultures and times. When the biblical Joseph in jail interpreted the dreams of Pharaoh's chief butler and baker, he saw into their personal futures: hanging for the baker and restoration of the butler to his former position. But these are predictions of private, individual "personal troubles." Later, when Joseph predicted the seven fat and seven lean years, he was forecasting events which affected the entire structure of the society, that is, "public issues" with consequences far beyond individuals. There is great importance for social welfare in predicting the future. The greater the extent to which social trends can be forecast, the greater the possibility for anticipation of future needs and the need for preparation to meet those needs.

Predicting the future is a serious matter. Consider the chagrin of the Western Union Company after it has been offered exclusive

[1] Robert L. Heilbroner, "Trying to Make Sense of It," *New York Times*, October 10, 1977, p. 29.

rights to the newly invented telephone and had turned them down. The president of the company, William Orton, when offered the telephone by Alexander Graham Bell asked, "What use could this company make of an electrical toy?" Different assumptions about the future led Sears-Roebuck and Montgomery Ward at the end of World War II to plan in different ways. Montgomery Ward, expecting a depression, saved its cash and did not expand, hoping to buy cheaply for expansion when the depression arrived. Sears-Roebuck assumed the future would bring a business boom, expanded, and captured a large part of the market.[2]

On the other extreme, it is fortunate that forecasts by the U.S. government in 1945 of huge unemployment were incorrect, as have been the predictions of the death of the world.[3]

Predictions of future trends can be useful for planning in many spheres. In business and industry, prediction of future population trends can anticipate resources needed and the numbers and location of potential purchasers. Great sums are expended by the U.S. intelligence community to predict the future intentions of nations in order to plan and prepare for anticipated actions. On a local level, decisions have to be made, for example, on where to erect a branch office of a bank, the best location for a quick-service food franchise, whether the town should build an extension to the high school or rent space. Planning is done in all parts of American society, including public and private domains, industry, business, agriculture, and such services as social welfare and education.

Planning has been viewed by some as an attempt to control peoples' lives, to relieve them of responsibility and decision-making. In one sense planning can be viewed as an attempt to control the future to the extent possible. This use of planning is clear and acceptable when we consider planning, let us say, for a space flight or building a healthy economy. Planning for social welfare does have the feature of trying to control the future by achieving particular goals, such as efficiency or effectiveness. However, the primary reason for planning in the social sphere is that "one seeks 'pre-vision' as much to 'halt' a future as help it come into being, for the function of prediction is not, as often stated, to aid social control, but to widen the spheres of moral choice."[4]

---

[2] *An Introduction to the Study of the Future*, Washington, D.C.: World Future Society, 1977, pp. 336–337.

[3] National Science Foundation, *Knowledge into Action: Improving the Nation's Use of the Social Sciences*, Washington, D.C.: U.S. Government Printing Office, 1969, p. 12.

[4] Daniel Bell, "Twelve Modes of Prediction," *Daedelus*, Vol. 93, No. 3, Summer 1964, p. 873.

From this latter point of view, planning is in fact an opportunity to expand options and thus provide greater freedom for personal responsibility and decision-making rather than less. If we can successfully anticipate the future and influence it, for example, provide appropriate and sufficient service for the population of aging persons in 1990, we increase the number of options available for individual choice by the aging. When they can freely choose between entering an institution and remaining at home with adequate support services, the planning which makes such individual and family decision-making possible expands the arena of freedom for people to determine their own lives and reduces the controls and constraints exerted on them.

There is the "self-fulfilling" prophecy where the prediction is itself a factor in making it accurate. For example, if leading pollsters predict an electoral victory for a given candidate, this may encourage voters to join the bandwagon and thus may increase the likelihood of the prediction being accurate.

But there is also the "self-defeating" prophecy where the prediction mobilizes a society to make the predicted outcome not come to pass. If it is predicted that 1000 people will die of starvation, this may cause new legislation specifically to thwart the predicted outcome. This is one of the benefits of prediction.

One example of early American social planning began during Herbert Hoover's Administration. President Hoover in 1929 called on a committee of scientists "to examine and to report upon recent social trends in the United States with a view to providing such a review as might supply a basis for the formulation of large national policies looking to the next phase in the nation's development."[5] Later, in his foreword to *Recent Social Trends,* the resulting study, Hoover suggested that the study "should serve to help all of us to see where social stresses are occurring and where major efforts should be undertaken to deal with them constructively."[6] Prediction and planning are needed more as functions of modern society than of particular ideologies or economic systems; in fact, they are requirements of all complex and technological societies.

Trends are important for social welfare just as they are important for other societal institutions. Social trends can indicate the general direction of future needs; for example, the following two predictions made in the early 1930s suggest trends extrapolated from then available information:

[5] *Recent Social Trends in the United States. Report of the President's Research Committee on Social Trends,* Vol. I, New York: McGraw-Hill, 1933, p. xi.
[6] Ibid., p. v.

1. Divorce is still increasing. Although the rate of this increase in the past decade has slowed up, a study of the long time trends gives no confidence in a prediction that the rate of divorce will decrease in the near future, though it must do so in the long run.[7]

Approximately 50 years later (the long run?), divorce has continued at increasing rates, although the anticipation had been for a diminished rate of increase. For social welfare such information and projections can suggest the kinds of social services needed: support for single-parent families, child care, marital counseling, Big Brother and Big Sister programs, and the kinds of training social workers need to deal with the results of this trend.

2. . . . an increasing number of women are joining the wage earning group. The rate at which they pass from the non-gainfully employed to the gainfully employed is not rapid, but it has been increasing . . . It is also clear that women are forming a steadily increasing proportion of the gainfully employed . . . the tendency seems to be away from the older agricultural and industrial pursuits, in the direction of office, store, and professional work.[8]

Although we look with hindsight, from the perspective of social welfare, the increase of women gainfully employed was the harbinger of shifts in employment patterns, family role adjustments, a need for child-care services, shifts in social security coverage and benefits, and so on.

Some planned events intended to deal with one set of issues may have secondary effects which may be either functional or dysfunctional, helpful or not helpful for the society. In regard to a more restrictive U.S. immigration policy implemented in 1924,

. . . immigration was no sooner restricted than the vacuum thus created drew hundreds of thousands of southern Negroes from the farm to the industrial cities, a movement with manifold repercussions upon the Negro population.[9]

The human needs created by this immigration policy shift are evident in the course of American history over the past half century. Although one could anticipate that mechanization of agriculture would force people off the land and to the cities insufficiently prepared to cope with complex urban life, it only became clear later that immigration policy, industrialization, and urbanization were intricately connected with major implications for social welfare and our society in general.

[7] Ibid., p. 708.
[8] Ibid., p. 748.
[9] Ibid., p. 555.

If the connections had been made between these separate events, if information had been available as to the likely consequences of their interactions, if resources were available, and if we willed doing something about the anticipated problems, it would have been possible for our society through social welfare to anticipate needs and to plan for meeting them to a greater degree than was actually done, possibly placing greater emphasis on prevention rather than "patch-up" work after the fact.

METHODS OF FORECASTING

Methods of forecasting the future range from the relatively simple to the extremely complex. The following listing of methods of forecasting is not meant to be complete but is meant to suggest something of the variety of methods currently used.

Trend curves are one kind of extrapolation technique. A trend curve suggests the long-term behavior of some societal feature and assumes the factors which produced the trend historically will continue to do so. In an earlier chapter we described a long-term trend in our society in which the government assumes more and more responsibility for social welfare services.

Correlation methods utilize correlations between an observable or measureable event and the topic to be forecast. Changes in the national economy are foreseen by particular indicators. When the national economy flags, recession of one degree or another begins. In a time of languishing economic activity, it is predictable there will be increasing unemployment and greater demand focused upon employment services and unemployment insurance systems. Such correlations may depend upon concurrent events or may be based upon the identification of precursors.

Causal models are based upon the assumption that the contributing variables are known and their interactional patterns are known so that the cause of one particular event is identifiable. Such models are now in the preliminary stages of development and have limited use in social welfare. For example, models of the economy of the United States can predict the response of the economy to tax cuts. Technological forecasts can be quite accurate, but sufficient accuracy has not been established yet in the social welfare sphere.

Scenarios are portrayals of the impact of a series of identified variables. Based upon particular assumptions, the forecasters may create a "best case" scenario in which the most favorable events occur or a "worst case" scenario in which whatever can go wrong does so. The scenario method can be a dramatic presentation of the consequences of the interaction of the important variables.

The *Delphi technique* depends upon expert judgment. A panel of experts may be asked to predict something in the future. Their responses are privately communicated to the coordinator of the inquiry, who compiles the responses and reports them to the panel members. They all in turn have an opportunity to revise their anonymous predictions without inhibition since no participants know the responses of any particular persons. This process is repeated as necessary to attain greater clarity about the issues being examined, views expressed by participants, and implications.

Computer simulation makes possible forecasts which are speedy and precise and can utilize large numbers of variables. Of course, as with manual computations, the validity, accuracy, and believeability of the input data are key factors.

Social welfare depends primarily upon extrapolated data when it wants to consider the future. The birthrate, for example, is an extrapolated statistic; that is, we must estimate what the rate will be in the future. Such an estimate is based upon present behaviors which are apt to change, trends in family size which may be short or long-lived, knowledge about current and future sources of child-bearing persons, and the like.

The predictions one makes depend, whether one is using simple intuition or highly sophisticated computers, upon the identification of important variables, knowledge about their interaction, and assumptions, among other things about the external factors which will impinge upon the factors and their interactions. Social trends especially have special complications.[10]

There are problems of accuracy in predicting the future for social welfare purposes. Not much work has been done in systematic evaluation of forecasting studies and their accuracy as proven by subsequent events. In fact, Daniel P. Harrison summarized the results of over 50 studies of forecasting accuracy:

> ... if one looks hard enough one can eventually find examples—in eleven of the fourteen types of forecasting (including combined forecasting methods) and find that the amount of error ranged between just a few percentage points (for example, with econometric models, survey forecasting, and biological growth curves) to over 40 percent (clinical prediction), depending on the method and time horizon used. This range of error, other things being equal, could be considered to be due to either methodological underdevelopment in a given type of forecasting method or to the intractability of the particular aspect of social pro-

[10] For an extensive listing and explanation of "Methods of Forecasting," see that chapter in *Introduction to the Study of the Future*, op cit., pp. 158–187.

cess being studied; probably both are true. "Hardware-oriented" technological forecasts seem to do better than social forecasts.

Social forecasts are prone to data problems in relation to the types, relevance, volume, and quality of the data available; the margin of error permitted (such as in life and death or summer camp attendance); and the measurement problems such as missing data, measurement imprecision, and assumptions used.

Extrapolation remains the basic forecasting method for social welfare purposes. However, straightforward extrapolation without other considerations can be extremely dangerous. If today there are 3 computer programmers in the United States and tomorrow there are 9 and the next day there are 27, one could predict from that series that within a short period of time almost everyone in the United States will be a computer programmer, but obviously there are limiting factors. It is precisely because of this assumption of a continuation of trends that demographic predictions often have been faulty. This method of extrapolation is one which has to be used most commonly in social welfare, but one can keep in mind that trends tend to be self-limiting.

The possibilities of prediction and ultimately of control remain speculative. As with many things, two points of view can be identified. For much of American history we have been an "optimistic" society. Especially during the progressive era (and extending into the second half of this century), American optimism combined with scientism and technology to assume that all problems could be solved if we only asked the right questions and found the correct formulas.

In recent years a new pessimism has arisen (could it have been forecast?), symbolized by the title of an article by Nathan Glazer, "The Limits of Social Policy." According to Glazer:

> It is illusory to see social policy only as making an *inroad* on a problem; there are dynamic aspects to any policy, such that it also *expands* the problem, *changes* the problem, *generates* further problems.[12]

On the one hand, there is the perspective that all problems are solvable. On the other, the solution of problems or their mere amelioration confound the hopes of the optimists by creating new problems. The place for cures becomes the place for new illnesses. A long time ago Florence Nightingale suggested that the first duty of a

[11] Daniel P. Harrison, *Social Science Frontiers, Social Forecasting Methodology: Suggestions for Research,* New York: Russell Sage Foundation, 1976, p. 56.
[12] Nathan Glazer, "The Limits of Social Policy," *Commentary,* Vol. 52, No. 3, September 1971, p. 53.

hospital is not to make patients sicker than when they came in. Now we know that staphylococcus infections picked up in hospitals is a serious consideration.

Somewhere between these two extreme positions probably lies the truth, that we have as a society significant abilities to anticipate problems and to solve them, but most significant problems are not simple to solve and solutions may create problems of their own.

With all the humility engendered by the above discussion we now seek to look at major social trends and at some of their implications for social welfare including trends related to growth and demography, productivity and the service economy, national society and centralized government, societal values and mores, marriage and divorce, ethnicity, and pluralism and comparative international developments.

GROWTH AND DEMOGRAPHY

Within a world context, projections of the future are essentially optimistic or pessimistic. In *The Limits to Growth*, Donella Meadows and others reached the conclusion that

> . . . if the present growth trends in world population, industrialization, pollution, food production, and resource depletion continue unchanged, the limits to growth on this planet will be reached sometime within the next one hundred years. The most probable result will be a rather sudden and uncontrollable decline in both population and industrial capacity.
>
> We can thus say with some confidence that, under the assumption of no major change in the present system, population and industrial growth will certainly stop within the next century, at the latest.
>
> The basic behavior mode of the world system is exponential growth of population and capital, followed by collapse.[13]

F. M. Esfandiary, a philosopher of the future, presents a different picture and suggests that

> . . . precisely because of the accelerating rate of change we urgently need plans for the coming years. Unfortunately most projections of the future are pessimistic. Western intellectuals in particular hobbled by puritan guilt and self-doubts flood the world with books and films and scenarios foredooming the future. To them our successes and potentials are not real. Only our failures. Their reactionary outlook has helped make people afraid of progress and the future. 'If the future is so bleak' is the unconscious reasoning 'why think about it? Safer to hide in the

[13] Donella H. Meadows et al., *The Limits to Growth*, New York: Universe Books, 1972, pp. 23, 126, 142.

womb of the past or of mother nature.' We must develop a bold new philosophy of the future. A hopeful outlook which can embolden people to want to face the future. To want to plan for it. More than ever we need short-range and long-range plans. Guidelines to help us steer our onrushing breakthroughs making them work for all humanity.[14]

Esfandiary laments pessimism and sounds a call for optimism about the future. Briggs, too, among others, has argued against the neo-Malthusians, those convinced that continued population growth and economic development will lead to starvation, exhaustion of resources, and the "collapse" of the world system. While pointing out that Malthus' eighteenth-century prediction that world population would outstrip food supply has proven false, Briggs cites evidence that the earth can support many times more people than it now does.[15]

Briggs has suggested that humankind has only scratched the surface of resources. Pollution can be controlled given the human will to do so. He also suggests that population growth is slowing. Citing United Nations population projections based on 1968 figures, he points out that in almost every case 1970–1972 actual census compilations were lower than the U.N. "low" projections. Furthermore, this drop was not due to starvation or malnutrition in any country.

Increasingly, demographers sense a self-limiting factor to population growth. In underdeveloped countries, modernism will tend to cut the death rate first, leading to dramatic increases in population growth. But this is temporary until the culture changes caused by modernism begin to result in smaller families. So as the economic situation improves, there will be frightening population spurts, but this may be the price of progress and only temporary.

Briggs also draws attention to the fact some agricultural economists have calculated the world has land which can be cultivated sufficient to feed 30 billion people at present U.S. levels of consumption with existing technology. On the basis of these optimistic projections, the Hudson Institute predicts the earth can support 15 to 20 billion people with an average income of $20,000 (current figures are 4 billion and $1200) and that it could function with present known technology without innovations yet unknown.

As Briggs has suggested, there is no necessity to believe the optimistic projections nor the neo-Malthusian predictions. But even Briggs assumes a certain reality which must be prepared for and

[14] F. M. Esfandiary, *Up-Wingers,* New York: John Day Company, 1973, p. x.
[15] B. Bruce-Briggs, "Against the Neo-Malthusians," *Commentary,* Vol. 58, No. 1, July 1974, pp. 25–29.

which has implications for everyone, rich and poor. He recognizes that

> . . . even with the most optimistic cut in the birth rate, there will be over five billion souls on this earth at the end of the century. These people must be fed, housed, and provided with a decent life. For them, a world of zero growth would be a world of conflict, an age of iron and blood. Only continuous growth can begin to deliver in modest degree, what the coming world will require by way of health, welfare, and human dignity.[16]

Such long-term considerations serve as assumptions for actions in the present. They form the stark background against which social welfare must operate. Limitations upon economic growth, and even upon population growth, will have future effects for social welfare. In his essay "Should the Poor Buy No Growth?" Willard Johnson argues that

> . . . a lack of continued growth, without substantial change in national policies to facilitate the transfer of wealth and income through transfer payments, tax reform and job development or vigorous antidiscrimination efforts would probably have disastrous consequences for blacks, and perhaps for the poor more generally.[17]

The line of reasoning of the neo-Malthusians, those who take the pessimistic approach, is congenial to those who are already prosperous; by the same token, those who are the "have nots" essentially have to opt for the "bigger pie" with more for everyone. If we believe the economy and world growth are to reach a stage of stasis, of steady-state, then wealth will be static as well. In this case, redistribution can only be resisted by those who are the "haves." John Rawls in *A Theory of Justice* has argued that equity should be based upon a reparations approach.[18] However, reparations or redistribution depend in either case—expanding economy and growth or contracting economy and limited wealth—on taking from the rich and giving to the poor. To the extent the "pie" is bigger and expanding, it seems more probable redistribution can be accomplished in that while the poor are given resources the wealthy continue to gain wealth, albeit at perhaps a diminished rate. Thus growth versus no growth is the fundamental issue which confronts the earth and our society and, in turn, social welfare provisions. Continued economic growth, hopefully in nonpolluting directions, seems to the authors to be prerequisite to improvements in social welfare.

[16] Ibid., p. 29.
[17] Willard R. Johnson, "Should the Poor Buy No Growth?" *The No-Growth Society*, Mancur Olson and Hans H. Landsberg (eds.), New York: W. W. Norton, 1973, p. 171.
[18] John Rawls, *A Theory of Justice*, Cambridge: Harvard University Press, 1971.

On a national level the issue of growth and shifts in the composition of the population are of immediate concern to the United States and to social welfare. The 1930s in the United States was a period of low fertility. However, following World War II the United States experienced a dramatic period of high fertility. As a result, while "from 1950 to 1960, the number of young persons aged 14 to 24 was almost constant, rising only slightly from 26.6 to 27.1 million, in the 1960 decade, reflecting the postwar baby boom, the cohort jumped 44 percent going from 27.1 million in 1960 to 39 million in 1969.[19]

The "bulge effect" of the baby boom created a need in serial order for more elementary classrooms, high schools, college facilities, and now produces marriages and the need for housing.[20] For many years in the future, this "bulging generation" will be a dominant factor in American life. For example, competition for better jobs and better pay are intense among those of the "baby boom" generation.[21]

Further, the population projections for persons 65 and over are for an

> increase until 2000, but at a declining rate as the relatively small birth cohorts of the 1920's and 1930's reach age 65. This age group constituted 10.3 percent of the total population in 1974 with the projected figures for 2000 ranging from 10.7 percent . . . to 12.5 percent. The population 65 years and over will grow rapidly after 2010, both in absolute numbers and as a proportion of the total population, with the entry of the baby boom cohorts into this age group.[22]

If one traces this bulge through all the phases of life from birth to death, it is possible to predict many of and the extent of the social welfare needs which have to be met. Beginning with social services related to childhood, the pattern of services needed by this large group of people shifts as they enter different periods of life: school, marriage, forming and raising families, and so on.

Regardless of the particular effect of the bulge upon the aging population around the end of this century, there are now 42 million persons over 55 years of age and close to 2 million over 85. It is

[19] Daniel Bell, *The Coming of Post-Industrial Society*, New York: Basic Books, p. 234.
[20] Eleanor Bernert forecasted in *America's Children* (New York: John Wiley, 1958) the need for services which would be generated by this "bulge" cohort.
[21] Stephen Good, "Baby Boom Execs Scramble for Jobs," *New York Post*, July 23, 1977, p. 10.
[22] U.S. Bureau of the Census, *Current Population Reports. Population Estimates and Projections. Projections of the Population of the United States: 1975 to 2050*, Washington, D.C.: U.S. Government Printing Office, 1975, p. 7.

expected that the population of aging will continue to grow.[23] From the social welfare perspective, one can anticipate the need for services to aging persons in their homes, other suitable options for housing, health care, and other services such as homemakers, "Meals-on-Wheels," friendly visitors, and financial supports. This trend can only be heightened by further advances in medicine, and therefore life span.

When one recognizes that a "slim" generation is passing through as the middle-aged population and paying taxes on earnings, but at the same time there is a substantial and growing aging population, the question arises as to how will social security be provided for the aging. With the recent shift to a lower birth rate, there is a change in the proportions of our population. Fewer people will be joining the work force, but more people will be entering retirement. Perhaps recent consideration of methods for changing retirement patterns, including alteration of rules for receiving social security after age 65, are related to this series of events.

In any case, as this chapter is being written, a major debate is going forward on how best to finance Social Security provisions. If early retirements continue as an important trend, this problem may be compounded.[24] Social Security has been a powerful weapon in combatting poverty. If the system is to be undermined, the fundamental social welfare supports in our society will be brought into question. Thus demography will play an enormously important role relative to social welfare provisions.

Since 1957 the American fertility rate has dropped from a peak to record lows. Zero population growth (the point at which deaths and births balance each other) seems to be an inevitable outcome.[25] Smaller families may have effects on child-rearing patterns, the middle-aged will have to bear the brunt of supporting the society as taxpayers, and mandatory retirement ages will have to be postponed.

Given minor changes in the death rate and net immigration, projections of future population can be made with confidence as to the number of survivors among persons now born. However, "because of wide fluctuations in the birth rate during the last few decades and uncertainties about how closely its future level will continue to approximate the present low level, the demographer is much less

[23] U.S. Bureau of the Census, *Current Population Reports, Demographic Aspects of Aging and the Older Population in the United States*, Washington, D.C.: U.S. Government Printing Office, 1976, p. 3.
[24] Jerry Flint, "Early Retirement is Growing in U.S.," *New York Times*, July 10, 1977, pp. 1, 22.
[25] "Looking to the ZPGeneration," *Time*, February 28, 1977, pp. 71–72.

confident about making projections of the population that is yet unborn."[26]

Are we truly headed toward zero or even negative population growth or is there a renewal of the birth rate? Such a fluctuation seems to have occurred, at least for the time being. The birth rate which reached new lows in the mid-1970s had been greeted eagerly by proponents of zero population growth. Others were concerned that the low birth rate would harm the economy and future of American society. The birth rate began to rise in the last part of 1976 and continued to rise in 1977. This discontinuity reversed a trend which seemed solidly established. One explanation for the reversal is the larger number of women between 15 and 44 years of age, many of them members of the bulge generation of the "baby boom" years. But while the American fertility rate is among the lowest in the world, the fertility rate (the rate at which women in the child-bearing age give birth) was up 5 percent in 1977 from a comparable period in 1976, a substantial increase.[27]

Another explanation offered for the renewal of the birth rate is that it represents a temporary "bump" in the curve based on the deferred patterns of giving birth among couples. According to this argument, once the "bump" is accommodated the long-term trend line will continue downward. Whichever way the birth rate moves — continuing downward, leveling off, or increasing—there are social welfare implications: size of tax force, family patterns, proportions of age groups within overall population, resources available for distribution, and other concerns such as living space and number of retirees.

Predictions of a reversal in birth trends had been made for some time. It remains to be seen what this alteration in birth rates will mean and what factors such as a revitalized economy, immigration, and the "surfacing" of several million illegal immigrants will produce. In regard to this latter point, according to Zero Population Growth, Inc., "illegal immigration is the biggest threat to hopes for population stability because it is an unplanned and uncontrolled source of growth."[28]

The complexity of such predictions is made clearer by this var-

[26] U.S. Department of Commerce, Bureau of the Census, *Population of the United States: Trends and Prospects: 1950-1990*, Washington, D.C.: U.S. Government Printing Office, 1974, p. 210.

[27] Robert Reinhold, "Birth Rate is Rising from 1976 Low," *New York Times*, July 24, 1977, pp. 1, 19.

[28] Ann Crittenden, "Illegal Immigration Called Threat to Hopes for Population Stability," *New York Times*, August 10, 1977, p. 32. For predictions of birth rate increases, see Linda Wolfe, "The Coming Baby Boom," *New York*, January 10, 1977, pp. 38–42.

iant understanding of the "baby boom" era which introduces additional variables. Richard Easterlin has hypothesized that

> ... the high wage and salary levels of persons twenty to twenty-nine years old was one of the prime factors sustaining the American baby boom of the 1950's. The number of persons in this age group was exceptionally low because of the small number of babies born during the Depression. The supply of new entrants to the labor force was, therefore, abnormally reduced during the 1950's, a period when demand for labor was high. Moreover, the group entering the labor force in the 1950's was exceptionally well educated in comparison with older age groups and thus had a competitive advantage in employment during a period in which educational qualifications became increasingly important.[29]

Thus labor demand, the importance of credentials, the size of the particular population cohort, and other factors combined to have an impact upon the baby boom. Not all of the factors could have been predicted. According to one view, it has been suggested that the grandparents of the "baby boom" generation had relatively few children and thus were able to help with resources needed for more children, including funds and time.

Birth rates declining or increasing, are results of economic conditions, and the values of society. The role of the family, the strength of ethnic values, and the trend to hedonism and self-fulfillment as life goals all will affect the birth rate. Prediction is difficult, but social welfare decisions need to be made nonetheless. How many obstetrical or pediatric beds, for instance, are needed for an adequate health care system?

Easier to do and equally necessary is to plan for the life stages of those already born, as described above.

PRODUCTIVITY AND THE SERVICE ECONOMY

Issues for social welfare also derive from the nature of productivity in American society. Leaving aside the nature of work (in itself a considerable issue for social welfare because of its impact on mental health, alienation, and family life), we want to at least note one dream which apparently must continue to be deferred.

Just a few years ago, predictions were being made that

> ... the traditional link between jobs and income is being broken. The economy of abundance can sustain all citizens in comfort and economic security whether or not they engage in what is commonly reckoned as

[29] David M. Heer, "Economic Development and the Fertility Transition," *Daedelus*, Vol. 97, No. 2, Spring 1968, p. 448.

work. . . . We urge, therefore, that society, through its appropriate legal and governmental institutions, undertake an unqualified commitment to provide every individual and every family with an adequate income as a matter of right.[30]

Similarly in 1853 an American writer predicted the day would arrive when "machinery will perform all work, automata will direct them. The only task of the human race will be to make love, study, and be happy."[31]

So far the automation revolution has not yet reached that millenium. Quite the reverse. In 1853 almost 33 percent of the total U.S. population was employed. In 1970 the figure was 36 percent.[32] Although some persons in some few industries (automotive workers, longshoremen) have reached a guaranteed annual wage, payment not to work has certainly not become a norm in our society. Planning for a guaranteed annual wage or minimum income cannot proceed on the assumption that automation per se will create so much wealth that everyone will be supported and there will necessarily be a rising proportion of nonworkers in the population and being "unproductive" will be acceptable. The sudden realization that energy is limited, that resources are finite, has led to a new appreciation that work is needed even in this society, if only the economy could be organized to handle full employment. To the extent that wealth is created through technological advances, the social welfare of the nation is a potential recipient of the "bigger pie." Nevertheless, social welfare has to compete among other "goods" within the society. Increasing productivity in itself does not mean greater emphasis upon social welfare concerns.

Furthermore, the issue of productivity enters the societal equation in other ways which affect social welfare. The shift from production of goods to the production of services is a part of the context for social welfare. Our society has become postindustrial, in the sense that it is no longer an industrial society in which the majority of the working classes are engaged in manufacturing or the production of goods. We have reached a high level of productivity so that it takes less than half of the work force to produce all the goods to supply the population. In the United States more than two-thirds of the work

---

[30] The Ad Hoc Committee on the Triple Revolution, "The Triple Revolution: An Appraisal of the Major U.S. Crises and Proposals for Action," *Poverty in America*, Louis A. Ferman, Joyce L. Kornbluh, and Alan Haber (eds.), Ann Arbor: University of Michigan Press, p. 457.

[31] Richard A. Peterson, *The Dynamics of Industrial Society*, New York: Bobbs-Merrill, 1973, p. 48.

[32] Ibid., p. 48.

force are employed in services and less than one-third makes goods for consumers.

The United States is the pioneer in such an economy. Following World War II it became the first "service" economy. As Victor Fuchs has pointed out, "Virtually all of the net increase in employment between 1947 and 1967 occurred in institutions that provide services—such as banks, hospitals, retail stores, schools." The *increase* in the field of education between 1950 and 1960 and the *increase* in the field of health were greater respectively than the total number employed in steel, copper, and aluminum industries and the total number employed in auto manufacture in either year.[33]

In a service economy there is inevitable inflation because of built-in labor-intensive industries. For example, if a factory manufactures 100 shirts per hour, a new invention may make it possible to create 200 shirts an hour, so then any one worker can be more productive. But there is no way a Mozart quintet can be played in less than a certain number of person-hours of work. Or there are natural limits to how many persons can be served by a barber during any one day. These latter two illustrations are of labor-intensive industries.

Productivity creates the "pie" which has to be divided up among the various demands within society. It is an open question as to how productive services can become. To what extent can teachers or sanitation workers be made more productive? Paraprofessionals can be used to increase the productivity of teachers, or television instruction can be used to increase their production. Ultimately, however, we are dealing with labor-intensive industries in which it is difficult to raise production. Therefore, there is a built-in inflation. Inflation can be "beat" only by getting more productivity in the same number of hours in labor-intensive work. A service economy is more prone to inflation than a manufacturing economy. Demand increases, but supply does not necessarily increase. With an increase in services, expectations also increase. In the public sphere this inflation requires raises in taxes and other costs, and wages in such an economy compete for money which is also needed for building hospitals, schools, and the like.

Higher taxes and general inflation create a difficult environment for social welfare. Since social welfare has to compete with other parts of the society for resources, this competition is minimized in an

[33] Victor R. Fuchs, *The Service Economy*, New York: Columbia University Press, 1968, p. 1. In the United States in June 1978, of employees on nonagricultural payrolls (86,-547,000), 70 percent (60,671,000) were employed in service-producing industries. U.S. Department of Labor, Bureau of Labor Statistics, *Employment and Earnings*, July 1978. Vol. 25, No. 7, Washington, D.C.: U.S. Government Printing Office, p. 73.

era of expanding productivity—"the larger pie"—and competition is made more difficult in an inflationary economy in which taxpayers and legislators become very much concerned with costs and priorities are given to defense-related expenses.[34]

All of the above suggests that social welfare goals can be met only if

1. Productivity can continue to be increased in manufacturing and farming.
2. Productivity can be increased even in the service areas such as sanitation and other areas where inertia or featherbedding fail to exploit possibilities.
3. Social welfare services themselves can be delivered more efficiently such as without the expense of means tests.

NATIONAL SOCIETY AND THE FAMILY

The United States has become a national society, one in which events in one part of the society can have immediate repercussions in every other part. A national economy, transportation system, and media of communication have served to develop a national interdependent society. Regions within the society continue to exist, but the degree of their interdependence is enormous.

In regard to mass media, people receive more and more information from central sources, that is, regional accents are disappearing, information is gotten from national newsweeklies and nationally distributed papers, less attention may be paid to local scenes and differences, and news is distributed from national sources such as the Associated Press.

As a people we are developing a mass culture; for example, we attend the same movies, see the same television shows, and in general are developing a culture of a single society with a single set of values.

Mobility has helped to create this national society. Twenty percent of the U.S. population moved in a one-year period near 1960. This rate compares to 11 percent in England and Wales and 8 percent in Japan. In the United States such long-distance movement is more associated with persons who possess higher rather than lower educational and occupational backgrounds. As educational and occupational levels have risen, the rate of long-distance migration, especially among men 25 to 34 years of age, has increased. In fact, peak movement occurs at age 22 "when just under 50 percent of men

---

[34] For an extended discussion of this problem, see Daniel Bell, *The Coming of Post-Industrial Society*, pp. 154–164.

move from one residence to another in the United Stated within a 12-month period."[35]

One of the inheritances we have received from the Great Depression of the 1930s is a managed economy. While management of the economy had its conscious beginnings during that decade, it became openly expressed through the passage of the Employment Act of 1946 which expressed the goal of full employment in our society and created the Council of Economic Advisors to the President. Through fiscal (governmental expenditures and taxes) and monetary (supply of money) policy, the government has managed the economy to a significant degree, further developing the interdependence of various regions and parts of the society.

There is also a tide of rising expectations. A mass production nation also has to ensure mass purchasing power. In addition, there is a pooling of risks and everyone is entitled to certain things. The way in which expectations are met, at least minimally, is through pooling the risks so that those who are unable to produce nevertheless are entitled to and provided with certain goods.

At the same time, there is a concern about individual rights and a concern for group rights. Freedom is no longer defined as freedom for the individual citizen alone, but the freedom for diverse groups to have equality of rights. Thus two separate trends are occurring: centralization of national government and some alienation which derives from that while, on the other hand, the greater expectation level and the greater desire for fulfillment of rights ("we want our group included too; we want a share of the pie") leads to consumerism because we now have a managed economy and no longer have many decisions being made in the marketplace.

There is stress between consumerism on the one hand and technocracy, expertise, and centralized government on the other. It used to be that if one wanted to buy shoes, the consumer (according to classical capitalist theory) had power to make purchases from the best shoe store, and if that shoe store did not serve peoples' needs, it would be considered inefficient and would not endure. The consumer had, according to this point of view, a certain power in the marketplace. Now we have environmental laws, a Federal Trade Commission, import controls, labor contracts, and rent controls, all of which dictate prices. So we have a cost-push economy in that certain built-in factors which are not controlled by supply and demand become crucial. But we do not have an economic theory for this kind of oligopoly. In the 1960s Keynesian economics worked, but the 1970s have experienced both unemployment and inflation, a phe-

---

[35] *Population of the United States: Trends and Prospects: 1950–1990*, p. 206.

nomenon for which knowlege is lacking. Lester Thurow had pointed out that theories are available for supply and demand determination of prices within competitive markets. However,

> . . . larger and larger fractions of the GNP are being produced in sectors (medicine, government, etc.) that are clearly not competitive profit-maximizing sectors. Many other industries have just a few competitors, and the GNP has become increasingly concentrated among the largest firms in the last two decades. To explain inflation economics needs an empirically useful theory of oligopolistic behavior. How do very large firms, unions, and nonprofit agencies act when they have few competitors or when they are not simple income or profit maximizers . . . If economics does not have a theory of price determination in oligopolistic situations or if prices are indeterminant in such situations, then it cannot have a useful theory of inflation.[36]

When consumers want to have power over decision-making, they have to organize to obtain seats on the Federal Trade Commission and on environmental councils and have to elect legislators who will pass laws concerning price controls. Since we no longer have a market economy, in the pure sense of the word, if you want to retain democratic freedoms along with a managed economy, there will be necessarily a clash between consumers and expertise, technicians, and the machinery of government. This appears to be a new kind of class warfare between the consumers and the experts. Consumers are forced to organize as a political force in order to have power against the technocrats.

In "The Cultural Contradictions of Capitalism" Daniel Bell discussed the development of hedonism (the pleasure principle) in our capitalist society. Capitalism was generated by and accompanied by the Protestant ethic (delayed gratification, put money in the bank, invest it, make it work for you, don't be profligate, spend little, idleness is the worst sin, be productive, work hard, and if you are successful you are blessed by God, but if not you are cursed by God and have not received grace). This ethic is part and parcel of the development of capitalism.

The contradiction, according to Bell, is that when capitalism works, as it had in the United States, the reverse situation is produced. The hedonistic ethic arises in which self-fulfillment, "do your

---

[36] Lester C. Thurow, "Economics 1977," *Daedelus*, Vol. 106, No. 4, Part 2, Fall 1977, p. 92. The persistent problem of inflation has been viewed by some as an "insoluble" problem analogous to the problem of unemployment in the 1930s. Different points of view exist as to the significance of inflation, causation, methods for dealing with the problem, and its ultimate potential impact on the democratic societies. See Leonard Silk, "Must Inflation Problem End in Disaster?" *New York Times*, June 23, 1977, p. D5.

own thing," becomes the result of and the keynote of an economy of abundance.[37]

The emphasis upon immediate gratification becomes more the American norm. The idea of delayed gratification, the traditional capitalist ethic, is less the common ideal of the American scene. If it feels good, it is right. Bell suggests this changed ethic is the result of the affluent postindustrial society, but it is a change which may undo society because when everyone is a hedonist, the common glue for a society may become weaker.

Patriotism and "old-time religion" may diminish in importance because members of the society think they are too sophisticated for them. The stature of sports heroes become diminished because sports are viewed as big business. The problem becomes agreement on what people can believe in. The immediate gratification syndrome is counter to a social responsibility orientation. In the first case, you are only responsible for yourself; if you are viewed as too responsible to others, you may be viewed as needing psychiatric care for being masochistic.

Several demographic facts appear to be related to a growing emphasis upon personal fulfillment in contradistinction to social responsibility. As a result, the crucible in which identity is primarily formed—the family—has been undergoing alteration. Changes in the general environment, including technological changes such as birth control methods, the women's movement, a questioning of traditional family patterns, and a search for personal fulfillment have led to changes in the family.

For the first time the number of divorces exceeded 1 million in 1975.[38] Since the mid-1950s there has been a two-thirds' increase in the divorce rate. Nevertheless, it is estimated that of persons 30 years or older close to 95 percent have married or will marry. Of that number, approximately 30 percent will divorce. But four of every five who divorce will remarry.[39] So marriage as a norm within the society seems secure.

However, changes are occurring which alter the traditional forms of marriage and of family life. The number of households with a female head increased by 30 percent between 1970 and 1975. During that same period the number of persons under 35 maintaining a household alone doubled from 1.5 million to approximately 3 million. There is also a tendency to postpone marriage. Among women

---

[37] Daniel Bell, "The Cultural Contradictions of Capitalism," *Capitalism Today*, Daniel Bell and Irving Kristol (eds.), New York: New American Library, 1971, pp. 27–57.
[38] U.S. Bureau of the Census, *Current Population Reports. Population Profile of the United States: 1975*, Washington, D.C.: U.S. Government Printing Office, 1976, p. 1.
[39] *Population of the United States: Trends and Prospects*: 1950–1990, p. 201.

20 to 24 years of age, 40 percent had not married in 1975, and 60 percent of the men had not done so.[40]

There have been increases in the number of divorced persons under 35 (26 per 1000 married persons under 35 in 1960 and 79 per 1000 married persons under 35 in 1975). Nevertheless, there are some positive signs regarding family life. Almost 95 percent of Americans marry at least once. Within five years most divorced persons remarry. Married persons are more likely to say they are "very happy" than single, widowed, or divorced men or women. Death rates are lower for married than for unmarried persons at all ages.

Today marriages may be more difficult to sustain. There is more acceptance of divorce as a way of dealing with unsatisfactory marriages. Marriages are confronting changing roles such as new opportunities for women which create tensions. Nevertheless, the proportion of children who live with at least one of their parents instead of relatives, foster parents, or in other situations has actually been rising. When compared to colonial times or the nineteenth century, American marriages are made at younger ages today. Husbands and wives spend more years together alone without their children. This latter change, along with the fact that 42 percent of married women worked in 1974, appear to be crucial changes which can alter significantly family life patterns of the future.[41]

Over the past 20 years marriages occur about one year later, families are having one less child, and more couples are surviving jointly for longer periods after their children marry. So the death of the American family as an institution seems prematurely reported. While there is disruption of family life, social welfare has a special concern about families under stress in our society.

There are estimates that one-fourth to one-third of all children live in conditions of poverty.[42] Poverty, therefore, is the greatest nemesis of the American family and children. An adequate income for all families is a pressing need in American society. Issues such as full employment, family or childrens' allowances, day care, housing, and tax policies are all related to the well-being of the American family. In addition to these foundation factors, there are social welfare implications which derive from divorce: women with children and without spouses, postponement of marriage, persons living alone and so forth. A number of services seem indicated including

[40] U.S. Bureau of the Census, *Current Population Reports. Population Profile of the U.S.: 1975*, Washington, D.C.: U.S. Government Printing Office, 1976, p. 1.
[41] Mary Jo Bane, *Here to Stay: American Families in the Twentieth Century*. New York: Basic Books, 1976, passim.
[42] Pamela G. Hollie, "Study Urges a U.S. Family Policy," *New York Times*, September 12, 1977, pp. 1, 54.

transitional counseling and supports premarriage, during marriage, at divorce, for remarriage, supportive services for single-parent families, and children and parents.

The future of the American family, the major institution for the socialization process and the place where one finds intimacy and relatively unconditional love and acceptance, does not appear to be in doubt as to its existence. What does appear to be changing are the dimensions of the family of the future: How shall families adjust to an increasing number of women working, shifting roles within the family, and more leisure time together after the children are gone? The future state of the family may depend in large measure upon the outcome of the argument between hedonism and cause-oriented existence.

As James Gannon has written, "A culture which glorifies individual independence, mobility, self-fulfillment and self-gratification isn't one which fosters the family values of authority, loyalty, self-denial and sharing."[43] To what extent will personal self-fulfillment precede the importance of family life? What effects upon children will the changes in family life bring? Social welfare through its services to families and individuals will play a role in helping people sort out their options and make choices as to the dimensions of their lives. The crucial issues will be what the family shall become and what kinds of American children (in the sense of values and identity) we shall choose to rear.

ETHNICITY AND PLURALISM

Ethnicity is a growing and visible phenomenon in American society. Ethnicity is an important ingredient in the formation of identity, both for families and for individuals. It is possible that ethnic group identity can serve as a counterforce against the encroaching national forces which make for a certain degree of homogenization. It is also possible that identification with an ethnic group serves to counterbalance feelings of alienation brought on in a technological and

[43] James Gannon, "1976: The Year of the Family," *Wall Street Journal*, September 15, 1976, p. 26. Regardless of the many changes taking place in American family life and predictions from a few people of the forthcoming demise of the family, the importance of the family as a societal institution continues to be stressed, for example, see Mary Jo Bane, op. cit.; Selma Fraiberg, *Every Child's Birthright: In Defense of Mothering*, Basic Books, 1977; Kenneth Keniston, *All Our Children: The American Family Under Pressure*, New York: Harcourt Brace Jovanovich, 1977; Christopher Lasch, *Haven in a Heartless World: The Family Besieged*, New York: Basic Books, 1977; and Robert M. Rice, *American Family Policy*, New York: Family Service Association of America, 1977.

enlarged society. The growing phenomenon of group identity and its emphasis in American culture as a political and social force also may serve as a means of expression and as a means for achieving meaning in people's lives.

The United States is a nation built on immigration from many lands by many different groups of people. Between 1830 and 1930, almost 40 million Europeans crossed the Atlantic Ocean to try to make lives for themselves in America.[44] Blacks were brought first as indentured workers and then as slaves. Mexicans inhabited the Southwest for centuries. Native Americans were here already.

Ethnic clashes have been part of American history, sometimes based on ideological conflicts but more often based upon economic competition, especially for jobs. Notwithstanding a history of intergroup conflict, there was much cooperation as well. Two group philosophies arose to point the way to the future. The *melting pot* theory held that Americans of whatever background would become "Americanized," a happy amalgam. Rudolph Vecoli has pointed out that as late as the end of World War II, W. Lloyd Warner, an outstanding sociologist, predicted: "The future of American ethnic groups seems to be limited; it is likely that they will be quickly absorbed."[45] This has not happened. Quite the reverse; there has been an acceleration of *cultural pluralism*, the concept that group identity should be maintained and that America can provide a supportive setting for group continuity and group expression within a diverse but democratic society.

While there may be a degree of truth to the melting pot theory (there is acculturation to a general American culture), the civil rights revolution of the 1960s, particularly the phenomenon of black pride, set up an explosion of ethnicity. Groups became more aware of their heritages; they became more sensitive to what they were losing as they ceded their traditions, language, and cultures to some mythical American ideal type.

It is clear that ethnic identities and cultures exist in our society of diversity. Assimilationist and antiassimilation biases coexist in modern America.

But there is, as Andrew Greeley has suggested,

> . . . a profound distrust of diversity based on anything other than social class, which is the only "rational" diversity. American theory endorses

[44] Stanley Feldstein and Lawrence Costello (eds.), *The Ordeal of Assimilation*, Garden City, New York: Anchor Books, 1974, p. 1.
[45] Rudolph J. Vecoli, "Ethnicity: A Neglected Dimension of American History," *Overcoming Middle Class Rage*, Murray Friedman (ed.), Philadelphia: Westminister Press, 1971, p. 160.

cultural pluralism, but our behavior insists on as much assimilation as possible as quickly as possible. Most Americans feel ambivalent about the fact of diversity and also about their own particular location in ethnic geography. We are torn between pride in the heritage of our own group and resentment at being trapped in that heritage. This ambivalence is probably the result of the agonies of the acculturation experience in which an immigrant group alternatively felt shame over the fact that it was different and unwanted and a defensive pride about its own excellence, which the rest of society seemed neither to appreciate nor understand.[46]

Whatever the personal ambivalences of individuals, ethnic groups occupy important positions in American society. One glance at the slates put forward by American political parties makes clear the attention given to "balanced" tickets, designed to appeal to various ethnic groups. One accompaniment of cultural pluralism is group conflict. Groups compete in society for power and resources, including social services. These conflicts range from the mundane to competition of immense importance for our society.

Daniel Bell has pointed out some of the complexities of this pluralist accommodation:

In the "real" world the problem of social priorities, of what social utilities are to be maximized, of what communal enterprises are to be furthered will be settled in the political arena, by "political criteria"—i.e., the relative weights and pressures of different interest groups, balanced against some vague sense of the national need and the public interest . . . one of the issues of a great society—one which can be defined as a society that seeks to become conscious of its goals—is the relationship, if not the clash, between "rationality" and "politics." . . . but we seem to be unable to formulate a "group theory" of economic choice. The impasse of social theory, in regard to social welfare, is a disturbing prospect at this stage of the transition to a communal society.[47]

Both things are true, we have a national society and we have pluralist groupings. Cultural pluralism, in fact, seems embedded in American society. The libertarian values of America support pluralism; pluralism suggests trade-offs and compromises; compromises between groups suggest political incrementalism, a strategy which operates to preserve the autonomy of multiple-interest groups smaller than the general population.[48] Thus one value supports

[46] Andrew M. Greeley, *Ethnicity in the United States*, New York: John Wiley and Sons, 1974, p. 17.
[47] Daniel Bell, *The Coming of Post-Industrial Society*, p. 307.
[48] David Braybrooke and Charles E. Lindblom, *A Strategy of Decision*, New York: The Free Press, 1970, p. 243.

another, pluralism reinforcing political trade-offs which, in turn, support the sustenance of ethnic pluralism.

On a personal level, however, Leonard Duhl has raised a question about the psychological implications of living in such a society of diversity. He mused at a conference on alternative futures:

> One of the really critical problems we are going to have to face is how to live with the differences encountered in a fantastically pluralistic society. How do you live with the anxiety of not really comprehending the thinking of people around you?[49]

This latter point is not simply one of psychology. Social services for ethnic groups is a matter of the distribution of resources. Which neighborhoods and people shall be served by what means are issues directly connected to questions of intergroup conflict and accommodation. Questions of poverty and inequality similarly have political implications. Which ethnic groups will control a school district? Which neighborhoods will have greatest access to manpower training funds? Given such powerful questions, the answers profoundly influence people's lives. With the perspective that ethnic identity is an important reality in relation to decision-making about services and control, American society has so far proven to be remarkable for its ability to manage these intergroup balancing acts.

One example of the way in which this conflict between groups is played out is the issue of quotas, goals, and affirmative action. The preferential treatment of one group can usually be done only at the expense of another group, to one degree or another. These issues translate group welfare into individual terms. Admission into professional schools has been one arena for intergroup competition where group interests and individual rights have clashed. Such issues remain to be worked out within an accommodation which enables our society to balance two "goods" simultaneously, the protection of individual rights and individual merit in contrast with group rights and justice for groups which have been discriminated against.

Concealed within this strain between groups in a pluralist society, there is at least one hopeful sign. The human psyche demands a sense of community. The development of ethnicity, women's groups, gay groups, and others may be indications that humankind is too vague an entity with which to identify oneself. A person must invent such a community, if it does not exist, so that people are parts of groups with a sense of responsibility. The rise of ethnicity and other groupings may be the response to alienation as well as the need for groups which will fight for one's rights. The future will unfold

---

[49] Leonard Duhl, "Toward the Year 2000," *Daedelus*, Summer 1967, p. 675.

whether ethnicity in our society is a passing fad because of alienation or a representation of an adjustment, a way in which people can express themselves and gain "their" share in this productive society.

THE NEW PROPERTY

Land, food, clothing, housing, automobiles, and other tangible goods have been the sign of wealth. One of the effects of a postindustrial society is the creation of a new kind of property.[50] Several issues for social welfare arise from the creation of this new form of wealth.

In a service economy there is a new property of credentials, licenses, and franchises so that now wealth is not measured just by a house or car, or even a savings account, but also by how many diplomas one has or whether one has a union card, and so forth. In a planned or semiplanned economy, more and more wealth is no longer in the area of "real" property, money, and tangible objects, but more in the area of entitlements. In fact, in some situations, such as union membership, it may be possible for you to get your son or daughter into the union, or children can be given the taxi medallion, for example, as an inheritance.

One of the consequences of trends in postindustrial society is that more and more of the "goods" of society will not be in tangible products but in access to the new property. The new property ranges from social insurances, pensions, access to training or education (free education has changed from a privilege to a right), subsidies to farmers or corporations, health, and other "properties." Citizens have a right to their entitlements such as unemployment compensation or Social Security or even to means-tested medical services or public assistance.

As a result of a suit in the State of Alabama, a U.S. court of appeals has upheld a ruling that mental patients as a class have a federal constitutional right to adequate treatment when they are committed against their will to state institutions.[51]

The new property, of course, has importance for all citizens but perhaps in several respects it holds special importance for social welfare. Social welfare must be concerned with helping people gain the rights to which they are entitled. Furthermore, within the social welfare professions (particularly social work) the new careers movement found great support as a device not to give people money per se so

---

[50] Charles Reich, "The New Property," in *The Public Interest*, Vol. 1, No. 3, 1966, pp. 57–89.
[51] "A Mental Patient's Rights to Adequate Care Upheld," *New York Times*, November 9, 1974, p. 34.

much as access to a new property, education, and jobs. In fact, social work as a profession and social services in many ways became restructured in order to accommodate the claimants of a new property, education.

All this is complicated for social welfare because in some instances social welfare personnel serve as the advocates for citizens to obtain their rights and entitlements; at other times, social welfare personnel are the controllers of the property itself.

The new property becomes a focus for conflict, however, when a union, perhaps dominated by one ethnic group, controls all entry to union membership and jobs. How our society will balance off such issues as the division of new property, especially where the property had been envisioned as an inheritance of real wealth, is a moot question. Needless to say such conflicts are powerful. But ultimately the conflicts which surround the new property relate to the issue of the "size of the pie." Only with an expanding economy can we ensure that our society is able to meet all the expectations to which citizens are legally and legitimately entitled while the number and types of entitlements are certain to increase in number.

HOW FAR CAN WE GO?

Inexorably the creation of the modern world has brought with it the welfare state. The evolution of modern society is accompanied by problems which seek solutions. According to Harold Wilensky,

> Whatever their economic or political system, whatever the ideologies of elites or masses, the rich countries converge in types of health and welfare programs, in increasingly comprehensive coverage, and, to a lesser extent, in methods of financing. The fraction of national resources devoted to these programs climbs, eventually at a decelerating rate.[52]

Social welfare in American society has developed in an unsystematic and disjointed manner. It has developed piecemeal and incrementally, attacking one problem, relatively unrelated to other problems which might contribute to the creation of the problem or which influence its dimensions. Eveline Burns has pointed out that "while past experience has taught us that there is no solution short of a comprehensive and well coordinated system (for absence of, or inadequacy in, one program serves only to overburden other parts of the system), a comprehensive set of measures could not be enacted overnight."[53]

---

[52] Harold L. Wilensky, *The Welfare State and Equality: Structural and Ideological Roots of Public Expenditures*, Berkeley: University of California Press, 1975, p. 86.
[53] Eveline Burns, "Social Security: What Should It Be?" *Social Welfare Forum*, 1973, New York: Columbia University Press, 1974, p. 117.

Reform efforts and incremental approaches to social welfare are sometimes dismissed as palliative, "first aid," and consequently short of the required mark. To the extent that social welfare is reactive and a markedly dependent variable within a society, it can be faulted for moving too slowly or not being sufficiently involved in change efforts. Eugen Pusic has suggested a variant understanding of the role of social welfare:

> . . . the declaration for social welfare is, essentially, a radical commitment. At the very least it questions the assumption of any established order that lack of success within its criteria must somehow be deserved. Be it through the providential withdrawal of divine grace or the equally providential lack of natural ability, those who fail are relegated to the place in society where they belong, the bottom. By trying to help the failures, the social worker implicitly expresses doubt in the well-foundedness of such judgments; otherwise why should he try to undo what God or nature have decreed? It is difficult, however, for any social worker who takes his vocation seriously not to take one further step; not to ask one further question. Is it not possible that the social order itself produces the failures by weighting the scales in favor of a privileged minority? Thus, to question the justice and humanity of the established order requires a moral choice and an act of courage.[54]

But the questions which are asked individually by social workers or collectively by social welfare are not asked within a vacuum. On the contrary, they are asked within the context of a national society at a particular time and state of development. Social welfare is in fact the collective supply of resources, a sharing of the burden or the risk. Nevertheless, as Bernice Madison has aptly suggested, two questions have to be asked: "What needs should be supplied by the collective action of the society and which left to individual effort? What can the society afford?"[55]

Thus, what should and can be done to eliminate poverty or to deal with other social problems? While change seems to be built into technological postindustrial society, a "backlash" appears to have grown toward social welfare provision in quite different societies. Wilensky suggests

> . . . a universal elite requirement for incentives fosters mass adherence to a success ideology, one source of the welfare backlash among modern segments of every rich country. . . . it is a mistake to peg "individualistic" values and beliefs as American or capitalist, and "collectivist" as

[54] Eugen Pusic, "Social Realities—A World View," paper presented at the XVIII International Congress of Schools of Social Work, San Juan, Puerto Rico, July 13, 1976, p. 10 (mimeographed).
[55] Bernice Madison, "The Welfare State: Some Unanswered Questions for the 1970's," *Social Service Review*, Vol. 44, No. 4, 1970, pp. 434–451.

European or socialist. Despite their apparent differences in welfare backlash, rich countries perhaps converge not only in types and coverage of welfare programs but also in the ideological reinforcements of those programs.[56]

Perhaps the effect of the welfare state is not as powerful as we thought. While much has been done which increases the welfare of the citizens of modern industrial nations, questions have arisen as to how much equality can be achieved. Disillusionment with the high taxes which support their national life-styles led in 1973 to Danish, Norwegian, and Swedish electoral upsets. Antitax votes were particularly important election factors in for example, Sweden where taxes account for 42 percent of the gross national product.[57]

Social attitudes and experiences in the social democracies have raised resistance to the level of taxation required to finance general welfare services. But resistance is not limited to taxes alone. Alva Myrdal has reported that although "wage policy is vital to the achievement of the Social Democrats' goal of equality," nevertheless "opposition has been very strong both from market forces and from 'institutional' factors, especially trade unions in the higher wage brackets."[58] Similar phenomena are found in Britain and elsewhere.

Taxpayer revolts, white-collar and professional strikes to widen income gaps between low and high status occupations, political campaigns which focus on welfare state issues, and linking benefits to earnings with tough eligibility requirements all are associated with a "backlash" phenomenon. In some respects the argument against the welfare state and its benefits is a "red herring" in the United States. For generations western Europe has developed a series of welfare functions. In the United States we have a long way to go to reach the point social welfare has achieved in many other nations. Although the United States has the world's highest per capita gross national product (GNP), as of 1966 twenty-nine nations spent more on social security as a percentage of their GNP, including nations from western and eastern Europe, Asia, and South America.[59]

Is the modern welfare state self-limiting as a result of the development of a "backlash" effect in which taxpayers revolt against higher taxes in times of rising inflation? To what extent can a viable

[56] Wilensky, op. cit., pp. 36, 39.
[57] "Socialism Is in a Rotten State in Denmark," *New York Times,* December 9, 1973, Section 4, p. 3. By comparison, direct and indirect taxes average 28 percent of GNP in the United States. Martin Schiff, "Social Dysfunctions and Myths," *American Journal of Economics and Sociology,* Vol. 34, No. 3, July 1975, p. 291.
[58] Quoted in William A. Robson, *Welfare State and Welfare Society,* London: George Allen & Unwin, 1976, p. 38.
[59] Wilensky, op. cit., pp. 122–124.

economy tolerate an ever-growing welfare state? Since inflation appears to be the accompaniment of a service society, does this preclude continued expansion of welfare services, broadly defined, at some point in the future? According to one observer,

> The real problem of British social spending is not that it expanded too quickly while the nation grew, but that it continues to expand while the economy has all but stopped. . . . Since the economy generated little new revenue, higher rates of taxation and double-digit inflation were inevitable, and they devoured disposable income. Like the sorcerer's broom in the fairy tale, the British welfare state, a manageable instrument in normal times, has proved to be a demonic one in the strained conditions the nation now confronts.[60]

Mass production demands mass purchasing power. Social welfare programs, particularly income maintenance programs, serve the society as stabilizers. Nevertheless, they must be funded, and these funds are made available through taxation of current or future generations. The complexity of modern society becomes focused on the issue of whether or not social welfare will expand or not. The decision is not simply one of social justice or morality but is part and parcel of an economic scene in which taxation grows and is resented, in which the middle classes and middle-aged are burdened with the tax load, and in which purchasing power has been diminished by inflation. Do these features of our modern society suggest there are inevitable limits to social welfare in the welfare state? If so, again the limits are those imposed by the size of the available pie and they are intimately related to issues of productivity, the engine which drives the entire society.

In any event the United States is so far from achieving welfare goals which others take for granted, that this question seems capable of being deferred for the present in America, at least in theory. Whether taxpayers will support the achievement of these welfare goals remains to be seen.

As noted in Chapter 7, according to Gilbert, since 1962 there has been a transformation of social services in the United States. The clientele has shifted from a selective to more universal inclusion, the nature of benefits provided has changed toward the "concrete" and greater diversity, the delivery auspices has altered from public to a public/private mix, population per se has become a more significant

[60] Leslie Lenkowsky, "Welfare in the Welfare State," *The Future That Doesn't Work: Social Democracy's Failures in Britain*, R. Emmett Tyrrell, Jr. (ed.), Garden City, New York: Doubleday, pp. 153–154.

factor determining funding patterns, and planning has become more decentralized.[61]

In Europe the basic point of departure for social welfare services has become a viable income maintenance level, basic health provision, and access to adequate housing. Further, an extensive series of services (health visitors, day care for young children, school meals, housing for the young and single, family vacations, housing for the elderly, and so on) have been instituted on a more or less universal basis.[62]

Whatever the degree of accuracy of Gilbert's assessment and the growth of social welfare services in Europe, counterforces in regard to social welfare simultaneously exist in the United States. Tax revolts in the United States and other nations showed great popular support despite their potential for destroying social welfare programs. At stake in new tax configurations are the relative powers of various groups; the roles of state, local, and national funding and power; and the nature of social services at every level.[63]

At the same time tax policy alters the nature of social services because of the demands of various parts of the population for fiscal relief, another trend has become visible in recent years which also will affect social welfare in ways yet undeveloped. The entire premise of progressive, liberal thought has become suspect, and questions of a serious nature are being asked about the limits of "doing good." The two-edged nature of social welfare has been recognized:

> . . . we can degrade people by caring for them; and we can degrade them by not caring for them; and in matters such as these there are neither simple answers nor simple solutions. We have gotten to this complex place, and we are not going to get away from it in a hurry. We belong to a reformist tradition, and long experience should have made us skeptical by now of some of our best-intentioned efforts. Caring for people in a concerted effort and not caring for them in a concerted effort are each of them, as matters of policy, interventions. All interventions have consequences, and one of the things we should learn to keep in the forefront of our consciousness is that the most important consequences of any intervention almost always turn out to be those consequences that were not intended or planned upon or could not have been calculated beforehand. Dependents, precisely because they are

---

[61] Neil Gilbert, "The Transformation of Social Services," *Social Service Review*, Vol. 51, No. 4, December 1977, pp. 624–641. While our perceptions vary somewhat from Gilbert's on the movement toward universal services, we agree with his analysis in general. See Chapter 7 of this book for a discussion of this point.

[62] Alfred J. Kahn and Sheila Kamerman, *Not For the Poor Alone: European Social Services,* Philadelphia: Temple University Press, 1975.

[63] John Herbers and Robert Lindsey, "California Tax Revolt Is Expected to Bring More Dependence on U.S.," *New York Times,* June 11, 1978, pp. 1, 34–35.

dependent and often unable to help themselves, deserve more than others to be protected from the unintended consequences of our benevolence and the incalculable consequences of our social good will.[64]

While questions are being raised about the efficacy of intervention, Mayer Zald predicts the welfare state is headed in the following directions: (1) no new large scale-redistribution program, (2) a major crisis related to female-headed households, (3) new programs minimize explicit redistribution effects, (4) large and costly programs will be trimmed to affect only the most desperately needy parts of the population, (5) labor-intensive social welfare services will find it increasingly difficult to be funded, and (6) the welfare state in Western industrialized nations will be in "low gear."[65]

These particular predictions of future trends may or may not prove to be true; the nexus between social welfare and our society may reflect deeper issues confronting our society. The evolution of modernity makes for conflict between individual, family, neighborhood, and the forces of bureaucracy. One set of ills of our modern age includes anomie, malaise, alienation, and a decline in the communal spirit. Peter L. Berger, among others, has recommended a greater emphasis on "mediating structures," those "institutions which stand between the individual in his private sphere and the large institutions of the public sphere." It is through life in the family, church, voluntary associations, neighborhood, and subculture that a balance can be obtained between the "little aggregations" of particularity, of pluralism, and of the universalism of the modern state. In fact, one of the strengths of American society is its ability to combine the power of the modern state with the energies of voluntary associations.[66]

A second but related group of issues revolves around the nature of social welfare in a capitalistic society. From the socialist point of view, social welfare in our society serves to repair, to contain, and to suppress the negative effects of the capitalistic system. Furthermore, the culture of capitalism leads to and depends upon an individualis-

[64] Steven Marcus, "Their Brothers' Keepers: An Episode from English History," *Doing Good: The Limits of Benevolence*, New York: Pantheon Books, 1978, pp. 65–66.

[65] Mayer N. Zald, "Demographics, Politics, and the Future of the Welfare State," *Social Service Review*, Vol. 51, No. 1, March 1977, pp. 121–122.

[66] Peter L. Berger, "In Praise of Particularity: The Concept of Mediating Structures," *Facing Up To Modernity*, New York: Basic Books, 1977, pp. 130–141, and Peter L. Berger and Richard J. Newhaus, *To Empower People: The Role of Mediating Structures in Public Policy*, Washington, D.C.: American Enterprise Institute for Public Policy Research," 1977. Also see Joseph L. Vigilante, "Back to the Old Neighborhood," *Social Service Review*, Vol. 50, No. 2, June 1976, pp. 194–208.

tic ideology and morality. These then call forth the need for a second set of social welfare measures to restore social morale and a sense of community.[67]

To what extent can a capitalistic society provide for a cooperative morality and for individualism, the enhancement of all individuals as opposed to the autonomy of some individuals? How can there be achieved a proper relation of individuals and society, freedom and planning, pluralism, and shared values? According to some, the issues of the welfare state shall not focus on totalitarianism/democracy but instead on the problems of modern industrial nations: bureaucratic responsiveness, citizen participation, and abolition of persistent poverty.[68] It is here, too, that Berger's emphasis upon "mediating structures" suggests the need for social workers and social welfare to work at the interface of the "little aggregations" and the forces of the state.

There are three additional points we wish to make regarding an international perspective on social welfare in the United States. First, international trends and comparisons do influence American social welfare, although we lag behind many other nations in this sphere. In terms of taxation, however, in a comparison of employee-employer payroll tax rates for all Social Security programs in 1973 only the United Kingdom among most western European nations and Canada and Japan had lower payroll tax rates than the United States. Citizens in some western European nations pay as much as five times the rate paid by Americans.[69]

Only Japan devotes a lower percentage of its gross national product to total expenditures for social security programs than the United States in a group including Belgium, Canada, France, the Federal Republic of Germany, the Netherlands, Sweden, and the United Kingdom. An important reason for the relative low standing of the United States is the absence on our national scene of a children's or family allowance, health insurance, and sickness benefits for short-term illness for wage and salaried workers.[70]

Second, the "blaming the victim" argument that poverty is the

---

[67] Robert L. Heilbroner, "Beyond the Welfare State" and "What is Socialism?" *Dissent*, Summer 1978, pp. 341–348.

[68] Norman Furniss and Timothy Tilton, *The Case for the Welfare State*, Bloomington: Indiana University Press, 1977.

[69] Martin B. Tracy, "Payroll Taxes Under Social Security Programs: Cross-National Survey," *Social Security Bulletin*, Vol. 38, No. 11, November 1975, p. 5.

[70] Research and Statistics Note, U.S. Department of Health, Education, and Welfare. Social Security Administration, "National Expenditures on Social Security in Selected Countries, 1968 and 1971," Department of Health, Education and Welfare Pub. No. (SSA) 74-11701, October 18, 1974.

result of a personal and individual character flaw has been transferred by analogy to explain the poverty of entire nations, a factor
which influences the international social welfare situation. Examples have been described of attitudes, beliefs, and modes of conduct
in developing nations which sound like a litany of the stereotypes
describing poor individuals and families in the United States and
some other Western societies. According to one observer the people
of developing nations show a

> . . . lack of interest in material advance, combined with resignation in
> the face of poverty; lack of initiative, self-reliance and of a sense of per-
> sonal responsibility for the economic fortune of oneself and one's fam-
> ily; high leisure preference, together with a lassitude often found in
> tropical climates . . . recognized status of beggary, together with a lack
> of stigma in the acceptance of charity; opposition to women's work out-
> side the household.[71]

In other words, according to this view, nations as well as individuals
create their own poverty through their lack of character. But Americans in our own era have begun to see how their personal life situations are determined by events and interrelationships which are
impersonal and structural "public issues" rather than personal, idio-
syncratic local and "private troubles."

Finally, American social welfare is affected by the international
context in which it exists. When Italian shoes, Japanese cars and
appliances, and German industrial tools, for example, are sold in the
United States, these goods affect the number and type of jobs available for American workers with immediate effects on working people and their families. The productivity of American workers and
inflation have serious consequences for American workers, families,
and social welfare. The strength of the American economy is influenced critically by its relationship to other nations. In fact, we live
in an interdependent world in which American social welfare is
closely interrelated with other parts of our society and, in turn, American society and social welfare are influenced by developments in
other nations. Perhaps we have reached a stage of recognized interdependence in which the nations of the world need to share the risks
through cooperative efforts to provide for the welfare of all people.
Just as we have begun to recognize how interdependent we all are
within one society, perhaps we will as a world recognize how human
welfare depends upon the interdependence of nations.

---

[71] P. T. Bauer, *Dissent on Development,* London: Weidenfeld and Nicolson, 1971, pp.
78–79.

Chapter 11
Alternative Programs to
Meet Social Welfare Needs

"No choice is a choice."

Yiddish Proverb

"Life's business being just the terrible choice."

Robert Browning
The Ring and The Book

At any given moment there are debates in legislative and administrative bodies over alternatives in social welfare programs. Old programs evolve; new programs are introduced. All citizens, and certainly social workers, need to have informed and intelligent opinions on alternatives.

In this chapter we want to help the reader to use the same analytical system introduced in Chapter 4, not just to understand what currently exists, but to develop opinions and to see which of several directions are preferable. We will accompany the reader through an anlysis of several programs, analyzing alternatives and developing a point of view.

The *structures* of social welfare programs and not just specific benefit levels or provisions are extremely important, in part because these programs tend to maintain their skeletal structures once in place. Since 1935 the Social Security system has been changed and improved many times. Still the changes have been incremental, and the Social Security system of the 1970s still operates within the general outlines of the 1935 enactments, with the basic inequities which have been pointed out almost since the system's inception.

There are so many social welfare programs that it is impossible here to analyze alternatives suggested for them all. For that reason we will focus on examples only of three types of programs: (1) economic security programs, (2) personal service programs, and (3) programs which have major elements of both (which is most often the case). Finally we want to point to examples of how the social work practitioner must make "social welfare" choices in day-to-day practice. Social policy decisions are made not only at the macrolevel but at the practice level as well.

ALTERNATIVES IN ECONOMIC SECURITY PROGRAMS—THE CASE OF SOCIAL SECURITY

The financing problems of the Social Security system are growing more serious with each passing year. Social Security is a system of financial support for retired workers, disabled workers, and dependent survivors of workers. These benefits are paid for by Social Security taxes levied upon employees, employers, and the self-employed and are discussed in Chapter 6.

To review that material: the Old Age, Survivors, Disability Insurance programs operate on the basis of current cost financing. In general, Social Security taxes collected currently are used to pay present benefits. Only when expenditures exceed income temporarily can the deficit be met from the limited trust fund reserves. But as benefit levels are improved by Congress, the more difficult question is "Where will the money come from for these increased benefits?"

Social Security deficits occurred in several years during the 1970s, precipitating a major congressional debate in 1977 to discuss ways of increasing income for the system. That debate highlighted the alternatives which remain as issues for the future. A number of factors led to the deficits and projected deficits in the system.

1. Congress underestimated the cost of benefits it had legislated in 1973 and overestimated the number of workers who would pay for the benefits issued. In an attempt to predict future Social Security benefit expenditures and tax yields, experts miscalculated the probable course of wages and prices.

2. The declining birthrate is another major factor. A declining birthrate results in a lower ratio of employees paying Social Security taxes to retirees collecting benefits. If the ratio of workers to retirees declines, there will be a shortage of funds in the future for the aged retirees.

3. Unemployment trends also influence Social Security. If

unemployment rises, there are fewer workers paying Social Security taxes and less money is pumped into the system. Consistent high unemployment therefore contributes to the deficit.

4. Improvements in medicine and other factors have increased the average life span of men and women. People now live longer and therefore collect benefits for a longer period of time. Additional benefits therefore must be issued, which increases the deficit.[1]

James B. Cardwell points out that the financing problems may have been blown out of proportion. "There is no reason whatsoever, for the kind of panic mongering that we have had in the press and on television."[2] It is impossible to predict with certainty the effect such factors as a declining birthrate or an average life span increase will have on the Social Security system. The predictions of a long-term future deficit may very well be overstated.

Eveline M. Burns explains how the very same factors which are assumed to increase the deficit could possibly have the reverse effect. Traditional economic theory states that a birthrate decline results in fewer workers supporting a greater number of retirees, thus increasing the deficit. The traditional theory is not necessarily a valid one in our present society. As Eveline Burns explains, "A lower birthrate would free more women for paid employment."[3] A low birthrate, then, would bring more women into the labor market. As employment would increase, Social Security tax yields would increase, and the deficit would be reduced.

We also should not be overly concerned about the increased average life span which results in retirees collecting benefits for longer periods of time. Burns perceptively notes that although improved health has increased the average life span, it also increases the worker's employability. If employees work for a longer period of time, beyond their initial eligibility for retirement, more money is pumped into the Social Security system and less is paid out.

There are other events which might occur in the near future which would increase employment:

> A raise in wages would tempt more people into the labor market . . . there might be a decline in the average rate of unemployment . . . or there might be a substantial increase in immigration.[4]

Furthermore, our present generation has assumed tax burdens

[1] Social Security Administration, *Social Security Bulletin*, February 1977, p. 40.
[2] James B. Cardwell, *The Future Role and Function of Social Security*, New York: Community Service Society, 1977, p. 21.
[3] Eveline M. Burns, *The Financial Problems of O.A.S.D.I.*, New York: Community Service Society, 1977, p. 11.
[4] Ibid., p. 12.

for purposes likely to increase the productivity of future generations. The present generation has extended educational opportunities increasing, for example, the proportion of youth who receive higher education:

> Our generation has devoted substantial tax money to research, for energy, health, computer science, and the like, the benefits of which will be reaped by future generations in the form of increased productivity—out of which, the present generation of producers might argue, they can well afford to support a large population of aged nonproducers.[5]

We can assume that the next generation will be wealthier as a result of our investments and will have little difficulty supporting the retirees of the present generation. Therefore the problem may be less acute than suggested by the "panic-mongerers."

Although the long-range Social Security problem may have been overstated, certain matters are clear: the small Social Security tax legislated in 1935 has escalated, to keep up with benefits, into a major and regressive tax burden. The increases legislated in late 1977 amounted to the largest peacetime tax increase in the nation's history. Therefore, a look at alternatives is needed.

There are proposals to eliminate payment of any benefits in excess of 100 percent of one's earnings and to freeze the monthly minimum benefit figure at current levels. Currently the Social Security benefits and the monthly minimum benefit figure are increased as the cost of living increases. Under the above proposal, no matter how high the cost of living were to rise, retirees could never receive benefits exceeding what they earned as workers. Another proposal is to freeze the minimum benefit.

Such measures would indeed reduce the Social Security financing problem but at the expense of vertical adequacy in benefits. Many retirees are currently receiving very low benefits, as the Federal Advisory Council noted:

> Millions of people are still receiving inadequate benefits . . . as demonstrated by the large number of people who must turn to the Supplementary Security Income Program, which is a program of means tested Welfare, in order to supplement their meager Social Security benefits.[6]

If the monthly minimum benefit figure is frozen, then in the event of high inflation, the aged who are struggling now will surely not be able to keep up with the rising cost of living.

---

[5] Social Security Administration, op. cit., p. 41.
[6] Federal Advisory Council, *Report of the Advisory Council on Social Security*, Washington, D.C., 1977, p. 28.

Another method to reduce the outgo would be to combine the Federal Employee Retirement Plan with the Social Security system. In our present system, federal employees have a separate retirement plan from which they are able to receive benefits after 20 years of work. Many of these employees retire from such jobs after 20 years and then work in another job just long enough to secure eligibility for regular Social Security. They then retire and collect benefits from both retirement plans. This practice is known as "double-dipping."

The suggestion is to combine these two systems and set up more comprehensive coverage. This would be a fair method to reduce Social Security benefits, because it seems unjust that federal employees can collect double benefits. Universal coverage would reduce Social Security outlays in future years. Furthermore, combining the two systems would help relieve the immediate problems, because the federal retirement fund now has a surplus.

Burns indicates that "the only drawback to this proposal is that in the past, Congress has been unwilling to act in the face of such opposition (Government employees)."[7] The advantages of the proposal remain unchallenged. The best Congress could do in 1977 was to set up a commission to look into the problem of dual retirement systems.

Another possible benefit of combining retirement systems is that it would make it more feasible to use the general revenues now supporting SSI to be contributed toward a higher minimum Social Security benefit. Primarily those receiving minimum benefits are the same ones receiving SSI assistance—except for the "double-dippers." Thus a major means-test selective program could integrate with a comprehensive program without much additional cost. The fear of giving more minimum income to the "double-dippers" is the major drawback to such a plan.

But all of these suggestions to reduce expenditures are limited in how much they would help in the problem. The Social Security system primarily has to look for sources to increase Social Security revenues. One traditional proposal is to increase the taxable "wage base" (tax limit) for the employer and employee. Employers and employees would pay taxes on a larger portion of salaries, and more revenue would be pumped into the system. This is one of the two major ways more income has been generated over the years.

The rich strongly object to this as a solution, at least beyond a certain point. Those who receive high salaries will not continue to support a program which would yield them so small a return on the increased taxes they would pay. The Federal Advisory Council

---

[7] Burns, op. cit., p. 24.

rejected this as a possible solution, asserting that "such a proposal would extend coverage to a level of income where enforced savings seem inappropriate."[8]

Social Security taxes have risen very rapidly in recent years to levels higher than most expected. "We may be approaching the limits of tax payer tolerance," writes Cardwell.[9] If high-salaried workers are forced to pay Social Security taxes at unacceptable levels, they can lobby together and disrupt the entire Social Security system. Furthermore, even for the nonrich, paying the same percentage on all income levels seems unfair, since general revenues collected from the income tax are based on higher tax rates with higher incomes. So the above is not so progressive, although it is less regressive than the following.

The major method of increasing income has been gradually to raise the tax rate. Such changes, however, make the Social Security tax even more regressive. Raising the tax rate forces the poor to pay greater proportions of their total salaries in Social Security taxes than the rich. Such a tax makes it difficult for the people whose income is insufficient to meet their needs.

In comparison with increasing the taxable wage base, raising the tax rate seems cruel and insensitive to the poor. Although there are objections mentioned earlier to a wage base increase, such an increase affects only 15 percent of all employees, high-salaried employees, who can afford the tax increase most easily. But increasing the tax rate forces the poor to struggle, making poverty and welfare problems worse. Still combinations of higher rates and higher bases of taxation are the way Congress has traditionally moved to increase Social Security income.

Of all the major solutions proposed, the most effective way to help to finance the Social Security system would be to draw funds from the general revenues. If funds from the general revenues were used, there would be no need further to raise the taxable wage base or the tax rate.

The United States thus far has financed Social Security almost entirely from payroll taxes levied on employers and employees. However, the idea of using general revenue is not a new one. In 1938 the Social Security Advisory Council agreed that in 1962 the federal government should help to finance the program out of the general treasury. It said:

> Since the nation as a whole, independent of the beneficiaries of the system, will derive benefit from the Old Age Security Program, it is

[8] Federal Advisory Council, op. cit., p. 23.
[9] Cardwell, op. cit., p. 21.

appropriate that there be Federal financial participation in the Old Age Insurance System by means of revenues derived from sources other than payroll taxes.[10]

The case for using general revenues to finance a portion of Social Security rests on the greater progressivity of the taxes which make up the general revenues, as compared to the wage and payroll taxes. In paying the income tax, the high wage-earner pays not only more money than the low wage-earner, but also pays a higher percentage of income in taxes, as opposed to the present regressive wage and payroll tax where *all* employees pay the same rate.

Cardwell, however, raises some objections to financing the deficit from the general revenue. He claims that the strength of the present Social Security system is its contributory policy. Since everyone currently contributes directly to the system (through the wage and payroll taxes), everyone has secured the right to receive benefits. But if Social Security were to be financed by the general income tax revenue, the contributory policy could be destroyed and Congress may feel people no longer have a "right" to receive benefits. If one year Congress sees a need to raise the defense budget, for example, it may decide to cut Social Security benefits.

Cardwell argues that once the contributory policy is destroyed, Congress will no longer recognize the public's "right" to receive Social Security and will manipulate the benefit structure according to its budget. In an effort to reduce the budget one year, Congress might withhold benefits from the rich. Cardwell fears that if there were serious financial problems in the government, Congress would set up a "means test" (as in public assistance) where each family must prove a need for Social Security in order to receive benefits. If a means test were established, the Social Security system as we know it would be destroyed.

However, most serious proposals suggest only *partial* support from the general revenues. Since there is no serious suggestion that the system be *wholly* financed from the general revenues, the important contributory policy would be maintained. Also, the possibility of a means test is highly unlikely. Burns refutes Cardwell:

> While the possibility of a means test might be conceded in a System with only limited population coverage, it is questionable whether it would be probable in a system of almost universal coverage.[11]

[10] Quoted in Office of Research and Statistics, Social Security Administration, Education and Welfare, *Reducing Social Security Contributions for Low Income Workers: Issues and Analysis*, 1977, p. 13.

[11] Burns, op. cit., p. 31.

Since almost everyone will be eligible for Social Security benefits in old age, Congress would be extremely reluctant to cut benefits, acting against such large opposition. The general revenue proposal does not suggest any real dangers to the Social Security system.

The Social Security system was established over 40 years ago and has become a basic "social utility" in our society. Just as such social utilities as fire services and police services are financed by the general revenues, the Social Security tax should be financed partially by the general revenues.

ALTERNATIVES IN PERSONAL SOCIAL SERVICE PROGRAMS

In this section we want briefly to examine alternatives in the operation of two parts of the personal social services system, that system as defined by Kahn and Kamerman (see Chapter 7). Alternatives in the personal social services differ from economic security programs in a major respect: there are seldom if ever either/or choices; instead, there are questions of how much of what is needed and affordable. For instance, in income maintenance one may favor either a negative income tax or a family allowance program. In the care of the aged it is clear that we need both institutional and community care. The question is how much social welfare resources should be invested in each. This complicates the problem for the social welfare student. In each situation there needs to be an analysis against the paradigm of horizontal and vertical adequacy, financial equity, coherence with other social programs, and latent consequences. It makes choices more difficult and less exact but nonetheless necessary.

The Case of Aging

Let us consider services for the aging as an illustration of one type of personal social services. There is a growing aging population caused by the increasing life span. The general expectation is that as one ages one can continue to be relatively independent and autonomous for an extended period. At the same time there is a gradual development of increasing dependency, physical and emotional. We live in a society where the extended family has broken down and in which our expectations for medical care have gone up. One result is that there has grown up a whole network and industry of nursing homes, public and private. The question is often posed: "Is it better to live in the community or in a nursing home?" However, it should be obvious that there is no single answer to this question. Nursing homes are appropriate for many people who become so dependent that only the intensive care possible in such a facility can make for survival. Nursing homes may also at times be the most economical form of care. One of the standard rules in social welfare has been that "outdoor relief" always costs less than "indoor relief." That is, parole and probation always cost less than incarceration. Community care for mental patients costs less than institutionalization in a mental facility, just as home relief always cost less than putting people in workhouses in the nineteenth century. In the same way, it is usually better for the elderly to be treated in the community than in a nursing home. However, there is a "tipping point" beyond which this truism is simply no longer true. If a person needs a whole battery of services—housekeeper, nursing, rehabilitation, and special technical and medical devices—a point is reached where it is more expensive to maintain a person at home that in an institution. One has to look at the whole range of options in deciding on what possibilities are best for the elderly. Some possibilities follow.

• *Congregate Living.* Three or four older adults take an apartment together, pooling their SSI payments so that they can afford a decent apartment often with the support of social services from a public or private agency.

• *Supportive Services.* Older people stay at home, make use of social groups, senior citizen centers, visiting homemakers, persons to do chores or escort services, nutrition programs such as meals on wheels, home attendants for medical care, and the like.

• *Apartment Complexes for the Elderly.* Units may sometimes be operated in conjunction with a nursing home. They centralize some of the above mentioned services, particularly medical, but still provide a modicum of independent existence and mobility.

• *Day Hospital.* The older adult stays home to sleep but receives medical services throughout the day in the nursing home. This alternative for persons with serious problems enables these persons to remain in the community for domiciliary purposes and some socialization. There is an interesting latent consequence to such programs. When they include the promise of institutionalization in the nursing home of choice if and when necessary, this availability keeps people out of institutions longer. Too often older people enter nursing homes before it is absolutely necessary in the fear that when the time comes they may end up in a nursing home not of their choice because the bed they seek will not be available. This kind of guarantee along with the day treatment can provide peace of mind and save the community money.

• *The Nursing Home Itself.* Such care has a variety of levels from health related care to skilled nursing facilities. Given these options one has to evaluate not what is best for society as a whole, because there is no answer, but which model from the above is best for a particular client, for a particular ethnic or other group, or for a particular neighborhood, community, or region. For each of these entities it is possible to examine the services to see which would be more adequate horizontally and vertically, which would provide the most equitable financing and priority use of funds, the cost and benefit efficiency of each alternative, and the coherence of particular programs with other programs and policies as well as latent consequences which derive from these choices. For instance, in a community which has few volunteer and mobile services but which has a strong central medical facility, the development of a nursing home and apartment complexes near the medical facility might be more desirable than in another community where there is a sophisticated network of mobile health services upon which could be piggybacked chore and escort services, Meals-on-Wheels, and the like. For people whose ethnic or cultural heritage implies that entering a nursing home or hospital means sure death, the choice has to be made in terms of elements more complex than dollars and cents. Some communities build magnificent nursing homes which provide first-rate vertical coverage for those who can attend, but at such a level of cost that it is impossible to expect decent horizontal coverage at that level of care. One has to consider the value of this kind of service as opposed to the alternative of less perfect care for the broad community of older adults. Thus the paradigm with which the student should now be familiar can now be a useful tool in evaluating which services are best for which populations among a variety of personal social services.

The Case of Community Mental Health

According to the Community Mental Health Center Act, 12 services should be provided through the local community mental health center:

1. Inpatient services
2. Outpatient services
3. Partial hospitalization services

4. Emergency services
5. Consultation and education services
6. Services for children
7. Services for the elderly
8. Screening services
9. Follow-up care
10. Transitional services
11. Alcoholism and alcohol abuse services
12. Drug addicition and drug abuse services

But there is no one program that can be right for all persons and all communities. Even the definition of area by geographical "catchment area" does not always make the most rational system; perhaps an ethnic or class population which is best served by a type of service may cut across the geographical lines of catchment areas. It might be that certain specialized services, perhaps in alcoholism, might be offered on a regional basis rather than being duplicated in a local area. There are latent consequences to the way services are funded. If, as has been the case, outpatient services are reimbursed on an interview-by-interview basis and other services are simply given a blanket allocation, there will be two latent consequences:

1. The service will tend to take the form of interviews, and outpatient services will deal less with having the social worker or other therapist go out into the community and help the client receive concrete services.
2. There will be an emphasis on these outpatient services for which there is reimbursement by the unit rather than for consultation and education which in the original thrust of the community mental health movement seem more important.

Thus funding patterns have to follow the stated priority of personal social services or else they subvert these priorities. If professional services are structured so that the highest paid professionals are, in the terms of the original idea behind community mental health, providing training to the "caretakers of the community," this will result in more horizontal adequacy and lower costs than if the highest paid professionals are doing one-to-one treatment. But as the community mental health centers have evolved along a medical model, it is the latter which has tended to develop. Therefore, in personal and social services one needs to look at the structure of the agency and the service and the way it is funded in terms of whether this aids or subverts the purposes of the service. In addition, as in aging, one has to see which of the services is most needed for which client and which community.

ALTERNATIVES IN ECONOMIC SECURITY/SOCIAL SERVICE PROGRAMS; THE CASE OF NATIONAL HEALTH INSURANCE

We live in a time of rising expectations. Fifty years ago few people thought they were entitled to health care as a human right; today people expect health care as a legitimate entitlement of all citizens. This prevalent attitude clashes directly with the economic principle of scarcity: there are only so many physicians, dollars, and other resources for health care.

Once we reach a minimum level of health care, advances in medical care itself seem to provide only marginal advances. Fuchs reports that

> . . . in developed countries the marginal contribution of medical care to life expectancy is very small. That is, variations in mortality across and within countries do not seem to be related to differences in the availability of physicians or other medical care inputs.[12]

The American experience illustrates this marginality. In 1900 the average life expectancy at birth was 49.2 years; by 1966 the average life expectancy at birth had increased to 70.1 years. This spurt in life expectancy was due to reductions in infant and child mortality. Thus 21 years were added to life expectancy at birth. However, *only 2.7 years were added to life expectancy at age 65.* For those who reached the age of 65, the remaining life expectancy in 1900 was 11.9 years; and the expectancy was 14.6 in 1966. Much of the credit for the increased expectancy at birth is due to vaccines and improved nutrition, personal hygiene, and environmental changes, including safe water and milk supplies and sewage disposal—public health measures rather than personal medical care.

The major point, of course, is that at this time the greatest influences upon health are outside the health care system. Only incremental changes can be anticipated for any of the indices of health such as life expectancy or infant mortality through changes in the health care system per se. Control of present health problems in our society depends on modifications of behavior and life-style. Such things as diet, moderate exercise, and adequate sleep are all crucial to current health care, but all of these are within the sphere of individual control and culture and not matters of health resources or system provision.[13] In fact, major causes of death today are automobile accidents and the results of smoking and drinking.

[12] Victor R. Fuchs, *Who Shall Live? Health, Economics, and Social Choice*, New York: Basic Books, 1974, p. 144.
[13] John Knowles, "The Responsibility of the Individual," *Daedelus*, Vol. 106, No. 1, Winter 1977, p. 61.

Nonetheless, medical care prolongs life, relieves pain, and cures illnesses. Furthermore, the health care industry is so big and important and raises so many problems of access and economics that we have to deal with it. The dimensions of the health care industry are staggering. In 1965 the national expenditure for health services was $39 billion. By 1975 the total was $119 billion.[14]

In 1974 about 11.6 percent of all federal outlays were spent on health-related matters.[15] Federal funds were spent on research, health labor-power training, services, prevention and control, support for construction projects, and improving the organization and delivery of services. Programs to improve the delivery of care were fostered through such activities as comprehensive health planning supportive of state and area planning efforts and regional medical program services.

Health expenditures reached the level of $119 billion in 1975 (8.3 percent of the gross national product). Nevertheless, in spite of changes, reforms, and the massive investment of funds,

> ... by far the largest component of medical care in the United States ... is the provision of ambulatory services to "private" patients by individual physicians in solo, partnership, or small-group practice ... on a fee-for-service basis, without effective quality control or accountability.[16]

Although the United States spends over 8 percent of its gross national product on health, perhaps spending as much of its wealth as any nation when all components of health expenditures are accounted for, it may not be a question of investing enough. It may not be a question of adding more dollars, but instead may require a better "payoff" for the dollars invested. The infant death rate in the United States (deaths per 1000 live births of infants under 1 year of age) was 16.6 per 1000 in 1976. Fifteen nations had better rates: Australia, Belgium, Canada, Taiwan, Denmark, Finland, France, West Germany, Japan, New Zealand, Norway, Spain, Sweden, Switzerland, and the United Kingdom. Life expectancy at birth for the United States was 67.4 years for males and 75.2 years for females in 1972. At least 19 nations have higher expectations for male longevity, and 5 nations have higher expectations for females.[17] All this is true

[14] John Knowles, "Introduction," ibid., p. 2.
[15] Louise Russell, Blair Bourque, Daniel Bourque, and Carol Burke, *Federal Health Spending 1969–74*, Washington, D.C.: National Planning Association, 1974, p. 112.
[16] H. Jack Geiger, "The Illusion of Change," *Social Policy*, Vol. 6, No. 3, November/December 1975, p. 31.
[17] U.S. Bureau of the Census, *Statistical Abstract of the United States: 1976*, Washington, D.C.: U.S. Government Printing Office, 1976, p. 871.

despite massive outlays of personal and governmental funds on the health-care industry.

Other nations seem to be moving ahead by various health indices. So we must look as a nation to the future. In spite of our awareness that major changes in the health of citizens will come more from changes in life-style than in the health system, we must look at the health care system and how that can be improved. We must do this because it is such a significant and rising portion of society's costs, because of our concerns about falling behind the advances of other nations, and because portions of our population— in the poverty areas—are still suffering from primitive conditions of health care, levels at which changes can make an important difference.

We can identify the seven components of an ideal health care system:

1. *Accessibility*. There would be no financial barriers, long waiting periods, lack of information, unavailability of local primary care, or the like.

2. *Single track*. There should not be one health care system for the poor and one for the rich. No health care services would carry a stigma with use.

3. *Comprehensiveness*. Coverage would be for a full range of services, not forcing consumers to use or physicians to prescribe less ideal or more costly service because it is "covered." Our health care system has been compared to purchasing a car part by part in different locations with the consumer needing to put the pieces together so they fit right. Over 70 percent of all American physicians are specialists. There is one MD for every 645 people. However, there is only one general practitioner or primary care physician for every 4771 persons. So a patient has to locate and deal with specialists of all kinds (for example, specialists within specialties such as pediatric cardiologists or urology of the newborn) and with pharmacists, nurses, technicians, and others.[18] A comprehensive system would manage to deal with the whole person, with a kind of case manager to integrate services for one person.

4. *Quality of care*. Good medical practice is required in an ideal system which means the right medicine, procedures, and personnel at the right time.

5. *Economical*. In the decade from 1965 following the enactment of Medicare, real health costs rose by 12 percent to 20 percent

---

[18] John H. Knowles, "Introduction—Doing Better and Feeling Worse: Health in the U.S.," *Daedelus*, Vol. 106, No. 1, Winter 1977, p. 2. Other than the physician, there are at least 425 technical health specialties. Geiger, op. cit., p. 33.

per year.[19] For September 1975 to September 1976, the Consumer Price Index increased by 5.5 percent. The Bureau of Labor Statistics estimated that during the same period hospital charges increased by 12 percent and physicians' fees by 11.6 percent.[20] Part of the explosion in medical costs is due sometimes to overuse of medical services. However, inflation, third-party payments, and other factors also play a part in these immense increases. An ideal health system has controls on costs built in.

6. *Accountability.* The professionals in the health care industry must be accountable to the public through professional review mechanisms, utilization reviews, professional standards review organizations, and professional associations, among other accountability devices. Malpractice should be guarded against without escalating costs as current malpractice mechanisms have done through the cost of lawsuits and defensive medicine.

7. *Resource development and planning.* Facilities must be built systematically in order to provide what is needed in regard to resources, including personnel.

8. *Public health perspective.* The focus would be on prevention, epidemiology, and life-style factors with a stress on primary prevention.[21] Incentives for this focus must be built into the system.

From the above list it is easy to see why we discuss national health insurance as a combined economic security/personal services program. Central is insuring against the economic risk of needing health care, but form of service delivery can be the critical difference between a plan which can work and one which is doomed to failure. After the adoption of Medicare and Medicaid in the mid-1960's, a general national health insurance seemed to be only a matter of time. In the more conservative atmosphere of the late 1970's there was

---

[19] Jerry L. Weaver, *National Health Policy and the Underserved. Ethnic Minorities, Women, and the Elderly,* St. Louis: C. V. Mosby, 1976, p. 122.

[20] Irene Oppenheimer, "Third-Party Payments," *Social Policy,* Vol. 8, No. 3, November/December 1977, p. 55.

[21] David A. Kindig and Victor W. Sidel have suggested the following criteria for national health insurance useful for deciding which program to adopt and assessing the attainment by enacted programs of their intended goals: "(1) Consumer participation and control. (2) No one desiring coverage should be excluded. (3) Services should be comprehensive and provide for continuity of service. (4) Services should be accessible and available. (5) No out-of-pocket expense to consumer at time of use. Out-of-pocket expenses to be paid by insurance program. Full protection against catastrophic expenses. (6) Quality control must be built into program. (7) Research into health care delivery and demonstration of new methods should be provided for." See "Impact of National Health Insurance Plans on the Consumer," *National Health Insurance,* Robert D. Eilers and Sue S. Mogerman (eds.), Homewood, Ill.: Richard D. Irwin, 1971, pp. 15–67.

growing fear that comprehensive national health insurance was more than government could afford. But while we may approach it in steps, most social welfare experts agree that the United States will ultimately have to join the other developed countries in having some kind of national health insurance. In spite of our progress, in 1975 about 6 million Americans below the poverty line were not covered by Medicaid, and over 70 percent of workers lose their medical coverage if they become unemployed. Even those insured are often covered inadequately.

In order to approach the goals for an ideal system, a variety of plans have been introduced. In each session of Congress different types of national health insurance plans are presented, differing only slightly from proposed plans which have preceded them. Changes in legislation come rapidly (notwithstanding ideological and economic conflicts), and at least some steps toward national health insurance may have been taken prior to your reading this.

The various plans presented tend to fall into four basic categories or approaches: *tax credit, catastrophic coverage, mixed public and private,* and *public insurance.*[22]

Tax Credit

Under the popular title *Medi-Credit,* a tax credit approach was supported by the American Medical Association and at other times has been introduced in Congress by a variety of representatives and senators. The basic concept is that some program would be established to allow credit against personal income taxes to offset the cost of premiums of private health insurance. Tax credits differ from tax deductions, which this would replace, in that they provide actual dollar amounts rather than percentages of income toward a given program. The poor would get a full tax credit for both catastrophic insurance and basic private medical insurance under the AMA plan, and the tax credit would gradually decrease in the percentage of the premium which the credit would cover as income rose. There also would be an opportunity for employers to deduct the cost of contribution to a plan as a business expense.

Among the various alternative tax credit approaches suggested was one introduced in Congress which would provide tax credit not simply for the premium of insurance but for the actual total medical costs of a family beyond 15 percent of its income in a given year.

[22] Karen Davis, *National Health Insurance,* Washington, D.C.: The Brookings Institution, 1975, uses similar categories to group the various proposals for National Health Insurance.

Eligibility would be for all U.S. residents on a voluntary basis, although it is anticipated that the benefits would motivate most Americans to join. The benefit structure would vary under the plans. The ones introduced usually have a deductible which the individual or family must pay and some coinsurance, a percentage of medical costs which the individual or family must pay to guarantee against abuses of the medical system. Usually covered are basic hospital costs, skilled nursing facilities, and personal physician services plus catastrophic coverage. The administration of these plans would be by the various private insurance carriers which would issue policies. As they do now, state insurance departments would certify carriers and approve policies. The Internal Revenue Service, as it administers the income tax, would handle the financial transactions. The financing of the plan would be from general revenues since the costs are built into the tax system.

There is nothing inherent in a tax credit approach that would make for limited benefits or for leaving the current medical system as is and uncontrolled. It is just that these plans have been introduced by those who favor the current "free enterprise" medical system, and so tax credits and leaving the delivery system as is tend to be joined. The tax credit approach could be horizontally adequate, although the plans as submitted all tend to be less than comprehensive vertically; that is, they do not provide for full and comprehensive medical coverage. The most severe criticism of the plan comes from its inability to control costs. It specifically mandates a hands-off approach to government controls and maintains all the problems in the health care system that are now extant, except for the broadened coverage. Although this is packaged as one of the least costly plans, it could ultimately drive up costs to the point where it is the most expensive. Its major advantage is that costs would come from the general revenues and that it is a plan acceptable to the current health care providers; that is, they would not be so negative as to work to sabotage the plan or magnify its flaws. Most liberals reject any plan which does not deal with problems which drive up health costs or with comprehensive planning needs or with the effects of third-party payments.

Catastrophic Coverage

The catastrophic approach is based on the notion that the nation cannot afford or is not ready for a comprehensive national health insurance, and it seeks to deal with that element which is most frightening to the vast middle range of the American population: the costs of catastrophic illness. Some versions of this plan include revision and improvements of the Medicaid system for the poor and greater incentives to private insurers for basic coverage of the middle class. But the heart of this plan is the fact that relatively inexpensively one could cover catastrophic medical costs, if families were expected to pay the first portion of normal medical care. Everyone now covered by Social Security or the dependents of such people would be covered by the catastrophic plan and eligible for the benefits. The benefits would include anywhere from 80 to 100 percent of the cost (depending on which catastrophic plan is being discussed) beyond a certain limit, say $2000 per family or 15 percent of annual income or the like. The plan would be financed by an additional tax on the Social Security–Medicare system, between three- and four-tenths of a percent of income. It would be administered in the same way as the Medicare program is currently.

The horizontal adequacy is good under a plan which covers all those covered by Social Security. The vertical adequacy leaves much to be desired. It does not solve the problems of the poor or of the many others ineligible for Medicaid and often not covered or not adequately covered by basic health insurance. It would be financed by an additional, regressive tax, albeit a small one, in the Social Security model. Although the Medicare administration provides some minimal control, it still does not seek to revise the health care system or provide incentives for prevention or lowered costs. It is a limited plan, and within its limits can accomplish what it sets out to do. It is one of the plans which is given some chance of success because it is limited in cost and is attractive to middle America, but it would only be one step along the way toward true national health insurance.

Mixed Public and Private

The third group of plans are the mixed public and private plans, and there have been many variations since one such plan was first advocated by the Nixon Administration in the early 1970's. The American Hospital Association and the Health Insurance Association of America also have submitted versions of this kind of approach which have been introduced by many different members of Congress. The basic feature of most of these plans is for federal requirements that employers provide basic health insurance plans for all employees, with certain minimal levels of coverage. The plans would be paid for by employer/employee contributions, and various kinds of incentives for employers and employees would be built into the various plans. Additionally, each of these plans has some system which would modify Medicaid so that low-income families or the unemployed also would be covered as well as the aged. Eligible under these plans would be almost all Americans, although under provisions of various types of coverage. The benefits vary by plan but usually include the broad range of institutional and personal services covered by Blue Cross/Blue Shield-type plans. The Nixon Administration plan and various of the others provide other kinds of incentives toward cost limitation and comprehensive care. There are fiscal incentives for health maintenance organizations—the kind of prepaid plans whereby physicians do better if the patient is kept healthy. The major drawbacks of these plans are that they are less than fully comprehensive, tend toward two- or three-tier systems with different kinds of means tests, and have an increasing bureaucratic maze. The limitations on the present free enterprise system are missing, and the third-party coverage that causes escalation is not adequately handled.

Public Insurance

This is also called, at least by its proponents, the comprehensive approach. Some such plan has been proposed regularly by the AFL-CIO and at various times has been propounded by Senator Edward Kennedy (although he also has lent his name to other plans at other times).

Every resident of the United States would be eligible for health care services. At present 25 million Americans have *no* medical insurance of any kind.[23] Services would be provided without a means test or waiting period and without deductions or coinsurance requirements. Services would include the entire range of health services including coverage for catastrophes.

The emphasis of such a plan would be upon prevention and early detection as well as treatment and rehabilitation. Certain limits would be set upon dental care, psychiatric visits, and the use of skilled nursing facilities.

Financed by payroll taxes and special health taxes on unearned income, general revenues also would be utilized to minimize the "tax bite." Despite the use of general revenues, the sense of contribution would be retained for most persons through the use of Social Security taxes partially to finance the plan. Costs would be spread over the entire population.

This type of plan would provide a single, unified, national health system with no means test and no two-tier system of care and entitlements, and as with Social Security there would be a tendency

[23] John Knowles, "Introduction," op. cit., p. 4.

to save administrative costs through the use of federal systems already in place. Access would be improved, particularly for those who have financial needs.

The federal government would take full responsibility for the administration of the plan with state cooperation. Compensation for all providers would be paid from the insurance funds. Private insurance carriers could provide health insurance supplements. These plans have been criticized because their costs have been viewed as very high. Proponents say that while the cost is high the plan replaces public and private expenditures which amounted to $119 billion in 1975.[24] The *net new cost* is viewed by others as only minimal, especially in light of the many strengths which accompany this kind of health insurance plan.[25]

With such a plan there would be federal involvement with policy, training, and planning. One criticism made is there would be overuse and abuse because use would be "free" and costs would be driven up. Citizens in other countries have found no great joy in going to physicians and have found they use health services only when needed, after an initial rush to use the new entitlements.

Criticism of this type of plan focuses upon the sweeping nature of the required changes in the health care industry, the fact that this plan is unabashedly a public program, the potential costs, and too many public controls for those who represent the private sector and advocates of "free enterprise."

Modifications of the public insurance plan also have been offered. Some have contributions based on income toward the cost of this plan by the families covered; that is, the first $100 or up to $1000 for higher income people per year would be covered by the family. Other variations have some kind of coinsurance or deductible provision, but what they all have in common is a single comprehensive plan covering all Americans with major federal involvement in the health care system. The major advantage is that it would make it possible to focus on what kind of care is best for people, and the major criticism is one of cost and of the dangers of moving toward a socialized system. Under the American system it is less likely that one of these plans as a whole will be adopted all at once (except perhaps for catastrophic insurance), but that parts of it may be adopted. For instance, there has been a call for an equivalent to Med-

[24] Ibid., p. 2.
[25] According to one estimate by the Department of Health, Education, and Welfare of those programs introduced in the 93rd Congress, the most comprehensive would have added approximately 13 percent to total health care expenditures. Cited by Rachel Boaz in "Fair Share in Health Care," *Jubilee for Our Times*, Alvin L. Schorr (ed.), New York: Columbia University Press, 1977, p. 213.

icare for the first five or six years of life, which would be a public insurance or comprehensive program but only for young children. This could be relatively low in cost, since there is less expensive and chronic illness among children and could be cost-saving in the long run to the extent that it is preventive.[26] But the issue of adequate operation of the health care system is a complex one and one that is likely to be with us for many years.

A comparison of various plans is shown in Table 11-1.

ALTERNATIVES FACING THE PRACTITIONER

Policy choices are not just made at the macrolevel, although as one reads about social programs the policy choices are most often discussed at this high level. But social workers at the line level and in supervisory positions also influence policy choices which affect services.

For example, the staff at a settlement house meets to set fees for a day camp service. There are serious policy decisions to be weighed. If no fee is charged, there will be insufficient funds to support fully the program, and few children will be served totally. Also, the day camp may take on a "charity" flavor in the locality, and those children who do attend may be stigmatized. If a high fee is charged, perhaps based on the full cost of the program, because 20 or 30 percent of the families can pay this full fee, there will have to be a means test for the other 70 or 80 percent of families to use the service. Stigma usually accompanies such tests, and some people will probably pay less than they should; others will forego the service rather than submit to a test.

Thus do problems of universal versus selective service touch every level. In the case cited, the staff may decide on a low fee for all. This gives clients the dignity of contributing to a service, brings in *some* income, and minimizes the number who cannot pay and need a means test. Or the decision may be for a higher fee to maximize income, with a low fee available on a simple declaration of need. But the choices are not simple. If the service is made universally available, this decision will reduce the question of stigma but also will reduce the possibility of aiming the program specifically at a group of children who may need the program and its services most. On the other hand, if the day camp is aimed at those children who are most needy, one sacrifices inclusivity for serving the needs of a

[26] One estimate of the cost of "kiddie care" (comprehensive health care for children) is $200 per child per year or about $7 billion per year. Joseph L. Vigilante, "Explorations into Health Care Policy," April 1977, p. 6, mimeographed.

Table 11-1 PLANS COMPARISONS

	TAX CREDIT	CATASTROPHIC	PUBLIC-PRIVATE	PUBLIC
ADEQUACY				
Horizontal	Some limitations (voluntary)	Near total	Near total	Near total
Vertical	Major gaps	Major gaps	Some limitations	Near total
FINANCING				
Equitable	Yes	Regressive	Mixed	Yes
Priority use of funds	Yes	Yes	Yes	Yes
EFFICIENCY				
Cost	Poor	Good	Poor	Good
Benefit	Good	Poor	Fairly good	Poor
COHERENCE WITH OTHER PROGRAMS AND POLICIES	Does not deal with health care system	Does not deal with health care system	Some incentives for preventive medicine	Potential for meeting national priorities
LATENT CONSEQUENCES	Escalating costs	Incentive to "tip" medical care into catastrophic levels	Cumbersome bureaucracy	Cumbersome bureaucracy

special group, thus running the risk of demeaning the quality of the service and perhaps fostering divisive feelings in the community. Serving the poor and serving the rich in such a situation may be a question of balance, not a question of either/or. But this too depends upon the goals which one has as a community for the service provided. The population served and the needs to be met determine, finally, what the choices and the shadings of choices will be.

Suppose a staff member of a community mental health center is seeking apartments for discharged mental patients. Because of community resistance to this kind of program, in spite of all the community education which has been attempted, she is having great difficulty in locating apartments for people waiting to be discharged from mental institutions. An urban university has space in its dormitories for a few such model situations, groups of three to four mental patients in a dormitory unit. For a variety of reasons the worker is reluctant. The dormitory community is less of a natural community than the surrounding neighborhood. It will be harder for the patient to integrate. There will be times when the dormitories are vacant and the patients will be living in a kind of a ghost town. Here the worker is struggling with the dilemma of vertical versus horizontal adequacy. If she maintains her principles about getting the best possible service, she will have less group homes available; or the ones she finds will be closer to the desirable pattern but more people will be left behind in the mental institution. If she sacrifices vertical adequacy for horizontal adequacy, more patients can be discharged to halfway houses and can have a chance at integration, but in a less desirable setting. One has to weigh the gains and losses in each case in making this kind of decision.

In another example a voluntary agency has set up a model program using young volunteers to provide escort services to the elderly. After a one-year trial period during which public officials are impressed with the program, an opportunity comes to receive a contract which will make it possible to pay small stipends to the volunteers for their travel time and incidental expenses. This would seem to enhance the program, to give it recognition and the possibility of new expansion. On the other hand, the worker considers that a latent consequence may be to professionalize the program, which has a certain desirable flavor because of the volunteer and sacrificial nature of the participation. Will this be a step toward eliminating the volunteers in favor of paid staff? Will it destroy the spontaneity? This potential latent consequence needs to be weighed in deciding whether or not to move ahead with the stipend program.

Again, suppose the parents of a day-care center are dismayed by the level of funding. The worker attempts to move them toward social action to pressure the state office to provide more adequate funding for the day care center. However, the parents, in part despairing of that kind of change, volunteer to do supplementary fund-raising and to provide all the amenities missing in the day-care center. Is this step to be encouraged? It could provide the improvement in services needed, but it is not equitably financed. What should be done?

All the above cases are attempts to illustrate that the "line" worker in day-to-day practice is faced with social welfare decisions not unlike those described on the macrolevel throughout this volume. This is not a text on practice methodology, and therefore we will not get into a description of *how* a worker effects social change and social policy. But it is important to know that workers are involved in social policy on the microlevel at least and that they need to be armed with analytic tools to help them decide on the directions in which they will press, using the skills learned in other courses and from other texts. How important this can be is perhaps best illustrated in the example in Chapter 7 of how guideline writers in the War on Poverty may have shaped the whole "maximum feasible participation" component of it in ways never anticipated by the legislators. One of the few articles which explores in-depth social work practice decisions and social work policy choices is "Direct Practice and Policy Decisions" by Dolgoff and Gordon.[27] The authors point out that the worker is making social policy decisions in:

1. The choice of treatment modality: whether the client group is seen individually or as a family for a short or long term is a policy choice of itself and will shape the nature of the agency service in the larger sense.
2. The choice of worker roles: the worker engaged in a lead poisoning detection and prevention project can deal essentially with information-giving, with treatment of those affected, or with advocacy to remove lead paint from the environment. The degree to which these various roles are played is a decision which is influenced at least in part by the worker herself.
3. The choice of intervention target: the worker may try to effect change in the client or in the larger social system that is causing a problem for the client.

[27] Ralph Dolgoff and Malvina Gordon, "Direct Practice and Policy Decisions," *Journal of Social Welfare*, Spring 1976, pp. 5–13. A major book on how lower level organizational participants develop change is by George Brager and Stephen Holloway, *Changing Human Service Organizations: Politics and Practice*, New York: The Free Press, 1978.

4. The choice of expected outcome: how one defines progress will very much feed back into the nature of the service. Is progress to be defined in terms of the development of certain social amenities in the community, in client satisfaction, or in outside expert evaluation of change in clients, or by what method?

Additionally there can be any combination of the above four choices in tandem which will lead to different worker decisions and will affect agency practice. The point can be summed up best by saying that what each social worker does in each situation makes a difference. Perhaps the point of this entire text has been that what each citizen and what each social worker knows can make a difference, and what that citizen or social worker does can contribute to the general welfare.

Index

family structure and, 135–138
geographical location and, 135, 136
income inequities and, 141–143
income transfer programs and, 143–146, 160–161
percentage of population in, 134, 136
rising expectations and, 146, 151–153
strategies for fighting, 157–163
unemployment and, 138, 156
war on, 38, 72, 80–83, 127, 163, 211–215, 335
working poor, 138–140
Poverty lines, 150–151
Prago, Albert, 63n
Prisons, 206
Private programs, 117–122, 208–211
Probation, 206
Productivity, 291–294
Professional association, development of, 241–242, 250
Professionalization, process of, 232–241, 249, 250
Professional orientation of programs, 125–126
Professional social workers, 273–276
Profit motive, 96
Progressive tax, 102n, 317, 318
Proprietary agency, 119
Protestant ethic, 9, 56, 62, 75, 86–87, 89, 296–297
Pruger, Robert, 259n
Psychoanalytic social work, 236–240
Psychosocial school, 239
Public assistance, 108–111, 114, 116, 122, 139–140, 181–189
   Aid to Families with Dependent Children (AFDC), 143, 149, 182–183, 185–188
   general assistance, 183–184, 186
   Supplemental Security Income for the Aging, Blind, and Disabled (SSI), 83, 143, 184–187, 189

Public insurance plans for national health, 330–333
Public-private plans for national health, 329–330, 333
Public sector, 117–120
Puerto Rican Social Service Workers, 242
Pullan, Brian, 51n
Pumphrey, Muriel W., 62n, 63, 64n, 229n, 236n
Pumphrey, Ralph E., 62n, 63, 64n, 229n, 236n
Purchase of service, 103–104
Pusic, Eugen, 305

Rabinowitz, Howard N., 72n
Racism, social work and, 276–277
Railroad Retirement Board, 220
Randall, J. G., 72n
Rawls, John, 287
Recent Social Trends, 280
Reconstruction, 72
Red Cross, 209
Rees, Albert, 84n
Regressive tax, 102n
Regulating the Poor (Piven and Cloward), 188
Rehabilitation, 161–162, 206
Reich, Charles, 153n, 303n
Rein, Martin, 149, 157, 186n, 262n, 268–269
Reinhold, Robert, 290n
Residency laws, 53, 59, 85
Residual programs, 106–110
Resnick, Herman, 259n
Revenues, general, 101, 195, 197, 317–318
Reynolds, Bertha, 240
Rice, Robert M., 299n
Richan, Willard C., 257–258, 259n
Richmond, Mary Ellen, 235, 236, 264, 265, 270
Riessman, Catherine, 14
Rights to social welfare, 108–109
Ripple, Lilian, 249n
Rising expectations, 146, 151–153, 295
Robins, Philip K., 84n